ENVIRONMENTAL LAW

NANCY K. KUBASEK, J.D.
Department of Legal Studies
Bowling Green State University

GARY S. SILVERMAN, D.Env.
Environmental Health Program
Bowling Green State University
Chapters 6 and 8

PRENTICE HALL, *Englewood Cliffs,*
New Jersey 07632

Library of Congress Cataloging-in-Publication Data

KUBASEK, NANCY.
    Environmental law / Nancy K. Kubasek, Gary S. Silverman.
        p.   cm.

    Includes bibliographical references and index.
    ISBN 0-13-285107-5
    1. Environmental law—United States.   I. Silverman, Gary.
II. Title.
    KF3775.Z9K83   1994
    344.73'046—dc20
    [347.30446]
                                                        93-4938
                                                          CIP

Acquisitions editor: Donald Hull
*Editorial/production supervision and
interior design:* Nancy DeWolfe
Cover design: Maureen Eide
Prepress buyer: Trudy Pisciotti
Manufacturing buyer: Patrice Fraccio

©1994 by Prentice-Hall, Inc.
A Simon & Schuster Company
Englewood Cliffs, New Jersey 07632

Printed in the United States of America
10 9 8 7 6 5 4 3 2

ISBN 0-13-285107-5 01

Prentice-Hall International (UK) Limited, *London*
Prentice-Hall of Australia Pty. Limited, *Sydney*
Prentice-Hall Canada Inc., *Toronto*
Prentice-Hall Hispanoamericana, S.A., *Mexico*
Prentice-Hall of India Private Limited, *New Delhi*
Prentice-Hall of Japan, Inc., *Tokyo*
Simon & Schuster Asia Pte. Ltd., *Singapore*
Editora Prentice-Hall do Brasil, Ltda., *Rio de Janeiro*

Contents

N

Preface

When I began teaching environmental law in 1982, there were very few such courses offered at undergraduate institutions. There were even fewer resources available for teaching them. My first semester I taught the course using one of the two available law school texts.

The next year I began putting together my own materials—materials that over the next few years evolved into an environmental law "text" designed especially for undergraduates that I made available to my students through a copy service. To improve the quality of the materials before attempting to publish them, I asked my colleague Dr. Gary Silverman, the director of our university's Environmental Health Program, to write the chapters on water quality control and management of waste and hazardous releases, areas in which he has special expertise.

The result is *Environmental Law*, a book designed to introduce those without any legal or special scientific training to the system through which our nation attempts to preserve the environment. Although this book was written for undergraduate students, it would be useful to anyone interested in learning about our system of environmental law. It also would be a helpful reference for anyone in business who is attempting to negotiate the morass of environmental regulations that affect businesses today.

Reflecting the fact that background knowledge is often important for understanding specific areas, this book provides two key types of background necessary for understanding environmental law. First, the initial chapters explain how our legal system functions in general. Second, the initial portions of the latter chapters provide the basic scientific knowledge necessary for understanding environmental law. Thus, the reader may gain a fundamental understanding of not only what the laws are but why they are needed.

Several people helped to make this book a reality, and I would like to thank them for their contributions. Thorough and insightful reviews were provided by the following professors:

James Carp, Syracuse University

William Clements, Norwich University

Frank Cross, University of Texas

David Hoch, University of Southwestern Louisiana

Mary Kieffer, Ohio University

Richard Kunkle, The College of St. Thomas

Patricia Tulin, University of Hartford

Their reviews led to vast improvements of the final version of this book. In fact, it is only because of a suggestion of these reviewers that a very important chapter of this book was written, the chapter on energy policy and natural resource protection.

The many drafts and redrafts of the chapters were typed by Joyce Hyslop and Tami Thomas. Once the book had neared completion, Shannon Browne compiled the index.

Several people at Prentice Hall were essential to bringing this project to completion. Eric Severson was the person I first approached about this project, and his enthusiasm was critical in my decision to try to publish the book. Donald Hull was an extremely helpful editor, and Nancy DeWolfe guided the book through production in rapid time. The appropriate and attractive cover was designed by Maureen Eide.

Finally, the students who used the preliminary drafts of this manuscript and offered helpful criticisms cannot be omitted. While they are too numerous to list by name, their contributions were invaluable.

I view this first edition as an attempt to satisfy the need for a basic introduction to environmental law. I realize, however, that there is always room for improvement. I also realize that in spite of the conscientious review of all stages of the book's production by many people, it is almost inevitable that mistakes have crept in, for which I accept responsibility. I would therefore appreciate readers' corrections and comments as to how future editions may better achieve the goals this book is designed to attain.

NANCY K. KUBASEK

1

AN INTRODUCTION TO THE LAW

A useful prelude to a functional understanding of environmental law is an appreciation of the U.S. legal system itself. The materials contained in Chapters 1 through 3 will help you gain that appreciation.

1

The American Legal System

SOURCES OF LAW

Environmental threats are reacted to within a particular context. Therefore, our legal system must be understood as a preface to outlining the possible reactions to environmental harm. The first step in the review is understanding the origin of our laws. Three articles of the U.S. Constitution create a federal government composed of three major branches: The legislative branch (under Article I) primarily creates laws; the executive branch (under Article II) primarily enforces laws; and the judicial branch (under Article III) primarily interprets laws. While performing their major functions as described in the relevant article, the executive and legislative branches also create law. Additionally, there is even a fourth source of law, administrative agencies. The following sections describe how each of these branches serves as a source of law. Table 1-1 shows where you can find the laws created by these branches of the federal government, as well as laws created by state and local governments.

The Legislature as a Source of Statutory Law

Article I, Section 1, of the U.S. Constitution states, "All legislative Powers herein granted shall be vested in a Congress of the United States which shall consist of a House and Senate." The process by which Congress makes a law (called a *statute*) is important to understand because Congress creates most environmental law. If we wish to change environmental laws, we must understand how to work through the legislative process. At every stage of the legislative process, groups that may be affected by a proposed law will seek to influence the proposal through lobbying. Some of these groups are highly organized forces

TABLE 1–1 Where to find environmental law

Level of Government	Legislative Law	Executive Orders	Common Law/ Judicial Interpretations	Administrative Regulations
Federal	United States Code (USC) United States Code Annotated (USCA) United States Statutes at Large	Title 3 of the Code of Federal Regulations Codification of Presidential Proclamations and Executive Orders	United States Reports (U.S.) United States Supreme Court Reporter (S.Ct.) Federal Reporter (F., F2d) Federal Supplement (F. Supp.) Environmental Law Reporter (ELR) Federal agency reports (titled by agency, e.g., FCC Reports)	Code of Federal Regulations (CFR) Federal Registrar
State	State code or state statutes (e.g., Ohio Revised Code Baldwin's)		Regional reporters State reporters	State administrative code or state administrative regulations
Local	Municipal ordinances		Varies; often difficult to find. Many municipalities do not publish case decisions, but keep them on microfilm. Interested parties usually must contact the clerk's office at the local courthouse.	Municipality administrative regulations

that attempt to influence any proposed environmental legislation in Congress. Other groups are loosely knit, ad hoc organizations that emerged to influence a particular proposal. Although most congressional lobbyists, especially those working on behalf of business interests, are paid professionals, a large number of lobbyists for environmental legislation are extremely committed volunteers.

The lobbying process with respect to environmental issues is somewhat complicated because it is not always a situation where business lobbyists are working against environmental lobbyists. Within the environmentalist community itself, divergent opinions concerning proposed legislation are frequent. Some more established groups such as the Defenders of Wildlife and the Environmental Defense Fund tend to take more moderate positions and are more open to ideas for cutting the costs of environmental regulation. Such groups' moderate stances have prompted some former members to join organizations that take more extreme positions, including some such as Earth First!, that have essentially given up on the governmental process and take their case directly to the media by staging protest actions.

Those in the moderate group see themselves as practical and effective. They believe that, especially in recessionary climates, you will be ignored if you do not take economic arguments into account. Those in the more extreme group perceive the moderates as having sold out. Some of them also believe that the best way to get on television, and thus generate public support for one's position, is by taking an extreme stance. Still others from both camps see the proliferation of environmental lobbying groups, even when they hold diverse positions, as being positive, because it means more voices sending the message to Congress that the public wants the environment protected.

In 1990, the major environmental groups spent approximately $217 million to support large Washington staffs of lobbyists, lawyers, fundraisers, and financial managers. This amount appears huge, but it is small in comparison to the amounts expended by various business interests to affect environmental legislation.[1] Nevertheless, from the amount spent by environmental lobbyists alone, you may infer that the lobbying effort is a very significant aspect of the political process.

The emphasis for environmental lobbyists has traditionally been in Washington. But during the 1990s, as action at the state level becomes more important, we may see greater emphasis on lobbying below the federal level. Many national organizations already have local affiliates that lobby state legislatures when their interests are affected. And in 1990, the Sierra Club set up a formal program to train state-level lobbyists and distribute a $100,000 fund to help local chapters develop effective lobbying programs at the state level.[2]

Steps in the Legislative Process. The federal legislative process is similar in many respects to the process followed by state legislatures, but each state constitution may require slightly different procedures. We focus on the federal process because it is the model on which state processes are based and because most environmental legislation is either federal or is modeled on federal law. The reason our environmental laws are primarily federal is that environmental problems do not recognize state borders and therefore a uniform approach is necessary.

All laws originate from legislative proposals called *bills*. A bill is introduced into the House or Senate by a single member or by several members. The bill itself may well have been drafted by a lobbyist. As explained, most environmental groups often have their own lobbyists who will attempt to persuade environmentally conscious legislators to introduce and support their bills. Various business interests also hire their lobbyists. Table 1-2 lists some of the more active lobbying organizations that influence environmental legislation.

Once introduced, a bill is generally referred to the committee of the House or Senate that has jurisdiction over the subject matter of the bill. For example, a bill seeking to provide subsidies to firms willing to get half their energy from solar power will be referred to the House Committee on Energy and Commerce, which will, in turn, refer it to an appropriate subcommittee. Table 1–3 lists some of the committees and subcommittees to which environmental legislation may be referred. In most cases a bill is simultaneously introduced into both the Senate and House and referred to the appropriate committee and subcommittee in each. Once the bill is referred, the subcommittee holds hearings on the bill, listening to testimony from all concerned parties and establishing a hearing record. Lobbyists will be active during this time, sometimes through testimony at congressional hearings.

Following these hearings, the bill is *marked up* (drafted in precise form) and then referred to the subcommittee for a vote. When the vote is affirmative, the subcommittee forwards the bill to the full House or Senate committee, which may accept the subcommittee's recommendation, put a hold on the bill, or reject it. If the House or Senate committee has voted to accept the bill, the com-

---

TABLE 1–2   Organizations engaging in environmental lobbying

Business Interests	Environmental Interests
Business Roundtable	Environmental Defense Fund
Chemical Manufacturing Association	National Audubon Society
National Chamber of Commerce	Natural Resources Defense Council
National Environmental Development Council	National Wildlife Federation
(a coalition of industries)	Sierra Club
Utility Air Regulation Group	Wilderness Society
(a coalition of utilities and	
trade associations)	

TABLE 1–3   Congressional committees and subcommittees influencing environmental legislation

Senate	House

Agriculture Appropriations
  Energy and Water Development
  Interior and Related Agencies
	Agriculture Appropriations
	  Energy and Water Development

Commerce, Science and Transportation
  National Ocean Policy
	Education and Labor
	  Health and Safety

Energy and Natural Resources
  Energy Regulation and Conservation
  Natural Resource Development and
    Production
  Water and Power
	Energy and Commerce
	  Energy Conservation and Power

Environment and Public Works Nuclear Regulation	Foreign Affairs

Finance
  Energy and Agricultural Taxation
	Government Operations
	  Environment, Energy, and Natural
	    Resources

Foreign Affairs	Interior and Insular Affairs
	  Energy and Environment
	  General Oversight, Northwest Power
	    and Forest Management
	  Mining and Natural Resources
	  Water and Power Resources

Labor and Human Resources	Merchant Marine and Fisheries
	  Oceanography
	  Panama Shelf/Outer Continental Shelf

	Public Works and Transportation Water Transportation

	Science and Technology
	  Energy Development and Applications
	  Energy Research and Production
	  Science, Research, and Technology

	Small Business
	  Energy, Environmental, and Safety
	    Issues Affecting Small Business

	Ways and Means

mittee reports it to the full House or Senate membership for a vote. Throughout this process, the bill may be amended several times in attempts to secure its passage. Sometimes opponents of a bill will also amend it, with the hope that their amendment will cause the bill to be defeated. Other times opponents will amend the bill in an attempt to water it down. As a bill is going through this process, interested parties may follow its progress in the *Congressional Quarterly Weekly*, a publication that keeps track of what is happening to proposed legislation. (Most university libraries subscribe to this publication.)

By the time the bill is passed by both the House and the Senate, a different version of the proposed law will usually have been adopted by each chamber. Therefore, the bill will need to go to a Senate-House Conference Committee where, after compromise and reconciliation of the two bills, a single bill will be reported to the full House and Senate for voting. Very often you will hear discussions in the media about differences between House and Senate versions of environmental laws that are making their way through this process. Often, one chamber's version will be supported by business interests and the other by environmental groups. The president will often throw his support publicly to one version or the other.

A final affirmative vote by both houses of Congress is required for a bill to become law. If passed, the bill is then forwarded to the president, who may either sign or veto the bill. When the president signs the bill into law, it becomes a statute. It then is written down and codified in the *United States Code* and the *United States Code Annotated.* If the president vetoes the bill, it may still become law if two-thirds of the Senate and House membership vote to override the veto. If the president takes no action within 10 days of receiving the bill from Congress, the bill becomes law without his signature. One exception to this procedure is that if Congress adjourns before the 10-day period has elapsed, the bill does not become law. The bill will have been *pocket vetoed* by the president—that is, the president will have "stuck the bill in a pocket" and vetoed it by doing nothing. Supporters will then have to reintroduce the bill during the next session of Congress.

The Judicial Branch as a Source of Case Law

The federal courts and most state courts (discussed in Chapter 2) constitute the judicial branch of government and are charged by their respective constitutions with interpreting the constitution and statutes on a case-by-case basis. Most cases interpreting these laws are reported in large volumes called *reporters,* compilations of federal or state *case law.* When two parties disagree about the meaning of a statute, they bring their case to the courts for interpretation. For example, if a bill to provide solar energy subsidies were signed by the president and became law, two parties might still disagree about its meaning and ask the federal courts to interpret it.

One disagreement that might arise under this bill could be the time limit within which the firm must obtain half its energy from solar power. Though you would think that something as important as a time for conversion would be clearly stated in the statute, such an omission is not unusual. Congress, especially in the environmental area, often makes very broad laws and leaves it to the courts to "fill in the gaps." As one senator said when Congress was about to pass the Superfund legislation, "All we know is the American people want these hazardous waste sites cleaned up. . . . [L]et the courts worry about the details."

Congress may have also made the law intentionally vague because a more specific bill could not garner sufficient support for passage. The sponsors may have specifics in mind, but they know there will be strong opposition to those details. So they water down the language in the bill and hope that the courts will interpret the law so as to impose those specifics the drafters had in mind. That strategy can be somewhat risky, because Congress never knows exactly how the courts will interpret a law. However, in the event that the judiciary interprets the law in a manner not intended by Congress, the legislative body can always amend the law, in effect overruling the judicial interpretation.

The judicial branch, when interpreting a law, sees itself as trying to ascertain congressional intent. The court first looks at the "plain language" of the statute, that is, words are given their ordinary meaning. The court then looks at the legislative history to determine the intent of the legislature. This history is found in the hearings held by the subcommittees and committees, as well as any debates on the Senate and House floors. Hearings are published in the *U.S. Congressional News and Administrative Reports* and may be ordered from the Government Printing Office or found in most university libraries in the government documents section. Debates about a bill are published in the daily *Congressional Record*, which may also be found in most libraries. When lawyers are arguing before the court on behalf of their interpretation of the law, many of their arguments will in fact be drawn from what is found in the *Congressional Record*. Thus, when trying to get a watered-down bill passed, its drafters will often try to insert language into the *Congressional Record* that would be supportive of their preferred interpretation of the law.

Not all judicially created law is based on a statutory or constitutional interpretation. Such laws for which there is no such basis are referred to as *common law*. Common law emerges from actual court cases. It develops when a problem arises for which there is no applicable statute or constitutional provision. We then have what is known as a *case of first impression*. Cases of first impression obviously provide judges with the greatest latitude to make law. The judge must create a law to resolve the problem. The rule laid down to resolve this case is called a *precedent*. If a similar case arises in the future, the courts have a tendency to follow the precedent. Very little environmental law, however, is created in this manner; most environmental law is based on statutes.

The rule that the court lays down when interpreting a statute or ascertaining the constitutionality of a statute is also known as a precedent. Such precedent will be relied on in the future when other judges are ruling on interpretations of statutes and the Constitution. This process of reliance on precedent is called *stare decisis*, which literally means "let the decision stand."

Not all precedents are equally important. The decisions of a court are binding precedent on only those courts on a lower level and in the same system. For example, precedents from Ohio's Supreme Court bind the Ohio Appellate and Ohio Trial courts. These precedents do not bind the Michigan courts. However, an

Ohio precedent may be used in a Michigan case as a persuasive device. In other words, lawyers in a Michigan case may point out how Ohio resolved the law and argue that the Ohio court's reasoning was logical and therefore should be adopted. Likewise, in the federal system, a Fifth Circuit Court of Appeals decision would not have any precedential effect on another circuit court appeal. However, the precedent would be binding on the district courts within the Fifth Circuit.

Although the process of stare decisis seems very straightforward, its application actually provides the judge with opportunity to implant his or her values on the law. Judges have discretion in part because no two cases are ever exactly the same. The judge therefore will usually be able to *distinguish* (a legal term) the case at bar from the case that others are arguing should provide the precedent. When distinguishing a case, the judge finds a difference between the case before him and the precedent-setting case significant enough to allow him to rule differently in the second case. In many cases one lawyer will be arguing that the case before the court is similar to the potential precedent, and the opposing lawyer will be trying to point out significant differences between the two.

Another factor making reliance on precedent less predictable than one might assume is that there are frequently conflicting precedents, especially at the trial and initial appellate levels. Finally, a judge may always simply overrule the clearly applicable precedent. Whereas the judge will generally cite some reason for overruling the precedent, such as changes in technology or community values since the precedent was established, she need not do so. She may simply say that the prior ruling was erroneous and that overturning the precedent is simply a matter of "correcting" the law.

The U.S. Supreme Court and most state supreme courts have what is generally known as the power of judicial review, that is, the power to determine whether a statute is constitutional. Although not expressly provided for in the Constitution, the Supreme Court established this right in the landmark case of *Marbury* v. *Madison*, making the Supreme Court the final arbiter of the constitutionality of every law. This power gives the Court ultimate power to restrict legislative and executive branch activity.

Because most environmental law is federal statutory law, and because the Supreme Court is the final arbiter of the constitutionality of laws, most decisions you will read about in this book will be from the Court. As you will see, through its case-by-case interpretation of the Constitution and statutes, the Supreme Court has established a line of authoritative cases on various environmental matters.

The Executive Branch as a Source of Law

The executive branch comprises the president, the president's staff, and the cabinet. The heads of all executive departments (e.g., the secretary of State, the secretary of Labor, the secretary of Defense, the secretary of the

Treasury) make up the cabinet. The executive office is composed of various bodies, such as the Office of Management and Budget (OMB) and the Office of Personnel Management (OPM). The executive branch is influential in the rule-making processes of both the legislature and administrative agencies. The president influences Congress by proposing legislation, publicly supporting or opposing proposed laws, and use of the veto. The OMB's role in influencing administrative regulations through cost-benefit analysis is detailed in Chapter 3. The executive branch exercises direct rule making through its power to make treaties and issue executive orders.

Treaty Making. The president has the power, subject to the advice and consent of the Senate, to make treaties. These treaties become the law of the land, based on the supremacy clause of the Constitution (Article XI), and supersede any state law. For instance, when President Reagan entered into the Montreal Protocol, a treaty mandating reductions in the production of chlorofluorocarbons and halons, that treaty became the law of the land, and its provisions superseded any existing federal or state laws inconsistent with the treaty. Thus, Congress could not subsequently pass a law that would allow the unlimited production of those chemicals. Treaty making is one of the few ways that the United States can influence the environmental policies of other nations.

Executive Orders. Throughout history, the president has made laws by issuing executive orders. For example, President Reagan, by virtue of an executive order, ruled that all executive federal agencies must do a cost-benefit analysis before setting forth a proposed regulation for comment by interested parties. In 1992, President Bush issued an executive order temporarily freezing the promulgation of new rules by administrative agencies, an act that had the potential to affect environmental law severely because agencies are constantly making rules implementing environmental laws.

The executive order as a source of law is also used by state governors to deal with emergencies and with budget functions. Often a governor will call out the National Guard by executive order or, in some states, implement particular aspects of the budget process. For example, a governor may order a freeze on hiring in the state university system or order an across-the-board cut in budgets in all state departments when quarterly tax revenues are lower than anticipated.

Administrative Agencies as a Source of Law

Less well known to the general public as a source of law are the federal regulatory agencies, among them the Environmental Protection Agency (EPA) and the Occupational Safety and Health Administration (OSHA). Congress has delegated to these agencies the authority to make rules governing the conduct of business and labor in certain areas. This authority was delegated because it was thought to accord with the public interest, convenience, and necessity. There was some concern, however, about the delegation of so much power to bodies with no elected representatives, so their rule-making processes (described in Chapter 3) are especially open to public participation. Proposed rules, as well as those rules finally implemented by an agency, must be published in the *Federal Register*, and the public must be given the opportunity to comment on these proposals.

Because of their substantial impact on the laws of this nation, administrative agencies sometimes represent what many observers have called a fourth branch of government. Because most of the federal environmental laws mandate the creation of many administrative regulations, we describe this fourth branch of government in greater detail in Chapter 3.

CLASSIFICATIONS OF LAW

Case and Statutory Law

As noted earlier, laws are classified as either case law or statutory law, depending on how they are made. Judges make case law; legislators make statutory law. We generally find statutory laws in codes and case law in case reporters. Even though this distinction is frequently made, it is important to remember that the two types of law are entwined through the process of statutory interpretation. We really do not know what a statute means until it is interpreted by the courts, whose judges attempt to construe congressional intent. Sometimes, as you know, the court may interpret the law in a manner not intended by Congress, and Congress may then respond by amending the statute to make its meaning clear.

Public and Private Law

Besides the statutory–case law distinction, another classification of law may be helpful in your study of environmental law, and that is the distinction between public law and private law. *Public laws* are those set up to provide for the public welfare, and they are generally administered by administrative agencies. These laws generally regulate classes of people or organizations. Environmental law is considered public law. Other branches of public law include securities law, labor law, and antitrust law. *Private law*, on the other hand, generally regulates the conduct between two individual parties. Sometimes private law may be used in environmental matters. For example, if a company does not properly test a chemical and consequently sells a product that injures a consumer, that consumer may be able to bring a private action for compensation against that company. Such a private action would be what is called a *tort*, or personal injury case. Other private law actions would include breach of contract and fraud.

Criminal Law and Civil Law

Perhaps an even more important distinction, however, is that between civil and criminal law. This distinction is important because the rules governing each are different, as are the outcomes sought in each case.

Criminal law comprises those federal and state statutes that prohibit wrongs against the state or society in general—conduct such as arson, rape, murder, forgery, robbery, and illegal dumping of hazardous waste. The primary purposes of criminal law are to punish offenders and to deter them and others from committing similar acts usually through imprisonment or fines. The prosecutor, the person initiating a criminal case, is the government, usually represented by a federal district attorney or a state prosecutor. The prosecutor is said to be representing society and the victim against the defendant, who is most likely to be an individual but may also be a corporation.

For purposes of both criminal and civil litigation, a corporation can sue and be sued, just like a person. Corporations, in the context of litigation, are sometimes referred to as artificial or juristic persons. If the corporation is a defendant, of course, it cannot be jailed. A fine will be imposed against the corporation in lieu of a jail term.

Crimes are generally divided into felonies and misdemeanors based on the severity of the harm the actions may cause. In most states, the more harmful *felonies* (e.g., rape, arson, criminal fraud) are commonly punishable by incarceration in a state penitentiary and by fines. The less harmful *misdemeanors* (e.g., shoplifting a magazine) are crimes usually punishable by shorter periods of imprisonment in a county or city jail, as well as by smaller fines. What may be a misdemeanor in one state could be a felony in another.

Civil law is usually defined as the body of laws regulating relations between individuals or between individuals and corporations. In a civil matter the party analogous to the prosecutor is the plaintiff. The plaintiff is usually seeking either compensation or equitable relief (an order for specific performance or an injunction). There are no divisions in civil law comparable to that between felonies and misdemeanors in the criminal system. In the civil system laws are divided by subject matter, with the most common civil matters being tort cases and contract cases. Other substantive areas of civil law include domestic relations (family law), bankruptcy, agency law, property, business organizations, sales, secured transactions, and commercial paper.

Most people consider being convicted of a crime much more serious than being found guilty of violating a civil law. There is much greater "societal scorn" heaped on the criminal. Also, it is only criminal law that threatens the defendant with the loss of liberty. For those reasons the defendant in a criminal case is given much greater procedural protections. First, although almost anyone can file a civil action against another person, before a criminal defendant can be tried for a serious federal crime, an indictment must be handed down against him or her. Most states also require an indictment by a grand jury when a defendant is charged with a felony. To get an indictment, the prosecutor must convince the *grand jury*, a body generally composed of 15 to 23 citizens, that the prosecution has enough evidence to justify bringing the potential criminal defendant to trial.

When a defendant is charged with a misdemeanor, a local judge or magistrate will fulfill a role comparable to a grand jury. This initial step provides a safeguard against political prosecution. It is necessary because even when one is ultimately found not guilty, the act of being tried for a crime still tarnishes the defendant's reputation, so we want to make the trial of an innocent party as rare as possible.

Another difference between criminal and civil law lies in the burden of proof placed on the party bringing the action. In both cases the party filing the action must prove his or her case. However, a person filing a civil case must prove that the defendant violated the law by a "preponderance of evidence," which can be thought of as proving that it is more likely than not that the defendant committed the act. If the defendant is charged with a crime, however, the prosecution must prove the defendant's guilt "beyond a reasonable doubt," a much more stringent standard. Some people think of the difference as being the need to prove a civil case by 51 percent and a criminal case by 99.9 percent.

Our primary concern with criminal law lies in the fact that violations of many environmental statutes constitute criminal offenses. As we examine specific environmental statutes, note that the same act often gives rise to both criminal and civil penalties. Criminal penalties are often imposed for acts referred to as willful or knowing violations. The most publicized trend in criminal actions today is the increasing use of imprisonment of corporate violators, including those who violate criminal provisions of environmental laws. Since new federal sentencing guidelines took effect in 1987, incarceration has increased and plea bargains involving probation and community service have been less frequent. Further, when a company criminally violates an environmental law, that firm may have all its government contracts suspended.

One recent trend in environmental law has been an increasing use of criminal sanctions. The first major increase in the use of criminal sanctions to enforce environmental laws occurred in 1982, when the Department of Justice (DOJ) created a separate Environmental Crimes Unit in its Land and Natural Resources Division, and the EPA established an office for Criminal Investigations. From 1982 on, there has been a steady increase in the use of criminal sanctions. In 1990, the EPA referred a record 65 cases to the Justice Department for criminal prosecution, surpassing the previous year's high of 60. A record 100 defendants were charged with crimes in 1990, and 55 were convicted and sentenced, with sentences averaging 1.8 years. The total amount of fines imposed in 1990 was $30 million. That amount was a substantial increase over the $13 million imposed in 1989. In one of the toughest criminal sentences handed down in an environmental case, a Pennsylvania waste-pit owner, William Fiore, was sentenced to serve 6 to 12 years in a state prison for deliberately piping 1.2 million gallons of toxic leachate into the Youghiogheny River near Pittsburgh. The largest criminal penalty ever assessed an individual for violating an environmental law was given in 1990 to a Wall Street trader. He was fined $2 million for filling wetlands without a permit.[3]

Thus, at least during the early 1990s, the EPA believes criminal penalties have an important role to play in environmental enforcement. This view seems consistent with that of the public but not with that of corporate executives. A poll reported in *The Wall Street Journal* on March 11, 1992, revealed that 75 percent of the general public believed that executives should be held personally liable for their environmental crimes, but only 49 percent of 500 executives of large corporations agreed. A majority of the public rated environmental crime as worse than price-fixing and insider trading, whereas 80 percent of corporate executives felt that the latter two were more serious.

A single act may lead to both criminal penalties and civil liability. For example, if a businessperson willfully violates the Resource Conservation and Recovery Act, both the person and the corporation may be subject to criminal penalties in the form of fines. In addition to criminal penalties, civil penalties may be assessed, and parties who were personally injured by the violations may also bring private civil damage suits.

The year 1990 was also a record year for the EPA in terms of civil enforcement, with the imposition of an all-time high of $38.5 million in civil judicial penalties and $22.8 million in administrative penalties. The largest settlement with a party charged with violating an environmental statute was reached when Texas Eastern Transmission Corporation paid a $15 million fine and agreed to perform $400 million in cleanup work at 89 sites in 14 states.[4]

The improved enforcement record of the early 1990s may be attributed to two factors. First, the administrator of the EPA, William Reilly, was determined to improve enforcement. Second, the EPA's enforcement budget was greatly increased. Figure 1–1 illustrates the increasing enforcement budgets. If budgets continue to increase, enforcement should continue at these record-setting levels. It is important to remember, however, that just because enforcement efforts have increased substantially, we are not necessarily anywhere close to prosecuting most violators of environmental regulations.

An important criminal law case that has helped to make criminal sanctions more of a deterrent than they otherwise might have been is the 1975 U.S. Supreme Court case of *United States* v. *Park*.[5] That case laid down the rule that a corporate officer can be held criminally liable for failure to correct a regulatory violation, even when that officer directed a lower-level employee to take corrective action. The test for liability laid down in that case was that criminal liability would be imposed when a person, by virtue of his or her position in a corporation, had the responsibility and authority either to prevent the violation or promptly correct it and failed to do so.

The defendant in such a case cannot avoid liability by claiming ignorance. If the person delegates responsibility, he or she is legally accountable for the actions or inaction of delegatees. Even when a statute requires knowledge for a criminal violation, the concept of knowledge may be interpreted very broadly, with presumed knowledge considered adequate under some statutes. For example, the Resource Conservation and Recovery Act imposes criminal liability on any person who "knowingly" transmits an RCRA hazardous waste to an unpermitted facility.

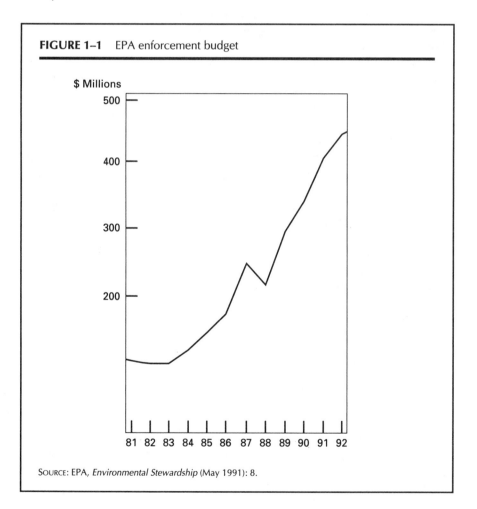

FIGURE 1–1   EPA enforcement budget

$ Millions

Source: EPA, *Environmental Stewardship* (May 1991): 8.

In the 1986 case of *U.S.* v. *Hayes International Corporation*,[6] a defendant had arranged to have a private hauler dispose of waste the company had generated, and was led to believe that the waste was being recycled. Only if the waste were being recycled did the hauler not need a permit under the act. The hauler in fact was not recycling the waste and did not have the appropriate permit. Despite the company's lack of actual knowledge that the hauler did not have a permit, both the company and its contracting officer were found guilty of violating the act. The Eleventh Circuit Court of Appeals upheld the convictions. The court created a presumption of knowledge on the part of those handling hazardous waste, and said that such presumed knowledge could be used to prove circumstantially a knowing violation of the act.

Firms are increasingly recognizing the potential for criminal liabilities being imposed on them. Because it is now clear that neither ignorance of the facts nor ignorance of the law is an excuse, corporations are beginning to encourage employees to take steps to protect themselves and their companies from liabilities. These steps are ones that should have been taken anyway, but often only a threat of prosecution motivates people.

First, employees in responsible positions are being encouraged to know the law. Second, when an official delegates a task mandated by an environmental regulation, he or she is advised to accompany that delegation with strict supervision to be sure that compliance occurs. In prudent corporations, all environmental policies of the company are being put in writing, as are all communications with regulatory agencies, especially when an agency is waiving a regulatory requirement. Individuals who disagree with directives with respect to environmental policies are being encouraged to make their objections known in writing to top corporate officials, who are encouraged to investigate such claims quickly. Prudent companies are also more carefully investigating those firms that they hire to do tasks that must be done in compliance with federal environmental regulations. Finally, firms are having periodic environmental audits by an outside consultant or environmental attorney. Such audits may uncover potential compliance problems. If the advice of the auditor is followed, a firm may be spared subsequent problems.

CONSTITUTIONAL PRINCIPLES UNDERLYING THE LEGAL SYSTEM

No discussion of the American legal system would be complete without a discussion of the constitutional principles on which this system is based. The Constitution, as originally drafted, was a conservative document. Most of those who attended the Constitutional Convention were men of wealth, and they understandably desired to protect their own interests. Because most of the drafters owned property, protection of private property was a major objective. Protection of private property interests, in turn, means the protection of business owners' interests.

The framers were also strongly influenced by the philosopher John Locke. Locke saw government as a *social compact* by which people, living in a state of nature, agreed to form a government that would make rules by which all would abide. To prevent this government from being oppressive, individuals, according to Locke, had to retain certain rights. These inalienable rights included the right to the pursuit of life, liberty, and property. The U.S. Constitution was perceived as the embodiment of our social compact.

Although it is generally true that business and private property interests have consequently been well served by many of the provisions of the Constitution, there have been exceptions. As the political makeup of justices on the U.S. Supreme Court changes, interpretation of the Constitution also changes. The concepts and constitutional provisions discussed briefly in the following sections are those that have had the greatest impact on the scope of congressional authority to regulate private property interests and on laws designed to protect the environment.

Federalism

Underlying the system of government established by the Constitution is the principle of *federalism,* which means that the authority to govern is divided between two sovereigns, or supreme lawmakers. In the United States these two sovereigns are the state and federal governments. One characteristic of federalism is its allocation of the power to control local matters to the local governments. This characteristic is embodied in the Constitution. Under the Constitution all powers not given exclusively to the federal government or taken from the states are reserved to the states. The federal government has only those powers granted to it in the Constitution. Therefore, whenever federal legislation affecting the environment is passed, the question of the source of authority for that regulation always arises. As will be revealed shortly, the commerce clause is the predominate source of authority for the federal regulation of business and thus the source of authority for most environmental legislation.

In some areas the state and federal governments have *concurrent* authority; that is, both governments have the power to regulate the matter in question. This situation arises when authority to regulate in an area has been expressly, but not exclusively, given to the federal government by the Constitution. In such cases, the states may regulate in the area as long as the state regulation does not conflict with any federal regulation of the same subject matter. A conflict arises when a regulated party cannot comply with both the state and the federal laws at the same time. When the state law is more restrictive, and so compliance with the state law automatically constitutes compliance with the federal law, the state law may still be valid. For example, as discussed in subsequent chapters, in many areas of environmental regulation, states may impose much more stringent pollution-control standards than those imposed by federal law. However, states cannot pass less restrictive laws.

The outcome of direct conflicts between state and federal laws is dictated by the *supremacy clause*. This clause, found in Article VI of the Constitution, provides that the Constitution, laws, and treaties of the United States constitute the supreme law of the land, "any Thing in the Constitution or Laws of any State to the Contrary notwithstanding." This principle is known as the principle of *federal supremacy*. Any state or local law that directly conflicts with the federal Constitution, laws, or treaties is void. Especially important for environmental law is the inclusion of rules established by federal administrative agencies as federal law.

Federal Preemption

The supremacy clause is also the basis for the doctrine of *federal preemption*. This doctrine is used to strike down a state law that does not directly conflict with a federal law but attempts to regulate an area in which federal legislation is so pervasive that it is evident that Congress wanted only federal regulation in that general area. It is often said in these cases that federal law "preempts the field."

Cases of federal preemption are especially likely to arise in matters pertaining to interstate commerce, where a local regulation imposes a substantial burden on the flow of interstate commerce through a particular state. This situation is discussed in greater detail in the next section. The law of federal preemption is one where there really are no broad principles to be applied; the court simply looks at each individual case to try to determine whether Congress intended to preempt the subject matter in question from state regulation.

The Commerce Clause

The primary powers of Congress are listed in Article I of the Constitution. It is important to recognize, before proceeding any farther, that Congress has only *limited* legislative power. Congress possesses only that legislative power granted it by the Constitution. Thus, all acts of Congress not specifically authorized by the Constitution or necessary to accomplish an authorized end are invalid.

The *commerce clause* provides the authority for Congress to pass most of the federal environmental regulations. Commerce refers to trade or exchange of goods or services. This clause empowers the legislature to "regulate Commerce with foreign Nations, and among the several States, and with the Indian Tribes." Depending on the ideological makeup of the Supreme Court, of course, interpretations of the specific boundaries of this clause vary.

Throughout history, interpretation of this clause has varied greatly. Today, the commerce clause is broadly interpreted. Any activity, even if purely intrastate, can be regulated by the federal government if it substantially affects interstate commerce. The effect may be direct or indirect. Thus, the federal government can regulate the price of milk both processed and sold in the same state. Intrastate milk competes with interstate milk, and thus the price of intrastate milk has an impact on the price of the interstate milk, thereby affecting interstate commerce.

Whereas many would argue that this broad interpretation of the federal government's ability to regulate Congress is so well established as to be unassailable, others still challenge some federal regulations on the grounds that such regulation is an attempt to affect private matters rather than interstate commerce. An example of such a challenge in the environmental arena is provided by the case of *Hodel* v. *Virginia Surface Mining and Reclamation Association, Inc.*[7] The *Hodel* case arose after Congress passed a statute establishing a number of requirements for strip mining, the most controversial being a provision that any land used for strip mining be returned to approximately its original state. The mining association argued that the principal purpose of the act was to regulate the use of private land, a matter that falls within the state's police power; thus the act could not have been designed to be a regulation of interstate commerce.

In setting forth its rule, the Supreme Court reiterated its broad interpretation of the commerce clause with respect to environmental matters, saying, "the court must defer to a congressional finding that a regulated activity affects interstate commerce if there is any rational basis for such a finding. . . . even activity that is purely intrastate in character may be regulated by Congress where the activity, combined with like conduct by others in similar situations, affects commerce among the States or within foreign nations." The Court in *Hodel* applied this test to the facts and found that Congress had a rational basis for determining that strip mining affects interstate commerce. Congress had relied heavily on the impact of mining on water pollution. The Court also pointed out the need for national standards in light of the difficulties states had encountered when attempting to regulate the problem. The Court also stated that characterization of a regulated activity as local was "irrelevant" if the purpose is to protect interstate commerce from adverse *effects.*

Most environmental regulation by the federal government, like the foregoing, is now presumed to be constitutional. In determining whether Congress has the authority to enact legislation under the commerce clause, the Supreme Court asks whether there is any rational basis for Congress to find that the activity to be regulated affects interstate commerce. If so, the Court asks whether there is any reasonable connection between the ends asserted and the regulatory scheme selected to achieve those ends. If both questions can be answered affirmatively, the legislation stands.

The Restrictive Effect of the Commerce Clause. In addition to being seen as a source of power for the federal government, the commerce clause is also interpreted as an implicit restriction on the states' authority to regulate matters affecting interstate commerce. After all, under the doctrine of federal preemption, if the federal government is supposed to regulate matters affecting interstate commerce, then the state should not regulate these matters. Thus states may not regulate interstate commerce.

This restriction has a history of changing interpretations so complex as to be beyond the scope of this book. Instead, we will focus on how the clause is being interpreted today. In brief, it is a violation of the commerce clause for a state to pass a law that on its face discriminates against interstate commerce. If, however, the legislation involves the state's engaging in a proprietary action (an action whereby the state is not functioning as a government but is acting more in the role of a business), the legislation will be upheld. If a statute does not appear on its face to be discriminatory but has discriminatory effects on interstate commerce, a balancing test is applied, balancing the impact of the state's regulation on interstate commerce with the state's justification.

The issue of whether a state regulation is a violation of the commerce clause arises frequently in disputes surrounding the regulation of waste. States are searching for ways to restrict the importation of out-of-state waste without violating the commerce clause and are generally not succeeding. The earliest such case that went to the U.S. Supreme Court was *City of Philadelphia* v. *New York.*[8] In that 1978 case a New York statute had prohibited the import of solid or liquid waste generated outside the state to be buried in a landfill in the state. The Court said that the state was attempting to slow or stop the flow of commerce for protectionist reasons, an action that is clearly in violation of the commerce clause, because (as explained earlier) interpretations of the clause prohibit states from passing legislation that inhibits interstate commerce.

Other states attempted to learn from New York's experience. Ohio's legislature, recognizing that a statute discriminatory on its face could still be upheld if (1) the law has a legitimate purpose, (2) the statute serves that purpose, and (3) there is no nondiscriminatory alternative that would serve the same purpose, tried to pass a law that would meet that exception. The Ohio statute imposed higher taxes on out-of-state waste. Ohio had three justifications: (1) the sheer volume of waste flowing into the state, (2) the higher costs of out-of-state waste inspection, and (3) the increased threat of hazardous material entering Ohio and the consequent difficulty of policing its transportation. In striking down the law, the lower court said that protecting the environment was no justification unless something other than the source was the reason for the different treatment. The court found the latter two justifications to be unsupported. The case was appealed in 1991, and the decision upheld in 1992.

Michigan also tried to circumvent the restrictive impact of the commerce clause. Its law, however, fared much better than Ohio's in the lower court. Michigan's Solid Waste Management Act gave each Michigan county the right to accept or reject waste from any outside source. Because the law classified waste by county, and thus treated inter- and intrastate waste the same, there was no problem, according to the lower court. The U.S. Supreme Court, however, did not agree.

Michigan's law, along with an Alabama law that imposed a $72 per ton tax on out-of-state toxic waste shipped to an Emelle, Alabama, commercial site, was struck down by the Supreme Court in the summer of 1992, with the court stating in the Michigan case that states could not adopt "protectionist" measures to stop waste being generated in other states from being shipped to their dumpsites. Even legitimate goals like protecting health and the environment could not be accomplished by economic protectionism.

In the 8–1 Alabama ruling, the High Court stated that Alabama could impose a special fee on the disposal of all hazardous material, not just out-of-state material, if indeed its goal was to reduce the volume of waste entering the Emelle facility. The Court said Alabama would have needed to show some distinction between hazardous waste generated inside and outside the state. In the 7–2 Michigan decision, the Court likewise said that its decision would have been different if the imported waste raised health or other concerns *not* presented by in-state waste. Chief Justice Rhenquist filed dissenting opinions in both cases and was joined by Justice Blackmun in his Michigan dissent. In the Alabama case, Rhenquist wrote that a state ought to be able to "take actions legitimately directed at the preservation of the state's natural resources, even if those actions incidentally work to disadvantage some out-of-state waste generators."[9]

While most states are struggling with trying to find a way to draft a constitutional law allowing them to keep hazardous waste outside their state, Rhode Island is trying do just the opposite: Rhode Island is trying to keep commercial trash inside the state. Rhode Island's Central Landfill cannot, by law, charge the state's municipalities more than $14 a ton to receive residential trash. Because that amount does not cover disposal costs, the landfill charges up to $59 per ton for commercial trash.

The high prices made Central Landfill noncompetitive with dumps in neighboring states, which was a boon to local trucking firms, as they were now hauling tons of wastes to landfills in neighboring states. Consequently, the state's Solid Waste Management Corporation decreed that all the state's commercial trash had to go to a state-licensed disposal site, which meant Central Landfill. A trucking firm claiming the regulation was ruining its business sued the state on the ground that the regulation violated the commerce clause. The district court judge agreed and issued an injunction in the summer of 1991.

Because trash disposal is such a major problem, and cases seeming to support a position that state restrictions on out-of-state waste disposal violate the commerce clause, Congress is coming under increasing pressure to pass some form of legislation that would override at least part of the Supreme Court's recent ruling and allow states to restrict the importation of waste. Measures that would allow states to restrict interstate transport of nonhazardous waste have been introduced in both the House and Senate, but thus far, have not been passed.

The Contract Clause

One of the Constitution's few explicit restrictions on the states' authority to regulate their citizenry is the *contract clause*. This clause provides that no state shall pass any law that impairs the obligation of any person under a contract. On numerous occasions, the Supreme Court has emphasized the importance of the inviolability of contracts. Thus, parties may enter into contracts feeling fairly secure that either their expectations will be fulfilled or they can obtain the appropriate remedy through the legal process.

Despite the Supreme Court's commitment to protecting the viability of the contract clause, the clause is not interpreted literally. Only those impairments that the courts interpret as unreasonable are prohibited by this clause. Thus, proving that a statute changes the rights or obligations of a party to a contract is only the first step in challenging the constitutionality of the statute in question. The next step is demonstrating that the impairment is unreasonable.

Changes in rules of civil procedure, statutes of limitations, and availability of attorneys' fees and punitive damages might impair the obligations of a contract by making its enforcement more difficult, but such changes are not considered unreasonable. The more troublesome cases arise when a new law substantially increases or decreases the performance obligations of one party to a contract, or as in the environmental case of *Blackstone Valley Disposal* v. *Rhode Island*,[10] the new law totally abrogates the contract.

In the fall of 1986, Blackstone, an out-of-state waste hauler entered into a contract with the Rhode Island Solid Waste Management Corporation (RISWMC), which allowed him to deposit Massachusetts waste at Rhode Island's Central Landfill, a state-subsidized landfill, so long as the amount of Massachusetts waste deposited did not exceed the amount of Rhode Island waste he collected. In 1987, the state of Rhode Island passed a statute prohibiting the deposit of out-of-state waste in the Central Landfill. The new law abrogated the contract between Blackstone and RISWMC, so Blackstone brought an action alleging, among other claims, a violation of the contract clause.

The Court found that the law did indeed cause a substantial impairment of the contract but refused to find a violation of the contract clause. The Court said that once substantial impairment was found, the Court must determine whether there was a significant and legitimate public purpose justifying the statute. Usually the courts require that the legislation be serving to remedy a broad social or economic problem, and that the state is exercising its police power and not legislating to benefit special interests. In this case, the Court found the state to be attempting to operate the landfill in a manner "designed to afford to the environment and to the citizens of the state who reside near the landfill the maximum protection which is available for the land disposal of rubbish." Citing protection of the environment as a broad societal interest well within the powers the state to protect, the Court upheld the regulation.

The Fourth Amendment

The Fourth Amendment protects the right of individuals to be secure in their persons, their homes, and their personal property. It prohibits the government from conducting unreasonable searches of individuals and seizing their property to use as evidence against them. If such an unreasonable search and seizure occurs, the evidence obtained cannot be used in a trial.

An unreasonable search and seizure is basically one conducted without the government official's having first obtained a warrant from the court. The warrant must specify the items sought as well as the persons and places to be searched. Government officials are able to obtain such a warrant only when they can show probable cause to believe that the search will turn up the specified evidence of criminal activity. Supreme Court decisions, however, have recently narrowed the protections of the Fourth Amendment by providing for circumstances in which no search warrant is needed. Improvements in technology have also caused problems in the application of the Fourth Amendment because it is now simpler to eavesdrop on people and to engage in other covert activities.

The Fourth Amendment applies to corporations as well as individuals. Fourth Amendment issues often arise when legislation authorizes warrantless searches by administrative agencies. For example, the EPA would prefer pollution-control regulations providing that when a firm is suspected of violating pollution limits, the EPA may conduct a surprise search to catch the violator. To the agency's dismay, the courts generally will not allow such warrantless searches. However, the standards for securing an administrative search warrant in such cases are much less stringent than in a criminal action. Generally, an administrative warrant requires a showing of a neutral enforcement plan that assures the court that selective enforcement will not occur.

The Fifth and Fourteenth Amendments

The Due Process Clause. The Fifth and Fourteenth Amendments are often spoken of together because both contain what is known as the *due process clause*, the provision that no person shall be deprived of his or her right to life, liberty, or the pursuit of happiness without due process of law. The Fifth Amendment is a prohibition on the federal government, and the Fourteenth restricts states. There are two types of due process: procedural and substantive.

Originally, due process was interpreted only *procedurally*. It required that a person whose life, liberty, or property would be taken by a criminal conviction be given a fair trial—that is, he or she was entitled to notice of the alleged crime and the opportunity to confront his or her accusers before an impartial tribunal. The application of procedural due process soon spread beyond criminal matters, especially after passage of the Fourteenth Amendment.

Today, the due process clause has been applied to such diverse situations as the termination of welfare benefits, the discharge of a public employee from his or her job, and the suspension of a student from school. It should be noted, however, that the form of takings (restrictions on property and liberty) to which the due process clause applies are not being continually increased. In fact, after a broad expansion of the takings to which this clause applied, the courts began restricting the application of this clause during the 1970s and are continuing to do so. The courts restrict the clause's application by narrowing the interpretation of property and liberty. This restricted interpretation is especially common in interpreting the due process clause as it applies to state governments under the Fourteenth Amendment.

What procedural safeguards does procedural due process require? That question is not easily answered. The procedures that the government must follow when there may be a taking of an individual's life, liberty, or property vary according to the nature of the taking. In general, as the magnitude of the potential deprivation increases, the extent of the procedures required also increases. For example, a student being suspended from the public school for three days would be entitled to fewer procedural guarantees than one being expelled for a year.

The concept of *substantive* due process refers to the basic fairness of laws that may deprive an individual of his or her liberty or property. In other words, when a law is passed that will restrict individuals' liberty or use of their property, the government must have a proper purpose for the restriction, or it violates substantive due process. What constitutes a proper governmental purpose is, of course, subject to interpretation by the courts. Originally, proper purpose was limited to those items within the traditional scope of the police power, that is, regulations that benefit the public health, safety, and welfare. The term *welfare* has been broadly interpreted, even in some cases to include such things as aesthetics.

In applying the concept of substantive due process, we usually say that the government cannot act arbitrarily and capriciously. When substantive due process analysis occurs, one asks whether the deprivation by the government involves the deprivation of a fundamental right. If so, the government cannot act unless it has a compelling reason to do so and there is not less restrictive means for satisfying this compelling interest. If there is an alternative way to achieve the same end that causes less deprivation, then there has been a violation. If the deprivation is for other than a fundamental right, the government action must be rationally related to a legitimate state end. In other words, the state end was an exercise of the police power, and the means will logically lead to the specified state end.

The Fifth Amendment further provides that if the government takes private property for public use, it must pay the owner just compensation. The language of the Fifth Amendment states "nor shall private property be taken for public use without just compensation." Although the Fourteenth Amendment does not contain such a clause, the Supreme Court has interpreted the Fourteenth as incorporating this clause through its due process clause. Unlike the privilege against self-incrimination, which does not apply to corporations, both the due process clause and the provision for just compensation are applicable to corporations. The latter provision is of great importance in numerous environmental cases, where representatives of the corporation frequently argue that the environmental regulations are so onerous as to constitute a taking of their land, for which compensation should be awarded.

In cases in which a party argues that regulations are so restrictive of private use as to constitute a taking of his or her private property for public use, the government will argue that the regulations are simply an exercise of its "police power," its power to protect the welfare of the citizens. In general, the courts seem to look at the diminution of the value of the property caused by the regulation and require compensation only when there has been a *drastic* reduction in the economic value of the property. In 1987, a 5-4 majority of the U.S. Supreme Court ruled that a state could impose restrictions on land use without having to compensate the owner for the land's reduced commercial value when the state "intends to prevent serious public harm."

This issue of when a regulation constituted a taking became increasingly debated during the early 1990s as states passed more regulations protecting wetlands that were often held as private property. The most significant case on this issue was argued on March 2, 1992, before the U.S. Supreme Court. The case, *Lucas* v. *South Carolina Coastal Council*,[11] involved a dispute between a beachfront property owner and the state of South Carolina over a law prohibiting permanent construction on any eroding beach. Lucas had bought two beachfront lots for $975,000 in 1986, prior to the passage of the law in question. Lucas, who had not yet begun construction on his property when the law was passed, lost the right to use his property for condominiums, so he challenged the law as constituting a taking without just compensation. The state court agreed with Lucas that the regulation denied him full value of his property and thus constituted a taking, so it awarded him $1.2 million in damages. The South Carolina Supreme Court, citing U.S. Supreme Court precedents, disagreed and overturned the lower court decision.

Lucas appealed the decision to the U.S. Supreme Court, which handed down its opinion on June 29, 1992. This opinion reversed the state supreme court in a 6–3 decision. The Court held that a state regulation that deprives a private property owner of all economically beneficial uses of property, except those uses that would not have been permitted under background principles of state property and nuisance law, constitutes a taking of private property for which the Fifth Amendment's takings clause requires payment. The Court stated that the South Carolina court erred in applying the principle that the takings clause does not require compensation when the regulation at issue is designed to prevent "harmful or noxious uses" of property.

Obviously, this decision was met with concern on the part of environmentalists, who fear that this ruling may lead to significant restraint on the part of state governments, which may fear that passing laws to protect state coastlines may now cost them millions of dollars. Even before a decision was handed down, however, the debate triggered legislature activity. Republican Senator Steve Symms of Idaho is attempting to gain support for a law that would require agencies to "assess" and "minimize" the potential for taking private property whenever a regulation is issued. Another legislative proposal being considered in the House would require federal agencies to compensate owners of wetlands when use of their property was restricted. Many environmentalists are understandably concerned about these proposals.

The Equal Protection Clause. The Fourteenth Amendment contains another clause that has been gaining importance in the environmental area since 1979: the Equal Protection Clause. This clause provides that no state "shall deny to any person within its jurisdiction the equal protection of its laws." These words provide the constitutional basis for concerns about environmental racism that are increasingly being raised by civil rights activists.

While many claim that the movement against environmental racism began to coalesce approximately 10 years ago in South Carolina when church-led black residents organized to protest the siting of a toxic landfill in the neighborhood, the movement started to achieve significant prominence in 1992.[12] During February of that year, the public became aware of an increasing array of statistics that appear to show that minorities receive less protection from environmental laws than whites do.

A study of EPA records by the *National Law Journal* revealed that there was a 506 percent disparity in fines assessed under the Resource Conservation and Recovery Act (the law regulating hazardous dumps) in predominately black versus predominately white neighborhoods. The average fine in white neighborhoods was $335,556, whereas the average fine in black neighborhoods was $55,318.[13] A former EPA attorney said he believed that statistic was the most telling with respect to environmental racism.[14]

There were also much lower fines for cases alleging multiple environmental law violations in black neighborhoods. Average fines for such violations were 306 percent higher in white neighborhoods during the past seven years.[15] Moreover, penalties for violations of the Clean Water Act were 28 percent lower in minority communities, while fines for violating the Safe Drinking Water Act and the Clean Air Act were lower by 15 percent and 8 percent, respectively.[16]

Final evidence comes from the Superfund program, or cleaning up hazardous waste sites. It took an average of 20 percent more time for a dump site in a minority neighborhood to be placed on the list for cleanup than one in a white neighborhood. Actual cleanup efforts also took longer to complete in minority neighborhoods. And, finally, the cleanup of minority sites was more often what many perceived as less effective "containment" action, which consisted of walling off the site. In white neighborhoods the site was more likely to receive "permanent" treatment such as removing the hazardous waste or treating it to eliminate the toxins.[17]

Of course, some argue that the conclusions being drawn of environmental racism are unfair. For example, one of the factors the law says must be considered in assessing the size of a penalty is the financial condition of the violating facility. Often the facilities in minority neighborhoods are also in economically depressed areas, so their penalties would be lower.[18] Others claim there is no evidence for this rationale.

Certainly, the issue of environmental racism is going to continue to be debated. And there are signs that the Clinton Administration may be examining the issue very closely. In December 1992, then–Vice President-elect Gore's transition team met with members of environmental justice groups to discuss this issue. That meeting was a sign that the issue may be given greater consideration in the 1990s.

A Constitutional Right to Environmental Protection?

Because as a nation we have a tendency to look to the Constitution to protect those rights most fundamental to us, it is only natural that when a concern for protecting the environment began to take the form of a national movement, people looked to the Constitution for a guarantee of a clean environment. Some legislators, in arguing for passage of the first major environmental statute, the National Environmental Policy Act, argued that a constitutional right to environmental quality in fact existed;[19] their claim, however, was not widely accepted. Some environmentalists had hoped to use the Ninth Amendment, broadly interpreted, to expand the right to privacy to include a right to a clean, unspoiled environment.

At least one case in which such a claim was made, *Tanner et al.* v. *Armco Steel et al.*,[20] a 1972 case, was unsuccessful. Still others have tried to argue that every time a governmental entity grants a permit to a polluting firm, that action constitutes state action, thereby subjecting the action to the possibility of being subject to claims of a violation of due process or an unconstitutional taking. The Supreme Court's reluctance to recognize such a right probably can be explained by two factors. First, there is nothing explicit in the Constitution or in its early interpretations to indicate that the drafters had any intention of protecting the environment. Second, from a practical perspective, it would be extraordinarily difficult for the courts to define the boundaries of such a right. Protecting the environment appears to be an area better left to legislators and administrative agencies.

In light of the failed attempts of parties to obtain judicial recognition of a constitutional right to a clean environment, at least one environmental group is attempting to generate support for a constitutional amendment that would guarantee a clean environment for future generations: the World Wildlife Foundation. Although its proposed amendment is not yet in final form, the basic rights of each individual to be protected would include: the right to clean air; pure water; productive soil; and the conservation of natural, scenic, historical, recreational, aesthetic, and economic values of America's natural resources. The amendment would prohibit any public or private entity from impairing these rights and place the responsibility for preserving and enforcing these rights on the federal and state governments.

The Public Trust Doctrine. The idea of the government as a trustee for environmental quality is not just an idea that environmentalists pulled from nowhere. The public trust doctrine is deeply imbedded in American law, forgotten for years but reborn in the 1970s. The concept traces its historical roots back to early Roman law where the doctrine of the public trust developed around the idea that certain common properties, like the air, seashores, and rivers, were held in trusteeship by the government for the free and unimpeded use of the public.[21] This doctrine was subsequently applied in England to give ownership of public lands to the king, but requiring that his subjects be given access to waterways for such purposes as fishing and trade.

This doctrine, on a limited scale, has been followed in the United States, primarily for rivers, shorelands, and natural areas, although its adoption has been on a somewhat piecemeal basis. The Northwest Ordinance of 1787, for example, stated that "the navigable waters leading into the Mississippi . . . shall be common highways and forever free . . . to the citizens of the United States." The leading case establishing this doctrine is the 1892 U.S. Supreme Court opinion in *Illinois Central Railroad Co.* v. *Illinois.* In 1869 the Illinois legislature passed a statute granting more than 1,000 acres of valuable land, including submerged lands under Lake Michigan and the shoreline along the city of Chicago's central city business district, to the Illinois Central Railroad Company. Four years later, the state passed another statute repealing this grant. It then filed an action to establish title to that property in the state's name.

The U. S. Supreme Court affirmed the state's title to the land, and in so doing explained the concept of holding title under the public trust doctrine:

It is a title that is held in trust for the people of the state that they may enjoy the navigation of the waters, carry on commerce over them, and have the liberty of fishing therein, freed from the obstruction or interference of private parties. . . . The control of the state for purposes of the trust can never be lost, except as to such parcels as are used in promoting the interests of the public therein, or can be disposed of without any substantial impairment of the public interest in the lands and waters remaining.

This precedent-setting case demonstrates the clearest application of the public trust doctrine: a situation where title to public lands is about to be transferred to a private entity. More difficult cases arise when control of the land is being diverted to a different governmental entity that intends to put the land in public trust to a more questionable public use, or, perhaps in partnership with a private entity, to develop and exploit the land for its economic value.

One example arose in Illinois in 1970 when the Chicago Park District proposed, among other endeavors, the transfer of 3.839 acres of city parkland to the Chicago Public Building Commission for the construction of a new school. Area property owners sued, arguing that the public trust doctrine required the state to retain the land in its use as parkland. The Illinois Supreme Court, in *Paepke* v. *Building Commission*,[22] disagreed, stating: "The mere dedication by the sovereign of lands to public park use does not give private property owners . . . the right to have the use continue unchanged. . . ."[23]

The Illinois court noted the conflict between those who wanted to preserve the parks in their pristine state and those administrators who, "under the pressures of the changing needs of an increasingly complex society, find it necessary, in good faith, and for the public good, to encroach to some extent upon lands heretofore inviolate to change," and held that the resolution of such conflicts is a matter properly given to the legislature and not the courts. And, in this case, the court found that the legislative authorization in question was sufficiently broad and comprehensive to allow the transfer.

In coming to its conclusion, the Illinois court cited with approval the approach developed by the Supreme Court of Wisconsin. That state approved proposed diversions in the use of public trust lands under conditions that demonstrated that

1. public bodies would control the use of the area in question;
2. the area would be devoted to public purposes and open to the public;
3. the diminution of the area of original use would be small compared with the entire area;
4. none of the public uses of the original area would be destroyed or greatly impaired; and
5. the disappointment of those wanting to use the area designated for a new use for former purposes was negligible when compared to the greater convenience afforded those members of the public using the new facility.

While noting that these standards were not controlling, the Wisconsin court found them to be a useful guide for situations similar to the immediate case.

A third type of case in which the public trust doctrine may come into play is where lands held in trust are threatened by proposed actions of the government. These cases often involve water pollution problems created by the government or developers. Most recently the doctrine has been applied in cases involving oil spills.

As you might infer from the foregoing discussion, the public trust doctrine is an important one in terms of public rights and responsibilities with respect to natural resources, even though it does not rise to the level of a constitutional protection. Questions as to its scope, balancing the interests of the competing publics, and the extent to which the qualities of the trusted property are to be preserved against short-term use, however, still remain. We shall refer to this important doctrine later in the book.

CONCLUDING REMARKS

After reviewing how our legal system is structured, you can begin to realize how complex a task it is to establish a comprehensive system of laws to regulate the environment. Because the United States is organized in accordance with the basic principles of federalism, we have, in essence, two parallel systems of government: a state and a federal system. Both are organized similarly, with legislative, judicial, and executive branches that are primarily responsible for, respectively, creating, interpreting, and enforcing the laws that govern our nation. A so-called fourth branch of government that combines all those governmental functions is now also fully functioning at both the state and local levels, and is especially important in making and enforcing environmental regulations.

The laws these governments make are both civil and criminal. Both are important in preserving the environment. These two parallel governmental systems often have overlapping responsibilities as dictated by the U.S. Constitution. But because the Constitution is a broadly worded document, subject to interpretation by the U.S. Supreme Court, it is not always clear where the lines of authority between the state and federal governments are drawn. The commerce clause gives the U.S. Congress the authority to pass environmental regulations, whereas the states rely on the police power that they retain under the Constitution to pass such laws. Where there is potential for conflict, the courts must intervene and draw boundaries, relying on interpretations of the Supremacy Clause and applying the doctrine of federal preemption.

The Constitution also protects individual rights. Often, in environmental matters, individuals will argue that the government's attempts to regulate or protect the environment have gone too far and have infringed on constitutional freedoms. Cases in which such claims have arisen in the environmental area include those questioning the need for search warrants and those questioning whether a regulation is so onerous as to constitute a taking.

Whereas this chapter has focused on the structure and lawmaking function of the government, the judicial function of our system merits special consideration. Thus, Chapter 2 takes an in-depth look at exactly how our legal system handles conflicts.

QUESTIONS FOR REVIEW AND DISCUSSION

1. Explain how statutory laws are created.
2. What does *stare decisis* mean?
3. Differentiate civil law from criminal law.
4. Explain the significance of the decisions in *U.S.* v. *Parks* and *U.S.* v. *Hayes International Corporation.*
5. What can corporate officials do to decrease their chances of being held criminally liable for violating environmental laws?
6. What is the relationship between the commerce clause and environmental law?
7. How does the Fourth Amendment affect enforcement of environmental regulations?
8. When does a regulation constitute an unconstitutional taking?

FOR FURTHER READING

(Note). "Criminal Sanctions for Environmental Crimes and the Knowledge Requirements: *United States* vs. *International Harvester.*" *American Criminal Law Review,* 25 (1988), 535.

Leon, Richard J. "Environmental Criminal Enforcement: A Mushrooming Cloud." *St. John's Law Review,* 63 (1989), 679.

McMurry, Robert, and Ramsey, Stephen. "Environmental Crimes: The Use of Criminal Sanctions in Enforcing Environmental Laws." *Loyola of Los Angeles Law Review,* 19 (1986), 1133.

Rebovich, Donald. *Dangerous Ground: The World of Hazardous Waste Crime* (New Brunswick, N.J.: Transaction Publishing, 1992).

Riesel, Daniel. "Criminal Prosecutions and Defense of Environmental Wrongs." *Environmental Law Reporter,* 15 (March 1985), 10065.

Szasz, Andrew. "Corporations, Organized Crime, and the Disposal of Hazardous Waste: An Examination of the Making of a Criminogenic Regulatory Structure." *Criminology,* 24 (1) (1986), 1.

Yeager, Peter. *The Limits of Law: Public Regulation of Private Pollution* (New York: Cambridge University Press, 1991).

NOTES

1. Thomas Arrandale, "The Mid-Life Crisis of the Environmental Lobby," *Governing,* 32 (April 1992), 36.
2. Ibid.

3. EPA, Environmental Stewardship (May 1991), 8.
4. Ibid., 9.
5. 421 *U.S.* 658 (1975).
6. 786 F2d 1499 (1986).
7. 452 *U.S.* 264 (1981).
8. 437 *U.S.* 617 (1978).
9. *Law Week*, 60 (1992), 4795.
10. 669 *F.Supp.* 1204 (1987).
11. *Law Week*, 60 (1992), at 4795.
12. Marianne Lavelle and Marcia Coyle, "Unequal Protection: The Racial Divide in Environmental Law," *National Law Journal* (September 21, 1992), 52.
13. Ibid.
14. Ibid.
15. Ibid.
16. Ibid.
17. Ibid.
18. William K. Reilly, "EPA's Reilly Replies to 'Unequal Treatment,' " *National Law Journal,* (Jan. 25, 1993), 16.
19. Congressional Record, December 20, 1969, pp. 40, 417.
20. 340 *F. Supp.* 532 (1972).
21. Joseph Sax, *Defending the Environment: A Strategy for Public Action* (New York: Knopf, 1970), p. 163.
22. 146 *U.S.* 387 (1892).
23. 263 N.E. 2d 11 (1970).

2

The Litigation Process and Other Tools of Dispute Resolution

Environmental problems are not resolved simply by the passage of environmental regulations. Once regulations are passed, disputes often arise over how the laws should be applied and whether a particular behavior constitutes compliance with the law. Thus, it is important to understand the way laws are interpreted and enforced. In our society such interpretation and enforcement occur primarily through the use of an adversarial system we commonly refer to as *litigation*. The first sections of this chapter explain how this system works and also point out some of the system's flaws. Increasingly, however, litigation is being viewed as a last resort, and alternative methods of dispute resolution are favored. Thus, latter portions of this chapter discuss how various other dispute resolution processes work.

THE ADVERSARY SYSTEM

An Introduction to the Adversary System

Our system of litigation is often referred to as an adversary system. In an adversarial system a neutral fact finder hears evidence and arguments presented by both sides and then makes an objective decision based on the facts and the law as presented by the proponents of each side. Strict rules generally govern the types of evidence that the fact finder may consider.

Theoretically, the adversary system is the best way to bring out the truth, because each side will aggressively seek all the evidence that supports its position. Each side will attempt to make the strongest possible arguments for its position and point out weaknesses of the arguments of its opponents. No shred of evidence will be overlooked, and no plausible argument will be unspoken. With all the best evidence and arguments presented, the truth, theoretically, will be easily discernible.

Criticisms of the Adversary System

Many people criticize this system. They argue that because each side is searching for only the specific evidence that supports its position, a proponent who discovers evidence helpful to the other side will not bring such evidence to the attention of the court. This tendency to ignore contrary evidence prevents a fair decision, one based on all the available evidence. Another argument of the critics is that the adversary process is extremely time-consuming and costly. Two groups of investigators are seeking the same evidence. Thus, there is a duplication of effort that lengthens the process and increases costs unnecessarily.

Still others argue that the adversary system, as it functions in the United States, is unfair. Each party in the adversarial process is represented by an attorney. Having the most skillful attorney is a tremendous advantage. Because the wealthier party can afford a better attorney, the system unjustifiably favors the wealthy. In the environmental area, the impact of this disparity can be seen when you consider a group of local citizens banding together to sue a corporation. The corporation may have its own staff of attorneys; and even if the firm has to hire outside counsel, it has the money to do so. The citizens' group, however, must get its money from donations. Often, if a company can tie up a group with a lot of pretrial motions, the costs of attorneys fees may be so high that the group may have to drop the lawsuit because it simply does not have the money to continue the action.

When used to resolve environmental disputes, the adversarial system is subject to these criticisms, as well as to others. However, perhaps the biggest criticism from environmentalists, as well as from some businesspersons, is that the adversarial process promotes strife between the parties as each seeks to be the "winner." What is really needed in many environmental cases is not a legal winner but, rather, a creative compromise. Such compromises are generally not discovered in a trial. Litigation is ideally suited for a yes–no decision; either the plaintiff or the defendant wins. In many cases what the parties want is some other objective. The defendant may want to create an industrial park in an area that the plaintiff believes should be preserved. Unfortunately, those kinds of cases are not so easily resolved through our adversarial process.

A closely related criticism is that the adversarial nature of the litigation process leads to bad feelings between two parties that really need to be able to get along with each other. When there is a conflict between a developer and conservationists, for example, many of their problems may result from an inability to discuss how a parcel of land could best be used. After a court fight, they are going to be even less able to talk to each other. Or what about an agency and a business it regulates? Litigation makes them view each other as enemies, not parties that will need to cooperate in the future.

THE U.S. DUAL COURT SYSTEM

Our adversary system is implemented through the court systems. As makes sense under federalism, we have a dual court system. The system is depicted in Figure 2-1.

The Federal Court System

Federal Trial Courts. Jurisdiction is the power of a court to hear a case and to render a decision. There are many different types of jurisdiction. The trial court is the court of *original jurisdiction*. This designation means that it is the court that has the power to initially hear and decide the case. In the federal court system, the trial courts are the *U.S. district courts*. The United States is divided into

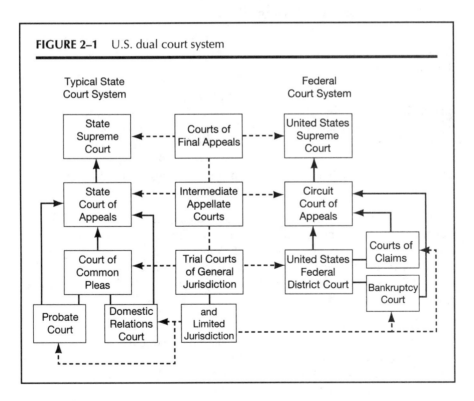

FIGURE 2–1   U.S. dual court system

96 districts, and each district has at least one trial court. Almost all cases arising under the federal environmental laws will generally be heard in the federal district courts.

Intermediate Courts of Appeals. The second level of courts in the federal system is made up of the *U.S. circuit courts of appeals.* The United States is divided into 12 geographic areas, including the District of Columbia, each of which has a circuit court of appeals. There are also federal circuit courts of appeals. Each circuit court of appeals hears appeals from all the district courts located within its area. Appeals from administrative agencies are heard by the federal circuit court of appeals.

Court of Last Resort. The U.S. *Supreme Court* is the final appellate court in the federal system. In some instances, the Supreme Court also hears cases from the court of last resort in a state system. As previously noted, the Supreme Court also functions as a trial court in an extremely limited number of cases, such as suits against ambassadors of foreign nations.

The State Court System

There is no uniform state court structure because each state has devised its own court system. All states, however, follow a general structure similar to that of the federal court system.

State Trial Courts. In state court systems, trial courts, or courts of original jurisdiction, are distributed throughout the state, usually by county. The names of these courts vary from state to state, including such titles as *courts of common pleas* or *county courts.* New York state uniquely calls its trial courts of general jurisdiction *supreme courts.* Cases involving state environmental laws will generally be brought in these state trial courts of general jurisdiction. Also, private tort claims involving environmental matters are usually brought in these courts.

Intermediate Courts of Appeals. Intermediate courts of appeals, similar to the federal circuit courts of appeals, exist in approximately half the states. These courts usually have broad jurisdiction, hearing appeals from courts of general and limited jurisdiction, as well as from state administrative agencies. The names of these courts also often vary by state. They may be called *courts of appeals* or *superior courts.*

Courts of Last Resort. In almost all cases filed in the state court system, the last appeal is to the state court of last resort. This court is frequently called the *state supreme court.* In some states, it is known as the *court of appeals.* In approximately half the states, this is the second court to which an appeal can be made; in the other half, it is the only appellate court.

Choice of Courts

Knowing that a case must be filed in a trial court does not tell the plaintiff which trial court will hear the case. The plaintiff must know which system is appropriate. The choice of which court system to enter is not purely a matter of deciding which forum would be the most desirable. Only in a limited number of cases does a party have the ability to choose between the federal and state systems. Even if a party does have that choice and chooses the state system, the other party may have the right to have the case removed to the federal system. The determination of which system may hear the case is a matter of subject matter jurisdiction. *Subject matter jurisdiction* is the power of the court to hear and render a decision in a particular type of case. Subject matter jurisdiction is extremely important because when a judge renders a decision in a case over which the court does not have subject matter jurisdiction, the decision is void, or meaningless. The parties cannot grant the judge such jurisdiction. It is determined by law as described in the following paragraphs. Figure 2–2 depicts the relationship among the types of jurisdiction.

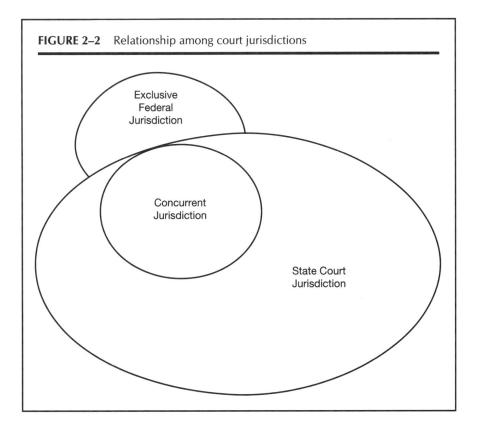

FIGURE 2–2   Relationship among court jurisdictions

Exclusive
Federal
Jurisdiction

Concurrent
Jurisdiction

State Court
Jurisdiction

Subject Matter Jurisdiction of State Courts. The state court system has jurisdiction over all cases not within the exclusive jurisdiction of the federal court system. Those cases falling within the exclusive jurisdiction of the federal courts are enumerated in the next paragraph. As the federal courts have exclusive jurisdiction over very few issues, unsurprisingly most litigation occurs in the state system.

Exclusive Federal Jurisdiction. A few types of cases may be heard only in the federal courts. Such cases are within the exclusive jurisdiction of the federal court system. If these cases were tried in a state court, any decision rendered by the judge would be void. Cases that fall within the exclusive jurisdiction of the federal courts include such matters as admiralty, bankruptcy, federal criminal prosecutions, claims against the United States, and claims arising under those federal statutes that include a provision for exclusive federal jurisdiction. Cases brought under such statutes must be filed in the federal district court or the appropriate federal court of limited jurisdiction. Thus, whenever an action based on a federal statute is anticipated, the statute should be read carefully to discern whether cases under the statute fall within the exclusive jurisdiction of the federal system. Many federal environmental statutes grant exclusive jurisdiction to the federal courts.

Concurrent Federal Jurisdiction. Many cases may be heard in either the federal or the state court. These cases are said to fall within the federal court's concurrent jurisdiction, meaning that both court systems have jurisdiction, so the plaintiff may file in the trial court of either system. There are two types of such cases. The first are *federal question* cases. If a case requires an interpretation of the U.S. Constitution, a federal statute, or a federal treaty, it is said to involve a federal question and may be heard in either state or federal court. Most federal statutes do not grant exclusive jurisdiction to the federal courts, so the case may be heard in state or federal court. Many federal environmental statutes give exclusive jurisdiction to the federal courts, but challenges to those that do not may be brought in state or federal court.

The second means by which a case may fall within the federal court's concurrent jurisdiction is through *diversity of citizenship.* If the opponents in a case are from different states, there is said to be diversity of citizenship. The diversity must be complete. If any two parties on opposing sides reside in the same state, diversity is lost. For example, if the plaintiff is an Ohio resident and one of the defendants lives in Michigan and the other in Indiana, diversity exists. However, if an Ohio plaintiff is bringing an action against a Michigan defendant and an Ohio defendant, there is not complete diversity and therefore no concurrent federal jurisdiction. Also, when the basis for federal jurisdiction is diversity of citizenship, there must be at least $50,000 in controversy.

When a case falls within the federal court's concurrent jurisdiction because of either a federal question or diversity of citizenship, the suit may be filed in either state or federal court. If the case is filed in state court, the defendant has a *right of removal*, which means that he or she may have the case transferred to federal court. If the plaintiff files in federal court, the case must be heard in that court.

Why should both parties have the right to have such a case heard in federal court? In certain cases a party may fear local prejudice in a state court. Juries for a state court are generally drawn from the county in which the court is located. The juries for federal district courts are drawn from the entire district, which encompasses many counties. Juries in state court are therefore usually more homogeneous than those of a district court. One problem that this homogeneity may present to the out-of-state corporate defendant occurs when the county in which the court is located is predominantly rural. If the case involves an injury to a member of this rural community, the defendant may feel that the jurors would be more sympathetic to the local injured party, whereas jurors drawn from a broader area, including cities, may be more likely to view the victim less sympathetically. City residents are more likely to work for a corporation and thus may not regard corporations as unfavorably as might rural residents.

Some people believe that because federal judges have more experience in resolving questions that require an interpretation of federal statutes, they are better qualified to hear such cases. Finally, if a party anticipates that it may be necessary to appeal the case to the U.S. Supreme Court, bringing the case first in a federal district court may save one step in the appeals process.

Venue. Subject matter jurisdiction should not be confused with venue. Once it is determined which court system has the power to hear the case, venue determines which of the many trial courts in that system is appropriate. Venue, clearly prescribed by statute in each state, is a matter of geographic location. It is usually based on the residence of the defendant, the location of the property in dispute, or the location in which the incident out of which the dispute arose occurred. When there are multiple defendants who reside in various geographic locations, the party filing the lawsuit may usually choose from among the various locales. If a corporation is being sued or filing an action, its residence is the place of the corporate headquarters, as well as where the firm has plants or offices. Thus, if a plaintiff residing in Wood County sued a defendant residing in Lucas County over an accident that occurred in Huron County, venue would be appropriate in any of those three counties and the plaintiff may file the case in any of them.

If the location of the court in which the case is filed presents a hardship or inconvenience to one of the parties, that person may request that the case be moved under the doctrine of *forum non conveniens*, which simply means that the location of the trial court is inconvenient. This is a motion that may be granted at the judge's discretion.

PRIMARY ACTORS IN THE LEGAL SYSTEM

An understanding of the structure of the legal system would be incomplete without an awareness of the primary actors within the legal system.

The Attorney

The party with whom environmental groups and business representatives usually have the most frequent contact is the *attorney*. Although the exact qualifications for being an attorney vary from state to state, most require that he or she have a law degree, have passed the state's bar examination, and be of high moral character. Attorneys are the legal representatives of the parties before the court. Some corporations have full-time attorneys, referred to as *in-house counsel*; other corporations send all their legal work to an outside law firm. Many large businesses have in-house counsel and also use outside counsel when a problem arises that requires a specialist. Many firms with large in-house staffs have one attorney who does only environmental law.

Attorneys are probably best known for representing clients in litigation, but they also provide other services. Attorneys represent their clients not only in courtroom litigation but also before administrative boards. Attorneys may serve as negotiators. For example, if a developer wants to undertake a project that the area's residents feel will not be environmentally sound, the residents may hire an attorney to negotiate with the developer to try to find an alternative plan. Attorneys also serve as advisers or counselors. Finally, the attorney may serve as a draftsperson, drawing up contracts and other legal documents.

Attorney–Client Privilege. The attorney can provide effective representation only when he or she knows all the pertinent facts. Clients who withhold information from their attorneys may cause irreparable harm if the hidden facts are revealed by the opposing side in court. To encourage client honesty, *the attorney–client privilege* was established. This privilege provides that information furnished in confidence to an attorney, in conjunction with a legal matter, may not be revealed by that attorney without permission from the client. This protection also extends to the attorney's work product under what is known as the *work-product doctrine.* The work product includes those formal and informal documents prepared by the attorney in conjunction with the client's case. Thus, if a client fears that his or her company is violating an environmental law and hires an attorney to determine whether the corporate behavior is unlawful, the lawyer may not be called to testify as to the work performed in analyzing the company's behavior.

The Judge

Although few people actually come into contact with a judge, the role of the *judge* is especially important in our legal system. The judge's function changes, depending on whether he or she is a trial or appellate court judge. A trial court judge presides over the trial, rules on all motions made in the case, and decides all questions of law, such as what evidence is admissible, what items may be obtained through discovery, and what law applies to the case. The judge explains the applicable law through the jury instructions. This judge makes sure that the case is heard with reasonable speed. If the parties waive their rights to a jury trial, or if, under the particular circumstances, they are not entitled to a jury, the judge also decides the facts in the case and renders a decision accordingly. A single judge presides over each case at the trial court level.

Although Thomas Jefferson said, "Ours is a government of laws, not of men," in reality, the "men" (and women) are as important as the laws. In an actual trial, the judge has a great deal of discretion when ruling on matters such as whether to admit a certain piece of evidence over the objection of opposing course. Thus, the careful litigant will always try to know something about the judge's ideology before bringing a case to trial. Certain courts earn reputations as being more pro- or antienvironment, and these reputations influence the types of cases brought to them. For example, the federal district court in Washington, D.C., is known for being pro-environment, so environmental activists file cases there whenever possible. Louisiana district courts have the opposite reputation, so business interests file in these courts whenever possible. As new appointments are made, the ideological makeup of courts may change, so attorneys must keep track of changes in the appointees.

Appellate judges serve on panels. They review lower court cases to determine whether errors of law were committed. Their review consists primarily of reading the transcript of the trial, reading written arguments by counsel for both parties, and sometimes hearing oral arguments from both parties' attorneys.

Aside from ideological differences, not all judges have equivalent knowledge about environmental issues. In an attempt to remedy the problem of a lack of understanding of scientific issues related to the environment, the Flaschner Judicial Institute in Boston and the Environmental Law Institute in Washington, D.C., have a two-day cram course in environmental law that they offer to judges all over the country. In May 1991, the first such course was taken by 48 state court judges in New England. The course was taught by both technical and legal specialists.

State court judges are usually elected, although some are appointed, whereas federal court judges are appointed by the president with the advice and consent of the Senate. Federal court judges serve for life; state court judges generally serve definite terms, the length of which varies from state to state. Because of the lifetime tenure of federal judges, many people argue that the most powerful act of a president is the appointment of judges.

The Jury

The *jury* is the means by which citizens participate in our judicial system. It has its roots in ancient Greek civilization, and it is often considered the hallmark of democracy. A jury is a group of individuals, selected randomly from the geographic area in which the court is located, who will determine questions of fact. There are two types of juries: petit and grand.

Petit Juries. Petit juries serve as the finders of fact for trial courts. Originally composed of 12 members, most juries in civil cases are allowed to have fewer members in many jurisdictions. Traditionally, jury decisions had to be unanimous. Today, however, more than half the jurisdictions no longer require unanimity in civil cases—a change made primarily to speed up trial procedures.

An important decision to be made by any party filing an action is whether to have a jury. In any civil action in which the plaintiff is seeking a remedy at law (money damages), a jury may hear the case. If both parties to the case agree, however, the jury may be waived and a judge decides the facts of the case. There is no rule about when a jury should be chosen, but a few factors should frequently be considered. One is the technical nature of the case. If a case is highly technical, it may be one that can be more fairly decided by a judge, especially one with expertise in the area in dispute. Another factor is the emotional appeal of the case. If the case is one for which the opponent's arguments may have strong emotional appeal, a judge may render a fairer decision. In most environmental law cases, the remedy being sought is an equitable one, such as the granting of an injunction, and whenever a court order, such as an injunction is being sought, no jury is allowed.

Grand Juries. Grand juries are used only in criminal matters. The Fifth Amendment requires that all federal prosecutions for infamous crimes (including all federal offenses that carry a term of imprisonment in excess of one year) be commenced with an indictment (a formal accusation of the commission of a crime, which must be made before a defendant can be tried for the crime) by a grand jury. This jury hears evidence presented by the prosecutor and determines whether there is enough evidence to justify charging a defendant.

Now that you understand how the court system is structured, and who the primary actors in the system are, it is time to examine how the court system works.

STEPS IN CIVIL LITIGATION

This section focuses on dispute resolution in the United States under the adversary system, in particular, examining the procedures used in a civil case. The rules that govern such proceedings are called the *rules of civil procedure*. There are federal rules of civil procedure, which apply in all federal courts, as well as state rules, which apply in the state courts. Most of the state rules are based on the federal rules. The procedures in a criminal case are very similar to those in a civil case except for the criminal issues of pretrial release of the defendant and sentencing.

The Threshold Issues

Prior to instigating litigation, a party must be sure that his case meets certain threshold requirements. These requirements are said to ensure that only those cases really requiring adjudication are before the courts and that both sides of the case are properly represented. These objectives are met by the threshold requirements of standing, case or controversy, and ripeness. It is the requirement of standing that is of greatest importance in environmental cases, so we will discuss this requirement first and also in the greatest detail.

Standing. *Standing* is said to be the legal right to bring a lawsuit. One who has standing is said to be a proper party to pursue the action. In most cases, one has standing when he or she is personally affected by the outcome of a case. The personal involvement is believed necessary to stimulate the party to put forth the best possible case.

An important issue, once thought settled, that is again controversial is whether citizens' groups (as opposed to individual citizens) incur sufficient personal injury to have standing to bring an environmental case. The role of citizens' groups in bringing about enforcement of environmental legislation is undeniable. Almost all environmental lawsuits (except for those brought by the EPA) are filed by citizens' groups. During the "environmental decade," 1970–80, when the initial environmental laws were being first interpreted, the most common lawsuit was a public interest group suing the government for allegedly abusing its discretion in administering environmental laws by not applying them with appropriate zeal.[1] And these cases were heard only because a long line of cases have granted citizens' groups the right to bring lawsuits to enforce environmental statues. However, with the more conservative, less activist courts ushered in by Reagan and Bush appointees, the broad standing granted to citizens' groups began to come under fire.

Conservatives have argued unsuccessfully for years that environmental groups should not be able to sue for harms that affect all citizens equally. Standing requires a particularized injury, and because everyone enjoys clean air and clean water, interest groups should not be allowed to sue to enforce these laws. This argument is now being heard anew.

The case that many had feared would begin the shrinking of the role of environmental interest groups in bringing environmental cases is *Lujan* v. *Defenders of Wildlife*,[2] argued before the U.S. Supreme Court on December 3, 1991. In that case, the Defenders argued that the Endangered Species Act of 1973 should apply to activities that the United States funds in foreign countries. The projects at issue involved the partial use of U.S. funds for an irrigation project in Sri Lanka and funds to rebuild the Aswan Dam on the Nile River, projects that threatened the endangered elephant in Sri Lanka, the crocodile in Egypt, and other species. Besides arguing on the merits, Lujan raised the standing issue, arguing that, at minimum, a group must show an injury-in-fact cause by the regulation that it is challenging. The Defenders argued that they have standing because they represent members of their organization who had personally visited the sites under regulation to study the endangered species that are to be regulated under the act, a basis for standing that would be sufficient under the traditional definition of standing recognized since the Supreme Court case of *Sierra Club* v. *Morton*.[3]

In *Sierra Club* v. *Morton*, the Sierra Club challenged a decision of the Forest Service and Department of the Interior to consider a proposal of Walt Disney Enterprises, Inc., to turn the Mineral King Valley, a national game refuge and quasi-wilderness area, into a resort. The Sierra Club alleged it had standing to seek the injunctions against granting the permits because its membership corporation had "a special interest in the conservation and the sound maintenance of the national parks, game refuges, and forests of the country." The High Court denied standing to the Sierra Club in that case, but the Court's reason for the denial set the basis for the broad interpretation of the standing requirement. The Court denied standing because the Sierra Club "failed to allege that it or any of its members would be affected in any of their activities or pastimes by the Disney development. Nowhere in the pleadings or affidavits did the Club state that its members used Mineral King for any purpose, much less that they use it in any way that would be significantly affected by the proposed actions of the respondents."

Thus, the holding in *Sierra Club* v. *Morton*, made it clear that an organization whose members would be adversely affected by failure to comply with an environmental statute would have standing, and that the requirement of a "particularized injury" was not going to mean that the petitioners had to be the only ones affected by the action. This holding was subsequently reinforced in *United States* v. *Students Challenging Regulatory Agency Procedures* (SCRAP 1).[4] In SCRAP 1, an unincorporated student group sought an injunction prohibiting the Interstate Commerce Commission from allowing the railroads to collect a 2.5 percent surcharge on goods being transported for purposes of recycling without first filing an environmental impact statement. The commission challenged the standing of the organization to bring the action.

The Supreme Court found a sufficient basis for standing in the student group's allegations that each of its members "suffered economic, recreational and aesthetic harm directly as a result of the adverse environmental effect of the railroad freight structure." The specific harms allegedly suffered were that members had to "pay more for finished products," and that each used "the forest, rivers, streams, and other natural resources surrounding the Washington Metropolitan area and at his legal residence, for camping, hiking, fishing, sightseeing, and other recreational and aesthetic purposes" and these uses were adversely affected by the increased freight rate. The group also alleged that members breathed air that was more polluted due to the rate increase, and that each member had to pay increased taxes because sums had to be expended to dispose of otherwise reusable waste materials. The Court found that the allegations of those specific harms were sufficient to deny a motion to dismiss for lack of standing.

Looking at these two primary precedent-setting cases on the issue of standing in environmental cases, many felt that the defenders' position in *Lujan* should prevail. However, the Supreme Court today is very different from the Court of the 1970s; the *Lujan* court chose to restrict the right of citizens to challenge the enforcement of environmental statutes by restricting the definition of standing.

Applying a rigorous standing test advocated by the Bush administration, the opinion of the 7–2 majority, written by Justice Antonin Scalia, said that the environmental group did not show that it would suffer an "injury in fact" or demonstrate "redressability." The High Court said that the group needed to demonstrate "not only that the listed species were in fact threatened by funded activities abroad, but also that one or more of [their] members would thereby be 'directly' affected from their 'special interest' in the subject." The Court held that it failed to demonstrate the latter.

Reaction to the decision from environmentalists matched the feelings expressed by the dissent. Justice Blackmun, joined by Justice O'Conner, wrote that the decision was "a slash and burn expedition through the law of environmental standing." He expressed fear that the decision would impose "fresh limitations" on Congress's authority to allow citizens' suits in federal courts for injuries that were "procedural" in nature.[5] Losing counsel for the Defenders was quoted as saying, "I've been in the environmental litigation business for 18 years, and this is an attempt by the Supreme Court to put us all out of business."[6] It's unlikely that his dire projection will come true, but we will have to wait to see how this case affects environmental litigation in the future.

Case or Controversy. The requirement that the courts render a decision only when there is a case or controversy before them may seem like a relatively simple matter. But in actuality, the term *case or controversy* is very imprecise and thus has been subject to changing interpretations. Today, the requirement appears to demand that the case have three essential characteristics. First, the affected parties must be in an adverse relationship to each other. Second, actual or threatened events must give rise to a live legal dispute. Finally, the courts must have the ability to render a final and meaningful judgment. Thus, the courts may give only judgments that solve an existing problem. They cannot provide advisory opinions or provide rulings with respect to hypothetical situations.

Ripeness. *Ripeness* simply means that there exists a present controversy for which a decision is needed. In other words, the decision must have the capacity to affect the parties immediately . This issue most often comes into play when one party argues that the issue is moot, or no longer ripe. For example, if a party wanted to stop a development because it would cause the loss of an endangered species habitat, but the project had already begun to the extent that the habitat had already been destroyed, the issue would be moot, so the court would not hear the case.

Pretrial

Informal Negotiations. For anyone involved in a dispute, the first step is to discuss the dispute with an attorney. It is important that the attorney be given all relevant information, even if it does not make the client look good. The more relevant facts the attorney has, the better the attorney's advice will be. Together, the attorney and the client may be able to resolve the dispute informally with the other party.

Initiation of a Legal Action. Once a party decides that an informal resolution is not possible, the parties enter what is often called the *pleading stage* of a lawsuit. Pleadings are papers filed by a party in court and then served on the opponent. The basic pleadings (described in detail later) are the complaint, the answer, the counterclaim, and the motion to dismiss. The attorney of the person who feels he or she has been wronged initiates a lawsuit by filing a complaint in the appropriate court. A *complaint* is a document that states the names of the parties to the action, the basis for the court's subject matter jurisdiction, the facts on which the party's claim is based, and the relief that the party is seeking. The party on whose behalf the complaint is filed is the *plaintiff.* The *defendant* is the party against whom the action is being brought. In most environmental cases, the plaintiff is a government agency. The second most common plaintiff is a citizens' group. The most common defendants are also government agencies, and second is corporations.

In determining the appropriate court in which to file the complaint, the attorney must determine which court has subject matter jurisdiction over the case. Once that determination has been made, the attorney must ascertain the proper venue for the case. The means used by the attorney to determine subject matter jurisdiction and venue were discussed earlier in this chapter.

The Court's Acquisition of Jurisdiction over the Person. Once the complaint is filed, the court *serves* a copy of the complaint and a summons on the defendant. Service is the procedure used by the court to ensure that the defendant actually receives a copy of the summons and the complaint. The *summons* is an order of the court notifying the defendant of the pending case and telling him or her how and when to respond to the complaint.

Personal service, whereby a sheriff or other person appointed by the court hands the summons and complaint to the defendant, has been the traditional method of service. Today, other types of service are more common. Residential service may be used, whereby the summons and complaint are left by the representative of the court with a responsible adult at the home of the defendant. Certified mail or, in some cases, ordinary mail is also used to serve defendants. When one thinks about how the rules of service would apply to a suit against a corporation, the question arises: How do you serve a corporation? The legal system has solved that question. Most states require that corporations appoint an *agent* for service when they are incorporated. This agent is a person who has been given the legal authority to receive service for the corporation. Once the agent has been served, the corporation is served. In most states, service on the president of the corporation also constitutes service on the corporation.

The purpose of service of the summons and the complaint is to give the defendant *notice* of the pending action. It also gives the court *jurisdiction over the person* of the defendant. This jurisdiction means that the court has the power to render a decision that is binding on the defendant. Traditionally, a defendant had to be served within the state in which the court was located in order for the court to acquire jurisdiction over the person of the defendant. This restriction imposed severe hardships when a defendant who lived in one state entered another state and injured the plaintiff. If the defendant never again entered the plaintiff's state, the plaintiff could bring an action against the defendant only in the state in which the defendant lived. Obviously, this restriction would prevent many legitimate actions from being filed.

To alleviate this problem, most states enacted *long-arm statutes.* These statutes enable the court to serve the defendant outside the state as long as the defendant has engaged in certain acts within the state. Those acts vary from state to state, but most statutes include such acts as committing a tort within the state or doing business within the state. Initially, such statutes were challenged as a denial of due process to the out-of-state defendant. Such challenges were usually unsuccessful.

Defendant's Response. Once the defendant has been properly served, he or she files an answer and possibly a counterclaim. An *answer* is a response to the allegations in the plaintiff's complaint. The answer must admit, deny, or state that the defendant has no knowledge about the truth of each of the plaintiff's allegations. The answer may also contain *affirmative* defenses, which consist of facts that were not stated in the complaint that would provide justification for the defendant actions *and* a legally sound reason to deny relief to the plaintiff. These defenses must be stated in the answer. If they are not raised in the answer, the court may not allow the defenses to be raised later. The defendant is required to plead his or her affirmative defenses in the answer in order to give the plaintiff notice of all the issues that will be raised at the trial.

When a defendant, on receiving the complaint, believes that even if all of the plaintiff's factual allegations were true the plaintiff would not be entitled to a favorable judgment, the defendant may file a *motion to dismiss.* There are no factual issues being debated, so the judge accepts the facts as stated by the plaintiff and makes a ruling on the legal questions in the case. Judges are generally not receptive to such motions, granting them only when "it appears beyond doubt that the plaintiff can prove no set of facts in support of his claim which would entitle him to relief."

If the defendant believes that he or she has a cause of action against the plaintiff, this will be included as a *counterclaim.* The form of a counterclaim is just like that of a complaint: The defendant states the facts supporting his or her claim and asks for the relief to which he or she feels entitled. If the defendant files a counterclaim, the plaintiff generally files a reply. A *reply* is simply an answer to a counterclaim. In the reply the plaintiff admits, denies, or states that he or she is without knowledge of the truth of the facts asserted by the defendant in the counterclaim. Any affirmative defenses that are appropriate must be raised in the reply.

After the pleadings have been filed, either party can file a *motion for judgment on the pleadings*. When such a motion is filed, the party is saying that even if all the facts are as alleged by the opposite side's pleadings, I should still win the case. Such motions are rarely granted.

Pretrial Motions. The early pleadings just described serve to establish the legal and factual issues of the case. Once these issues have been established, either the plaintiff or the defendant may file a motion designed to bring the case to an early conclusion or to gain some advantage for the party filing the motion. A *motion* is simply a request by a party for the court to do something. A party may request, or move, that the court do almost anything pertaining to the case, such as a motion for some form of temporary relief until a decision has been rendered. For example, if a suit is brought over the right to a piece of property, the court may grant a motion prohibiting the current possessor of that property from selling it.

Discovery. Once the initial pleadings and motions have been filed, the parties gather information from each other through *discovery*. At this stage a party is frequently asked by her or his attorney to respond to the opponent's requests for information about the case. There are a number of tools of discovery through which these requests are made. One of the most common is *interrogatories*—a series of written questions that are sent to the opposing party, who must truthfully answer them under oath. Interrogatories are frequently accompanied by a *request to admit certain facts*. The attorney and the client work together to answer these interrogatories and requests for admission of facts.

A *request to produce documents* or other items is another tool of discovery. Unless the information requested is privileged or is irrelevant to the case, it must be produced. Photographs, contracts, written estimates, and forms that must be filed with governmental agencies are among the items that may be requested. One party may also request that the other party submit to a mental or physical examination. This motion will be approved only when the party's mental or physical health is at issue in the case.

Finally, testimony before trial may be obtained by the taking of a *deposition*. At a deposition, a witness is examined under oath by the attorneys. A court reporter (stenographer) records every word spoken by the attorneys and witnesses. The testimony is usually transcribed so that both parties have a written copy. When a person is to be deposed in a case, it is very important that he or she and the attorney talk extensively about what kinds of questions may come up at the deposition and how such questions are to be answered. The party who requested the deposition is not only seeking information but is also laying the groundwork for identifying any inconsistencies that may arise between a person's testimony at the deposition and in court. If such inconsistencies exist, they will be brought to the attention of the fact finder and may result in a loss of credibility for the courtroom testimony.

Depositions may also be used when a potential witness is old or ill and may die before the trial. They are useful if witnesses may be moving or for some other reason may not be available at the time of the trial.

As a result of discovery each party should have knowledge of most of the facts surrounding the case. This process is supposed to prevent surprises from occurring in the courtroom. Parties must comply with requests for discovery, or the court may order that the facts sought to be discovered be deemed admitted as if they had been proved. Thus, it is important that anyone involved in litigation produce for the attorney all requested discovery material. An attorney who feels that certain material should not be discovered makes arguments about its lack of relevance to the case, but if the court disagrees, the information must be supplied.

Pretrial Conference. If the judge finds that questions of fact do exist, he or she usually holds a pretrial conference. This is an informal meeting of the judge with the lawyers representing the parties. At this meeting, they try to narrow the legal and factual issues and to work out a settlement if possible. When the lawsuit begins, there are many conflicting assertions as to what events actually led to the lawsuit. Questions about what actually happened are referred to as *questions of fact.* Many times, as a result of discovery, parties come to agree on most of the facts. Remaining factual disputes may often be resolved at the conference. Then the only questions left are how to apply the law to the facts and what damages, if any, to award. By the time of the pretrial conference, each party should have determined the limits of any settlement to which he or she is willing to agree and should have communicated those limits to his or her attorney, who may be able to reach a settlement at the conference. Judges frequently try very hard to help the parties reach agreement before trial. If no settlement can be reached, the attorneys and the judge discuss the administrative details of the trial, its length, the witnesses, and any pretrial stipulations of fact or law to which the parties can agree.

The Trial

Once the pretrial stage has concluded, the next step is the trial. As noted earlier, if the plaintiff is seeking a legal remedy (money damages), he or she is usually entitled to a jury trial. The judge is the fact finder when an equitable remedy (an injunction or other court order) is being sought or the parties have waived their right to a jury. For example, when a plaintiff in a negligence action against a manufacturer that produced a toxic substance requests a judgment for $10,000 in medical expenses, he or she is seeking a legal remedy and is entitled to a jury trial. But a plaintiff seeking an injunction to prohibit the construction of a dam that would destroy the habitat of an endangered species is requesting an equitable remedy and is not be entitled to a jury. It is important for a person filing an action to determine at the outset whether a jury is desirable, because a jury must be demanded in the complaint.

The stages of a trial are jury selection, opening statements, plaintiff's case, defendant's case, conference on jury instructions, closing arguments, and post-trial motions.

Jury Selection. An important part of a jury trial is the selection of the jury. A panel of potential jurors is selected randomly from a list of citizens. In the federal court system, voter lists are used. In a process known as *voir dire*, the attorneys and/or the judge question potential jurors to determine whether they could render an unbiased opinion in the case. In most states each attorney is allowed to reject a minimal number of potential jurors without giving a reason. These rejections are called *peremptory challenges*. Attorneys are given an unlimited number of challenges for cause. *For cause* dismissals are used when questioning reveals a fact that would make it difficult for the potential juror to be impartial. For example, the potential juror may have brought a similar lawsuit against one of the defendant corporations five years ago.

Jury selection is deemed so crucial to the litigation process that some law firms hire psychologists or jury selection professionals to assist them in the voir dire process. In fact, there is a great deal of debate about whether jury selection is indeed a science, and what impact jury selection has on the outcome of a case. If jury selection is indeed a science, and the use of jury selection consultants can influence the outcome of a case, there are important implications for environmental litigation. The party with the greater financial resources would enjoy a distinct advantage in the courtroom. In most cases the advantaged party would be a corporate defendant. In any event, enough people believe that jury selection is a science that jury consultant firms are springing up across the country.

Their services are varied, and even go beyond jury selection to helping lawyers anticipate jury behavior once jurors are selected. Their fees are not cheap, often ranging from $40,000 to several million dollars per case.[7] Some of the more commonly sought services of jury consultant firms are community surveys, jury selection assistance, mock juries, and shadow juries.[8] A community survey is a survey of potential juries, the results of which are used to develop a profile of the ideal juror. Jury selection assistance includes the consultant's providing questions for voir dire and even, if allowed in the state, sitting in on the questioning. A mock jury is a jury selected to match the profile of the actual jury. The lawyers then "rehearse" their case before the mock jury, and get feedback from the mock jury as to which arguments, evidence, and witnesses were persuasive and which were harmful to their case. Based on that feedback, the lawyers may alter their trial performance.

A shadow jury is also selected to match the profile of the actual jurors. But the shadow jurors sit in on the actual trial. At the end of each day, they meet to discuss what transpired during the trial and how the day's events affected their evolving opinion. Lawyers may alter their next day's presentation to try to remove doubts or change undesirable perceptions created that day. After trial, the shadow jury deliberates briefly to try to give the lawyers a preview of what the actual verdict will be. Based on input from the shadow jury, the lawyers may either go to opponents with a last-minute settlement offer, or they may reject any settlement proposals they receive.

Opening Statements. Once a jury has been impaneled, or selected, the case begins with the opening statements. Each party's attorney explains to the judge and the jury what facts he or she intends to prove, the legal conclusions to which these facts will lead, and how the case should be decided.

Plaintiff's Case. The plaintiff then presents his or her case, which consists of examining witnesses and presenting evidence. The procedure for each witness is the same. First, the plaintiff's attorney questions the witness in what is called *direct examination.* Then the opposing counsel may *cross-examine* the witness; only questions pertaining to the witness's direct examination may be asked. The plaintiff's attorney then has the opportunity for *redirect examination,* to repair any damage done by the cross-examination. The opposing counsel then has a last opportunity to cross-examine the witness to address facts brought out in redirect examination. This procedure is followed for each of the plaintiff's witnesses.

Immediately following the plaintiff's case, the defendant may make a *motion for a directed verdict.* In making such a motion, the defendant is stating to the court that even if all the plaintiff's factual allegations are true, the plaintiff has not proved his or her case. For example, as will be discussed in Chapter 4 to prove a case of nuisance, the plaintiff must prove that the defendant used his own property in a manner that interfered with the plaintiff's use or enjoyment of her property. If the plaintiff offers no evidence of how her use or enjoyment of her land had been diminished, then there can be no judgment for the plaintiff. In such a case a motion for a directed verdict would be granted and the case dismissed. Such motions are rarely granted because the plaintiff will usually introduce some evidence of every element necessary to establish the existence of his or her case.

A motion for a directed verdict also may be made by either party after the presentation of the defendant's case. The party filing the motion (the moving party) is saying that even if the judge looks at all the evidence in the light most favorable to the other party, it is overwhelmingly clear that the only decision the jury could come to is that the moving party is entitled to judgment in his or her favor.

Defendant's Case. If the defendant's motion for a directed verdict is denied, the trial proceeds with the defendant's case in chief. The defendant's witnesses are questioned in the same manner as were the plaintiff's, except that the defendant's attorney does the direct and redirect examination and the plaintiff's attorney is entitled to cross-examine the witnesses.

Conference on Jury Instructions. If the case is being heard by a jury, the attorneys and the judge then retire for a conference on jury instructions. Jury instructions are the court's explanation to the jury of what legal decision they must make if they find certain facts to be true. Each attorney presents to the judge the set of jury instructions he or she feels will enable the jury to accurately apply the law to the facts. Obviously, each attorney tries to state the law in the manner most favorable to the client. The judge confers with the attorneys regarding their proposed instructions and then draws up the instructions for the jury. Attorneys listen very carefully to the instructions the judge gives because one basis for appeal of a decision is that the judge improperly instructed the jury.

Closing Arguments. The attorneys' last contact with the jury then follows. The attorneys present their closing arguments. The party who has the burden of proof, the plaintiff, presents the first closing argument; the defendant's closing argument follows. Finally, the plaintiff is entitled to a rebuttal. The judge then reads the instructions to the jury, and the jurors retire to the jury room to deliberate. When they reach a decision, the jurors return to the courtroom, where their verdict is read.

Posttrial Motions. The party who loses has a number of options. A *motion for a judgment notwithstanding the verdict (judgment N.O.V.)* may be made. This is a request for the judge to enter a judgment contrary to that handed down by the jury on the ground that as a matter of law the decision could only have been different from that reached by the jury. For example, if a plaintiff requests damages of $500 but introduces evidence of only $100 worth of damages, the jury cannot award the plaintiff $400 in damages. If they do so, the defendant would file a motion for a motion notwithstanding the verdict. Alternatively, the dissatisfied party may file a *motion for a new trial* on the ground that the verdict is clearly against the weight of the evidence. If neither of these motions is granted and the judge enters a judgment in accordance with the verdict, the losing party may appeal the decision.

Appellate Procedure

As discussed previously, the court to which the case is appealed depends on the court in which the case was originally heard. A case heard in a federal district court is appealed to the U.S. circuit court of appeals for the geographic region in which the district court is located. If heard in a state trial court, the case is appealed to that state's intermediate appellate court or, if none exists, to the state's final appellate court.

To appeal a case, the losing party must allege that a prejudicial error of law occurred during the trial. A *prejudicial error* is one that is so substantial that it could have affected the outcome of the case. For example, the judge may have ruled as admissible in court certain evidence that had a major impact on the decision, when that evidence was legally inadmissible. Or the party may argue that the instructions the judge read to the jury were inaccurate and resulted in a misapplication of the law to the facts.

When a case is appealed, there is not a new trial. The attorney for the appealing party (the appellant) and the attorney for the party who won in the lower court (the appellee) file briefs, or written arguments, with the court of appeals. They also generally present oral arguments before the appeals court. The court considers these arguments, reviews the record of the case, and renders a decision. The decision of the appellate court can take a number of forms: The court may accept the decision of the lower court and *affirm* that decision. Alternatively, the appellate court may conclude that the lower court was correct in its decision, except for granting an inappropriate remedy, and so it will *modify* the remedy. If the appellate court decides that the lower court was incorrect in its decision, that decision will be *reversed.* Finally, the appeals court may feel that an error was committed, but it does not know how that error would have affected the outcome of the case, so it will *remand* the case to the lower court for a new trial.

Although the appeals procedure may sound relatively simple compared to the initial trial procedure, appeals require a great deal of work on the part of the attorneys. They are consequently expensive. Thus, when deciding whether to appeal, a party must consider how much money he or she wishes to spend. In some cases, it may be less expensive to pay the judgment than to appeal.

However, a more important factor to consider when deciding whether to appeal may be the precedential value of the case. The case may involve an important new issue of law that a party hopes may be decided in her or his favor by an appeals court. If she or he anticipates similar prospective suits, it may be important to get a favorable ruling. If the case appears to be strong, an appeal may be desirable. If the case is weak, the wiser move may be to accept the lower court decision and wait for another opportunity to get an appellate ruling. Remember, an appellate precedent carries more weight than a trial court decision.

Appellate courts, unlike trial courts, are usually composed of at least three judges. There are no juries. The decision of the court is determined by the majority of the judges. One of the judges who votes with the majority records the court's decision and their reasons in what is called the *majority opinion.* These have precedential value and are used by judges to make future decisions and by attorneys in advising their clients as to the appropriate course of behavior in similar situations. If any of the judges in a case agrees with the ultimate decision of the majority but for different reasons, he or she may write a *concurring opinion*, stating how this conclusion was reached. Finally, the judge or judges disagreeing with the majority may write their *dissenting opinion*, giving their reasons for reaching a contrary conclusion. Dissenting opinions may be cited in briefs by attorneys arguing that the law should be changed. Dissents may also be cited by an appellate judge who decides to change the law.

In many important U.S. Supreme Court cases, there is one majority opinion accompanied by several concurring and dissenting opinions. A case that has only one majority opinion signed by all the judges is considered much stronger—and potentially longer lasting than a majority opinion accompanied by numerous concurring and dissenting opinions. For most cases only one appeal is possible. In some states, where there is both an intermediate and a superior court of appeals, a losing party may appeal from the intermediate appellate court to the state supreme court. In a limited number of cases a losing party may be able to appeal from a state supreme court or a circuit court of appeals to the U.S. Supreme Court.

Appeal to the U.S. Supreme Court. There are two types of appeals to the U.S. Supreme Court: appeal by *writ of certiorari* and *appeal as of right.* The former is the more common type of appeal. To appeal by writ of certiorari, the losing party files a petition with the Supreme Court in which he or she argues that the issue on which the appeal is based either presents a *substantial federal question* or involves a matter that has produced *conflicting decisions from the various circuit courts of appeal* and is in need of resolution. The Supreme Court reviews the petition and may decide to review the case if at least four justices are convinced that it is a matter in need of resolution.

It is often difficult to predict whether the Court will hear a case. A federal question is simply an issue arising under the federal Constitution, treaties, or statutes. Substantiality is more difficult to define. If the decision would affect a large number of people, or is likely to arise again if not decided, it may be considered substantial. If the Supreme Court refuses to hear a case, such refusal has no precedential effect.

In a limited number of cases the losing party is entitled to nondiscretionary *appeal as of right.* When parties are entitled to an appeal as of right, they file a notice of appeal, and the Supreme Court must review the case on its merits. For example, if a state supreme court holds that a federal statute is unconstitutional, this ruling can be appealed as of right. In both appeals by writ and as of right, the appeal may be limited to the Court's simply reviewing the transcript of the lower court case. It is up to the Court to determine whether it wants to hear oral arguments and read written briefs.

ALTERNATIVES TO CIVIL LITIGATION

The litigation process seems extremely time-consuming and expensive to many people, so unwieldy that they have turned to other means to resolve their disputes. In the environmental arena the two main alternatives are mediation and arbitration. Both these alternative methods share certain advantages over litigation. Generally, they are less expensive and less time-consuming, and the formal hearing times and places can be set at the parties' mutual convenience. The persons presiding over the resolution process can be chosen by the parties and, in many cases, are more familiar with the area of law over which the dispute arose than would be a randomly assigned judge. These alternatives may also prevent adverse publicity, which could be ruinous to a business. They may also result in the preservation of confidentiality, which may be extremely important when a company's trade secrets are involved.

The following detailed examination of these alternative dispute-resolution methods should help you understand the types of situations wherein each of these alternatives may be preferable to litigation. One problem that sometimes arises in the decision to use an alternative form of dispute resolution is that in many cases an alternative may benefit one party, whereas litigation may be more beneficial to the other.

Arbitration

Arbitration—the resolution of a dispute by a neutral third party outside the judicial setting—is one of the most well-known alternatives to litigation, although not the most common form used to resolve environmental matters. The arbitration hearing is somewhat similar to a trial, but there is no prehearing discovery process. The stringent rules of evidence applicable in a trial are generally relaxed in arbitration. Each side presents witnesses and evidence, and the parties are given the opportunity to cross-examine their opponent's witnesses. The arbitrator frequently takes a much more active role in questioning the witness than would a judge. An arbitrator who needs to know more information will generally ask for that information from witnesses.

Unlike at a trial, there is usually no official record of the hearing. However, the parties and the arbitrator may agree to have a stenographer record the proceedings at the expense of the parties. The arbitrator and each of the parties usually take their own notes of what transpires. Although attorneys may represent parties in arbitration, notes are not required. Often, to save money, a party may consult an attorney to help plan the arbitration strategy, but the party would appear at the arbitration without the lawyer. Individuals may represent themselves or may have someone else represent them. In some cases, the arbitrator may request written arguments from the parties. These documents are called *arbitration briefs*.

The arbitrator usually provides a decision for the parties within 30 days of the hearing. He or she may provide the reasons for the decision but is not required to do so. The decision rendered by the arbitrator is much more likely to be a compromise decision than is the decision handed down by a court, for a number of reasons. First, the arbitrator is not as constrained by precedent as are judges. The arbitrator is interested in resolving a factual dispute, not in establishing or strictly applying a rule of law, although of course he or she cannot render a decision that is clearly contrary to the law. Second, the arbitrator may be more interested than a judge in preserving an ongoing relationship with the parties. A compromise is much more likely to achieve this result than is a clear win-or-lose decision. Obviously, if the evidence overwhelmingly favors one party, the arbitrator will rule in that party's favor, but most cases are not so clear, and arbitrators will generally try to give each party something. Finally, because an arbitrator frequently decides cases in a particular area, he or she wants to maintain a reputation of being fair to both sides so as to be selected to decide future cases.

The decision rendered by the arbitrator is legally binding. The decision may be appealed through the court system, but judges will only rarely overturn an arbitrator's decision. Usually the only basis for overturning the decision is that the arbitrator exceeded the bounds of his or her authority. Such a high standard for review almost seems to give an arbitrator more power than the trial court!

Methods of Securing Arbitration. There are three basic methods by which parties can secure arbitration. One means is by inclusion of a *binding arbitration clause* in a contract. Such a clause provides that all or certain disputes arising under the contract are to be settled by arbitration. The clause should also include the means by which the arbitrator is to be selected. More than 95 percent of the collective bargaining agreements in force today have some provision for arbitration.

If no arbitration clause is included in a contract and a dispute arises over its terms, the parties may secure arbitration by entering into a *submission agreement.* This is a written contract stating that the parties wish to settle their dispute by arbitration. It usually also states the means by which the arbitrator will be selected and the limits of the arbitrator's authority. For example, in a tort case, the arbitrator may be limited to awarding the plaintiff up to *x* amount of dollars.

If the parties have entered into a submission agreement or have included an arbitration clause in their contract, they will be required to resolve their disputes through arbitration. Both federal and state courts must defer to arbitration if the contract in dispute contains a binding arbitration clause.

Selection of an Arbitrator. Once the decision to arbitrate has been made, an arbitrator must be selected. Arbitrators are generally lawyers, professors, or other professionals. They are frequently selected on the basis of their special expertise in some area. If the parties have not agreed on an arbitrator before a dispute, they generally use one of two sources for selecting an arbitrator: the Federal Mediation and Conciliation Service (FMCS), a governmental agency, or the American Arbitration Association (AAA), a private, nonprofit organization.

When the disputants contact one of these agencies, they receive a list of arbitrators along with a biographical sketch of each. Once the arbitrator has been selected, the parties and the arbitrator agree on the time, the date, and the location of the arbitration. They also agree on the substantive and procedural rules to be followed in the arbitration.

Disadvantages of Arbitration. The most significant reason for not using arbitration would probably be that the decision does not create a legally binding precedent, which may be important in many cases. Less importantly, a party may want the publicity generated by a lawsuit, which arbitration does not usually provide. Another problem with arbitration is that the lengthy court procedures that arbitration omits serve to protect parties from surprise and unfair admission of questionable evidence. The protection of thorough review on appeal is also lost.

Mediation

Since the mid-1970s, mediation has increasingly been used to resolve environmental disputes, especially those involving complex issues and multiple parties with different interests. Between 1974 and 1984, mediation was used to solve approximately 160 environmental disputes involving matters that ranged from air quality to land use to toxic waste. Mediation differs from arbitration and litigation in that the mediator makes no final decision. The mediator is simply a facilitator of communication between disputing parties. Mediation is an informal process in which the two disputants select a party, usually one with expertise in the disputed area, to help them reconcile their differences. Although there is no guarantee that a decision will be reached through mediation, if a decision is reached, the parties generally enter into a contract that embodies the terms of their settlement. If one party does not live up to the terms of the settlement, that party can then be sued for breach of contract.

Advantages of Mediation. Among environmentalists, agency employees, and businesspersons, mediation has both its supporters and its detractors. And although not all environmental issues are suitable for mediation, clearly all environmental issues are not appropriate for litigation, either. The primary advantage of mediation is that because of its nonadversarial nature, it tends to preserve the relationship between the parties to a greater extent than would a trial or an arbitration. Thus, it is used more and more frequently in cases where the parties will have an ongoing relationship once the immediate dispute is settled. Many times in community disputes, the parties will frequently find themselves in conflict. Conceivably, mediation could help each understand the other a little better, so future disagreements might be resolved more easily.

A second advantage is that mediation can be quicker. With the ever-increasing federal court caseload, delays are inevitable. Mediation can be almost instantaneous, once a mediator is agreed upon. Because many environmental issues demand a quick response, mediation may be desirable. Mediation may be less expensive than litigation. At minimum, mediation eliminates the cost of hiring expensive expert witnesses to testify at the trial. An extremely complex mediation may cost thousands of dollars, but an expensive lawsuit may run into the millions.

Another reason why mediation may be desirable for environmental problems is that in many cases the environmental issue does fit neatly into the two-party, right-wrong mode of litigation. Many times the environmental matter may involve numerous groups with varying interests. What is needed is a creative solution that takes into account multiple interests. Mediation provides a forum where an unlimited number of interests can be heard, and a solution other than a "winner take all" judgment for the plaintiff or no liability for the defendant can be attained. And even if a solution cannot be reached, mediation will have at least served to help educate the parties as to the others' position. And in the future, if the parties have to deal with each other, they may be a little more understanding and be able to work out problems together.

Disadvantages of Mediation. Sometimes mediation is clearly not appropriate. If you want to establish a precedent-setting interpretation of a case, you have no choice but to go to court. A related problem is that mediation may produce more inconsistent outcomes. Arguably, this disparity of outcomes resulting from a matter's being mediated in many places could be considered unfair.

Also, if part of a party's objectives include getting publicity that it hopes will turn public opinion against a project strongly enough to block the project, then, again, mediation is not appropriate. In many environmental disputes, the greatest benefit of litigation for a citizens' group may be in creating public awareness that it hopes will lead to public pressure to prohibit some action.

Finally, no one can be forced to mediate. If one person whose interests are affected chooses to not mediate, even if 20 other affected interests agree to a mediated solution, the party who did not participate may still raise the issue through litigation. And sometimes those involved in the mediation may not be aware of an affected party who consequently is not included in the mediation. That party may later litigate. Even worse, a party who wants to tie up a project may agree to mediation and go through the process, fully intending *not* to reach any agreement. The party is simply "tying the case up" in mediation. Once the other party realizes what is going on, the case may then be litigated, but by that time there has been a costly delay.

Critics of mediation often argue that the informal nature of the process represses and denies certain irreconcilable structural conflicts, such as the inherent strife between developers and environmentalists. They also argue that this informal process tends to create the impression of equality between the disputants when no such equality exists. The resultant compromise between unequals is an unequal compromise, but it is clothed in the appearance of equal influence. Despite these criticisms, mediation does have its place in the resolution of environmental disputes. It will probably always be a supplement to, and not a replacement for, litigation.

CONCLUDING REMARKS

You now understand how the U.S. dual court system is structured and functions. Dispute resolution through our courts is an adversarial process, so disputes are managed by two conflicting parties, represented by lawyers, each of whom tries to bring out the strongest evidence and make the best argument for his or her side. A neutral third party, either a judge or jury, will decide who is the winner.

This adversarial process, however, is not well suited for many disputes, especially environmental ones. It is time-consuming, publicity-generating, does not lead to compromise resolutions, and often worsens the relationship between two parties who must work with each other in the future. Because of these problems, alternatives to litigation increasingly are being used to resolve environmental disputes. Some of the more common alternatives include arbitration, and mediation. Mediation is probably the most common because it preserves the parties' relationship and also allows the easiest inclusion of a multiplicity of interests.

Once you appreciate how the dispute resolution systems function, there is only one more area of the American legal system that you need to understand before you are ready to explore environmental law: administrative law. Chapter 3 introduces this important system of law.

QUESTIONS FOR REVIEW AND DISCUSSION

1. Explain what is meant by an adversary system and justify the use of such a system.
2. Explain the problems associated with reliance on the adversarial process to resolve environmental disputes.
3. Distinguish subject matter jurisdiction from jurisdiction over the person.
4. Explain the various roles a lawyer may play.
5. Distinguish a grand jury from a petit jury.
6. Explain the significance of the standing cases such as *Lujan* v. *Defenders of Wildlife* and *Sierra Club* v. *Morton*.
7. Trace the steps of a civil lawsuit.
8. Explain and critique the primary alternatives to litigation.

FOR FURTHER READING

(Comment) "Calm after the Storm: Grandmother of Environmental Lawsuits Settled by Mediation." *Environmental Law Reporter*, 11 (1981), 10074.

Hoban, Thomas, and Richard Brooks. *Green Justice: The Environment and the Courts.* Boulder, Colo.: Westview Press, 1987.

(Note) "Lujan v. National Wildlife Federation: The Supreme Court Tightens the Reins on Standing for Environmental Groups." *Catholic University Law Review*, 40 (1991), 443.

Sax, J. "The Public Trust Doctrine in Natural Resource Law: Effective Judicial Intervention." *Michigan Law Review*, 68 (1970), 471.

Singer, D. "The Use of ADR Methods in Environmental Disputes." *Arbitration Law Journal*, 47 (March 1992), 55.

Stone, Christopher. *Should Trees Have Standing? Toward Legal Rights for Natural Objects.* Los Altos, Calif.: William Kaufmann, 1974.

Wenz, Peter. *Environmental Justice.* Albany: State University of New York Press, 1988.

NOTES

1. Lettie Wenner, *The Environmental Decade in Court* (Bloomington: Indiana University Press, 1982).
2. 405 *U.S.* 727 (1972).
3. 405 *U.S.* 727 (1972).
4. 412 *U.S.* 669 (1973).
5. M. Coyle, and M. Havelle, "Eco-Groups' Standing Curtailed," *National Law Journal* (June 1992), 3.
6. Ibid.
7. Emily Couric, "Jury Sleuths: In Search of the Perfect Panel," *National Law Journal* (July 21, 1986) p. 1.
8. Ibid.

3

The Law
of Administrative
Agencies

Environmental law is classified as a branch of administrative law. This classification means that these laws are overseen by a body known as an administrative agency, and that many of the specific regulations in this area are also established by this agency. Because environmental law falls within this classification, some basic understanding of administrative law is necessary.

The first part of this chapter explains how administrative agencies are created. Next, their primary functions, rule making, adjudication, and administrative activities are described. The third section focuses on the ways in which the primary branches of the U.S. government control these agencies. The chapter concludes with a description of some of the major agencies affecting the environment.

The first federal administrative agencies were created by Congress near the end of the nineteenth century and the beginning of the twentieth. They were the Interstate Commerce Commission (ICC) and the Federal Trade Commission (FTC). Congress felt that the anti-competitive conduct of railroads and other corporations could best be controlled by separate regulatory bodies with defined statutory mandates. Following the crash of the stock market and the Great Depression of the 1930s, Congress saw a need for additional agencies that could assist in guiding market decisions in the public interest. Since then, numerous agencies have been created whenever Congress believed there was an area that required more intense regulation than Congress could provide.

An administrative agency is generally defined as any body created by a legislative branch (e.g., Congress, a state legislature, or a city council) to carry out specific duties. Most agencies, however, are not situated entirely in the legislative, the executive, or the judicial branch of government. They generally have legislative power to make rules for an entire industry, judicial power to adjudicate (decide) individual cases, and executive power to investigate corporate misconduct. Numerous agencies play a role in creating and enforcing environmental regulations; especially important is the Environmental Protection Agency (EPA).

CREATION OF ADMINISTRATIVE AGENCIES

Congress creates most administrative agencies through statutes called *enabling legislation*, although the president sometimes creates administrative agencies through an executive reorganization plan. Generally, the enabling statutes contain broad delegations of congressional *legislative power* to agencies for the purpose of serving the "public interest, convenience, and necessity." This power to create rules is sometimes referred to as *quasi legislative* because the agency's rule-making authority is limited in scope to the authority it is granted by Congress. Using this mandate, a particular administrative agency issues rules that control individual and business behavior. In many instances, such rules carry civil, as well as criminal, penalties.

When passing an enabling statute, Congress also delegates *executive power* to agencies to investigate potential violations of rules or statutes. Through enabling statutes, Congress also delegates *judicial power* to settle or adjudicate individual disputes that an agency may have with businesses or individuals. For example, the EPA administrator, using the congressional mandate under the Clean Air Act, sets forth rules governing the amount of certain hazardous air pollutants that may be emitted into the atmosphere. Using these standards, another branch of the EPA sends investigators to inspect a plant suspected of violating the act. If the inspector finds a violation and the EPA imposes a penalty, the plant operator will most likely contest the imposition of the fine, and a hearing will be held before an administrative law judge employed in another division of the EPA.

Because legislative, executive, and judicial powers have traditionally been placed in separate branches of government by the Constitution, the role of administrative agencies has led some to state that an unofficial "fourth branch of government" really exists. Although there is a semblance of truth to that characterization, administrative agencies are not in fact another branch, primarily because all their authority is simply delegated to them and they remain under the control of the three traditional branches of government. They are not as independent as the term "fourth branch of government" might imply.

FUNCTIONS OF ADMINISTRATIVE AGENCIES

Administrative agencies perform the following functions: rule making; adjudication of individual cases brought before administrative law judges by the staff of an agency; and administrative activities.

Rule making

Americans are probably most familiar with administrative agencies because of their rule-making powers. Administrative agencies are granted the authority to perform the legislative function of making rules or regulations by the enabling statutes that bring them into existence. For example, the enabling statute creating the Occupational Safety and Health Administration gave the secretary of Labor authority to set "mandatory safety and health standards applicable to businesses affecting interstate commerce." The secretary was given the power to "prescribe such rules and regulations that he may deem necessary to carry out the responsibilities under this act." In some cases, the procedures for implementing the rule-making function are spelled out in the enabling act. When this is not done, one of three alternative models for rule making may be used: informal, formal, or hybrid.

One reason for the creation of administrative agencies has been the idea that they could be staffed with people who had special expertise in the area the agency was regulating and therefore would be capable of knowing what types of regulations were necessary to protect the citizens in that area. Also, because they were not elected, agency employees, in their rule-making capacity, would not be subject to political pressure. Agencies would also be able to act more swiftly than Congress in enacting laws. Today, administrative agencies actually create more rules than Congress and the courts combined.

As you read about the administrative rule-making procedures, compare them to the legislative process. You may notice that it is really much easier for the public to participate in agency rule making. One reason for the relatively great opportunity for public participation is concern on the part of Congress that people would be upset about laws being made by individuals who were not elected.

Informal Rule Making The primary type of rule making used by administrative agencies is informal, or notice-and-comment rule making. As provided by Section 553 of the Administrative Procedure Act (APA), informal rule making applies in all situations where the agency's enabling legislation or other congressional directives do not require another form. An agency initiates informal rule making by publishing in the *Federal Register* the proposed rule, along with an explanation of the legal authority for issuing the rule and a description of how one can participate in the rule-making process. Following this publication, opportunity is provided for all interested parties to submit written comments. These comments may contain data, arguments, or other information a person believes might influence the agency in its decision making. Although the agency is not required to hold hearings, it has the discretion to receive oral testimony if it wishes to do so. After considering the comments, the agency publishes the final rule, with a statement of its basis and purpose, in the *Federal*

Register. This publication also includes the date on which the rule becomes effective, which must be at least 30 days after publication. Figure 3–1 depicts this process.

Informal rule making is most often used because it is more efficient for the agency in terms of time and cost. No formal public hearing is required, and no formal record need be established, as would be true in formal rule making. Some people, however, believe that informal rule making is unfair because parties who are interested in the proposed rule have no idea what types of evidence the agency has received from other sources with respect to that rule. Thus, if the agency is relying on what one party might perceive as flawed or biased data, that party has no way to challenge those data. A second type of rule making, formal rule making, avoids that problem.

Formal Rule Making. Section 553(c) of the APA requires formal rule making when an enabling statute or other legislation requires that all regulations or rules be enacted by an agency as part of a formal hearing process that includes a com-

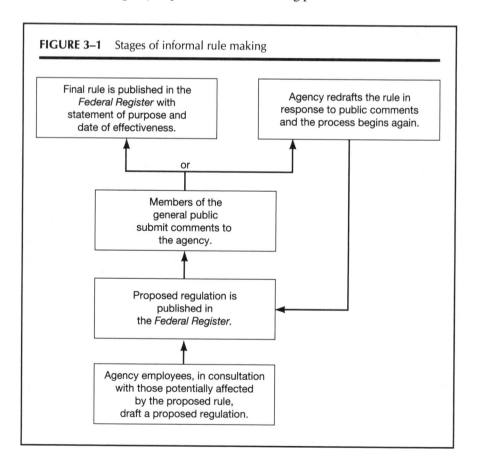

FIGURE 3–1   Stages of informal rule making

Final rule is published in the *Federal Register* with statement of purpose and date of effectiveness.

Agency redrafts the rule in response to public comments and the process begins again.

or

Members of the general public submit comments to the agency.

Proposed regulation is published in the *Federal Register.*

Agency employees, in consultation with those potentially affected by the proposed rule, draft a proposed regulation.

plete transcript. This procedure is initiated in the same manner as is informal rule making, with publication of a notice of proposed rule making by the agency in the *Federal Register*. The second step in formal rule making is a public hearing at which witnesses give testimony on the pros and cons of the proposed rule and are subject to cross-examination. An official transcript of the hearing is kept. Based on information received at the hearing, the agency makes and publishes formal findings. On the basis of these findings, an agency may or may not promulgate a regulation. If a regulation is adopted, the final rule is published in the *Federal Register*. Because of the expense and time involved in obtaining a formal transcript and record, most enabling statutes do not require a formal rule-making procedure when promulgating regulations. If a statute is drafted in a manner that is at all ambiguous with respect to the type of rule making required, the court will *not* interpret the law as requiring formal rule making.

Hybrid Rule Making. After agencies began regularly making rules in accordance with the appropriate procedures, the flaws of each type of rule making became increasingly apparent. In response to these problems a form of hybrid rule making became acceptable to the courts and legislature. Hybrid rule making is an attempt to combine the best features of both. The starting point, publication in the *Federal Register* is the same. This publication is followed by the opportunity for submission of written comments, and then an informal public hearing with a more restricted opportunity for cross-examination than in formal rule making. The publication of the final rule is the same as for other forms of rule making.

Exempted Rule Making. Section 553 of the APA contains an exemption from rule making that allows an agency to decide whether public participation will be allowed. The APA exempts public rule-making proceedings with regard to "military or foreign affairs" and "agency management or personnel." Exemptions are also granted for rule-making proceedings relating to "public property, loans, grants, benefits or contracts" of an agency. Military and foreign affairs often need speed and secrecy, which are incompatible with public notice and hearings. Other exemptions are becoming more difficult to justify in the eyes of the courts unless they meet one of the exemptions to the Freedom of Information Act discussed later.

Also exempted from the rule-making procedures are interpretive rules and general policy statements. An interpretive rule is a rule that does not create any new rights or duties, but is merely a detailed statement of the agency's interpretation of an existing law. These interpretive rules are generally very detailed, step-by-step statements of what actions a party would take to be considered in compliance with an existing law. Policy statements are general statements about directions in which any agency intends to proceed with respect to its rule-making or enforcement activities. Again, these statements have no binding impact on anyone; they do not directly affect anyone's legal rights or responsibilities.

A final exemption is when public notice and comment procedures are "impracticable, unnecessary, or contrary to the public interest." This exemption is used most commonly when either the issue is so trivial that there would probably be very little, if any, public input, or when the nature of the rule necessitates immediate action. Whenever an agency chooses to use this exception, it must make a "good cause" finding, and include in its publication of the final rule a statement explaining why there was no public participation in the process.

Judicial Review of Rule Making. Following the promulgation of a regulation by an administrative agency and its publication in the *Federal Register*, the regulation becomes law. Often, however, regulated interests may not be happy with a law that an agency promulgates. These disgruntled parties have two options. First, they may immediately bring an action in the federal district court to have the law invalidated. An alternative approach is just to ignore the law. When the agency tries to fine the party for violating the law, the party's defense would be that the rule was not valid. If the administrative law judge upholds the rule, the party may appeal the case to the federal district court and on through the appeals process.

Generally, appellate courts have accepted an agency-promulgated regulation as law unless a business, other groups, or individuals affected can prove it is invalid for one of four reasons. One reason is that the congressional delegation of legislative authority in the enabling act was unconstitutional because it was *too vague* and did not properly limit the agency's actions in any way. An unlimited delegation of legislative authority would obviously be unconstitutional. A second claim is that an agency action *violated a constitutional standard*, such as the right to be free from unreasonable searches and seizures under the Fourth Amendment. For example, if an agency like OSHA promulgated a rule that allowed its inspectors to search a business property at any time without permission of the owners, and without an administrative search warrant, this law would be struck down as a violation of the Fourth Amendment.

A third alternative is to show that the act of an agency was *beyond the scope of power* granted to it by Congress in its enabling legislation. In other words, the agency passed a rule that it had no authority to delegate. Finally, a party could demonstrate that the agency *did not follow the proper procedures* in promulgating the rule. For example, the agency was required by its enabling statute to engage in formal rule making but instead followed informal rule-making procedures.

You are correct if you believe that these four circumstances seem highly unlikely. It is very unusual for a court to strike down an administrative rule. Despite the low success rate of such challenges, firms continue to challenge agency rules. For example, approximately 80 percent of the rules made by the EPA from 1987 through 1991 have been challenged in court. Even if such a challenge is not successful, it still buys time for the firm. The firm may be able to get a temporary injunction prohibiting enforcement of the law until there is a final decision in the case. Many times the appeals process will last for years; the resulting delay can save a firm a substantial amount of money, especially when the cost of compliance is high.

Regulated Negotiation. The exceedingly high number of challenges to regulations, as well as a growing belief that structured bargaining among competing interest groups might be the most efficient way to develop rules, has stimulated interest in a number of agencies in a relatively new form of rule making, often referred to as *reg-neg*. Each concerned interest group and the agency itself sends a representative to bargaining sessions led by a mediator. After the parties achieve a consensus, that agreement is forwarded to the agency.

The agency is then expected to publish the compromise as a proposed rule in the *Federal Register* and follow through with the requisite rule-making procedures. The agency, however is not bound to do so. If it does not agree with the proposal the group negotiated, the agency is free to try and promulgate a completely different rule or a modification of the one obtained through the negotiation. The reasoning behind reg-neg is similar to that supporting the increased use of mediation. If the parties can sit down and try to work out a compromise solution together, that solution is much more likely to be accepted than one handed down by some authority. The parties who hammered out the agreement now have a stake in making it work because they helped to create it.

Admittedly, reg-neg is not possible in all situations. If, for example, there were an unmanageably large group of interests that would have to be represented, or if any possible compromise would have to result from one group backing away from a fundamental principle, or if two groups feel so antagonistic toward each other that they are unable to rationally sit down and talk, reg-neg would probably not even be worth trying.

Problems Associated with Rule Making. Although there is an expediency associated with this process of rule making, critics are quick to point out that some problems are associated with this process. Agency employees are not subject to the same political pressures as legislators, but they are not necessarily unbiased "scientists." Many of the people with the necessary expertise to regulate specific areas come from the industry they are now going to be regulating. And if they are going to leave government service someday to return to the private sector, they will most likely return to the very industries that they are regulating. Many people believe that it will be difficult for regulators to ignore their past and potential ties to industry and pass the regulations that are in the public interest, especially when the regulations would increase costs to the industry or are opposed by the industry for other reasons. When people are discussing an agency in which they perceive this problem as existing, they will often refer to the agency as being a "captured" agency.

The counterargument is that those who have been deeply involved in an industry know it best. Only those with personal experience can really understand whether a proposed regulation is workable.

Rule making in the environmental area is especially difficult, because there is so much uncertainty surrounding the causes and consequences of pollution. There is often a significant time lag between exposure and the resultant detrimental health effects or ecological changes, making it difficult to ascertain the impact of a given pollutant. There is very little agreement as to how much certainty is needed before a regulation should be imposed. And even when we have a little knowledge about a single pollutant's effects, we know less about synergistic effects, that is, the effects brought about by the interactions of various pollutants.

Another problem associated with environmental rule making is that though many of the costs of regulation are borne immediately, the benefits flow primarily to future generations. Thus, many people question how much the present generation can be asked to sacrifice for future generations. This question becomes complicated by the fact that sometimes those costs are borne by those with the least economic and political power.

Regulators in the environmental area are confronted with a difficult task. With respect to almost every standard they set, they must balance the risk to society with the cost of expenditures for pollution-control equipment. And they know that almost every standard they set is going to be challenged in court by the regulated industries, which will see the standards as too stringent, and the environmental groups, which will see them as too weak.

An issue that has been increasingly arising in debates over environmental policies is the impact that the costs of compliance will have on the competitiveness of U.S. firms in a global economy. Certainly, the competitiveness of U.S. firms is an important concern. After all, it affects our standard of living. Further, our standing in the global markets also affects our worldwide influence in international affairs. Yet, as with the health impact of pollutants, the effects of pollution-control compliance on global competitiveness are unknown. We can gather data on costs of pollution-control equipment in the United States, but we do not know how much other nations' industries spend. Nor do we know how much increased efficiency the pollution-control equipment generates.

As you will read in Chapter 10, differences in environmental regulation has become an issue in trade agreements. We know that some firms have left the United States to go to less developed countries where there are less stringent pollution-control regulations. But not all firms that move do so just to avoid environmental regulations. Some may also be seeking cheaper labor or material costs.

Finally, regulators must be sensitive to the role the economy plays in the public's willingness to accept or support environmental regulations. When the economy is flourishing and unemployment is low, there is much greater acceptance of regulations. When unemployment is high, people are much more reluctant to accept regulations that they believe might cause some workers to lose their jobs and/or cause the prices of products to rise.

Adjudication

In addition to rule making by state and federal administrative agencies, adjudication of individual cases is another important agency activity. The number of cases heard by administrative law judges is extremely high: In 1983, one-third more cases were referred to administrative law judges than were filed in the federal district courts. The APA again sets forth the steps for adjudication, which can be modified by an agency's enabling statute. APA Sections 554, 556, and 557 set out the minimum standards for adjudication whenever an agency's adjudication is "required by statute to be determined on the record after opportunity for an agency hearing."

An agency adjudication is generally preceded by an investigation and the filing of a complaint with an administrative law judge (ALJ) by the agency staff. The party against which the agency is taking the action is entitled to notice of the time and place of the hearing, the authority the agency is relying on, and the "matters of fact and law asserted." A hearing is then conducted by the ALJ, after which an initial decision is issued by the ALJ. An appeal to the full commission or the head of an agency may then be filed. That decision may then be appealed to the circuit court of appeals. Figure 3–2 illustrates the steps of this administrative adjudication process.

The Environmental Protection Agency (and approximately eight other federal agencies) has so many appeals that a special board has been set up within the agency to handle certain types of appeals. On March 1, 1992, a special three-person board began operation to handle appeals of penalty decisions made by EPA administrative law judges and appeals of permit decisions in the EPA's 10 regions. This board was created in anticipation of a crush of environmental disputes that are expected to be heard by administrative law judges and then appealed in the mid- and late-1990s. With over 100 appeals per year during the early 1990s, the administrator of the EPA already had been forced to delegate authority to senior attorneys in the agency to help decide appeals.

The administrative adjudication process is extremely important because most agencies rely primarily on administrative actions to enforce their regulations. This enforcement strategy is especially true in the environmental area. Administrative actions are often preferred to taking a violator to trial because administrative actions are generally quicker, less expensive, and less resource-intensive than a trial. An administrative proceeding may be handled by an agency employee, whereas in order to prosecute a violator in court, a federal agency must turn the case over to the Justice Department and a state agency must refer the case to the state attorney general.

As a result of an administrative action, an agency can issue a compliance order, which may require immediate action by a violator, or a timetable that must be followed in moving toward compliance. The order may contain daily penalties for noncompliance or include provisions for suspension or revocation of a violator's operating permit under appropriate circumstances.

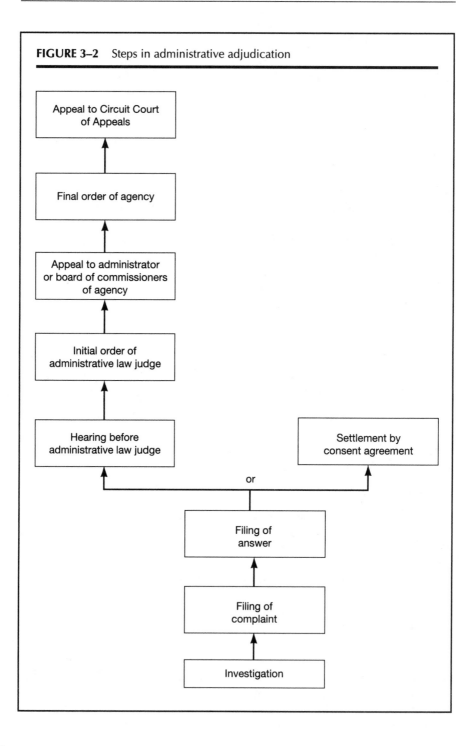

FIGURE 3–2   Steps in administrative adjudication

Administrative agencies may also issue corrective orders. These orders are comparable to court orders for specific performance. For example, a corrective order may require a violator that has released water containing waste into a river to install equipment that would filter out the waste before the water is released.

Penalties for Noncompliance. Each of the environmental laws that you will be reading about contains provisions for administrative, civil, and criminal actions. Generally, administrative penalties are less than civil and criminal penalties. By providing lesser penalties for administrative actions, violators are encouraged to settle early. In one EPA case, a violator was encouraged to settle for a $200 agency fine. The violator refused, and the case was turned over to the Justice Department. The federal district court awarded the statutory penalty of $10,000.[1]

In light of the substantial difference between administrative penalties and civil and criminal awards, it is not surprising that violators are often willing to settle for small administrative penalties. Table 3–1 shows the difference between judicial and administrative penalties assessed for fiscal years 1978 through 1989.

Citizen Rewards. As you will discover as you read more about specific environmental laws, often violations are discovered not by the agencies themselves but by citizens. In order to motivate citizens, most federal and state agencies

TABLE 3–1 Penalty Assessments in civil cases referred to the Department of Justice by the Environmental Protection Agency and in cases handled administratively by the EPA, fiscal years 1978–89

Year	Civil Judicial	Administrative	FY Total
FY78	1,313,873	25,000	1,338,873
FY79	4,028,469	56,800	4,085,269
FY80	10,570,040	159,110	10,729,150
FY81	5,634,325	742,910	6,377,235
FY82	3,445,950	949,430	4,395,380
FY83	5,461,583	2,419,898	7,881,481
FY84	3,497,579	3,385,344	6,882,923
FY85	13,071,530	9,707,480	22,779,010
FY86	13,178,414	7,449,993	20,628,407
FY87	17,507,499	6,818,374	24,325,873
FY88	24,976,221	11,786,300	36,762,521
FY89	20,700,000	12,900,000	33,600,000
Total	128,204,193	56,400,639	184,604,832

SOURCE: U.S. Environmental Protection Agency, Office of Enforcement and Compliance Monitoring, Information Sheet (Washington, D. C., 1990).

involved in environmental enforcement have various types of reward programs to encourage them to bring forth evidence in cases of environmental violations. The EPA, for example, administers Superfund Citizen Award Provision, paying up to $10,000 for information leading to a successful criminal prosecution.

Administrative Activities

Executive and independent agencies perform a variety of less well known but equally important tasks. These include advising, conducting research, issuing permits, and managing property.

One of the most common ways individuals come into contact with agencies is when agencies *advise* businesses and individuals as to whether the agency considers an activity legal or illegal. Agencies also *conduct studies* of industry and markets. For example, the FTC, OSHA, and the FDA conduct studies to determine the level of economic concentration, safety in the workplace, and whether drugs are harmful to the public. Also, agencies *provide information* to the general public on various matters through hotlines (see Table 3–2), publications, and seminars. Agencies also devote much of their time to *issuing licenses or permits.* The EPA, for example, helps protect the environment by requiring certain environmentally sound activities before granting permits. Finally, agencies often are responsible for *managing property.* The Government Service Administration (GSA) is the largest landlord in the country. It buys, sells, and leases all property used by the U.S. government.

LIMITATIONS ON AGENCIES' POWER

Statutory Limitations

Certain federal statutes restrict the power of administrative agencies. One of these limiting statutes, the Administrative Procedure Act, has been discussed previously. Its rule-making procedures, for example, mandate public involvement. Two other acts are especially helpful in keeping agency action open to the public, preventing secret, arbitrary, or capricious activity: the Freedom of Information Act of 1966, as amended in 1974 and 1976, and the Government in Sunshine Act.

The Freedom of Information Act requires federal agencies to publish in the *Federal Register* places where the public can get information from the agency. The act requires similar publication of proposed rules and policy statements. Finally, it requires the agencies to make such items as staff manuals and interpretations of policies available for copying to individuals, upon request. The Government in Sunshine Act requires agency business meetings to be open to the public if the agency is headed by a collegiate body. A collegiate body consists of two or more persons, the majority of whom are appointed by the president

---

TABLE 3–2 Environmental hotlines for federal government agencies

Consumer Product Safety Commission
    For information or to report a product with an actual or
    potential hazard
	(800) 638-2772

National Institute for Occupational Safety and Health (NIOSH)
    For questions concerning workplace health hazard
    evaluations
	(800) 35-NIOSH

National Response Center Hotline
    To report a release or spill of oil or hazardous waste
    materials anywhere nationwide
	(800) 424-8802

Occupational Health and Safety Administration (OSHA)
    To register a complaint about health or safety violations
    in the workplace
	(800) 582-1708

U. S. Environmental Protection Agency Safe Drinking Water Hotline
    For questions about drinking water standards and
    contaminants
	(800) 426-4791

RCRA - Superfund Hotline
    For general information on Superfund sites and hazar-
    dous waste laws
	(800) 424-9346

Emergency Planning and Community Right-to-Know
    For questions about the national right-to-know law
    and state and local emergency planning efforts
	(800) 535-0202

U.S. Federal Bureau of Investigation
    To report potential criminal violations of environmental
    laws
	(800) 582-1766

---

with the advice and consent of the Senate. This open-meeting requirement applies only when a quorum is present. The law also requires agencies to keep records of closed meetings.

In addition, private citizens can sue the government for damages caused by improper acts of employees of federal administrative agencies through the Federal Tort Claim Act of 1946. This act forces an agency to waive sovereign immunity for its tortious actions and those of its employees. Tortious actions under this act include assault, battery, abuse of prosecution, and false arrest. For example, if an inspector from the EPA illegally enters a business property and pushes the owner who is trying to block the door, and if the owner is injured from the assault, the EPA inspector, as well as the agency, may be held liable.

Institutional Limitations

Executive Branch. The power of administrative agencies is limited by the executive branch through (1) the power of the president to appoint the heads of the agencies; (2) the power of the Office of Management and Budget (OMB) to recommend a fiscal year budget for each agency; and (3) presidential executive orders. As already discussed, the president appoints the head of each agency, as well as some lower-level heads of departments and divisions that do not fall under the federal civil service system. Presidential appointees usually have the same philosophical bent as the chief executive and are often of the same party. Each president thus gains some influence over both independent and executive agencies.

As you will see in greater detail later in this chapter, the chief executive's ability to appoint an agency's head and to make recommendations can have a powerful, long-lasting effect on an agency. It is the agency's head who sets the tenor of the agency. It is the head of the agency, for example, who decides whether the agency is going to aggressively pursue violations of regulations. The importance of the heads of agencies is reflected by the vigor with which interested parties lobby the president when he is making such appointments. A minor issue in election campaigns, in fact, is sometimes the question of the type of person the candidates would select to head various agencies.

The executive branch also restricts agencies through its Office of Management and Budget. This office reviews agencies' budgets and makes recommendations with respect to their need for greater or lesser funding. Two of the most powerful agencies with respect to enforcing environmental policies, the Environment Protection Agency and the Council on Environmental Quality, were forced to curtail their actions severely as a result of President Reagan's budget and personnel decisions for 1980–88.

The issuance of executive orders can also have a major impact on agencies' activities. One of the most significant of such orders is Executive Order 12291, issued by President Reagan on February 17, 1981. This order mandated that a cost-benefit analysis be performed by executive agencies for every regulation they enacted. This mandate is set forth in Section 2 of the order, which reads as follows:

> In promulgating new regulations, reviewing existing regulations, and developing legislative proposals concerning regulation, all agencies, to the extent permitted by law, shall adhere to the following requirements:
>
> (a) Administrative decisions shall be based on adequate information concerning the need for and consequences of proposed government action,
>
> (b) Regulatory action shall not be undertaken unless the potential benefits to society for the regulation outweigh the potential costs to society,
>
> (c) Regulatory objectives shall be chosen to maximize the net benefits to society,
>
> (d) Among alternative approaches to any given regulatory objective, the alternative involving the least net cost to society shall be chosen; and
>
> (e) Agencies shall set regulatory priorities with the aim of maximizing the aggregate net benefits to society, taking into account the condition of the particular industries affected by regulations, the condition of the national economy, and other regulatory actions contemplated for the future.

The order also spells out the procedures for ensuring that this mandate is carried out. Regulatory Impact Analyses (RIAs) must be prepared for all proposed and final "major" (costing over $100 million) rules. All notices of proposed rule making and final rules (along with RIAs) must be submitted to the OMB, which is given the authority to ensure that the cost-benefit analysis was correctly prepared and that the regulation is indeed cost-effective. The limitation contained in the first paragraph, to the extent permitted by law, saves a number of environmental regulations from this cost-benefit scrutiny. Congress may include in statutes granting the EPA authority to pass certain types of regulations a provision that a cost-benefit analysis is not to be taken into account when setting standards under that law.

Soon after taking office in 1989, President Bush found an additional way for the executive branch to influence administrative agencies. He created the White House Council on Competitiveness. Headed by Vice President Dan Quayle, and consisting of several high-ranking cabinet officials, the council ostensibly was designed to enable the administration to "speak with one voice on issues involving international competitiveness."[2] During the summer of 1990, President Bush gave the council a mandate to push for deregulation. The council was to review new regulations, and any that would impose more costs on business than the benefits generated to the rest of society were to be held up or revised.

Although some Democrats labeled the Council on Competitiveness "sinister," and others claimed its actions were "Orwellian," "nothing short of treason, and perhaps illegal," defenders of the council claimed the body has clear authority to review regulations under Executive Order 12291. And regardless of one's attitude toward the legitimacy of the council, no one would attempt to deny its impact. Some claim it became a forum for appeals on any rules that were the subject of disputes between the EPA and other agencies. The council, either alone or in concert with other agencies, helped to kill a proposal to require recycling at municipal incinerators, softened a plan to improve visibility at Grand Canyon by reducing sulfur dioxides from a nearby power plant, and postponed an EPA plan to discourage the incineration of lead batteries, a source of toxic pollution.[3]

Legislative Branch. Congress limits the authority of administrative agencies through (1) its oversight power; (2) its investigative power; (3) its power to terminate an agency or amend its enabling statute; (4) its power to approve or disapprove budgets; and (5) its power to advise and consent on the president's nominations for heads of administrative agencies.

When Congress creates an agency, it delegates its legislative power over a narrow area of commerce or human rights. Each year, using its oversight power, it determines, through one of its oversight committees, whether the agency has been carrying out its mandated function. If, for example, the House Energy and Commerce Committee, through its subcommittee on Consumer, Finance, and Telecommunications, finds that the Securities and Exchange Commission is not enforcing laws against insider trading and fraud, the committee investigates and orders the SEC to do so. As we shall discuss, during the 1980s, there were numerous committee hearings at which the head of the EPA was called to testify as to why the agency did not appear to be fulfilling the tasks assigned to it.

The greatest limitation on agency power by Congress, however, lies in its right to approve or disapprove any agency's budget. If Congress disagrees with the agency's action or the OMB's proposed budget, it can slash the budget, raise it, or refuse to budget the agency. The latter action shuts the agency down.

Judicial Branch. As explained earlier in this chapter, the courts can curb excesses of the administrative agencies' rule-making and adjudication functions by reversing or modifying such actions. The U.S. Supreme Court case of *Citizens of Overton Park* v. *Volpe* [4] clearly stated that all agency action is subject to judicial review unless there is a statutory prohibition or "agency action is committed to agency discretion by law." This agency discretion exception has been interpreted very narrowly. The scope of review set forth in this case is that agency action must be set aside if it is arbitrary or capricious, unconstitutional, outside the scope of the agency's authority, or in violation of procedural requirements.

The power of the judiciary to control the rule-making actions of administrative agencies was demonstrated by a recent U.S. court of appeals ruling in *AFL-CIO* v. *OSHA.* [5] In that case, OSHA had undertaken its most extensive rule-making effort ever, promulgating permissible exposure limits (PELS) for 428 toxic substances. OSHA had promulgated only 24 substance-specific health regulations by 1989. In an effort to speed up its rule-making, OSHA attempted to engage in "generic rule making."

Section 3(8) of the Occupational Safety and Health Act (OSH Act) defines an "occupational health and safety standard" as "a standard which requires conditions or the adoption or use of one or more practices, means, methods, operations, or processes, reasonably necessary or appropriate to provide safe or healthful employment and places of employment." The Supreme Court interpreted that provision to require that, prior to the promulgation of any new permanent health standard, OSHA make a threshold finding that a significant risk of material health impairment exists at the current levels of exposure to the toxic substance in question, and therefore a new, lower threshold is reasonably necessary or appropriate to provide safe or healthful employment. Any subsequent standard the EPA promulgates must also comply with Section 6(b) 5 of the act, which requires that a standard adopted must prevent material impairment of health "to the extent feasible."

Industry petitioners argued that OSHA's use of generic findings, its lumping together of so many substances in one rule making, and the short time for public comment created a record that was inadequate to support the rule making. The union argued that the procedure resulted in standards that were inadequate to protect employee health.

The Court, in looking at OSHA's record, agreed with the industry position. The Court said that OSHA had a responsibility to quantify, or explain to a reasonable degree, the risk posed by each toxic substance. OSHA's discussions of individual substances contained summaries of various studies of that substance and the health effects found at various levels of exposure, but made no estimate of the risk of contracting those health effects; instead, OSHA provided a conclusory statement that the new limit would reduce the "significant" risk of material health effects, without any explanation of how the agency determined what was significant. There were no reasons given for why the particular standards were set. For most standards, a few studies were cited, with no explanation of why the study mandated the standard. For some, no studies were cited. The Court also faulted OSHA for failing to establish the economic and technical feasibility for each standard.

Thus, though the courts do not tend to scrutinize carefully the evidence agencies rely on, agencies must act in accordance with their statutory mandates. As the Supreme Court said in *AFL-CIO* v. *OSHA*, an agency cannot shortcut the proper rule-making procedures by attempting to combine multiple substances in a single rule making. Besides demonstrating the courts' power over agencies, this case also points out one of the dilemmas agencies sometimes face. They are often given a tremendous number of standards to set, and in order to save valuable time, they may wish to act with less than the maximum possible attainable evidence. Yet, in their haste to regulate, they may find that they have overstepped their authority.

IMPORTANT AGENCIES AFFECTING
THE ENVIRONMENT

Currently more than 100 federal agencies are in operation, as well as countless state agencies. Often, when there is a federal agency, there will also be comparable state agencies to which the federal agency will delegate much of its work. For example, the most important federal agency affecting environmental matters is the Environmental Protection Agency. Every state has a state environmental protection agency to which the federal EPA delegates primary authority for enforcing environmental protection laws. However, if at any time the state agency fails to enforce these laws, the federal EPA will step in to enforce them. Because the EPA is the primary agency responsible for enforcement of environmental laws, we devote the greatest attention to that agency. Other agencies that affect the environment are briefly introduced, either in the text or in Table 3–5 on p. 85.

Executive vs. Independent Agencies

Agencies are classified as either executive or independent. *Executive agencies* are sometimes seen as less stable in terms of their regulatory policies because the administrators of these agencies, who are appointed by the president with the advice and consent of the Senate, may be discharged by the president at any time, for any reason. Generally, whenever a new president is elected, he will place his appointees in charge of executive agencies. These agencies are generally located within the executive branch, under one of the cabinet-level departments. Hence, executive agencies are often referred to as cabinet-level agencies. An example of a traditional executive agency is the Federal Aviation Agency, located within the Department of Transportation.

Although executive agencies are usually led by an administrator, it is a board of commissioners, one of whom is the chair, that is generally in charge of an independent agency. The president likewise appoints the commissioners of *independent agencies* with the advice and consent of the Senate, but these commissioners serve fixed terms and cannot be removed except for cause. No more than a simple majority can be members of any single political party. Serving fixed terms is said to make them less accountable to the will of the executive. These agencies are generally not located within any department. Examples of independent agencies are the Federal Trade Commission and the Interstate Commerce Commission.

One other difference between these two types of agencies is the scope of their regulatory authority. Executive agencies tend to have responsibility for making rules covering a broad spectrum of industries and activities. Independent agencies, often called commissions, tend to have more narrow authority over many facets of a particular industry, focusing on such activities as rate making and licensing. Executive agencies have a tendency to focus more on "social" regulation, whereas independent agencies are more often focused on what we refer to as primarily "economic" regulation.

Hybrid Agencies. Some agencies do not fall clearly into one classification or the other. Created as one type of agency, the body may share characteristics of the other. The EPA, for example, was created as an independent agency, not located within any department of the executive branch. Yet it is headed by a single administrator who serves at the whim of the president. During the early 1990s, in fact, there were discussions of the need to transform the EPA into a cabinet-level executive agency. (These initiatives did not get beyond the discussion stage.) Another example is the "independent" Federal Energy Regulation Commission, which has the typical structure of an independent agency, yet is located within the Department of Energy.

The Environmental Protection Agency

History. By a presidential reorganization order, the Environmental Protection Agency was created in 1970 as an independent agency. This new agency was to take over functions that were formerly carried out by the Federal Water Quality Administration in the Department of the Interior; the National Air Pollution Control Administration and the Food and Drug Administration in the Department of Health, Education, and Welfare; and the Atomic Energy Commission, among others. Its mission was to control and abate pollution in the areas of air, water, solid waste, pesticides, radiation, and toxic substances. Its mandate was to mount an integrated, coordinated attack on environmental pollution in cooperation with state and local governments. In 1973, the EPA had 8,200 employees. By 1982, it had grown to be one of the largest federal agencies, with 12,623 employees, and by 1992, it had more than 17,000 employees. It has also been one of the most controversial agencies, having most of its actions criticized by either business groups, environmentalists, or both. The EPA has often been in conflict with the executive branch and with Congress.

The EPA's first head was William Ruckleshaus, under whose three-year tenure the agency served as a vigorous enforcer of air and water quality standards. As Congress passed more and more environmental regulations, the agency expanded and was given increasing amounts of responsibility. In September 1973, Ruckelshaus was succeeded by Russell Train, who ran the agency during three more years of growth. Next, under the leadership of Carter appointee Douglas Costle, the EPA continued to grow as the new administrator attempted to streamline its regulatory process and make the agency more cost-effective.

President Reagan's tenure proceeded to demonstrate how effectively an agency can be gutted by an executive hostile to the agency's mission. During his first three years in office, Reagan cut the EPA's research budget by 50 percent, cuts from which the agency has not yet recovered. He also appointed Anne Burford (then Anne Gorsuch) to head the agency. According to Toby Moffett, chair of the House Government Operations Subcommittee on Environment, Energy and Natural Resources, Burford used private meetings, reorganizations, budget cuts, and pledges of selective enforcement to emasculate the laws the EPA was duty-bound to execute. Whether his statement is exaggeration or not, it is certainly true that during that time, when the EPA was being asked by Congress to do more, it was doing less; few environmental regulations were being issued. Burford requested budget cuts, and old-timers at the agency were quitting out of frustration. In addition, there was a 70 percent drop in enforcement actions in 1981.

At first Congress went along with the president's program, but as the EPA began to fail to live up to its mandate, Congress tried to push the agency back on its former course. The conflicts between the agency and Congress, as well as among agency employees, reached their zenith between October 1981 and July 1982, when officials of the agency were called to testify before congressional oversight committees more than 70 times! Alleged mismanagement at the EPA continued until finally, in February 1983, several top EPA officials were fired. A subsequent report of the House Energy and Commerce Committee's Oversight and Investigations Subcommittee reported that, under Burford's tenure, EPA officials had violated their public trust by manipulating the Superfund cleanup for political purposes, engaging in unethical conduct, and generally disrupting the country's public health and environment.[6]

The revitalization of the EPA did not begin until after March 1983, when Anne Burford resigned. She was replaced by the former administrator William Ruckelshaus, who was followed in 1984 by Lee Thomas, who began once again to increase the number of agency enforcement orders and environmental regulations. Thomas was followed by William Reilly. Reilly, the former head of the Conservation Foundation and World Wildlife Federation, described himself as a "conservationist" rather than an "environmentalist" because the latter has an "anti-industry, anti-growth" ring to it that he does not feel describes him.[7] However, he was willing to fight executive branch efforts at deregulation. The EPA's budget improved somewhat under the Bush administration, although the agency's 1990 budget, in constant dollars, actually increased by less than 20 percent over 1972 levels. This increase, however, is very modest indeed in light of all of the new environmental regulations the EPA has been given responsibility for since 1972. If we exclude the staff employed under the Superfund, the EPA's staff was actually smaller at the end of the 1980s than it was at its inception.

Where exactly is the EPA now? The agency, even in the best of times, has tended to be very reactive, responding to the public's concerns as revealed through congressional enactments. Generally the agency has seen its role as enforcing specific pollution-control laws, not as being in the forefront of generating new policies to prevent problems from arising. A report of the Science Advisory Board (SAB) to the director of the EPA, completed in September 1990, may help the agency become more effective. The SAB made 10 recommendations in its report (see Table 3–3).

In January 1993, President Clinton nominated Carol M. Browner to head the EPA in what is hoped to be an era of greater cooperation among Congress, the executive branch, and the agency. Browner was the former head of the Florida state EPA, as well as the legislative director for Vice President Gore when he was a senator. At Browner's confirmation hearing, Max Baucus, chair of the Senate Environment and Public Works Committee stated, "For the past several years, Congress and the Administration have been paralyzed by gridlock, particularly when it comes to environmental policy. . . . Now the American people expect all that to change."[8] The only promise that the new administrator seemed to give was to provide a regulatory climate not hostile to business. Depicted as practicing a pragmatic, cost-conscious brand of environmentalism, she may have been chosen for her appearance of "balance." By not being clearly aligned with either environmental or business extremists, she may be perceived as being able to balance the interests of the two groups and thereby turn the agency into a more effective regulator. She claims that her experience with the Florida EPA has taught her that we can "ease the regulatory burden on business without compromising the environment." It remains to be seen whether she will be able to guide the EPA successfully through the 1990s.

TABLE 3–3   Recommendations of the Science Advisory Board

---

1. *EPA should target its environmental protection efforts on the basis of opportunities for the greatest risk reduction.* Since this country already has taken the most obvious actions to address the most obvious environmental problems, EPA needs to set priorities for future actions so the Agency takes advantage of the best opportunities for reducing the most serious remaining risks.

2. *EPA should attach as much importance to reducing ecological risk as it does to reducing human health risk.* Because productive natural ecosystems are essential to human health and to sustainable, long-term economic growth, and because they are intrinsically valuable in their own right, EPA should be as concerned about protecting ecosystems as it is about protecting human health.

3. *EPA should improve the data and analytical methodologies that support the assessment, comparison, and reduction of different environmental risks.* Although setting priorities for national environmental protection efforts always will involve subjective judgments and uncertainty, EPA should work continually to improve the scientific data and analytical methodologies that underpin those judgments and help reduce their uncertainty.

4. *EPA should reflect risk-based priorities in its strategic planning processes.* The Agency's long-range plans should be driven not so much by past risk reduction efforts or by existing programmatic structures, but by ongoing assessments of remaining environmental risks, the explicit comparison of those risks, and the analysis of opportunities available for reducing risks.

5. *EPA should reflect risk-based priorities in its budget process.* Although EPA's budget priorities are determined to a large extent by the different environmental laws that the Agency implements, it should use whatever discretion it has to focus budget resources at those environmental problems that pose the most serious risks.

6. *EPA—and the nation as a whole—should make greater use of all the tools to reduce risk.* Although the nation has had substantial success in reducing environmental risks through the use of government mandated end-of-pipe controls, the extent and complexity of future risks will necessitate the use of a much broader array of tools, including market incentives and information.

7. *EPA should emphasize pollution prevention as the preferred option for reducing risk.* By encouraging actions that prevent pollution from being generated in the first place, EPA will help reduce the costs, intermediate transfers of pollution, and residual risks so often associated with end-of-pipe controls.

8. *EPA should increase its efforts to integrate environmental considerations into broader aspects of public policy in as fundamental a manner as are economic concerns.* Other Federal agencies often affect the quality of the environment, e.g., through the implementation of tax, energy, agricultural, and international policy, and EPA should work to ensure that environmental considerations are integrated, where appropriate, into the policy deliberations of such agencies.

9. *EPA should work to improve public understanding of environmental risks and train a professional workforce to help reduce them.* The improved environmental literacy of the general public, together with an expanded and better-trained technical workforce, will be essential to the nation's success at reducing environmental risks in the future.

10. *EPA should develop improved analytical methods to value natural resources and to account for long-term environmental effects in its economic analyses.* Because traditional methods of economic analysis tend to undervalue ecological resources and fail to treat adequately questions of intergenerational equity, EPA should develop and implement innovative approaches to economic analysis that will address these shortcomings.

Structure of the EPA. When the EPA was created, the agency was structured to bring regulatory authority over all forms of pollution control within one federal body—research, standard setting, monitoring, enforcement, policy setting. This integrated management ideal, however did not materialize, partly because of the agency's structure and partly because of its tremendous size. Basically, the EPA is headed by an administrator who is responsible for overall policy setting. The agency has a deputy administrator who helps the administrator. Under the administrator and deputy are six assistant administrators, three of whom are in charge of the "functional" missions of the EPA: research and development, planning and management, and enforcement, which apply to all EPA activities. The other three have "program" responsibilities. They are responsible for each of the agency's regulatory programs. What ends up happening is that there is little coordination among the various departments. Figure 3–3 diagrams the structure of the agency.

There is also, as with other agencies, an office of administrative law judges. These administrative law judges, like others in their profession, are fiercely independent and do not always side with the EPA's enforcement officers. The EPA is frequently represented before these justices by attorneys from the Department of Justice's Land and Natural Resources Division. Finally, the EPA has 10 regional offices throughout the country (see Table 3–4). Many of these offices are staffed with competent employees concerned about the environment and skeptical of industry. Unlike many other government agencies, the EPA does not have a substantial number of employees who come from industry.

Interagency Cooperation

One of the ways the EPA can be more effective is to coordinate its enforcement efforts better, not just within the agency itself but with other agencies as well. A joint venture with OSHA proved to be fairly effective. During the spring of 1991, agents from the two agencies jointly conducted surprise inspections at 29 of the nation's 140 hazardous waste incinerators run by some of the biggest corporations. As a result of the sweep, corporations were charged with 395 violations of federal standards. The EPA referred 52 violations to state authorities for enforcement actions, and OSHA assessed fines totaling $92,220 on incinerator operators. Perhaps fear of these new, coordinated sweeps may make plant operators a little more concerned about following federal health, safety, and environmental laws.

Many other federal agencies also aid in protecting the environment, although not always so directly. Many of these agencies are housed within departments that also play significant roles in regulating the environment. For example, the Departments of the Interior and Energy play significant roles, as does the

FIGURE 3–3 Environmental Protection Agency

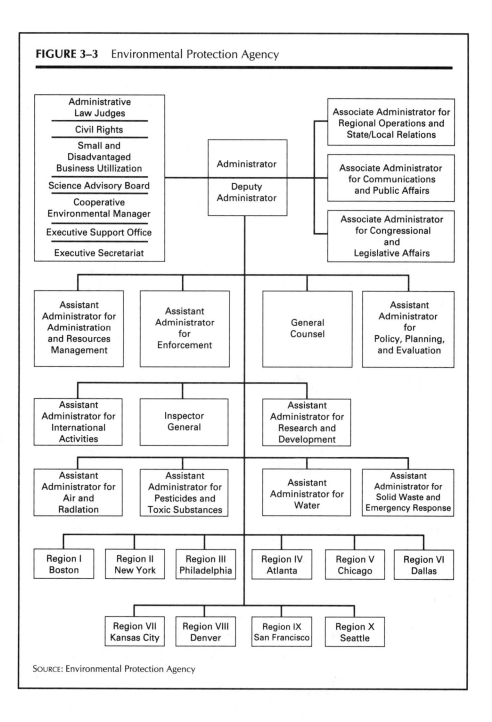

SOURCE: Environmental Protection Agency

TABLE 3–4   Environmental Protection Agency regional offices

	Region	States Included
Region I	Boston, Massachusetts JFK Federal Building, 02203 (617) 565-3424	Connecticut, Massachusetts, Maine, New Hampshire, Rhode Island, Vermont
Region II	New York, New York 26 Federal Plaza, 10278 (212) 264-2515	New Jersey, New York, Puerto Rico, Virgin Islands
Region III	Philadelphia, Pennsylvania 841 Chestnut Street, 19107 (215) 597-9370	Delaware, Maryland, Pennsylvania, Virginia, West Virginia, District of Columbia
Region IV	Atlanta, Georgia 345 Courtland Street N.E., 30365 (404) 347-3004	Alabama, Florida, Georgia, Kentucky, Mississippi, North Carolina, South Carolina, Tennessee
Region V	Chicago, Illinois 230 S. Dearborn Street, 60604 (312) 353-2072	Illinois, Indiana, Michigan, Minnesota, Ohio, Wisconsin
Region VI	Dallas, Texas 1445 Ross Avenue, 75202 (214) 655-2200	Arkansas, Louisiana, New Mexico, Oklahoma, Texas
Region VII	Kansas City, Kansas 726 Minnesota Avenue, 66101 (913) 551-7003	Iowa, Kansas, Missouri, Nebraska
Region VIII	Denver, Colorado 999 18th Street, 80202 (303) 293-1692	Colorado, Montana, North Dakota, South Dakota, Utah, Wyoming
Region IX	San Francisco, California 1235 Mission Street, 94103 (415) 556-5145	Arizona, California, Hawaii, Nevada, American Samoa, Guam, Northern Mariana Islands
Region X	Seattle, Washington 1200 6th Avenue, 98101 (206) 442-1465	Alaska, Idaho, Oregon, Washington

National Oceanic and Atmospheric Administration. The remainder of this chapter introduces some of these important agencies. Additional agencies that affect the environment are listed in Table 3–5. As you begin to concentrate on learning about various environmental laws, the roles of many of these agencies will be discussed.

The Department of the Interior and Its Agencies

Created as a cabinet-level department in 1845, the Department of the Interior is to natural resources what the EPA is to the regulation of pollution. It is responsible for seeking an optimally healthy balance between economic growth and the preservation of natural resources. As you might imagine, Inte-

TABLE 3–5 Federal agencies that play a role in environmental regulation

Agency	Primary Environmental Responsibility
Army Corps of Engineers	Regulates construction projects on navigable waterways; regulates transportation and dumping of dredged materials into navigable waterways; and undertakes projects to prevent flooding, supply water for industrial and municipal use, create recreational areas, and protect wildlife and shorelines of oceans and lakes.
Federal Energy Regulatory Commission	Issues licenses for hydroelectric power; is responsible for the safe operation of dams.
Federal Maritime Commission	Certifies the financial responsibility of vessels that carry oil or other hazardous materials to cover costs of cleaning up their spills in navigable waters.
Materials Transportation Bureau	Develops and enforces operating safety regulations for the transportation of all materials by pipeline; carries out inspection compliance and enforcement actions for transportation of all hazardous materials by air, water, highway, and rail.
National Institute for Occupational Safety and Health	Researches and develops occupational safety and health standards.
National Oceanic and Atmospheric Administration	Describes, monitors, and predicts conditions in the atmosphere, ocean, sun, and space environment; disseminates environmental data; and manages and conserves living marine resources and their habitats.
Nuclear Regulatory Commission	Licenses the construction and operation of nuclear facilities and the possession, use, transportation, handling, and disposal of nuclear materials.
Office of Conservation and Renewable Energy	Directs energy conservation programs and conducts studies.
Office of Surface Mining and Reclamation	Protects against adverse effects of coal mining; establishes standards for surface effects of coal mining; and promotes reclamation of previously mined lands.
Office of Water Research and Technology	Supervises and conducts research related to the nation's water quality.
Soil Conservation Service	Administers programs to develop and conserve soil and water resources.
U.S. Geological Survey	Maintains data center that conducts and sponsors research to apply data findings in mapping, geography, mineral and land resources, water resources, rangeland, and environmental monitoring.
Water and Power Resources Services	Develops and manages water and power resources in the western states.

rior is frequently a battleground between environmentalists and conservationists who want to preserve natural resources and those who want greater access to natural resources, such as those in the timber and cattle industries, mining operations, and sportsmen. State governments, especially in the West, also want to gain greater control of the public lands and natural resources within the department's control. Through its various agencies, the department is responsible for the management of more than 549 million acres of public land, administration of Indian lands and federal Indian programs, conservation and management of wetlands and estuaries, and protection and preservation of wildlife, including endangered species.

Bureau of Land Management. Created in 1946, the Bureau of Land Management is the largest landholding entity in the United States—responsible for the management of natural resources on about 15 percent of the country, more than 350 million acres. About half of the land managed by this agency is in Alaska, and most of the remaining lands are in the 12 most western states. Much of the land is designated for recreational use; some has been designated for conservation as wilderness. Natural resources include such items as timber, minerals, oil and gas, geothermal energy, wildlife habitats, endangered plants and animals, vegetation, and wild and scenic rivers.

U.S. Fish and Wildlife Service. Probably most well known for its role in the "spotted owl controversy" in which the Fish and Wildlife Service listed the owl as endangered, this agency is responsible for safeguarding and improving wildlife and wildlife habitat in the National Wildlife Refuge System. Since 1983, this system has grown to 472 national wildlife refuges, waterfowl production areas in 166 counties, and 51 coordination areas. The agency is responsible for protecting migratory and game birds, fish, and endangered and threatened species. The agency is also responsible for enforcing regulations for hunters, as well as preserving wetlands as natural habitats.

National Park Service. This agency administers programs that conserve scenery, natural and historic objects, and wildlife in the national parks. It also is responsible for the management of 80 million acres of land.

The Department of Agriculture and Its Agencies

U.S. Forest Service. This agency manages the nation's forests and grasslands. It is responsible for 33.6 million acres of wilderness areas. Like the Department of the Interior, this agency has to confront competing interests of those who want to conserve and those who want to exploit our natural resources, but focuses its energies on those resource uses that occur in the forest, such as lumbering, mining, farming, and grazing. The agency is currently embroiled in controversy for such actions as clearcutting, selling public timber below cost, and constructing roads for lumber companies in national forests.

The Department of Labor and Its Agencies

Occupational Safety and Health Administration. OSHA is primarily responsible for promulgating and enforcing rules that affect the health and safety of the workplace. A sister agency, the National Institute for Occupational Health and Safety (NIOSH), is responsible for doing research related to occupational health and safety that may be used by OSHA and the EPA in setting health and safety standards.

Mine Safety and Health Administration. This agency develops and promulgates health and safety standards for mines. It enforces standards, proposes penalties for violators, and investigates accidents. It works with states to help develop mine health and safety programs.

Independent Agencies

Consumer Products Safety Commission (CPSC). CPSC is responsible for passing and enforcing regulations that protect consumers. This mandate makes the CPSC responsible for making sure that consumer products do not contain carcinogens or other toxic chemicals.

Food and Drug Administration (FDA). This agency is well known for its role in ensuring that our food and drugs do not contain toxins and are not adulterated. The FDA works with the EPA in trying to ensure that the food we eat is not contaminated by pesticides.

CONCLUDING REMARKS

Administrative agencies have enormous impact, given their authority to establish and enforce regulations. Remember, however, that their power is constrained by all of the traditional branches of government. Also, much of our environmental law is, in fact, administrative law, developed and enforced by agencies, especially the EPA.

One of the most significant aspects of administration law is the way in which administrative regulations are created. The three processes by which these regulations can be created all invite public participation, all begin by publication of the proposed rule in the *Federal Register*, and all conclude with publication of the final rule in the *Federal Register*. If these legally binding regulations are not created following the proper steps, they will be struck down by the courts.

Now that you understand how the administrative law system functions, you are ready to begin study of that specialized area of law on which this book focuses: environmental law.

QUESTIONS FOR REVIEW AND DISCUSSION

1. Distinguish formal from informal rule making.
2. Explain when rule making is exempt from public participation.
3. Explain the use of reg-neg.
4. Describe the grounds for which a rule made by an administrative agency can be overturned.
5. Trace the steps of adjudication that must be followed by an administrative agency.
6. Why should anyone in a heavily regulated industry be familiar with the *Federal Register*?
7. How do legislative, executive, and judicial branches each restrict the activities of administrative agencies?
8. Describe the structure of the EPA.

FOR FURTHER READING

Aman, Alfred. *Administrative Law in a Global Era* (Ithaca, N.Y.: Cornell University Press, 1992).

Durant, Robert. *When Government Regulates Itself: EPA, TVA and Pollution Control in the 1970's* (Knoxville: University of Tennessee Press, 1985).

Gellhorn, Ernest, and Richard B. Stewart. *Administrative Law and Process in a Nutshell.* (St. Paul, Minn.: West Publishing Co., 1990).

NOTES

1. *CEQ, Twentieth Annual Report,* 1990, p. 204.
2. Jeffrey H. Birnbaum, "White House Competitiveness Council Provokes Sharp Anger among Democrats in Congress," *The Wall Street Journal,* July 8, 1991, p. B1.
3. Ibid.
4. 401 *U.S.* 402 (1971).
5. 61 LW 2042 (1992).
6. Donald J. Rebovich, *Dangerous Ground: The World of Hazardous Waste Crime* (New Brunswick, N.J.: Transaction Publishers, 1992).
7. Barbara Rosewicz, "Environmental Chief Clashes with New Foe: Deregulation Troops," *The Wall Street Journal,* March 22, 1992, p. 1.
8. Phillip Davis, "Browner Short on Specifics in Confirmation Hearing," *Congressional Quarterly Weekly,* January 16, 1993, p. 127.

II

THE ENVIRONMENTAL LAWS

The second part of this book provides the basics of the most influential environmental laws and introduces troublesome dilemmas arising from implementation of the laws. With the exception of Chapter 4, which discusses the basics of environmental policy, each chapter first introduces the primary environmental problems the law must resolve, providing the scientific knowledge necessary for you to understand the problem. Then later sections of each chapter describe the laws themselves.

4

An Introduction to Environmental Law and Policy

The area of law you are now beginning to study is one of extremely recent development. Twenty years ago there would not have been any law school or undergraduate courses in environmental law, because there was no such cohesive body of law. Environmental regulation has evolved over that brief period of time from reliance on tort law to an emphasis on end-of-pipe controls through direct regulation and finally into an emphasis on pollution prevention.

Prior to the existence of a cohesive set of environmental laws, how, you may wonder, did we keep the ravages of pollution from degrading the quality of our water, air, and land? The answer is that we didn't. Without protective legislation, lakes and rivers became unfit for fishing and swimming, the air in many cases became severely degraded, forests were destroyed, and valuable land was eroded. Today we are still paying the costs of cleaning up our mistakes from this era of minimal regulation.

In the first section of this chapter we examine the justifications that led to the adoption of the regulations designed to repair the ravaged environment and prevent its future degradation. We then examine alternative ways to provide that protection. The third section then traces the evolution of environmental policy. Finally, the remaining two sections discuss the two major environmental policy statutes.

THE NEED FOR REGULATION

Some believe that we did not need to enact environmental protection laws because tort law would protect the environment to the extent that it needed protection. In fact, for a while, tort law was the way we feebly controlled pollution, and it was in a tort class where protection of the environment was discussed, if at all, in law school. But the dying streams and polluted skies made it evident that tort law was not working, and thus the adoption of environmental regulation was seen as necessary.

Tragedy of the Commons

Many times when people seek to justify environmental regulation, they do so using a story told by Garrett Hardin entitled "The Tragedy of the Commons."[1] The tragedy develops this way: Picture a huge, lush pasture open to everyone. Many people survive by raising cattle; they take their cattle to the common pasture to graze. Each herdsman keeps as many cattle as possible. For a while, disease, famine, and tribal wars keep the number of cattle down to a reasonable level. Eventually, however, the day of reckoning comes. There is just enough land to support all of the cattle.

The rational herdsman, however, asks himself, "What is the utility of adding one more animal to my herd?" Because the herdsman receives all the proceeds from the sale of the animal, he has powerful incentive to add to his herd. The negative effect of adding one more animal is the harm that results to the other herdsmen from resultant overgrazing. Because all herdsmen share in this negative effect, the negative consequences to the individual herdsman are minimal. Consequently, herdsmen tend to keep adding to their herds. As the same conclusion is reached by each herdsman, each continues to increase his herd without limit. But the space for the herd is limited. Herein lies the tragedy. They are locked into a system that guarantees the destruction of the commons and thus their own ruin. Hardin thus concludes, "Ruin is the destination to which all men rush, each pursuing his own interest in a society that believes in the freedom of the commons. Freedom in a commons brings ruin to all."[2]

How, you may ask, is the tragedy of the commons related to environmental protection? Without environmental laws, the rational manufacturer finds that because the cost of a polluted river is borne by everyone, he pays only a fraction of the cost of dumping waste products into a stream. On the other hand, if he chooses to not pollute by properly treating his waste, he bears the whole cost of proper disposal. Therefore he will pollute. Because the calculations are the same for everyone, we are trapped in a system of destroying our environment as long as we behave only as independent, rational free enterprisers.

Just as with the tragedy of the commons, as long as there were few polluters relative to the size of the water and air, the absorptive capacities of these resources were not taxed and there were no problems. As population and industry increased, environmental tragedy emerged. Rivers became polluted, as did the air and the land. Nature's absorptive capacities were exceeded in many areas.

Free Rider Problem

Rather than using analogies like the tragedy of the commons, some people justify the need for environmental laws by pointing out that clean air and clean water are *public goods*. Public goods are goods that have the characteristic of *nonexclusiveness*—that is, once they are produced, others cannot be excluded from using them. Thus, when someone pays to produce the good, not only the payer but everyone else gets to use it. Those who do not pay become *free riders*. They get benefits paid for by others. No one, therefore, is going to pay for clean air and water, because every rational person would prefer to be a free rider. Each person will pollute and let everyone else pay to clean up the environment. The problem is that as everyone seeks to become a free rider, no one but a few "irrational" saints will be willing to pay for clean air and water. Thus our environment will become degraded.

Pollution as an Externality

One common justification for any government intervention into the market is to eliminate negative externalities. Third parties have no impact on market prices; either government gives their interests a voice in production decisions or they have no voice. Thus, some argue that the government needs to step in to impose the costs of pollution on the polluting firm, so that it will have to increase the price of the product to reflect the true costs of producing the product. If the producer must pay to properly dispose of the hazardous waste created by the production of the product, citizens who would have otherwise been adversely affected by the improper waste disposal will not have to pay by incurring losses to their health. The important point here is that the marketplace by itself has no mechanism for achieving this objective of improved waste disposal.

An Environmental Ethic

Proponents of an environmentalist perspective believe that too often important decisions affecting the environment are made while taking into account only short-run impacts and economic factors, with little concern for the ongoing maintenance and enhancement of the viability of ecosystems.

Environmentalists are heavily influenced by ecology, the study of the relationships of living organisms to their environments. In ecology, land is viewed as a biotic pyramid:

> Plants absorb energy from the sun. That energy flows through a circuit called the biota, which may be represented by a pyramid of layers. The bottom layer is the soil. A plant layer rests on the soil, an insect layer on the plants, a bird and rodent layer on the insects, and so on up through the various animal groups to the apex layer, which consists of larger carnivores. ...Land, then, is not merely soil; it is a

fountain of energy flowing through soils, plants and animals. Food chains are the living channels which conduct energy upward; death and decay return the energy to the soil. The circuit is not closed. ...[I]t is a sustained circuit, like a slowly revolving fund of life."[3]

When a change occurs in one part of the circuit, all other parts of the circuit must respond. Most changes that occur through evolution happen slowly, thus giving the circuit time to adapt. The more gradual and less violent the change, the more likely the successful readjustment in the pyramid.[4] The fear of ecologists is that humankind now has the capacity to make rapid changes in the circuit, and we do not know how the pyramid will respond. A substance we use to kill one harmful rodent may be absorbed into the food chain, causing death or mutation up the chain. When returned to the soil, that chemical may poison the soil, thus making plant growth impossible and resulting in a lack of food for insects, rodents, birds, and their predators in that area.Thus, the ecologists warn, we must be careful before we take steps that may interrupt ecological systems. The consequences of our actions may be graver than we had anticipated. The unregulated marketplace again has little incentive to heed these fears.

Some environmentalists point out that as the dominant species in the ecosystem, with all our knowledge and power, we have a duty or responsibility to care for that ecosystem, to preserve it for future generations. We have an ethical obligation to past and future generations to be careful stewards of the legacy we have inherited. Some also make a sort of environmental noblesse oblige argument. Because our species has gone beyond mere acquisition of food, clothing, and shelter, and we can understand the way ecosystems work, we have the special duty to preserve those systems. Because we have superior understanding, we have special responsibilities to consider the long-run impacts of our behavior. Finally, it is argued by many environmentalists, we must recognize that we are not the measure of all things. We are but a small part of the universe and have no right to destroy a significant portion of it to satisfy our own selfish desires.

As you read environmental cases, notice that while the courts attempt to focus purely on the law, there are times when they go beyond a strict interpretation of the law. There are occasions when you will see the influence of the ecological perspective on a judge's decison making.

ALTERNATIVE WAYS TO CONTROL POLLUTION

Tort Law

As mentioned earlier, tort law was the first way we attempted to control pollution, and it still provides a limited means of control. However, a number of limitations make tort law unavailable in many cases and unsatisfactory as an overall means of pollution control.

Under tort law, the typical action brought to control pollution is a nuisance case. An action for *nuisance* can be brought whenever there is an *unreasonable interference with the use and enjoyment of another's land*. When someone interferes with a person's use of his or her land, the one interfering can be sued for nuisance. The person suing can receive an injunction requiring that the nuisance be stopped. Because pollution of the air and water is clearly an interference with others' use and enjoyment of their land, nuisance would seem an ideal solution. The person who has been harmed by pollution could bring an action seeking an *injunction*, a court order prohibiting the polluting behavior and/or providing *money damages* for the harm caused.

The case of *Boomer* v. *Atlantic Cement Company*[5] reflects some of the problems of using tort law. In *Boomer*, the defendants operated a large cement plant near Albany. They were sued by neighboring landowners who alleged injury to property from dirt, smoke, and vibrations emanating from the plant. The plaintiffs sought permanent injunctions and damages. After trial, a nuisance was found, and temporary damages were granted but the request for an injunction was denied. The appellate court granted the injunction *unless* the defendants paid permanent damages of $185,000 to compensate for the plaintiff's economic loss. Given the relatively small amount of the monetary damages award, the injunction was essentially denied.

The ground for the denial of injunction, notwithstanding the findings that, first, there was a nuisance and, second, that plaintiffs had been damaged substantially, was "the large disparity in economic consequences of the nuisance and of the injunction." In denying the injunction on this ground, the court admitted that it was "overruling a doctrine which has been consistently reaffirmed in several leading cases in this court and which has never been disavowed here, namely that where a nuisance has been found and where there has been any substantial damage shown by the party complaining, an injunction will be granted." The rule in New York had previously been that such a nuisance would be enjoined even if a marked disparity had been shown in economic consequences between the effect of the injunction and the effect of the nuisance.

The court noted that defendant's investment in the plant was in excess of $45 million and that it employed 300 people. The court was convinced that the technology did not exist to enable the plant to operate without creating a nuisance; nor was the technology likely to be developed within the foreseeable future. The court made it clear that it was now going to balance the harm created by the nuisance with the costs of ceasing the nuisance. If the economic costs were great, no injunction would be granted. Thus, because pollution control <u>is</u> expensive, after *Boomer*, nuisance became an ineffective way to stop pollution. At best, tort law could be used to get damages to clean up some of the pollution's harm.

Problems with Using Tort Law. The major problem reflected in *Boomer* is the court's reluctance to grant injunctions, the only remedy that really controls pollution because what you really want to do is to stop the pollution. However, courts will now balance the economic harm caused by the nuisance against the costs that would result from the injunction. If the harm from the injunction would be greater, then the courts will simply award *permanent damages*. The problem with this approach is that it allows the pollution to go on unabated. It leaves the injured party without a remedy for unforeseen future harms. And if the landowner sells the property to someone else, the courts could rule that the subsequent landowner can bring no action because permanent damages had already been awarded. And once the damages have been assessed, there is no motivation for the polluter to stop polluting.

Another problem is that of *standing*. Recall from Chapter 2 that standing is the legal right to bring an action. Standing in a nuisance action is somewhat different than standing in most other cases. For purposes of standing, nuisance is classified as being either private or public. A *private* nuisance affects only a single or limited number of persons, or affects one person in a unique way. When a nuisance is private, the affected individuals have standing to sue. If the nuisance affects a large number of persons, it is deemed a *public* nuisance. Only a public official can bring suit for a public nuisance. Herein lies the main problem with using nuisance law to control pollution. Most pollution is a public nuisance. Public officials, who are generally elected, may be very reluctant to bring a nuisance action against a major corporation in the town for several reasons. For one, the polluter means jobs, and public officials do not want to be accused of driving jobs out of town. Also, they do not want to anger a powerful constituent that may be responsible for sizable campaign contributions.

A third problem with using tort law is the difficulty of proving one's case. Remember that in a civil action the burden of proof is on the plaintiff. If there are multiple polluters, it is difficult to prove which one caused the damage. If seven factories are located along the stream that flows across your land, how do you demonstrate that the toxic chemical from the tire plant killed the fish?

Another problem is a comparative lack of resources. In the rare instance where a nuisance is private, the plaintiff needs money to bring the action, and many do not have the money to bring such an action. Remember, many firms would have an in-house lawyer who could spend lots of time filing interrogatories and motions that would drive up the cost of the lawsuit. Finally, tort law is problematic in that it is reactive. The problem must exist before the law comes into effect. Ideally, the law should prevent the creation of the problem.

Subsidies and Emissions Charges

Two alternative means of protecting the environment are subsidies and emission charges. As we shift toward pollution prevention in the 1990s, we shall see the increasing use of these tools. *Subsidies* exist when the government pays, either directly by grants or indirectly by tax relief, to encourage pollution control. For example, the government might pay for one third of the cost of installing a newly developed pollution-control device. Subsidies are most likely to be effective when the polluter knows that eventually it is going to be forced to clean up the problem. So, if the company takes care of it now, the government will help pick up the tab. If it waits until the government chooses to impose a tighter standard, no subsidy will be available. One interesting outcome of the use of subsidies is that sometimes a firm that is able to control its emissions better because of technology installed with a subsidy may start to pressure the government to impose even stricter emissions limitations on that industry.

Traditionally subsidies have not fully covered the costs of reducing pollution, so businesses were likely not to use the subsidies because they did not wish to pay for pollution control when their competitors did not. In some respects this type of thinking is encouraged by a business climate in which managers are evaluated based on the bottom line at the end of the quarter or year. Our country's managers simply do not focus on the long-run calculations of benefit and cost.

Another alternative is to require *emissions charges*. In essence, we are saying that the air and water belong to the community, so if you want to use them, you must pay the owners, that is, the community. The larger the per unit fee, the more effective the charges are in reducing levels of emissions. The charges theoretically encourage development of pollution-control technology, because if a competitor could discharge less, it would lower costs and increase profits.

Emissions charges, however, are not without their problems. First, it is very difficult to monitor the emissions. Second, it is also difficult to know how to set the fee. If the fees are too low, firms will simply continue to pollute, paying the price. If there are few firms in the industry, they may even tacitly agree simply to pass on the fees to consumers. If the fees are too high, and alternative technology to reduce emissions is extremely expensive or not available, only a few firms may be able to survive, thereby creating a monopoly. In such an event emissions charges can be a stimulus to concentrated economic power.

A related alternative is for the government not only to sell permits but let the polluters trade these permits among themselves, sometimes referred to as *emissions trading*. The total amount of pollution would thus be controlled by the initial distribution of permits. Firms then possess incentives to reduce their emissions using low-cost methods so they can sell their permits. The total amount of pollution can be reduced by gradually reducing the number of permits issued. Again, there are problems with this method. The government may find monitoring difficult. A second problem is that new entrants into an industry may be restricted by difficulty in obtaining a permit.

Green Taxes

A way to help control pollution that has not been attempted to any great extent in the United States is the use of green taxes. A *green tax* is a tax on polluting behaviors, the revenues from which may be funneled into environmental programs. Supporters of green taxes argue that these taxes correct the market's failure to value environmental services. They also seem to be somewhat effective in discouraging polluting behavior if they are set at a high enough level. In the United Kingdom, for example, a higher tax on leaded gasoline increased the market share of unleaded gas from 4 percent in April 1989 to 30 percent in March 1990. The United States is attempting to discourage the use of ozone-depleting chlorofluorocarbons (CFCs) with a tax it imposed in late 1989 of $3.02 per kilogram, increasing to $6.83 per kilogram by 1995 and to $10.80 per kilogram by 1999. A comprehensive set of green taxes could help shape our nation's behavior, while at the same time raising substantial revenues that could be used for environmental projects.

Direct Regulation

The primary means of protecting the environment is direct regulation, or command-and-control regulation. By *direct regulation*, we mean the setting of standards and mandating compliance through threat of fines for violations. Standards may be set in terms of levels of technology that must be used or total emissions allowed. The focus of the remaining chapters is primarily on direct regulation.

These regulations are often referred to as end-pipe regulations because they tend to concentrate on controlling pollutants toward the end of the manufacturing process. These direct regulations have been the focus of most environmental legislation. As the final section in this chapter reveals, however, we are beginning to shift away from the end-pipe regulations traditionally identified with direct regulation and toward ways of making it economically beneficial for firms to evaluate their entire production process in search of avenues whereby fewer pollutants would be created in the first place.

EVOLUTION OF OUR ENVIRONMENTAL POLICY

The Origins of Our Environmental Policy

When we think about our government, we generally do not think about our government's policies. We do not have national policies on many issues; our policy, if you can call it a policy, with respect to most issues has been laissez-faire, or "government hands off." Minimal government intervention, especially in business affairs, traditionally has been seen as desirable by those in power in this country. We are, for example, the only industrialized nation that does not have a coherent industrial policy. However, if there is any area in which our country has seemed to have adopted a national policy, it is with respect to the environment.

As noted earlier, before 1970, the United States did not really have any sort of environmental policy. To a large extent this absence of environmental regulation, as well as subsequent increases in regulation, reflected the state of scientific knowledge. We were not even aware of many environmental problems. Further, we did not have the ability to detect and measure low levels of chemical contaminants. For example, the ability to measure levels of many contaminants has gone from parts per thousand to parts per million.

We also did not have the computer technology available to do the types of modeling that today allow us to project the long-run impacts of certain levels of contaminants on the human environment. And even, in some cases, when we determined that a given level of pollution was harmful, we did not have the technology immediately to reduce emissions levels. Once the technology was developed, it was sometimes more costly than expected. Very frequently, the cleaner the environment became, the more costly the technology for smaller and smaller reductions of emissions.

As mentioned in Chapter 2, our system of government also helped to slow the evolution of environmental policy. Strong constituencies were needed to get the legislative and executive branches moving together toward protecting the environment. And once the laws were passed, they were still subject to the courts' interpretation. And, as we saw in Chapter 2, the ideology of the majority of justices can change, and thus environmental policy as enforced by the courts may change.

Finally, our environmental policy is influenced by our values, the long ingrained values of our culture, as well as more temporary values that seem to change over time in response to economic conditions. Our independence has always encouraged a hands-off policy toward business, which would tend to explain our lack of an earlier environmental policy. However, as our economy became stronger, other values, especially those reflecting a desire for an improved quality of life, became more dominant and encouraged the adoption of policies more favorable to the environment.

The Seventies: The Environmental Decade

The environmental movement of the early 1970s was inspired to a great extent by three books. Perhaps the most influential of these was Rachael Carson's *Silent Spring*, which made people aware of the effects of pesticides on birds and other wildlife. The other two were Paul Ehrlich's *The Population Bomb*, which alerted us to the potentially adverse impact that our rapidly increasing population could have on our natural resources, and Barry Commoner's *The Closing Circle*, which explained ecological principles in terms that laypeople could understand.

Also influential in generating public interest in preservation of the environment were a few cataclysmic events, such as the 1969 oil spill in Santa Barbara, California. On April 22, 1970, the first Earth Day was celebrated, and there were "teach-ins" about environmental problems across the nation. These events created the public pressure that caused policymakers in all branches of government to perceive environmental issues as politically emergent. Seeing almost unprecedented public support for a strong environmental policy, lawmakers set about adopting tough environmental regulations, often without fully considering the costs and technological feasibility of implementing such regulations.

In terms of institutionalizing an environmental policy that would have a long-run impact, two actions were probably the most significant. One was the creation of the EPA, to bring the coordination of environmental policy under the control of one agency. The other was passage of the National Environmental Policy Act (described later in this chapter), which requires every federal agency to consider the environmental impacts of every major activity it undertakes.

The years from 1969 through 1979 saw the passage of 27 laws designed to protect the environment, as well as hundreds of administrative regulations. The decade of the 1970s, under this new environmental policy, witnessed vast improvements in the quality of the air, water, and land, even though many of the goals established by these laws had not been completely attained.

The Decade of the 1980s

By 1980, concern was growing over the costs of regulation in general. The economy was not in good shape, and Reagan was elected under a banner of deregulation. As part of his general policy of "getting government off the back of business," Reagan appointed conservatives to head the EPA and the Interior Department, as well as to serve in key positions in these and other agencies that played significant roles in setting out and enforcing environmental policy. Many of these newly appointed officials in fact came from businesses, legal foundations, or firms that had fought the regulations they were now supposed to enforce. Subsequently, many, with their deregulatory ideas, drove a number of senior executives and professionals out of the environmental agencies.[6]

Reagan also reduced the staffs of many agencies, in particular cutting EPA personnel by 20 percent.[7] Further reductions in enforcement were assured by cutting the EPA's budget by more than one third, when adjusted for inflation, between 1981 and 1983.[8] Funding for conservation programs in the Interior Department, as well as for renewable energy programs, was also reduced. Reacting to less money and staff for enforcement, business soon recognized that there had been a shift in environmental policy and felt less constrained by environmental regulations.

At first, Congress went along with the administration's relaxation of environmental policies. After two years, the public, at the instigation of numerous environmental groups, began to make its dissatisfaction known. In March 1982, 10 environmental and conservation groups issued an "indictment" of Reagan, alleging that he had "broken faith with the American people on environmental protection" by taking or proposing "scores of actions that veered radically away from the broad bipartisan consensus in support of environmental policy that has existed for many years," and citing 227 ways that the administration had subverted environmental policy.[9]

Congress, perhaps in response to a perception that the public disapproved of the administration's lax attitude toward the environment, began to oppose the administration's policies toward the environment by holding several oversight hearings on the EPA's handling of specific environmental matters. Congress also voted to strengthen a number of environmental laws that came up for renewal during the 1980s. In many instances the laws may have been stronger than they would have been with a more pro-environment president because of congressional belief that it needed to draft strong laws that could not be watered down by a weakened EPA.

Thus, the 1980s saw a reduction in funding for environmental programs and a relaxation in their enforcement, along with cutbacks in the budgets and staffs of agencies established to protect the environment. Much of the administrative burden associated with environmental policy was shifted to the states. However, by the end of the decade, there seemed to be a renewal of environmental vigor on the part of Congress.

The 1990s

As the 1990s approached, there seemed to be renewed interest in having a strong policy to protect the environment. "Green" products began cropping up all over. Major firms, such as McDonald's, started advertising that they were changing their products to become more environmentally friendly. Public opinion polls began to show more interest than ever in environmental protection. Further, enforcement at the EPA was given renewed attention. Both 1990 and 1991 produced record numbers of prosecutions and fines for environmental violations. Congress also seemed to be continuing its environmental support by passing a strong Clean Air Act.

Thus, there were many indicators that the 1990s would see a strengthening of an environmental policy that had been weakening during the 1980s. Not all indicators were pointing in that direction, however. President Bush's appointee to head the EPA, William Reilly, though a disappointment to many environmentalists, was proving to be a bit more pro-environment and not quite pro-business enough for the president, so there were numerous conflicts within the executive branch: between the president, his Competitiveness Council, and the Office of Management and Budget on the one side and the EPA on the other.

Also, by the 1990s, many federal courts were dominated by conservative appointees. Early cases indicated that these new appointees were not necessarily going to be as willing as previous courts to take pro-environmental positions. And even the newly constituted U.S. Supreme Court indicated that it was going to give much less weight to preserving environmental values, even going so far as to overturn past precedents that it saw as having given too much protection to environmental concerns.

As the economy continued to slump during the early 1990s, people again became more concerned about the costs of environmental regulations. They also started to recognize that once the initial gains had been made in the 1970s and 1980s, future incremental gains were going to be much more costly. And each incremental gain would also provide fewer visible benefits. These factors helped to create a shift in environmental policy away from the end-pipe regulation toward more pollution prevention and the use of more cost-effective ways to reduce pollution. As mentioned earlier, one of the factors that helped stimulate a concern for the environment during the late 1960s and early 1970s was the fact that the economy was doing well; there was money available to be spent. At the beginning of the 1990s, the economy was not in good shape.

An Increasing Use of "Market Forces." Part of this shift of environmental policy in the 1990s appears to be toward greater use of "market forces." This term covers a broad range of strategies. Proponents of this trend are careful to point out that the term is not a code word for deregulation. Rather, they insist, it is a way of using the market forces to encourage pollution prevention.

One example of this type of market force incentive is the passage of "bottle bills," bills that require certain types of beverages to be sold in recyclable or reusable bottles. Consumers must pay a deposit for such bottles, which will be refunded when the bottles are returned. Consumers will be much more likely to recycle when there is a financial incentive to do so. At least nine states have such laws. Another example is what Seattle is doing in charging for refuse pickup based on poundage. If consumers pay by the pound to have their trash carted away, they will be motivated financially to reduce their trash. Pollution taxes and refundable deposits on hazardous materials are two other market-oriented incentives. Maine and Rhode Island, for example, impose refundable deposits on automobile batteries. What all these strategies have in common is that they make the polluter pay—and thus, theoretically, encourage reduction in pollution in order to avoid the costs.

Two of the more controversial strategies are pollution charges and marketable emissions permits. The former is an alternative to ordering plants to cut emissions by a specific amount. Instead, every unit of pollution discharged is taxed, thus giving an incentive to the firm to cut emissions. Critics, however, point out that for this scheme to work, the taxing agency would need detailed information about a company's costs to make possible the setting of fees at a level that would discourage pollution. Marketable emissions permits were mentioned in an earlier section of this chapter. Governments would set overall emissions targets and then issue permits to meet those targets. If a firm could reduce its emissions below its target, it could sell unused credits to other firms. Some have even suggested using marketable permits to solve global problems, awarding marketable permits, for example, to countries that take steps to preserve forests. The first major experiment in marketable emissions permits is taking place under the Clean Air Act of 1990.

Described in detail in Chapter 6, this policy is designed to alleviate one of the frequent criticisms of direct regulation, that the regulations do not take into account the differences among various competitors' compliance.

Many of these new strategies are detailed in Project 88, a public policy study sponsored by two U.S. senators, Timothy Worth of Colorado and the late John Heinz of Pennsylvania. This project is the most comprehensive review of potential market-oriented policies.

Voluntary Programs. Another shift in environmental policy is toward more voluntary programs on the part of businesses to reduce pollution. One example of such a program is the 35/50 Project, a voluntary project in which more than 600 companies were asked to reduce voluntarily their emissions of 17 high-priority chemicals. The goal for the project is to achieve a one-third reduction of these emissions by 1992 and a 50 percent reduction by 1995. By April 1991, more than 100 companies had expressed interest in the project.

Another example of such voluntary projects is the Green Lights Program. When a company agrees to participate in this voluntary project, it signs an agreement with the EPA committing itself to surveying all its facilities and installing new lighting systems that maximize energy savings as long as the new systems do not compromise lighting quality or profitability. In return, the EPA provides the company the information and technical support it needs to install the requisite lighting. By April 10, 1991, 50 corporations had become partners in the program, and approximately 75 percent of these were Fortune 500 firms.

It is difficult to project what environmental law developments will occur in the mid- and late 1990s. However, in 1992 democratic presidential and vice-presidential candidates who were characterized by their opponents as "environmental extremists" were elected. Vice president Gore had, in fact, written a book suggesting ways to improve environmental quality. When asked by an interviewer from *The Wall Street Journal* what recent event helped shape his vision of American society, Gore replied, "The UN Conference on Environment and Development conducted in Rio de Janeiro."[10]

Articles appearing soon after the election indicated that corporate environmental lawyers were taking the election of the new presidential team as a signal, at minimum, of renewed environmental enforcement. For example, in the *National Law Journal,* in an article entitled "Girding for a Change," the author opened by warning readers, "For the general counsels at the nation's corporations, the transition period between the last weeks of President Bush's tenure and the first months of a Clinton administration calls for a thorough re-examination of their companies' overall compliance program."[11] According to more than two dozen regulatory and compliance experts from private law firms, corporations, public interest groups, and law schools who were interviewed for the story, the new administration will bring new rules and an overall boost in enforcement.

While enforcement in all regulatory areas was predicted to increase, the greatest increases were expected to come in the environmental area.[12] Whether these predictions will prove true remains to be seen.

NATIONAL ENVIRONMENTAL POLICY ACT

We begin our study of environmental regulations by examining the two major policy statutes: the National Environmental Policy Act (NEPA) of 1970 and the Pollution Prevention Act of 1990. Enacted 20 years apart, these acts when contrasted give a sense of the history and future direction of our environmental policies.

The National Environmental Policy Act was signed into law on January 1, 1970, and may be characterized as a planning statute. It does three things directly:

1. Establishes the Council on Environmental Quality (CEQ), the federal watchdog of environmental policy;
2. Requires federal agencies to take environmental consequences into account when they make certain decisions, which prior to NEPA, they *could not* do because consideration of such effects was rarely listed in agencies' enabling acts as a factor to be taken into account in agency decision making; and
3. Requires that an Environmental Impact Statement (EIS) be prepared for every major legislative proposal or other federal agency action having a significant impact on the quality of the human environment.

Council on Environmental Quality

The least controversial aspect of NEPA was its first mandate: the creation of the Council on Environmental Quality (CEQ). The CEQ was made up of three persons, one of whom was designated the chair. The role of the council was primarily advisory, mainly advising the president about environmental matters. For over twenty years, the CEQ gathered and analyzed data, informed the president about the progress the nation was making toward cleaning the environment, and recommended legislation that needed to be passed and issues that needed attention. Every year the CEQ used the data it gathered to publish the *President's Annual Report on Environmental Quality*, which was available to the public.

The CEQ also helped federal agencies to meet their EIS requirements under NEPA by reviewing drafts of these statements. The CEQ established regulations pertaining to NEPA procedures. For example, in 1986, the CEQ amended 40

CFR 1502.22 to require the EPA to disclose when there is incomplete or inade-quate data to fully discuss potential adverse impacts.

The chair of the CEQ had additional duties. He or she attended meetings of the President's Domestic Policy Council when environmental matters were dis-cussed, represented the president at international conferences, and drafted memos and executive orders related to the environment. The chair also coordi-nated federal agency activities involved with the World Commission on Envi-ronmental Development (WCED), an offshoot of the United Nation's General Assembly that conducts research on environmental topics.

The CEQ was decimated during the 1980s. Adjusted for inflation, the CEQ's budget dropped from $4.1 million in 1975 to $700,000 by 1990, an 83 percent decline. Its staff fell from 57 in 1977 to 11 by the late 1980s.[13] With such dras-tic cuts in budget and personnel, it became increasingly difficult for the CEQ even to produce its mandated annual report, which continued to diminish in size, and fell several years behind schedule toward the end of the 1980s.[14] Many had hoped that the CEQ would return to its earlier form when Clinton was elected. But President Clinton surprised many by instead moving to abolish the CEQ in February 1993 and proposing a new Office of Environmental Policy, designed to have broader influence than the CEQ. The head of this new office would be a deputy assistant to the president. Kathleen McGinty, a former Sen-ate staff aide to Albert Gore, was appointed to fill this new position. Among her tasks would be sitting in on meetings of the Domestic Policy Council, the National Security Council, and the Economic Policy Council.

Environmental Impact Statement (EIS)

Far more controversial than the creation of the CEQ was the requirement of the Environmental Impact Statement (EIS). This requirement has a widespread impact on several government agencies, as well as on private firms seeking to do business under governmental agency contracts or licenses. Although the process has been criticized by many affected groups, most studies of NEPA's effectiveness have concluded that it has forced greater governmental awareness and more careful planning in many agencies. To get an idea of the impact of the EIS process, examine Table 4–1, which lists the number of EISs filed by federal agencies during the years 1979 through 1990.

Several major issues pervade an analysis of the EIS requirement, ranging from who must file the EIS and when, to disputes over what must be included in the statement, to whether the process is effective.

Threshold Considerations. Every time a federal agency undertakes an activity, it must decide whether to file an EIS. Filing an unnecessary EIS is a waste of time and money. Failure to file a necessary statement can be equally or more expen-

TABLE 4–1 Environmental impact statements filed by federal agencies

Agency	1979	1980	1981	1982	1983	1984	1985	1986	1987	1988	1989	1990
Agriculture	172	104	102	89	59	65	117	118	75	68	89	136
Commerce	54	53	36	25	14	24	10	8	9	3	5	8
Defense	1	1	1	1	1	0	0	0	2	0	0	0
Air Force	8	3	7	4	6	5	7	8	9	6	11	19
Army	40	9	14	3	6	5	5	2	10	8	9	9
COE	182	150	186	127	119	116	106	91	76	69	40	46
Navy	11	9	10	6	4	9	8	13	9	6	4	19
Energy	28	45	21	24	19	14	4	13	11	9	6	11
EPA	84	71	96	63	67	42	16	18	19	23	25	31
GSA	13	11	13	8	1	0	4	0	1	3	0	4
HUD	170	140	140	93	42	13	15	18	6	2	7	5
Interior	126	131	107	127	146	115	105	98	110	117	61	68
Transport-ation	277	189	221	183	169	147	126	110	101	96	90	100
TVA	9	6	4	0	2	1	0	1	0	0	0	3
Other	98	44	76	55	22	21	26	15	17	20	23	18
Total	1,273	966	1,033	808	677	577	549	521	455	430	370	477

Notes: Years refer to calendar years. Number of EISs includes draft EISs, EIS supplements, and final EISs filed during the specified year. Some proposed projects may have several draft and final EISs filed over a period of years. COE = U.S. Army Corps of Engineers; HUD = Department of Housing and Urban Development; EPA = U.S. Environmental Protection Agency; GSA = General Services Administration; TVA = Tennessee Valley Authority.

SOURCE: U.S. Environmental Protection Agency, Office of Federal Activities, unpublished data, 1991; reprinted in CEQ, *Environmental Quality*, 22nd annual report (1992).

sive if someone challenges the lack of an EIS and seeks an injunction in court. However, it is not always easy to know when an EIS is required. NEPA specifies three conditions that must be met for an EIS to be required. First, the activity must be *federal.* A federal activity is fairly broadly defined. If, for example, a private sector construction firm wants to construct a building that requires a government license or if the project is going to be partly financed by a government loan, the licensing or lending agency is undertaking a federal activity.

Whether an EIS is required for a federal activity depends on whether the other two criteria are met. The federal activity must be *major.* There are no dollar guidelines as to what is a major activity. The courts generally say that the activity requires a substantial commitment of resources, with resources being broadly defined to include both financial and human resources. A substantial commitment of either type of resource is sufficient.

The third criterion is that the proposed activity must have a *significant impact on the human environment.* The term "significant impact on the human environment" is so ambiguous that it initially generated substantial litigation. Then, in 1979, the CEQ tried to resolve some of the controversy by adopting a series of guidelines for the implementation of NEPA's procedural provisions. In these guidelines, the CEQ tried to define better what was meant by "significant impact." The CEQ stated that determining the significance of an impact necessitated examining both the context and the intensity of the action. Looking at the context was said to require consideration of both the short- and long-term effects of the activity, and looking at the impact of the activity on the local area, the region, and society as a whole.

Examining the intensity of an activity was said to involve 10 factors: (1) both beneficial and detrimental effects; (2) the degree to which the public health and safety will be affected; (3) unique characteristics of the geographic area that may be affected by the activity; (4) the degree to which the effects of the activity are likely to cause controversy; (5) the degree to which the effects on the human environment are highly uncertain or unique; (6) the degree to which the activity is likely to set a precedent for future actions; (7) whether insignificant effects from this activity, when combined with insignificant effects from other activities; will constitute significant effects; (8) the degree to which the act may affect places of scientific, historic, or cultural significance; (9) the degree to which an act may adversely affect an endangered species; and (10) whether the act threatens any law designed to protect the environment.[15]

Even with this "clarification" by the CEQ, it is still sometimes difficult to know whether an EIS is necessary. A demonstration of that difficulty can be made by examining two very similar cases. After reading the descriptions, try to decide whether the court in either case required an EIS.

Both cases involved the Department of Housing and Urban Development (HUD). In case 1, HUD was preparing to loan a developer $3.5 million to construct a high rise in an area of Portland where there were no other high rises.[16] In case 2, HUD was preparing to insure a developer's $3.7 million loan to construct a 272-unit apartment complex in Houston on a 15-acre lot.[17] Must HUD file EIS in both cases, either case, or neither case? The court in the first case required an EIS; the court in the second case did not.

There were two primary reasons for the different outcomes: First, the activity in case 1 was major, whereas the second was not. Though both involved millions of dollars, the actual transfer of money was likely to be much greater in the first case than in the second, because the former required the actual lending of money whereas the latter was only a guarantee of a loan.[18] The only way the transfer of funds would occur would be if the developer failed to pay the loan. Because of the careful screening of candidates for insured loans, failure of repayment did not appear likely. Second, the impact of the first activity was more significant. In the first case, the use was for a unique activity, whereas in Houston, where there was no zoning as the city developed, building a housing complex was not unique, regardless of where it was.[19] There was also the possibility that building one high rise in Portland might set a dangerous precedent, leading to overcrowding in the area. Another factor, not mentioned in the statement of the case, was that there was organized opposition to the high rise in Portland.

Other less significant factors that may have an impact on whether an EIS is required include the jurisdiction and the time.[20] Recall from your previous reading that most attorneys who do environmental work are quite aware of the fact that certain judges or courts tend to hand down more pro-environmentalist decisions than do others. In fact, in situations in which a corporation with operations in many states is being sued, and the company would fall within the jurisdiction of multiple courts, the plaintiff will carefully examine rulings of all those courts so that the case may be filed in the most environmentally friendly one.

Time may have an impact in three ways. First, though judges are supposed not to be influenced by the public, they would not be human if they were totally unaffected by public opinion. Thus, at a time when there is strong public sentiment in support of environmental protection, judges may be moved slightly toward requiring EISs in close cases. A second factor is that during a time period when the federal courts are dominated by judges appointed by a strong environmentalist president, judges may be more likely to require EISs because appointees have a tendency to have political values similar to those of the president who made the appointments. Finally, the prevailing political climate may influence federal judges who are desirous of appointments to higher courts. They may not want to displease the president and jeopardize their chances for prospective appointments.

In any situation in which the need to file an EIS is questionable, some analysis of the significance of the impact of an activity must obviously take place. If an agency decides that no EIS is necessary, although it believes others may disagree, the agency may try to protect itself by filing a Finding of No Significant Impact, or FONSI. This document states the reasons why the agency believes no EIS is necessary. The FONSI is usually accompanied by an environmental assessment that provides the evidence and analysis for the agency's decision.

Once the agency decides that it needs to file an EIS, certain procedural steps must be followed. These procedures are detailed in the following section.

Procedure under the EIS Requirement. One of the major criticisms of the EIS process is related to the time-consuming nature of the procedures necessary for preparing an EIS. Initially, the agency required to file the EIS will assemble a team of specialists to prepare a draft report. In many cases, this team will consist of outside consultants, many of whom may have a vested interest in preparing positive assessments so that they will be able to secure contracts from the agency in the future. Next, a draft version will be circulated within the agency, to be reviewed by several parties. There may frequently be disputes between those reviewers who are pro-agency or pro-industry and those who are more environmentally concerned. The draft may be revised as a result of these initial comments.

Following the agency's completion of that draft, the document goes to the CEQ for review and comments. Then, in accordance with the Administrative Procedure Act's rules for informal rule making, the draft is published in the *Federal Register* for public comment. Many other agencies will submit comments at this time, as will citizens' groups and business interests.

After the public comments have been received, a similar process will be followed for the final draft. If a draft has been severely criticized, the agency is faced with the difficult decision of whether to try to "repair" the heavily criticized draft or draft an entirely new document. This type of dispute can tie up an agency for weeks or months. Preparing a new draft is time-consuming and costly, because all the steps have to be repeated with the new statement. However, proceeding with an inadequate EIS may lead to a successful legal challenge by parties opposed to the action. Once the agency is satisfied with its final draft, it publishes it in the *Federal Register*. For a routine EIS, this entire procedure may take from six to nine months. Court challenges may tie up this process for a year or longer.

After publication of the final draft, the sufficiency of the draft may be challenged in court. Also, the failure to file an EIS when required may also be challenged. This process of judicial review of the EIS has led to criticism by environmentalists. When reviewing the EIS, the court generally operates in an administrative law tradition, which means that the court will *not* substitute its judgment for the agency's. As long as the agency followed the proper procedures and included the requisite elements in the EIS, the court will allow the EIS to stand and the agency action to occur. Under no circumstances can a party contest the weight given by the agency to any adverse consequences listed in the statement. The court will never forbid an action on the grounds that the consequences are too severe.

Even if the court finds that the EIS was inadequate, the only remedy is a temporary injunction of agency action until a proper EIS has been filed. This limited power of the courts has led many to argue that the filing of an EIS is a "toothless" requirement. As a consequence of the court's limited remedies, a party who challenges an EIS may hope for one of three outcomes: First, the party seeking to take the action for which the EIS was required will decide to modify the project to save time or to avoid adverse publicity. Second, the delay might give the party challenging the action enough time to rally persuasive public opposition to the project. Finally, the delay may make the project too costly, so it may be dropped.

You might think that given the limited remedy available under NEPA, few challenges would be filed. However, between 1974 and 1985, roughly 120 NEPA cases were filed each year. Most cases did not result in injunctions being issued. In fact, no injunctions were granted until 1979, when the courts responded favorably to 12 of the 139 requested injunctions. From 1980 to 1985, the number of injunctions issued ranged from 8 to 21. Of course, just because an injunction was not issued, the case was not necessarily ineffective.

TABLE 4–2   Plaintiffs for NEPA lawsuits, 1990

Plaintiffs	Number of Cases
Environmental groups	38
Individuals or citizens' groups	38
State governments	5
Local governments	9
Business groups	5
Property owners or residents	13
Indian tribes	2
Other	2
Total	112

SOURCE: CEQ, *Environmental Quality,* 22nd Annual Report (1991).

We do not know how many court challenges or threatened challenges led to voluntary modifications of agency plans. Sometimes the very act of preparing the EIS causes an agency to change its plans. For example, a spokesperson for the Army Corps of Engineers stated that in 1972, EISs caused the corps to drop 24 projects temporarily, indefinitely delay 44, and significantly modify 197.

The most frequent plaintiffs in challenges to EISs are citizens' groups and environmental groups. Table 4–2 lists the plaintiffs in NEPA lawsuits filed in 1990. The most frequent defendants tend to be the Department of Transportation, the Department of the Interior, the Army Corps of Engineers, and the Federal Energy Regulatory Commission. Table 4–3 details the number of cases filed, injunctions granted, and most frequent plaintiffs, defendants, and types of complaints from 1974 to 1985.

Contents of the EIS. Whether an agency voluntarily prepares an EIS or is required to by the courts, certain elements must be contained in the document: (1) a statement of environmental impacts (positive and negative) of the proposed action; (2) any unavoidable adverse environmental impacts should the proposal be implemented; (3) alternatives to the proposal (including taking no action); (4) the relationship between short-term uses of the environment and enhancement of long-range productivity; and (5) any irreversible commitments of resources. The suggested format for the EIS is given in Table 4–4.

POLLUTION PREVENTION ACT

The first environmental protection laws used a very directive approach. The EPA was to establish standards, and the other agencies and businesses were to meet those standards. Many of the early regulations, as you shall see when you read about specific laws in subsequent chapters, were "command

TABLE 4–3   Cumulative NEPA Litigation Survey, 1974–1985

Year	Cases Filed	Injunctions	Most Frequent Defendant	Most Frequent Plaintiff	Most Common Complaint	Second Common Complaint
1974	189		DOT, HUD			
1975	152					
1976	119		DOT, DOI, HUD	Citizens' and environmentalist groups	No EIS	Inadequate EIS
1977	108		DOT, DOD, DOI	Cit. & env. gr.	No EIS	Inadequate EIS
1978	114		DOT, DOD, DOI, HUD, EPA	Cit. & env. gr., individuals	No EIS	Inadequate EIS
1979	139	12	DOT, HUD, DOI, DOAg, DOD	Env. gr., cit. gr. & ind.	No EIS	Inadequate EIS
1980	140	17	DOT, DOI, DOD, HUD, EPA	Ind. & cit. gr., env. gr.	No EIS	Inadequate EIS
1981	114	12	DOD, DOT, DOI, DOAg, HUD, NRC	Env. gr., ind. & cit. gr.	No EIS	Inadequate EIS
1982	157	19	DOI, COE, DOT, DOAg, HUD, EPA	Ind. & cit. gr., env. gr.	Inadequate EIS	No EIS
1983	146	21	DOI, DOT, DOA, FERC, NRC	Ind. & cit. gr., env. gr.	No EIS	Inadequate EIS
1984	89	14	DOAg, DOI, DOT	Env. gr., ind. & cit. gr.	Inadequate EIS	No EIS
1985	77	8	DOT, DOI, COE, FERC	Env. gr., ind. & cit. gr.	No EIS	Inadequate EIS

SOURCE: Annual Report, Council on Environmental Quality, Appendix B, p. 241 (1986).

and control" (dictated standards) or "end of pipe" (using technology to treat the waste or pollutant just before it was emitted). And, in fact, these are still the primary types of regulations today. The Pollution Prevention Act, however, recognizes that these end-pipe regulations may not be enough, so we are going to have to find ways to prevent the creation of pollution in the first place.

Initially great gains were made using these strategies. Relatively minor investments led to dramatic decreases in pollutants. However, after 20 years of implementation of these end-pipe controls, it became increasingly costly to get increasingly smaller reductions of pollutants. Whereas $1 million might have decreased a firm's emissions of a pollutant by 80 percent, the tailpipe controls

TABLE 4–4　Format of environment impact statements

Item	Length	Contents Include
1. Cover sheet	Up to 1 page	Title and locations of proposed action; locale involved; agencies; names and addresses of persons who can supply further information; relevant dates; one-paragraph abstract of statement.
2. Summary	Up to 15 pages	Summary of statement stressing major conclusions, areas of controversy, and issues to be resolved.
3. Table of contents		
4. Purpose and need for action		
5. Alternatives, including proposed action		Heart of the statement. Rigorous evaluation of all alternatives, including why some were eliminated from consideration; including alternative of no action; identifying agencies' preferred action; and including appropriate mitigation actions.
6. Affected environment	No longer than necessary	Succinct description.
7. Environmental consequences		Discussions of direct and indirect effects and their significance; energy requirements; possible conflicts with land-use plans of other governmental bodies; depletable resource requirements and conservation potential of alternatives; urban quality; historical and cultural resources; and means to initiate impacts if not already discussed.
8. List of preparers	Not to exceed 2 pages	Names and qualifications.
9. List of agencies, organizations, and persons to whom copies are to be sent		
10. Index		
11. Appendixes (if any)		Material prepared in connection with EIS that is analytical and relevant to any decisions to be made and substantiates any analysis fundamental to the EIS.

needed to decrease that pollutant by only 10 more percent might cost the firm an additional $2 million. It gradually became apparent to Congress that a new approach was necessary. That new approach was embodied in the Pollution Prevention Act of 1990, passed by Congress on October 27, 1990. In its findings, presented in Section 2 of the act, Congress stated:

(1) There are significant opportunities for industry to reduce or prevent pollution at the source through cost-effective changes in production, operation, and raw materials use. Such changes offer industry substantial savings in reduced raw material, pollution control, and liability costs as well as help protect the environment and reduce risks to worker health and safety.

(2) The opportunities for source reduction are often not realized because existing regulations, and the industrial resources they require for compliance, focus upon treatment and disposal, rather than source reduction; existing regulations do not emphasize multi-media management of pollution; and businesses need information and technical assistance to overcome institutional barriers to the adoption of source reductions practices.

(3) Source reduction is fundamentally different and more desirable than waste management and pollution control. The Environmental Protection Agency needs to address the historical lack of attention to source reduction.

The wisdom of these findings is supported by an article in *The Wall Street Journal.* According to the article, chemical companies, traditionally a group with an oft-criticized record on the environment, are making a major shift and beginning to see waste as avoidable and efficient. The more unusable by-products a process creates, the less efficient it may be. For example, at one Du Pont plant, which generated 110 million pounds of waste annually, engineers adjusted their production process to use less of one raw material, and slashed the plant's waste by two-thirds. The resulting savings from the change in process amounted to $1 million a year.[21]

As a result of its findings, Congress established the following policy: "Pollution should be prevented or reduced at the source whenever feasible; pollution that cannot be prevented should be recycled in an environmentally safe manner, whenever feasible; pollution that cannot be prevented or recycled should be treated in an environmentally safe manner whenever feasible; and disposal or other release into the environment should be employed only as a last resort and should be conducted in an environmentally safe manner." To implement this new policy, the administrator of the EPA is required to establish a separate office within the agency to serve as administrator under the act.

The act also authorizes the provision of matching grants to states for programs to promote the use of source reduction techniques by business. The amount budgeted for these grants was $8 million for each of fiscal years 1991, 1992, and 1993. To collect and compile information generated by the grants and to disseminate this information, the administrator is authorized to establish a clearinghouse to serve as a center for source reduction technology transfer.

Finally, certain biennial reports are required of the administrator of the act. These reports are to include such information as analysis of grant results, identification of industries and pollutants that require priority assistance in multimedia source reduction, and evaluation of data gaps and duplication of data collected under federal environmental protection acts.

Because this act is relatively new, we cannot yet assess its effectiveness. (Some people believe it will have no real effect.) It is clear, however, that many industries are already beginning to move in the direction of pollution prevention. As you shall see as you read the remainder of this book, while we have set forth this policy of pollution prevention, and are increasing the use of incentives to prevent creation of pollutants, our primary mode of protecting the environment is still the command and control approach.

CONCLUDING REMARKS

The primary justifications for environmental protection range from the analogy of the tragedy of the commons, to economic justifications to arguments from an environmental ethos. Taken together, these justifications seem to provide strong support for many of the regulatory programs you are going to be studying.

You have been introduced to various strategies that are adopted to protect the environment, such as tort law, emissions fees, permits, subsidies, and green taxes. In addition, the 1990 Pollution Prevention Act encourages initial prevention and voluntary actions. However, our main approach to environmental problems continues to be direct regulation, which is the focus of the remainder of the book. Chapter 5 examines our approach to controlling air quality. We concentrate on air quality first because the Clean Air Act was the first major end-pipe pollution-control law, and subsequent acts for other protected resources were modeled loosely on it.

QUESTIONS FOR REVIEW AND DISCUSSION

1. Explain the relationship between the tragedy of the commons and the need to control pollution.
2. Explain what a free rider is and how that concept is related to environmental law.
3. Why is tort law alone an ineffective way to control pollution?
4. Explain the advantages and disadvantages of using emissions charges and subsidies to control pollution.
5. What factors influence the development of environmental policies?
6. Explain when an Environmental Impact Statement must be filed.

7. What must be contained in an EIS?

8. What is the purpose of the 1990 Pollution Prevention Control Act?

FOR FURTHER READING

Brooks, Richard O. "A New Agenda for Environmental Law." *Journal of Law and Litigation,* 6 (1991):1.

(Comment). "NEPA's Role in Protecting the World Environment." *University of Pennsylvania Law Review,* 131 (1982):353 .

(Comment). "NEPA Violations and Equitable Discretion." *Oregon Law Review,* 64 (1986):497 .

Hawkins, Keith. *Environment and Enforcement: Regulation and the Social Definition of Pollution.* New York: Clarendon Press, 1984.

(Note). "Legal Institutions and Pollution: Some Intersections Between Law and History." *Natural Resources Journal,* 15 (1975):423 .

Yeager, Peter. *The Limits of the Law: The Public Regulation of Private Pollution.* New York: Cambridge University Press, 1991.

NOTES

1. Garrett Hardin, "The Tragedy of the Commons," Science, 162 (1968), 1243 .

2. Ibid.

3. Aldo Leopold, *A Sand Almanac,* 1968 ed. New York: Oxford University Press, (1948), 214–20.

4. Ibid.

5. 287 NYS 2d 112 (1967).

6. Norman Vig, "Presidential Leadership: From the Reagan to the Bush Administration," in *Environmental Policy in the 1990's: Toward a New Agenda,* ed. Norman Vig and Michael Kraft. (Washington, D.C.: Congressional Quarterly, 1990.)

7. Ibid.

8. Ibid.

9. Ibid.

10. "Getting Personal," *The Wall Street Journal,* January 20, 1993, p. R3.

11. Margaret C. Fisk, "Girding for a Change," *National Law Journal,* December 14, 1992, p. S1.

12. Ibid.

13. Michael Kraft and Norman Vig, "Environmental Policies from the Seventies to the Nineties," in *Environmental Policy in the 1990s: Toward a New Agenda,* ed. Norman Vig and Michael Korda.

14. Ibid.

15. 40 C.F.R. § 1508.27.

16. *Goose Hollow Foothills League* v. *Romney,* 334 F. Supp 877 (1971).

17. *Hiram Clarke Civic Club* v. *Lynn,* 47 F2d 421 (1973).

18. David Firestone and Frank Reed, *Environmental Law for Nonlawyers* (South Royalton, VT: Soro Press, 1983).

19. Ibid.

20. Ibid.

21. Scott McMurray, "Chemical Firms Find That It Pays to Reduce Pollution at the Source," *The Wall Street Journal,* June 11, 1991, p. A1, col. 6.

5

Air Quality Control

When people think about air quality problems, they often think of bumper-to-bumper traffic spewing exhaust on a freeway or steel mills with smokestacks blackening the air with soot. The first major air pollution control act, the Clean Air Act of 1970, was designed to remedy such problems. This act was passed because people no longer considered visible pollution to be evidence of economic progress but rather as a problem in need of a regulatory solution. Although this first major statutory response did significantly improve air quality, air pollution is still one of the most serious environmental problems in the United States. As recently as 1990, the EPA estimated that more than 100 million Americans lived in areas where air pollution levels exceed federal ambient air quality standards.[1]

To understand the current approach to air quality control, we first need to understand which pollutants we are trying to restrict, and why we need to control them. The first section provides this information. Whereas these "criteria pollutants" have been the initial focus of regulation, other air quality problems must be remedied, and these are introduced in the second and third sections. A fourth section explains the early and unsuccessful approach initially adopted to protect the air. Finally, the last section explains the current approach.

THE MAJOR AIR POLLUTANTS

Every minute of the day, vast quantities of pollutants are pouring into the atmosphere. These pollutants come from both natural and human sources and are normally cycled and destroyed through natural processes. However, the quantity of man-made pollutants has begun to overload the atmosphere's self-cleansing processes, causing damage to the environment and health problems. Although we shall discuss the primary harm caused by each individual pollutant, you should be aware that much damage also comes from the interactions of these pollutants.

The first six air pollutants we will discuss are currently regulated by Congress under the Clean Air Act. They are referred to under the act as criteria pollutants. It is these criteria pollutants that were initially perceived as the major air quality problem, and so were the initial focus of governmental efforts to improve the quality of our air. Many people still regard the regulation of these pollutants through the establishment of ambient air quality standards to be the heart of air pollution control in the United States. A brief summary of the problems caused by these pollutants is presented in Table 5–1.

Sulfur Dioxide

Sulfur dioxide (SO_2) is a highly corrosive gas that can be transported long distances in the atmosphere because it bonds to particles of dust, smoke, or aerosols. Volcanic emissions are the largest natural source of atmospheric sulfur dioxide, although decaying organic matter and sea spray are also important. However, slightly more than half the approximately 170 million tons of SO_2 emitted globally each year come from man-made sources. The major human source of sulfur dioxide is the burning of fossil fuels to generate electricity. The United States relies on these fuels for 90 percent of its energy needs. From 1940 to 1986, fuel combustion from utilities caused about 67 percent of

TABLE 5–1   Problems associated with criteria air pollutants

Pollutant	Problems
Sulfur dioxide	Causes lung and respiratory tract damage, and contributes to acid rain, which damages trees, buildings, vegetation, and aquatic life.
Nitrogen oxides	Causes lung and respiratory tract damage, and contributes to acid rain and smog.
Carbon monoxide	Replaces oxygen in bloodstream, causing angina, impaired vision, poor coordination, and lack of alertness. Contributes to formation of ozone.
Ozone	Irritates eyes, reduces lung function, increases nasal congestion, and reduces resistance to infection.
Particulates	Reduces resistance to infection, irritates the eyes, ears, and throat, and causes temporary or permanent lung damage.
Lead	Damages neurological systems and kidneys.

SO_2 emissions; nonutility fuel combustion from stationary sources caused 14 percent of the emissions, industrial processes another 15 percent, and transportation about 4 percent.

Since 1900, the global output of sulfur dioxide has increased sixfold.[2] However, between 1974 and 1987, most industrial nations lowered their SO_2 emissions in urban areas through direct regulation and also by a shift away from heavy manufacturing toward burning lower sulfur coal. In the United States there has been a reduction from 28.3 million metric tons of sulfur dioxide emitted in 1970, to 23.9 metric tons emitted in 1980, and 20.4 million metric tons emitted in 1987.[3]

The primary health danger from SO_2 is damage to the lungs and respiratory tract. In combination with nitrous oxide, SO_2 also contributes to the creation of acid rain, which causes harm to vegetation and buildings. Acid rain is discussed in greater detail later in this chapter.

Nitrogen Oxides

Nitrogen oxides (NO_x) refers to two harmful gases: nitric oxide (NO) and nitrogen dioxide (NO_2). Nitric oxide, almost immediately upon release, is converted into nitrogen dioxide.

On a global basis, about half the approximately 150 million tons of NO_x emitted annually comes from natural sources, predominantly lightening and decomposing organic matter. The other half comes from human activities, with motor vehicles the largest source. Power plants and industrial emissions also make substantial contributions. Though industrialization and development have led to substantial NO_x emissions in the United States, new technology has resulted in a decrease from peak discharge levels. For example, there was about a 15 percent rise in man-made emissions of nitrogen oxides between 1970 and 1978, increasing from approximately 18.1 million metric tons to about 21.1 million metric tons. Discharges then began to decline (falling to 19.1 million metric tons in 1983), but a gradual increase may now be evident, with reported emissions of 19.3 and 19.5 million metric tons in 1986 and 1987, respectively.[4]

The primary negative health effects from NO_x mirror those of SO_2: damage to the lungs and respiratory tract. In combination with other air pollutants, NO_x contributes to depletion of the ozone layer, acid deposition, and smog.

Carbon Monoxide

A third harmful gas is carbon monoxide (CO). Unlike most air pollutants, an estimated 60 percent of CO comes from natural sources. The major man-made source is the incomplete burning of fuels by motor vehicles in some urban areas. Other human sources of CO include wood stoves, incinerators, and industrial processes. Over the past 15 years, the United States, Japan, and Germany have reduced their CO emission. In the United States, 98.7 million metric tons of CO were emitted during 1970; that amount steadily declined year after year, primarily as a result of automobile emission controls. Emissions fell to 61.4 million metric tons during 1987.[5]

Carbon monoxide traditionally has been perceived as the least harmful of the criteria pollutants in terms of its effect on human health, but increasing evidence suggests that it does present a serious health risk. When carbon monoxide is inhaled, it replaces oxygen in the bloodstream, causing angina, impaired vision, poor coordination, and lack of alertness. It may temporarily reduce one's attention span and problem-solving abilities. CO has been implicated in some accidents caused by decreased attention and reduced sensory ability. The health effects are especially severe for people who have heart and lung problems. Some animal studies have also indicated that CO can damage the central nervous system of offspring who had chronic prenatal exposure to the pollutant. CO contributes to the greenhouse effect and to the formation of ozone, itself an air pollutant.

Ozone

Some people argue that ozone is the most intractable and widespread pollution problem. Ozone, as a pollutant at low altitudes—not to be confused with the ozone layer of the atmosphere, which actually protects life on earth—is not directly emitted into the air as are most of the other pollutants with which the Clean Air Act is concerned. Rather, ozone is a gas formed when nitrogen oxides react with oxygen in the presence of sunlight, a reaction that can be enhanced by the presence of reactive hydrocarbons and other pollutants commonly found in urban environments. Chemically, ozone is a form of oxygen that has three oxygen atoms instead of two.

We cannot measure emissions of ozone, so we examine the *concentration* of ozone in the air. The EPA considers the maximum safe level to be .12 ppm (parts per million). During 1988, 96 U.S. regions exceeded this standard on some days. Concentrations vary significantly from region to region, however, and even from day to day in the same place, depending on such factors as weather and the amount of industrial activity.

Ozone causes eye irritation, nasal congestion, asthma, reduced lung function, possible damage to lung tissue, and reduced resistance to infection. Ozone harms vegetation by damaging plant tissue, inhibiting photosynthesis, and increasing plant's susceptibility to disease and drought.

Particulates

A fifth criterion pollutant is particulates. Particulates as a pollutant refers to solid and liquid materials, varying in size from aerosol to large grit and suspended in the air. The primary man-made sources of particulates are steel mills, power plants, cotton gins, smelters, cement plants, and diesel engines. Other sources include grain elevators, demolition sites, industrial road-work, construction work, and wood-burning stoves and fireplaces. Natural sources include soil erosion and pollen. Emissions controls have drastically reduced the amount of suspended particulates emitted into the atmosphere from man-made sources in the United States from 21.6 million metric tons in 1960 to 7.0 million metric tons during 1987.[6]

The health impacts of particulates vary, depending on the particulates' size, shape, and chemistry. Fine particles pose a much greater risk to human health than do those with a diameter greater than 10 micrometers. The larger particles can be filtered out by the body's defense mechanisms, whereas the finer ones may pass through the defense mechanisms and travel into the lungs where they may become embedded. Once in the lungs, the particulates may lead to respiratory illness or lung or other systemic damage. Evidence for this contention is available in a demonstrated statistical correlation between high levels of particulate matter in the lungs and hospital admissions for pneumonia, bronchitis, and asthma.[7] Some particulates are carcinogenic; others may merely irritate the eyes and throat.

Lead

The first five air pollutants were regulated as criteria pollutants under the Clean Air Act of 1970. Lead is the only pollutant to be added to the initial list of criteria pollutants. Lead emissions result primarily from burning leaded gasoline. It is also present in paints and leaded pipes.

We can see the greatest impact of regulation on pollution levels when we look at lead emissions. In 1970, 203.8 thousand metric tons spewed forth from human sources in the United States. By 1980, this amount had fallen to 70.6 thousand metric tons, and by 1987, to 8.1 thousand metric tons.[8] These dramatic reductions resulted primarily from a prohibition of leaded gas.

Lead is of concern because it can harm the neurological system and kidneys of humans and animals. It can also inhibit respiration and photosynthesis in plants and block the decomposition of microorganisms.

AIRBORNE TOXINS

Another substantial group of pollutants causes both long- and short-term harm when emitted in small concentrations. Generally refered to as airborne toxins or toxic air pollutants, this group is large and not well defined, and we know relatively little about their effects on health. Most of what we do know about their toxicity comes from studies of industrial workplaces, where these pollutants may be present in elevated concentrations, and from animal studies.

It is estimated that at least 189 toxic air pollutants are currently, or will be by 1999, regulated under the most recent Clean Air Act amendments. Some toxic pollutants of high concern are benzene, primarily from chemical and plastics plants; vinyl chloride, from similar sources as benzene; chlorinated dioxins, from sources such as chemical processes and high-temperature burning of plastics in incinerators; asbestos; beryllium; mercury; arsenic; radionuclides; and coke oven emissions. These are the only toxic air pollutants regulated prior to the passage of the 1990 Clean Air Act amendments.

SOME SIGNIFICANT AIR QUALITY PROBLEMS

In recent years the focus of attention has shifted somewhat away from questioning how to control conventional and toxic pollutants to more global air quality problems. These international issues are the concern of this section.

Acid Deposition

The existence of acid deposition or acid precipitation has been known for years. Only recently, however, has acid deposition been recognized as a problem. Acid deposition is a process that begins with the emission of sulfur dioxide or nitrogen oxides. These pollutants interact with sunlight and water vapor in the upper atmosphere to form sulfuric and nitric acids, which fall to earth as acid snow or acid rain. Sometimes the compounds may dust other airborne dry particles and fall as "dry deposition."

Acidity is measured on a pH scale that ranges from 0 to 14, with 7 being neutral, higher levels being basic, and lower levels indicating acidity. "Pure" rain, uncontaminated by human or natural sulfates, has a pH of about 5.6. Figure 5–1 depicts a pH scale and shows where various substances would fall on such a scale. Most rain is slightly acid. Acid precipitation begins to become a problem when the pH levels begin to fall below 5. Rainfall with a pH level as low as 4.3 has been measured in parts of Canada and the United States.

As noted, a primary cause of acid precipitation is sulfur dioxide emissions. According to the National Commission on Air Quality, between 75 and 90 percent of the sulfate concentration of rain falling on any state in the eastern half of the United States is attributable to sources outside those states. This export of acid gases has resulted from the use of tall smokestacks (over 500 feet high), which use smelters and electric utilities to disperse their emissions into the upper reaches of the atmosphere. Unfortunately, the result has simply been to spread the acidic deposition over greater areas. Ohio, Indiana, Illinois, and Kentucky alone are responsible for nearly one-fourth of the SO_2 production in the United States, primarily from the burning of coal to generate electricity.

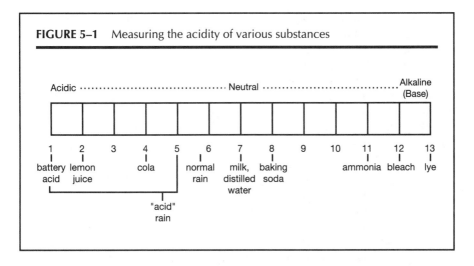

FIGURE 5–1   Measuring the acidity of various substances

The extent of harm caused by acid rain depends on the amount of acid deposition in an area and the sensitivity of the area. The Midwest has heavily alkaline soils that can buffer the effects of acid rain. Lakes that lie on limestone, sandstone, or other alkaline foundations, primarily those located in the western and midwestern regions of the nation, are likewise resistant to damage from acid deposition. Regions where lakes and soils lie on granite or thin glacial tils have much lower buffering capacity and thus are more susceptible to damage.

Perhaps one of the reasons we have been reluctant to recognize the problem of acid rain is that some of its worst effects are in Europe and Canada rather than in the United States. Eighty percent of the lakes in Norway are considered dead or in critical condition, and more than 300 lakes in Ontario have a pH level below 5.0. In the United States damage to waterways seems to be concentrated along the eastern seaboard, especially in the Adirondacks.

Considerable debate exists over exactly how acid deposition causes harm. The primary harm attributed to acid rain is damage to aquatic life, including the elimination of several species of fish and invertebrates in acidified regions. (When the pH of a lake falls below 5, most of its fish cannot survive.) Some fish taken from acidified lakes have high concentrations of mercury and other heavy metals that have been leached from the underlying soils, which makes them unfit for human consumption. Furthermore, acid precipitation erodes stone buildings and monuments.

Depletion of the Ozone Layer

We have previously discussed how ozone is a pollutant in the air we breathe. However, in an upper layer of the atmosphere, the stratosphere, between 9 and 30 miles above the surface of the earth, ozone acts as a filter to help prevent ultraviolet (UV) radiation from reaching the earth. Ultraviolet radiation is known to cause skin cancer in humans, be harmful to plant life, and potentially cause severe disruptions to the ecosystem.

There is growing and alarming evidence that the ozone layer is being depleted in several areas. Originally the major concern was about the "hole" developing in the atmosphere over Antarctica; during the past 20 years, ozone levels over Antarctica dropped by more than 50 percent, as measured during the spring. The "hole" is clearly visible by satellite measurement. Greater concern, however, was aroused by a 1988 study that showed a 2 percent decline in the ozone layer worldwide since 1969. The decline has been as much as 3 percent over some urban areas in North America and Europe, and greater than 3 percent over some parts of Australia, South America, and New Zealand.

The primary causal factor for the decline in the ozone layer is chlorofluoro-carbons (CFCs), substances for which emissions increased 28 percent from 1970 to 1985. CFCs are compounds made of chlorine, fluorine, and carbon that have been used as aerosol propellants, coolants, sterilizers, solvents, and blowing agents in foam production since their development in the 1920s. These compounds do not break down in the lower levels of the atmosphere. Instead, they rise up to the stratosphere where they are broken down by ultraviolet light. When broken down, the chlorine reacts with ozone (O_3) to convert it back into molecular oxygen (O_2) with two atoms, thus destroying the ozone layer. What is even worse is that the chlorine molecule acts as a catalyst and moves on to destroy ozone molecule after ozone molecule. A chlorine atom from a single fluorocarbon molecule can destroy as many as 20,000 ozone molecules. Seventy-five percent of the world's production of this hazardous compound is in the United States and Europe.

A second man-made compound contributing to the depletion of the ozone layer is halon. Halons are used primarily in fire-extinguishing foams. Halons contain bromine, which also acts as a catalyst to deplete the ozone layer. There is some evidence from laboratory tests that nitrogen oxides may also remove ozone from the stratosphere. As you may recall, nitrogen oxides are released primarily by the burning of fossil fuels. They also come from the use of nitrogen-rich fertilizers.

The Greenhouse Effect

Probably the most controversial air quality problem is the greenhouse effect. Everyone basically agrees on the definition of the greenhouse effect; the controversy centers on whether such an effect is occurring, and if so, at what rate and with what consequences.

The greenhouse effect occurs when carbon dioxide, methane, CFCs, nitrous oxide, and traces of a few other gases act in a manner analogous to the glass in a greenhouse. Visible light passes through the layer of gas to the earth's surface, heating it. The warmed surface then radiates energy back out toward space, but the greenhouse gases capture some of this heat, which warms the atmosphere. A certain amount of greenhouse effect is necessary because without it, earth would be a frozen planet like Mars, with an average temperature of about 0° F. The question scientists are grappling with is whether increases in the amount of carbon dioxide in the atmosphere (primarily from the burning of fossil fuels and the destruction of rain forests) have created a warming trend that may cause an increase of 6° Celsius over the next century.

The evidence is not clear. A recent study in the United States (2 percent of the earth's surface) found that temperatures had not increased during the past 100 years. However, the global average air temperature at earth's surface has increased 0.5° C over the past century. Also, between 1982 and 1988, ocean surface temperatures, as monitored by satellite, increased by approximately 0.1° C per year. And, finally, a study by the British Meteorologist Office estimates that temperatures may rise only 1.5°F over the next five years.

Possible effects of rising temperatures. A 1988 study by the American Association for the Advancement of Science predicted that an "equivalent doubling" of CO_2 will raise the average global temperature 2 to 5° C, with the middle and upper latitudes (including North America, Europe, and Asia) warming at twice the global average.[9] The warming could have an effect on precipitation. Some areas in the higher latitudes, such as the Soviet Union and Canada, could receive more rain and snow. Some wet tropical areas could receive more rainfall. The midwestern United States could become hotter and drier. There could also be an increase in the frequency and severity of hurricanes and other tropical storms because of increased ocean temperatures.

According to the EPA, sea levels could rise 7 feet (2.2 meters) by the year 2100 as a result of the expansion of water as it warms, perhaps exacerbated by the melting of polar ice. This rise in sea levels could displace populations in some coastal areas, such as in Egypt and Louisiana. Some low-lying river deltas and floodplains where rice is currently grown would be inundated with water and lost.

Global warming could have an impact on forests because trees are sensitive to climate variation. If warming spreads at the faster rate projected by some scientists, many forests could be devastated. Trees now living at the warm, dry fringe of their forest habitat would face conditions for which they are unsuited, and die. There could be some expansion to fringe regions previously too cold for the forests. However, this growth would be limited by the normally slow rate of seed migration or be blocked entirely by human development (roads, towns, and agriculture).

Agriculture might also be affected. Precipitation patterns could change, and much of the midwestern United States could experience long, dry summers with insufficient rain to raise traditional crops of corn and wheat. Irrigational practices might help mitigate these changes, but would increase costs and disrupt current farming practices.

Indoor Pollution

Indoor pollution has only recently received much attention. This type of pollution occurs when airborne toxins, irritants, and other air pollutants become trapped inside buildings; and the problem has been exacerbated by the construction of energy efficient buildings. The EPA has estimated that as many as 30 percent of new and remodeled buildings have indoor air quality problems.

Poorly ventilated buildings trap airborne pathogens, such as bacteria, fungi, and viruses; radioactive gases, such as radon; a wide range of inorganic compounds like lead and mercury; and organic compounds like formaldehyde and chloroform. Many of these harmful pollutants are caused by indoor smoking, the use of wood stoves and space heaters, chemicals on furniture finishings, and the use of cleaning solvents, wood finishing products, and air fresheners. Figure 5–2 illustrates some of these sources of indoor pollution.

In the short run, these pollutants can cause "sick building syndrome," which is associated with runny noses; headaches; eye, nose, and throat irritations; fatigue; lethargy; irritableness; dizziness; and nausea. In the long run, they may lead to impairment of the nervous system and cancer.

Indoor pollutants are a special problem for the old and young, who spend a more than average amount of time indoors. The average person in the United States still spends 90 percent of his or her time indoors, consequently exposing himself or herself to indoor pollutants.

One indoor pollutant discovered in the 1960s that presents a special problem because it is naturally occurring is radon. Radon is a gas emitted as a result of the radioactive decay of radium-226, found in a wide variety of rocks and soil. Radon enters homes through cracks in the foundation and structure and is trapped in buildings with poor ventilation. Research by the EPA in 34 states revealed that one in five homes had excessive levels of radon. When radon is inhaled, radon particles release radiation that can damage lung tissue and cause cancer. The EPA estimates that radon may be responsible for between 5,000 and 20,000 lung cancer deaths per year.

THE INITIAL APPROACH TO AIR QUALITY CONTROL

Now that we understand some of the air quality problems, we shall examine how the United States has attempted to address those problems. The central legislation, and the law we shall focus on, is the Clean Air Act and its amendments. Although we often think of the Clean Air Act of 1970 as the first piece of air quality regulation, there actually has been small amounts of regulatory activity in this area since the late 1800s. No legislation was very effective, however, until the Clean Air Act.

The first air quality laws were actually ordinances passed by the cities of Chicago and Cincinnati in the 1880s, followed by Pittsburgh and New York in the 1890s. These laws attempted to regulate smokestack emissions, the most vis-

FIGURE 5–2   Air pollution in the home

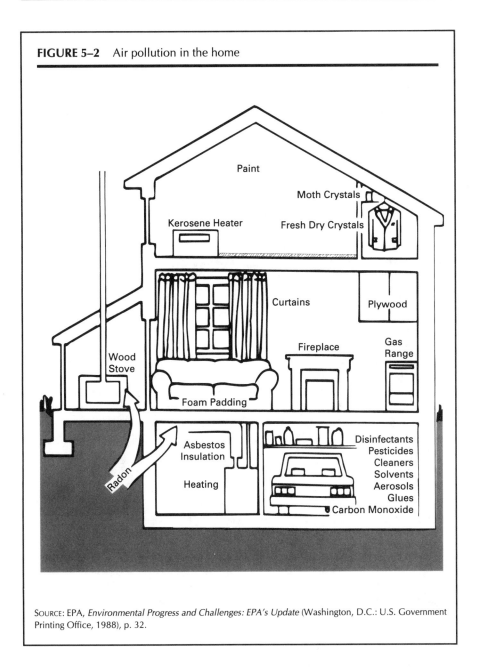

SOURCE: EPA, *Environmental Progress and Challenges: EPA's Update* (Washington, D.C.: U.S. Government Printing Office, 1988), p. 32.

ible type of air pollution. In the 1890s, the state of Ohio passed a law to regulate smoke emissions from steam boilers. Finally, in 1952, Oregon became the first state to pass a comprehensive air pollution law and establish a state air pollution control agency.

Air Pollution Control Act of 1955. The main function of the first piece of federal clean air regulation was simply to provide federal money for research into air pollution control. It authorized the surgeon general to investigate complaints of pollution problems brought by state or local governments.

Motor Vehicle Control Act of 1960. In 1960, Congress recognized that automobiles were causing air quality problems. Motor vehicle emissions of carbon monoxide, hydrocarbons, and nitrogen oxides were blamed for 60 percent of all air pollution. Congress passed the Motor Vehicle Act of 1960, which authorized research into the air pollution effects of motor vehicles.

Clean Air Act of 1963. The first national air quality act was the Clean Air Act of 1963. This act, however, did not mandate any reduction of pollution. There were four major features to this act.

First, it authorized the surgeon general to conduct investigations into specific or local pollution problems at the request of any state or local government, and it permitted the secretary of HEW to make such investigations on his own initiative if the pollution affected a state other than the state that was the source of the pollution. However, any recommendations following the investigations were advisory only; the states could ignore them.

Second, the act expanded the research and technical assistance programs established under the Motor Vehicle Act of 1955, and provided grants to state and local governments to aid them in developing and improving their control programs. Third, it provided for the development of air quality criteria by the secretary of HEW. These criteria were to reflect scientific knowledge of the effects of various pollution concentrations. Again, the criteria were advisory only: States did not have to adopt air quality standards based on the information in the criteria documents.

Finally, the 1963 act provided for federal abatement of action in cases where the health and welfare of citizens was being endangered by air pollution. The secretary of HEW could convene a conference on his own initiative when the pollution was interstate; it could be convened at the request of the governor for intrastate problems. The conference would issue a technical report on the problem, and the secretary would recommend an enforcement action by state or local authorities. If these actions were not taken within six months, the secretary (in case of interstate pollution, or at request of governor in the case of intrastate pollution) could request the U.S. attorney general to bring suit on behalf of the United States to abate the pollution. The attorney general was authorized to request only a cease and desist order, which, if not followed, could be punished as contempt of court. These conferences and their enforcement practices were cumbersome, time-consuming, and largely ineffective. From 1963 to 1970, fewer than 12 conferences were held, and only one enforcement action was brought in court.

If you take just a minute to examine the major provisions of this act, you can probably tell what the primary criticisms were. Two obvious problems were the failure of the act's standards to be mandated and its ineffective enforcement. In addition, the act did not define air pollution, stating only that the statute's purpose was to prevent and control air pollution. It is difficult to control a problem when one is not sure what the problem is. Also, the act's limited enforcement was hampered by a requirement that the courts take into consideration the practicability and economic and physical feasibility of stopping pollution. Such a requirement is seen by many as defeating the purpose of the law. They argue that effective statutes must be "technology forcing," that is, they must require polluters to develop the necessary technology if it does not presently exist.

Motor Vehicle Air Pollution Control Act of 1965. This act authorized the secretary of HEW to prescribe "standards applicable to any class or classes of new motor vehicles or new motor vehicle engines." There was no express prohibition of state controls, but there was stress on the need for uniformity. This act was not particularly effective because it required that consideration be given to economic and technological feasibility of obtaining the standards. Industry could reasonably, if inaccurately, argue that current practices were already selected on the basis of economic and technological practicalities.

1967 Air Quality Act. The 1967 amendments to the Clean Air Act of 1963 (1967 Air Quality Act) provided the first comprehensive federal scheme of air pollution control. This was the first act to establish an orderly procedure for adoption and achievement by states of ambient air quality standards. Under this act, HEW was to designate broad "atmospheric regions" in which meteorology, topology, and other factors influencing air pollutant concentrations were similar (10 regions covering the entire nation were so designated). Next, HEW was to designate "air quality" regions based on jurisdictional boundaries, urban-industrial concentrations, and other factors, including atmospheric areas necessary to provide adequate implementation of air quality standards. Regions could include portions of more than one state. The purpose of the act was to create regions within which pollution could be regulated with an integrated set of controls.

Once HEW made the appropriate designations, states were required to adopt ambient air quality standards for the air quality regions, defining permissible concentrations of pollutants. The standards were to be based on HEW criteria documents defining adverse effects of various pollutants and describing pollution-control techniques. Standards were subject to HEW approval. If states failed to establish adequate standards, HEW could promulgate standards after a process of consultation and a public hearing. Finally, states were to adopt, subject to HEW approval, state implementation plans designed to ensure that the state's air would meet the ambient standards. The plan would designate sufficient limitations that would be imposed on the sources of air pollution within each region to ensure that the permissible atmospheric concentrations of pollutants were not exceeded. The means for enforcement was the conference. Under this act, federal auto emissions controls were made preemptive of state's controls. In other words, states could not meet the standards by imposing more restrictive limits on auto emissions.

The 1967 Air Quality Act was a significant improvement over previous legislation. To some degree it reflected growing awareness that purely local regulation could not control the pollution problem. Unfortunately, the act was relatively ineffective in achieving rapid and effective control of air pollution. A number of reasons for its relative ineffectiveness have been proffered by academics who study regulation. Some attribute the failure to the emphasis on air quality regions, which cut across established state and jurisdictional lines; consequently, it was difficult to obtain agreement on standards or implementation plans.

There were also numerous delays in implementing the steps of the act, such as delays by the federal government in designating regions and issuing criteria documents. States delayed adoption of plans due to a lack of personnel, information, and political will. Despite a 15-month deadline, by spring of 1970, not one state had adopted a full-scale set of standards or an implementation plan. Another reason for the act's ineffectiveness was that, like previous air quality regulations, this act failed to define air pollution. Reductions in pollution were less likely because the act imposed economic and technological feasibility conditions on the standards. And finally, the legislation left extensive discretion to the states.

THE CURRENT APPROACH TO AIR QUALITY CONTROL

After years of ineffective legislation, the Clean Air Act of 1970 was passed. Arguably, several factors led to the development and passage of this law. First, congressional dissatisfaction with the lack of progress was high. Despite an increasing federal role and rising public concern, most indices showed more emissions and a decline in ambient air quality. Second, state governments responsible for enforcement of pollution-control policies were perceived as weak and vulnerable to industry "blackmail." A related concern was the fact that strict regulations in some states but not in others could put some firms at a competitive disadvantage. Further, the HEW division responsible for federal air pollution programs was seen as lacking in zeal. It was especially sympathetic to auto manufacturers' standards rather than forcing the industry to improve technology. Finally, political considerations may have played a role. A democratic Congress could blame failures on the Nixon administration. Congress could mandate sweeping changes. If the timetable were unmet, Congress could blame Nixon; if it were met, Congress would take credit.

This act created a new partnership between state and federal governments, giving the states primary responsibility for directly monitoring, controlling, and preventing pollution while assigning responsibility to the federal EPA for establishing the standards the states must enforce, conducting research, and providing financial and technical assistance to the states. When necessary, the federal

EPA steps in to aid the states in implementation and enforcement of regulations. This act, as amended in 1976 and 1990, governs air quality today.

It is easiest to examine the act and its amendments by dividing it into five sections: national ambient air quality standards, new source performance standards, no significant deterioration policy, mobile source emissions standards, and hazardous air toxins standards.

National Ambient Air Quality Standards

The centerpiece of the Clean Air Act is the national ambient air quality standards (NAAQS's). Under the 1970 act, the administrator of the EPA is required to determine which pollutants emanating from numerous and diverse mobile and stationary sources have an adverse impact on human health and welfare and to establish ambient air quality standards for these pollutants. The term *ambient air quality* refers to the quality of air representatively sampled from an area. In order to make it easier to measure and monitor air quality, the EPA divided the United States into 247 air quality regions. Each region would have common pollution sources and characteristic weather. We can then refer to the air quality of the various regions.

The EPA initially determined that carbon monoxide, sulfur dioxide, hydrocarbons, total suspended particulates, nitrogen dioxide, and ozone required regulation. The hydrocarbon standard was subsequently dropped and lead added. Prior to setting standards, the EPA prepares a criteria document for each pollutant that contains the scientific evidence of the negative health effects of each pollutant and the methods for controlling the emissions of each pollutant. For each of these criteria pollutants, the administrator must set two standards: primary and secondary ambient air quality standards. Primary standards are necessary to protect human health. Human health is interpreted to include the health of the most sensitive individuals, such as children and the elderly. Secondary standards are sufficient to protect public welfare. Public welfare includes visibility, plant life, and animal life. Every five years the evidence for the standards must be reviewed and new data analyzed to ensure that the standards are still valid.

State Implementation Plans. Once the federal EPA issues the standards, in accordance with APA rule-making procedures, responsibility then passes to the states. The EPA, in coordination with the states, established air quality regions, with each state representing at least one region. The states are required to develop state implementation plans (SIPs) that provide means for attaining the NAAQS's within the air quality regions in the state. The states are essentially free to use any types of restriction they desire. They can impose stiff emissions controls on certain types of industrial plants and virtually no restrictions on others.

At least in theory, there are strict guidelines for the SIPs. An SIP for a criteria pollutant is to be submitted to the federal EPA for approval within nine months

18 months for a plan to meet the secondary standard.) The EPA must approve or reject the plan within four months. If an inadequate or incomplete SIP is submitted, the EPA must promulgate a plan or part thereof for the state. Or the EPA can cut off funding for highways within the state or ban construction in nonattainment areas.

As noted, SIPs are to provide for attainment of a NAAQS within three years of the date of its promulgation. A two-year extension upon request of the governor is possible if the technology for certain sources is unavailable.

The Problem of Nonattainment. For the criteria pollutants described, after extensions the deadline for attainment under the 1977 amendments was January 1, 1987. One month after that deadline, the EPA estimated that 80 million people were living in areas that did not have healthy air. In other words, these people were living in areas where the NAAQS's were not met. An air quality region is defined as not in compliance when the second-highest one-hour average concentration per day exceeds the NAAQS. Figure 5–3 demonstrates how the emissions of criteria pollutants have declined as the states attempt to meet the NAAQS's.

By 1987, the emissions of all of the criteria pollutants had been significantly reduced from the amount emitted in 1977. Unfortunately, during 1988 and 1989, levels of ozone and particulates had started increasing once more, and nitrate oxide emissions had leveled. In 1989, 81 cities were still unable to meet all of the NAAQS's[10] and suffered no consequences for their failure to do so. In 1990, the EPA estimated that 74.4 million people still lived in areas where at least one NAAQS was violated.[11]

The greatest successes were attained in meeting the NAAQS's for lead and nitrogen oxides. The most difficult problem remaining is attainment of ozone standards. The current standard for ozone is .12 ppm, measured as an average over an hour. Most urban areas in the United States exceed that standard at times and are thus said to be in nonattainment.

The 1990 amendments to the Clean Air Act address the problem of ozone nonattainment. Ozone nonattainment areas are divided into five classes, depending on the degree to which the pollutant is exceeding the standard: marginal, moderate, serious, severe, and extreme. Each class has a deadline for attainment, ranging from 3 years for the marginal class to 20 years for the extreme class. Interim goals have been set for all classes, except marginal. How the nonattainment areas will meet these goals has not yet been determined, because the states will have to set forth the means of attainment in their revised SIPs. One certainty, at least according to most commentators, is that to meet the standards tens of thousands of never before regulated small and mid-sized businesses are going to have to be regulated.

Permit Program. One of the ways these smaller firms may be regulated is by the permit system added by the 1990 amendments. This permit system, one of the big changes imposed by the 1990 Clean Air Act Amendments, is modeled after the one imposed by the Clean Water Act of 1972 for water pollutants. Under

FIGURE 5–3 U.S. air pollution trends

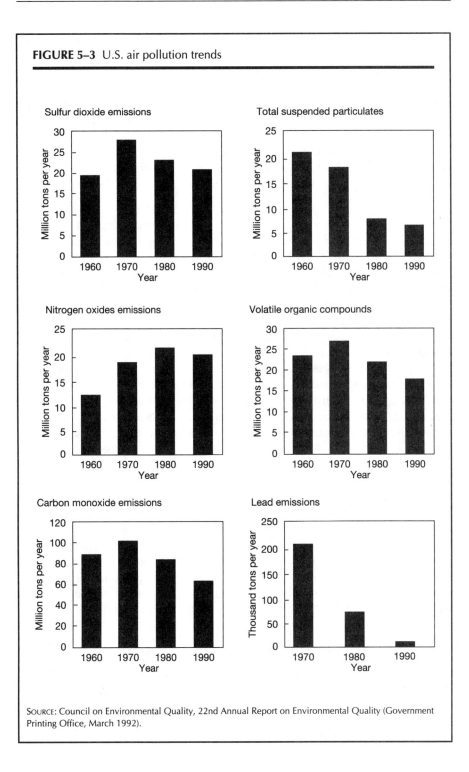

SOURCE: Council on Environmental Quality, 22nd Annual Report on Environmental Quality (Government Printing Office, March 1992).

the one imposed by the Clean Water Act of 1972 for water pollutants. Under the 1990 amendments, all large, and many small, sources of air pollution will be required to obtain five-year permits that spell out limits on the pollutants they emit. Many people believe that these permits will be a source of litigation. Industry will seek favorable permits, environmentalists will challenge them, and once the permits are issued, environmentalists will attempt to make sure plants operate in accordance with their permits.

Challenges to permits themselves must be made in hearings prior to the issuance of the permits. Once a permit is issued, a "permit shield" arises. As long as a plant is operating in accordance with its permit, it cannot be in violation of the Clear Air Act.

No Significant Deterioration (NSD). Focusing on nonattainment areas sometimes causes us to overlook the fact that some air quality regions already met or were cleaner than the NAAQS. The existence of these clean regions presented Congress with a problem. Should the air quality in these areas be prevented from deteriorating at all? Such a policy would maximize the preservation of a clean environment for future generations. Many living in clean areas, however, opposed such a policy, arguing that it would, in effect, be punishing them for not polluting. A no-degradation policy might prohibit them from bringing in substantial new industries.

Congress reached a compromise with the NSD policy. All "clean" air quality regions were to be designated Class I, II, or III. Class I air was the most pristine, and there would be only minimal increases in ambient concentrations permitted. Class II air would be allowed a moderate amount of degradation, consonant with moderate, well-controlled growth, and remain significantly cleaner than required under the NAAQS's. Class III areas would be allowed slightly more deterioration from new sources, and in some cases allowed to degrade to the level of the secondary standards.

Originally, all clean air quality regions were initially designated Class II. The state, once it had conducted a public hearing on the matter, could petition the EPA for reclassification. The EPA generally approved requests for reclassification as long as there was no evidence that the state acted capriciously or arbitrarily. The 1977 amendments required mandatory Class I designation for all international parks; natural wilderness areas and national memorial parks exceeding 5,000 acres; national parks exceeding 6,000 acres; and all areas designated Class I under the 1970 act. Such areas cannot be reclassified by the EPA.

New Source Performance Standards

While each state decides how it will meet the NAAQS's, there is one matter over which the states really have no control, and that is the new source performance standards (NSPS's). These standards are said to be "technology forcing" because they require industry to use a certain level of technology that may or may not be in use at the time the standard is promulgated.

Under the Clean Air Act, Section III, the EPA is directed to set forth technology-based new source performance standards for categories and classes of new sources of air pollutants. New sources include both newly constructed plants and older plants that have been modified after the date of the effective regulation. The standard of performance is defined by the act as a standard for the emission of air pollutants that reflects the degree of emissions limitation achievable through the application of the best system of emissions reduction that (taking into account the cost of achieving such reduction) the administrator determines has been adequately demonstrated.

Thus, for every category of stationary sources, the EPA must establish NSPS's for the various criteria pollutants. Obviously, this task is a very difficult one. The standard "adequately demonstrated" is certainly ambiguous. Another issue is what should be considered as falling into the same category? Are all metal smelters the same, or should there be separate standards for zinc, lead, copper, and aluminum smelters?

Whenever there is obvious ambiguity in a statute, that law invites litigation. Owners of plants subject to NSPS's have not been reluctant to challenge NSPS's and have met with varying degrees of success. An early case that addressed the issue of adequate demonstration was *Portland Cement Association* v. *Ruckelshaus*.[12] This case, referred to as *Portland Cement I*, arose when the EPA was promulgating new source performance standards for the cement industry. The cement manufacturers' association argued that EPA's proposed standards were too stringent because the technology demanded had not been "adequately demonstrated."

The association believed that "adequate demonstration" implied that it would be possible for *any* cement factory currently in existence to meet the new standards. The court rejected this argument, stating that Section II "looks toward what may clearly be projected for the regulated future, rather than the state of the art at the present, since it is addressed to standards for the new plants—old stationary source pollution being controlled through other regulatory standards." In justifying its decision, the court explained that the issue was really one of the performance level that was "achievable." The justices noted that the senate report drafted in conjunction with passage of this Clean Air Act provision made it clear that it did not require the technology actually to be in "routine use" at a plant when the standard was promulgated, but must be available for installation in new plants.

Seven years later, in *National Lime Association* v. *Environmental Protection Agency*,[13] the court gave further guidance as to what constituted "adequately demonstrated" technology. In rejecting standards the EPA had promulgated for lime manufacturing plants, the court reasoned as follows:

> Our review has led us to conclude that the record does not support the "achievability" of the promulgated standards for the industry as a whole. This conclusion is a cumulative one, resulting from our assessment of the many points raised by the industry at the administrative level and in this court; no one point made is so cogent that remand would necessarily have followed on that basis alone. . . . The

Agency's failure to consider the representativeness—along various relevant para-meters—of the data relied upon is the primary reason for our remand. The locus of administrative burdens of going forward or of persuasion may shift in the course of a rulemaking proceeding, but we think an initial burden of promulgating and explaining a nonarbitrary, non-capricious rule rests with the Agency and we think that by failing to explain how that standard proposed is achievable under the range of relevant conditions which may affect the emissions to be regulated, the Agency has not satisfied this initial burden.

Bearing this initial burden will involve first, identifying and verifying as relevant or irrelevant specific variable conditions that may contribute substantially to the amount of emissions, or otherwise affect the efficiency of the emissions control sys-tems considered. And second, where test results are relied upon, it should involve the selection or use of test results in a manner which provides some assurance of the achievability of the standard for the industry as a whole, given the range of variable factors found relevant to the standards' achievability.

The court went on to say that the EPA should have included its rationale for why it believed the standard was attainable, and remanded the case for a more adequate explanation or, if necessary, for supplementary data to justify the stan-dard in terms of the "representativeness" of the sources tested. The court held that test results were not necessarily required, but the agency's assumptions should be stated, and where possible, test data used to verify the assumptions.

Comparing the two opinions, one gets the distinct impression that today the courts are willing to give the EPA much less discretion with respect to deter-mining the feasibility of attaining a standard.

Mobile Source Performance Standards

One of the most successful aspects of the Clean Air Act, and prob-ably the most controversial, is the mobile source performance standards, also referred to as the auto emissions standards. The mobile source performance standards are primarily designed to reduce the emissions of hydrocarbons, car-bon monoxide, and nitrous oxides. The reductions are controlled primarily through the Federal Motor Vehicle Control Program. Under this program, the EPA sets national emission standards for fuel evaporation, CO, NO_x, VOC, and particulates. Car manufacturers must design cars to meet the standards. Since the first standards were set, there has been a running battle between the manu-facturers and the EPA over whether standards are too stiff. The manufacturers have generally succeeded in getting deadline extensions, but then eventually meet the once allegedly "unattainable" reductions.

One of the greatest successes of the EPA's regulation of mobile sources was the mandated reduction of lead content in gasoline. Beginning in 1975, the EPA started requiring the use of lead-free gasoline in new cars. By 1985, the EPA required a reduction of lead content in gasoline from an average of 1.0 gram per gallon to 0.5 gram per gallon and to 0.1 gram per gallon in 1986. Today, more than 70 percent of the gasoline sold is lead free.

Title II of the 1990 Clean Air Act amendments contains new tailpipe emissions standards, rules requiring the reformulation of gasoline, and provisions to force automakers to design and manufacture cars that can run on alternative fuels.[14] Other sections of these amendments require additional controls to reduce vehicle-related smog. By 1998, manufacturers must have reduced all new vehicles' exhaust emissions of nitrogen oxide by 60 percent of 1990 levels; emissions levels of other pollutants must be reduced by 35 percent. To ensure that manufacturers meet these standards, the EPA will certify a prototype of each new model that has emissions controls effective up to 50,000 miles. The EPA may also pull a model off the production line for testing. Any time the EPA discovers that a model in actual use does not meet the standards, it may order a recall and the repair or replacement of emissions control equipment at the manufacturer's cost. Additional measures under the 1990 amendments include the requirement for vapor recovery equipment on gasoline pump nozzles and mandatory auto inspection and maintenance.[15]

The EPA, in June 1991, took one of its first steps toward implementing this act by proposing rules to mandate the sale of cleaner gasoline in the most severely polluted cities. These rules required that oxygenated gasoline (gasoline blended with an oxygenate such as ethanol) be sold in 41 cities that had carbon monoxide problems by November 1992. The rules also mandated that by January 1995, gasoline reformulated to reduce the emission of ozone-forming hydrocarbons must be available for sale in the nine smoggiest cities. These cities—Baltimore, Chicago, Hartford, Houston, Los Angeles, Milwaukee, New York, Philadelphia, and San Diego—account for almost 25 percent of the country's gasoline consumption. As might be expected, the oil refiners immediately predicted that they will be unable to meet the demand for the oxygenated gasoline mandated by the new rule. Of course, the ethanol producers anticipated no difficulty in meeting demand for the new product. If supply is a problem initially, however, cities may request, with proof of a distribution problem, a one- or two-year exemption.[16]

National Emission Standards for Hazardous Air Pollutants

The sections of the Clean Air Act that we have discussed so far are directed primarily toward reduction of conventional air pollutants. Toxic, or hazardous, pollutants, substances that in low concentrations can cause serious long- and short-term damage to human health and the environment, are also regulated under the act. Table 5–2 lists the harms caused by some of these toxic pollutants.

Under the Clean Air Act of 1970, the EPA was given the authority to issue national emissions standards for hazardous or toxic pollutants. The EPA began

TABLE 5–2 Health effects of regulated hazardous or toxic air pollutants

Pollutants	Health Effects
Asbestos	A variety of lung diseases, especially lung cancer
Benzene	Leukemia
Vinyl chloride	Lung and liver cancer
Beryllium	Primarily lung disease; also damage to liver, spleen, kidneys, and lymph glands
Mercury	Damage to the brain, kidneys, and bowels
Radionuclides	Cancer
Arsenic	Cancer
Coke oven emissions	Respiratory diseases, cancer

SOURCE: Adapted from EPA, *Environmental Progress and Challenges: EPA's Update* (Washington, D.C., 1988), p. 13.

this process by publishing a list of those airborne chemicals that cause or contribute to air pollution that may be "reasonably anticipated to result in an increase in mortality or an increase in serious irreversible or incapacitating reversible illness." Within 180 days of listing a pollutant, the EPA must publish in the *Federal Register* a proposed regulation of the pollutant that includes an emissions standard, along with a notice of a public hearing that will take place within 30 days. Once the EPA has published its proposed regulation, it has another 180 days within which to establish an emissions standard. The EPA, in setting the standard, should consider information received at the public hearing. If that information convinces the EPA that the chemical clearly is not hazardous, then no standard will be issued.

The EPA must set a standard that will provide an "ample margin of safety" to protect the public's health. If setting such a standard is not feasible, the EPA may instead promulgate a design, equipment, work practice, or operational standard that will adequately protect the public health.

These standards apply to both new and existing sources, however, the EPA may grant a waiver of up to two years for an existing source if two conditions exist: The source must need the time to implement the necessary controls, and the source must be able to protect the public health in the interim. The president may also exempt a source for up to two years (and for one or two additional two-year periods) if the necessary technology to meet the standard is not available and the operation of the source is needed for national security.

Although this act sounds as if it would be very effective because it allows the EPA to move quickly, many believe that the EPA has not carried out the congressional intent with respect to toxic or hazardous air pollutants. A national inventory of toxic air pollution by a House of Representatives subcommittee found that 2.4 billion pounds of hazardous pollutants were emitted in 1987.[17]

The EPA's first national survey of cancer risks from toxic industrial pollutants found that more than 200 plants in 37 states posed threats more than 1,000 times higher than levels considered acceptable by federal standards.[18] Further, while Congress directed the EPA to regulate toxic pollutants, of an estimated 200 air pollutants that the agency has deemed hazardous, only eight had been regulated by 1989.[19] Those eight are asbestos, beryllium, mercury, vinyl chloride, benzene, radionuclides, arsenic, and coke oven emissions.

One of the problems that the EPA has with regulating toxic pollutants is that risk assessment, the process by which the agency decides whether a chemical poses a risk to human health, is a difficult and complex process (discussed in more detail in Chapter 7). Often scientists will disagree about the risk assessment for a particular substance because of the assumptions that must be made to do the assessment. Many of these assumptions are related to the degree to which inferences can be made from animal experimentation. In addition, the agency must also consider the social and economic costs and benefits of the controls needed to reduce the exposure.

1990 Air Toxins Program. Frustrated by the EPA's limited regulation of air toxins, Congress included a strict new air toxins program in Title III of the 1990 amendments. The program is designed to force both large and small industrial plants to reduce significantly their emissions of 189 pollutants listed as hazardous by the EPA. The law imposes strict deadlines on the EPA, forcing the agency to issue at least 25 new rules for reducing hazardous pollutants from new and existing sources.

One of EPA's first tasks under the new law is to designate categories and subcategories of the sources that will be regulated under the first round of program regulations. By November 15, 1992, the EPA must have published a schedule for the issuance of standards for each category and subcategory. This schedule will tell firms whether their standards will be promulgated within two, four, seven, or ten years after enactment of the 1990 amendments.

For major sources—any sources that emit or have the capacity to emit either 10 tons per year of a toxic air pollutant or 25 tons of a combination of toxic pollutants—the EPA will determine the standard of maximum achievable control technology (MACT) for each toxic pollutant emitted. For *existing* facilities, MACT is defined as the emissions reduction that the best performing 12 percent of similar facilities have attained, assuming there are at least 30 such facilities. (If fewer than 30 facilities exist, the EPA will use the five best facilities.) For *new* facilities, MACT is the best emissions control any facility in that category or subcategory is achieving. For area sources, those emitting fewer pollutants than the major sources, the EPA has the discretion to order lower standards. EPA may require area sources to meet generally achievable control technologies (GACT) or management practices.

By November 15, 1992, the EPA must have promulgated standards for at least 40 categories and subcategories. By November 15, 1994, it must have set standards for 25 percent of the sources; by November 15, 1997, an additional 25 percent; and the remainder, by November 15, 2000. By November 1996, the EPA must have evaluated the risk to the public from air toxins that will remain after MACT controls are in place. Based on its evaluation, it is to make recommendations to Congress for further regulation.[20]

By November 15, 1992, the EPA must have begun to promulgate an accident prevention program. By this date, the agency must have published a list of 100 substances that may be reasonably anticipated to cause death, injury, or serious adverse effects to humans or the environment, and must establish threshold quantities for each substance. Within a year, the agency's accident prevention program must be complete. The program must include release prevention, detection, and correction requirements, which may include such requirements as monitoring, training, and record keeping. Different sources may be required to meet different requirements.[21]

THE 1990 CLEAN AIR ACT AMENDMENTS

Though many provisions of the 1990 Clean Air Act amendments are detailed in the preceding sections, other aspects are not. The reason for this omission is that many of the regulations that will result from this act are yet to be written.

Until the passage of the Clean Air Act amendments of 1990, the EPA would generally issue seven or eight regulations a year for *all* environmental matters. As a result of this act, however, within two years the agency will be required to issue 50 major regulations and 30 minor ones, a massive undertaking, especially in light of the fact that, in the past, approximately 80 percent of the EPA's regulations were challenged in court. It is highly unlikely, therefore, that the mandated rules will, in fact, be drafted by the statutory deadline.

To attempt to prevent such litigation and implement the amendments as soon as possible, the EPA is trying a somewhat different approach to rule making under the amendments. It is using reg-neg, (see Chapter 4) whereby it tries to meet formally and informally with industry and environmental groups affected by the law during the early stages of drafting the rules, in an attempt to gain some early consensus.

Acid Rain Control Program

One of the more noteworthy aspects of the Clean Air Act amendments of 1990 is the acid rain control program. Accepting scientific evidence that the way to control acid rain is to reduce sulfur dioxide emissions, Congress imposed a program of controls that would cut these emissions in half by the year 2000. To accomplish these reductions, a limited number of allowances are to be created under Title IV of the amendments. Each allowance will authorize its holder to emit 1 ton of sulfur dioxide per year. The allowances will be issued by the EPA using a formula specified in the statute. The first phase of reductions begins January 1, 1995, and affects 110 of the highest-emitting electricity generating plants. The second, more stringent phase of the program, goes into effect January 1, 2000, and affects a much larger number of plants. After that date, the EPA will not be allowed to issue more than 8.95 million allowances annually. This limitation in the sulfur dioxide emissions will be cut in half by this date.

Once an allowance is "used up," the allowance is surrendered to the EPA and no longer exists. If a plant emits less sulfur dioxide than is permitted by its allowances, the plant may sell or transfer its unneeded allowances, or may "bank" them for the next year. If a plant's emissions exceed its allowance for a given year, the plant owners must secure additional allowances or face fines of up to $2,000 per ton of excess emissions, plus possible civil and criminal penalties. Violators will also face a reduction of their next year's allowances.

On December 3, 1991, the EPA issued proposed rules for the trading program that requires over 300 pages in small type in the *Federal Register*. Many utilities are skeptical of the program, but the EPA is committed to making it work. It will probably take years for the success or failure of the program to be known.

Enforcement of the 1990 Act

Whether, and to what extent, the Clean Air Act of 1990 is successful depends to a great extent on how the states implement and enforce the act. Many critics say that the states failed to attain the goals established by the SIPs to a large extent because, first, the states were so slow to develop and approve the plans, and second, there was much confusion of what was required from each specific source. Under the new act, whereby each source will ultimately need a permit that will specify all the regulations applicable to that source, as well as emissions limits, monitoring requirements, and maintenance procedures, there will be less confusion as to what requirements each source must meet.

Enforcement may also be strengthened because most criminal violations under the new act are now felonies; violations under the previous act were generally considered misdemeanors, and were, therefore, not of much interest to the Justice Department. Under the 1990 Act, the EPA may file a civil action in a federal district court against any owner or operator of a stationary source who "knowingly violates any requirement or prohibition" in an applicable SIP or permit or violates any provision of the act. The EPA may seek a permanent or temporary injunction to obtain compliance with the SIP, permit, or law, or may seek civil damages of up to $25,000 per day per violation. The EPA may also seek criminal penalties of fines or prison terms of up to five years against violators of the act. The agency may also issue an administrative order and impose a civil penalty of up to $25,000 per day for each day of violation if it acts within one year of the violation. Administrative penalties are sometimes viewed as a superior alternative simply because they are easier to obtain.

To help the EPA in its enforcement efforts, the act grants the agency the authority to award up to $10,000 to any person (excluding a government official acting in an official capacity) who "furnishes information or services which lead to a criminal conviction or judicial or administrative civil penalty"[22] for any violation of the act.

Finally, the 1990 amendments contain citizen suit provisions. Any person can bring an action in a federal district court against state and federal officials who fail to take an action required under the law and against any source believed to be in violation of the act, a regulation, or its permit. The court may order the EPA to perform its duties and impose civil penalties; emissions standards may be enforced. Costs of litigation may be awarded to the initiator of the citizen's suit when deemed appropriate by the court.

SOLUTIONS BEYOND THE CLEAN AIR ACT

Some pollution-control problems are addressed by the Clean Air Act and its amendments, but others are not. Two problems that could not be addressed nationally because they are global problems requiring international solutions are depletion of the ozone layer and global warming. Both are in fact being resolved on an international level through treaties (see Chapter 10) which will have the end result of substantially reducing, if not eliminating, by the year 2000 emissions that cause these problems.

Problems of indoor pollution likewise require a different type of solution than traditional regulation. A nontraditional approach was attempted through the 1986 Radon Gas and Indoor Air Quality Act, which directed the EPA to implement a public information and technical assistance program. Under this act, the EPA is conducting research to try and identify and rank the risks posed by various indoor pollutants and to discover better ways to diagnose building-related diseases and correct their causes. The agency's current emphasis is on education, and it has prepared several documents offering guidance on construction of new homes and rehabilitation of old ones to reduce the risks from indoor pollution. A campaign to encourage the public to test for and repair radon problems has begun. A radon hotline has been set up, and a list of more than 1,000 EPA-approved radon contractors has been made. Meanwhile, the EPA is still exploring strategies to try to reduce the risk from radon and other indoor pollutants.

CONCLUDING REMARKS

Conventional air pollution, indoor air pollution, toxic emissions, acid rain, the greenhouse effect, and depletion of the ozone layer are the primary air quality problems facing the nation today. We began to address these pollution problems seriously with the 1970 Clean Air Act. This act, which has been amended twice, still provides the basic structure for attempts to improve air quality. Over the course of the past 20-some years, some major improvements have been made in air quality, although there is still a long way to go. But with the passage of the 1990 Clean Air Act amendments, which bring more sources under regulation, impose more stringent steps toward controlling acid rain and air toxins, provide compliance deadlines that at least appear to be more reasonable than some imposed by the earlier Clean Air Act, and strengthen enforcement provisions, we can be hopeful that air quality will continue to improve.

Now that you understand the basic scheme for regulation of air quality, you are ready to move on to water quality. As you examine the way we protect water, try to identify those aspects of the approaches to the two different mediums that are alike and those that are different.

QUESTIONS FOR REVIEW AND DISCUSSION

1. List and describe the harmful effects of the six conventional air pollutants.
2. Explain the difference between a conventional air pollutant and a toxic air pollutant.
3. What is acid deposition?
4. Why is the thinning of the ozone layer a problem?
5. Conceptually, how did the regulation of air quality from 1970 to the present differ from air quality legislation prior to 1970?
6. How is the treatment of existing air pollution sources different from the treatment of new sources of air pollution?
7. What is the significance of an area being designated a Class I air quality control region?
8. How does the 1990 air toxins program differ from the program for controlling air toxins established under the previous Clean Air Act?

FOR FURTHER READING

Ackerman, Bruce, and William Hassler. *Clean Coal and Dirty Air: Or How the Clean Air Act Became a Multibillion Dollar Bail-Out for High Sulfer Coal Producers and What Should be Done About It.* New Haven: Yale University Press, 1981.

Brownlow, Andrew, and Jim Falk. *The Greenhouse Challenge: What's To Be Done?* New York: Viking Penguin, 1989.

Brunhee, Jutta. *Acid Rain and Ozone Layer Depletion.* Dobbs Ferry, N.Y.: Transnational Publishers, 1988.

Bryner, Gary C. *Blue Skies, Green Politics* (Washington, D.C.: Congressional Quarterly Press, 1993).

Durenberger, David. "Air Toxics: The Problem." *EPA Journal* (February, 1991):30.

Fisher, David. *Fire And Ice: The Greenhouse Effect, Ozone Depletion, and Nuclear Winter.* New York: Harper Collins, 1990.

Liroff, Richard. *Reforming Air Pollution Regulation: The Toil and Trouble of EPA's Bubble.* Washington, D.C.: World Wildlife Fund, 1986.

Welburn, Alan. *Air Pollution and Acid Rain: The Biological Impact.* New York: Wiley, 1988.

NOTES

1. Gary Bryner, *Clean Air Act of 1990* (Washington, D.C.: Congressional Quarterly, 1993).

2. CEQ, *Environmental Quality, 20th annual report,* 1991, p. 470.

3. Ibid.

4. Ibid.

5. Ibid., p. 472.

6. Ibid., p. 471.

7. C. Arden Pope III, "Respiratory Disease Associated with Community Air Pollution and a Steel Mill, Utah Valley," *American Journal of Public Health,* May 1, 1989, p. 623.

8. Ibid., p. 470.

9. Paul C. Waggoner, ed. *Climate and Water: Report of the American Association for the Advancement of Science Panel on Climatic Variability, Climate Change, and the Planning and Management of U.S. Water Resources.* (Washington, D.C.: AAAS, 1988).

10. Pope, op. cit., p. 471.

11. EPA, *National Ambient Air Quality and Emissions Trends Report, 1990* pp.1-3.

12. 486 F2d 375 (D.C. Cir. 1973).

13. 627 F2d 416 (D.C. Cir. 1980).

14. Bruce Ingersoll, "EPA Proposes Rules on Sale of Cleaner Gas," *The Wall Street Journal,* June 12, 1991, p. 3.

15. Ibid.

16. Ibid.

17. David Wollin, "Air Toxins Laws Force Industries to Plan Ahead," *National Law Journal,* May 13, 1991, p. 25.

18. Ibid., p. 26.

19. Ibid.

20. Ibid.

21. Ibid.

22. Clean Air Act amendments, §701, amending §§113(c) and (d) of the Clean Air Act of 1970.

6

Water Quality Control

Controlling water quality means different things to different people. For instance, it includes providing good-quality drinking water—knowing that when you turn on the tap, the water is safe to use for cooking, washing, and drinking without the need for special precautions. It means that local streams, lakes, ponds, rivers, and ocean beaches are places where you can safely swim, boat, and fish. It means that fish and other aquatic organisms are healthy. To the farmer, it means that irrigation water does not have excess amounts of salts or residuals of pesticides or pathogens. Increasingly, protecting water quality also means protecting underground aquifers, sources of groundwater vital to much of the population. To meet the need for protecting water for so many uses, a variety of complex laws and regulations have been developed.

To understand water *quality* control, we must also understand water *quantity* control. Many parts of the world have plenty of water, but face critical shortages in obtaining water of adequate quality. Consider, for instance, the southern California coast. Although the ocean is a huge potential water supply to Los Angeles and the rest of the western coastal zone, this water is not able to support agriculture or to be used for domestic purposes. Although technology does exist to desalinate ocean water, it is neither economically nor environmentally feasible to produce enough fresh water from the ocean to contribute substantially to southern California's water supply. Instead, the region must compete for limited freshwater supplies and look to mechanisms for maximizing the utility of sources currently available.

In this chapter we first examine the basic measures of water quality and the significance of various pollutants. With that background, we turn to discussion of how water supply is controlled, focusing on the differences between western water law with that brought from Europe and now common in the East. Finally,

143

we examine the two major federal laws, the Federal Water Pollution Control Act and the Safe Drinking Water Act, that provide the basis of the system used in the United States to protect this vital resource.

THE MAJOR WATER POLLUTANTS

Any system for classifying pollutants must be somewhat arbitrary, particularly when concerned with water quality from a number of perspectives. Critical water quality parameters may be very different for people and for fish, for industries and for ecosystems. By organizing pollutants into some kind of a system, we can gain enough understanding of their potential effects to see the need for a regulatory program.

Pathogens

Throughout the United States, most people are not worried that drinking tap water or being near surface water will lead to disease. Yet the World Health Organization reports that almost one-fourth of the world's populations suffers from one of four water-related diseases: gastroenteritis, malaria, river blindness (onchocerciasis), or schistosomiasis.[1] Some estimate that waterborne diseases are responsible for about 25 million deaths annually in the underdeveloped regions of the world.[2] In contrast, only 564 waterborne disease outbreaks, affecting approximately 140,000 people, were reported in the United States between 1971 and 1988. However, the number of reported diseases is rising dramatically although it is unclear whether morbidity is increasing, or just the reporting of disease.[3]

The kinds of pathogens responsible for waterborne disease include bacteria, viruses, protozoa, and parasitic worms. Bacteria are microorganisms that are ubiquitous in the environment. The human body harbors hosts of bacteria, particularly in the gastrointestinal tract. Although many bacteria are useful to bodily functions (e.g. the active *Lactobacillus bulgaricus* cultures in yogurt aid digestion), some are incompatible with good health. Because of the great diversity of organisms potentially found in water, it is impractical to monitor water for each specific type of pathogen. Thus, groups of bacteria called coliform or fecal coliform are routinely monitored to indicate potential contamination. Cholera, typhoid fever, shigellosis, and bacterial gastroenteritis are among the more important waterborne bacterial diseases. They are transmitted through contact with water contaminated by wastes from infected individuals. These diseases, characterized by severe diarrhea, can result in death (particularly for the very young and very old or those suffering from other stresses such as malnutrition).

Viruses are simpler organisms than bacteria. They are quite small, and lack many of the basic components that are normally thought necessary for life. Viruses do not live independently, but invade host cells, take over their host's reproductive processes, and produce new viruses. Unlike bacteria, viruses are not normally flora of the human system. Only infected individuals are carriers. Virus usually are more difficult to detect and destroy than bacteria. Infectious hepatitis and viral gastroenteritis are the primary viral-caused waterborne diseases. Both diseases can be quite severe, even resulting in death. These diseases may occur from drinking water that standard tests indicate is safe from bacterial contamination. No routine tests are available to search directly for the presence of viruses.

Protozoa and parasitic worms are more complex organisms than either bacteria or viruses. Backpackers have probably heard about the protozoan *Giardia lamblia*, and how contracting giardiasis from drinking visually pure water from apparently pristine locations can result in severe and prolonged diarrhea. Schistosomiasis is a good example of an extremely debilitating disease in which larvae invade the body, develop into worms, and cause chronic inflammation and pain. This disease is epidemic in much of the tropics. It is seldom fatal itself, but can so weaken victims as to make them very susceptible to other diseases.

Conventional Organics

Other pollutants from organic sources can adversely affect water quality, without being directly responsible for disease. Wastes resulting from such operations as food processing, petroleum refining, and municipal wastewater treatment can result in serious harm to aquatic ecosystems. These wastes often have relatively large amounts of residual organic matter that is digested by aquatic bacteria and other microorganisms. To use this food, dissolved oxygen is taken from the water. If the amount of food exceeds the supply of dissolved oxygen, the water turns anoxic. Anoxic water may smell terrible (often like rotten eggs) and kill desirable organisms such as fish. Large amounts of organic material may support large populations of nuisance organisms, such as filamentous bacteria (e.g., *Sphaerotilus natans*), which can clog water supply screens, and look and smell quite objectional.

This type of organic pollution is typically quantified through a measure of the amount of oxygen needed for all of the organic material to be decomposed as it is used as food. The most common of these measures are biochemical oxygen demand (BOD) and chemical oxygen demand (COD). The higher these demands, the more conventional organics are in the water. If the oxygen demands are known, and the rate of oxygen entering the water can be measured or calculated, accurate predictions can be made of the resultant oxygen content.

Oil and grease is frequently used as a measure of a group of organic materials that share similar analytical properties. It includes a variety of materials, from extremely toxic materials like benzene to benign plant waxes. Nevertheless, it is a useful measurement because of the simplicity of analysis and the utility in indicating the gross level of organic pollution.

Toxic Organics

Some organic compounds are extremely toxic and so create problems at very low concentrations. Common examples are polychlorinated biphenyls (PCBs), dioxins, and many solvents and pesticides. Most of the toxic organics of greatest concern in water are not naturally occurring but are products of chemical synthesis from industrial operations.

Trace toxic organics generally are analyzed individually or in fairly narrowly defined groups. They are often difficult (and expensive) to measure at the extremely low concentrations of concern, and they may have a variety of by-products of varying toxicity. Analytical chemistry has advanced considerably in the last few decades in its ability to detect and quantify these materials, and progress is continuing. However, less progress has been made in determining the implications of trace levels of synthetic toxic organic chemicals in the environment and in drinking water.

Many trace organic toxics are very slow to degrade and thus remain stable in the environment for extended periods of time. Some become concentrated in plants and animals as they move up through the food chain; very low levels in water lead to medium levels in aquatic plants and relatively high levels in aquatic animals. Furthermore, the effects of contamination often are expressed only after a considerable period of time. These characteristics greatly complicate efforts to relate exposure to effects and to understand the relationship between a given dose and a probable outcome.

The effects of trace organics on human health are quite variable. Many organics are thought to be carcinogens, and regulatory decisions often react to this threat. However, other effects may include mutagenesis, teratogenesis, nervous system damage, and damage to the liver and other internal organ systems.

Ecological effects may be even more variable and difficult to detect. For example, DDT, a herbicide now outlawed for use in the United States, was found responsible for interfering with the ability of several species of birds (including bald eagles, pelicans, and peregrine falcons) to metabolize calcium. Eggs were laid with shells so thin that they were broken by the nesting parents. Though not directly fatal to adults, the continued use of DDT would have led to the extinction of several of these desirable species.

Nutrients

Unfavorable conditions resulting from too much life can result from organic material developing in situ, as well as caused by waste. If excess fertilization occurs in a water body, photosynthesis by organisms such as algae and rooted aquatic vegetation can proceed at a rapid rate. As the vegetation becomes increasingly luxuriant, it can become a problem. When vegetation dies (or at night when photosynthesis cannot occur), oxygen may be used faster than it can be replenished. Ensuing anoxic conditions destroy favorable life forms, result in objectionable tastes and odors, and encourage undesirable species.

Excessive fertilization can occur when nutrients are added to a system. The nutrients most often effective in stimulating growth are nitrogen and phosphorus. Too much pollution from nutrients, causing overfertilization and too much vegetative growth, results in *cultural eutrophication.* This condition can be caused by water running off well-fertilized agricultural fields, from water containing high levels of phosphorus-based detergents, or from a variety of industrial processes. A difficult but vital concept to understand fully is that conditions favoring life can be just as bad for an ecosystem as conditions that are toxic to life.

Nitrogen can more directly affect public health. Excessive levels of nitrate, the form of nitrogen usually predominant in surface water and groundwater (unless subject to gross contamination), can cause methylmeglobenemia, a blue baby disease. In infants, excessive nitrate in the diet reduces the capacity of the blood to transport oxygen (turning the blood a bluish color), which disrupts normal central nervous system development and functioning. Nitrogen thus presents a dual threat—the risk of toxicity and the risk of cultural eutrophication.

Heavy Metals

Another important group of toxic water pollutants are the heavy metals. Substances such as mercury, cadmium, and lead are important to our industrialized society, yet they are extremely hazardous if not controlled properly. Similar to toxic organics, metals can present significant problems at extremely low concentrations.

While some waters have naturally high concentrations of a metal or metals, most problems with high concentrations result from discharge from industrial wastewaters or other anthropogenic sources. Heavy metals are usually found in the environment at levels below that which will cause any adverse effects. To make heavy metals useful, they are mined, concentrated and refined. Residuals from this process, and from the subsequent use of the end products, can result in elevated concentrations that are toxic and able to cause significant harm.

Probably the most well-known incident resulting from heavy metal exposure in a nonoccupational setting is the mass illness resulting from mercury poisoning in the Japanese village of Minamata during the 1950s. A plastics factory was discharging mercury-laden waste into the Minamata River and Minamata Bay. Villagers began to experience vague symptoms of irritability, lethargy, headaches, blurred vision, numbness in their arms and legs, loss of coordination, and dry mouths. These symptoms of mercury poisoning predominated in the families of fishermen, who consumed large amounts of fish. Examination of fish and shellfish tissue from the bay revealed extremely high levels of mercury. Although it is difficult to attribute adverse health outcomes to a specific source of chemical exposure, researchers commonly attribute about 50 deaths and more than 100 severe poisoning cases to this contamination. The effects will haunt this community for generations, as an extremely high rate of congenital defects have been linked to the mercury contamination. The Minamata tragedy is not an unusual incident, with little opportunity for occurrence elsewhere; similar outbreaks have been reported in such disparate areas as Sweden, Iraq, and Pakistan.

Other Measures

A variety of other properties are used to characterize water and determine its most suitable uses. Mineral content is an important measure of the suitability of a water supply for agricultural use, as well as potability. One common measure of minerals is water hardness, the sum of the dissolved calcium and magnesium. In hard water, soaps do not sud, and scums are often formed. Another common measure is alkalinity, which indicates the stability of water to changes resulting from addition of acids (e.g., from acid rain).

The gross level of materials in water can also be determined in terms of solid content. Total dissolved solids refers to the material that cannot be easily filtered out of water. Conversely, suspended solids refers to contaminants that can be readily removed through filtration. An alternative measure is turbidity, which indicates the amount of material in water that reflects light.

The pH of water is used in a number of applications. Either a very low pH (indicating acid conditions) or a very high pH (indicating basic conditions) is unfavorable to most life. However, a neutral pH of 7 (neither acid nor base) is not synonymous with normal or good quality. For example, noncontaminated rainwater is slightly acid, with a pH around 5.6, whereas treated domestic supplies are commonly released from a treatment plant with a pH greater than 8.

SOME SIGNIFICANT WATER QUALITY PROBLEMS

Degradation of water quality can adversely affect both human health and ecosystems. Regulatory attention has been directed to both areas, although much more focus is given to pollutants that have a direct link with human health risk.

Trace Organics

Although the threat of pathogens in drinking water supplies continues to be an important issue, in the United States more attention is given to chemical contamination. In particular, the relationship between chemicals used to destroy pathogens and the risk associated with the residual chemicals and their by-products remains of high concern. Chlorine has been widely used since before the turn of the century to destroy pathogens in drinking water, and it is responsible for a large reduction in morbidity and mortality due to waterborne disease. However, as water is chlorinated, trace levels of organic by-products are formed called trihalomethanes (THMs). THMs are thought to have the poten-

tial to cause cancers; the most well known of the THMs is chloroform. Researchers are at work looking for alternative disinfectants and treatment techniques that adequately destroy pathogens (at a reasonable cost), without leaving residual chemicals that might damage human health. Regulators are discussing appropriate standards for THMs and other disinfectant residual chemicals. Clearly, however, it is not a viable alternative to stop using disinfectants in drinking water supplies, with a subsequent return to massive outbreaks of cholera, typhoid fever, and other waterborne diseases.

A variety of other organics that may be toxic at trace levels in water are also being actively investigated and regulated. For example, organic solvents have been found to contaminate important groundwater aquifers serving hundreds of thousands of people. Major sources of drinking water have been lost in Long Island, New York, and the San Gabriel Valley, California, among others. This type of pollution is generally undetectable by human senses, with adverse health effects occurring long after initial exposure.

Perhaps even more difficult to perceive is the significance of trace levels of organics in waters not used for drinking. PCBs and other toxic organics are found frequently in sediments from drainages of many industrialized areas; it is unclear what this means to the ecosystems. In fact, there is substantial controversy about whether it is better to leave contaminated sediments in place or to resuspend chemicals as contaminated sediments are dredged and removed.

Lead

As a contaminant of water, lead has been the focus of substantial attention. In fact, as the major sources of airborne lead are being controlled (leaded gasoline and lead-based paints; see Chapter 5), the relative contribution of lead exposure from water may be increasing.

Lead interferes with a variety of bodily functions. We know that lead interferes with heme synthesis, a process necessary for formation of red blood cells (*hemo*globin), and reduces the blood's ability to transport oxygen. Lead poisoning is linked to a variety of health problems, including interference with the function and development of the central nervous system. Lead is particularly worrisome for children, because exposure has been related to reduced intelligence. Other physiological problems include anemia, kidney damage, impaired reproduction function, interference with vitamin D metabolism, and elevated blood pressure. We do not have a clear understanding of the quantitative relationship between lead dose and resultant adverse health effect. Some people argue that any amount of lead in the body increases health risk, others argue that below a defined threshold level, lead is innocuous in the body.

Lead in a domestic water supply has two primary origins: the source water and the plumbing system. The EPA has assessed the prevalence of lead in raw (untreated) water supplies and has found that about 250 surface water systems and 600 groundwater systems had water leaving treatment plants with lead concentrations greater than 5 micrograms per liter. This means that less than 1 percent of the public water supplies in the United States, serving a population of less than 3 percent of the 226 million people on public systems, have potential lead contamination from these sources. More concern is expressed over lead leaching into water from plumbing systems. Lead solders and fluxes used to connect copper pipes can contain up to 50 percent lead. Brass and bronze alloys used in faucets and other fixtures can contain large amounts of lead. The EPA has estimated that about 10 million lead service lines are in use in the United States, and that about 20 percent of all public water systems have at least some lead service connections or lines within their distribution system.

Considerable debate has raged about how best to control lead in drinking water systems. Most control strategies focus on ensuring that water quality is adequate as it leaves the treatment plant, which assumes that significant deterioration will not occur prior to its use. However, lead content can change considerably during the delivery process, depending on the specific plumbing system (both in the public system and in the individual building). Thus, lead must be monitored at targeted high-risk interior taps throughout the service area.

Radon and Other Radionuclides

Interest in possible contamination by radiation has increased considerably over the last several years. Multiple factors are driving this heightened interest, including the disaster at Chernobyl, media attention to development of low-level radioactive waste disposal sites, and renewed efforts to develop nuclear power plants. An important additional factor is a new awareness of radon, an invisible, odorless gas that is almost ubiquitous.

Most human exposure to radiation comes through inhalation. As shown in Table 6–1, a fairly small percentage of radiation exposure comes from ingestion. Water containing elevated radon concentrations presents a threat largely from the radon gas released when water is exposed to the atmosphere (e.g., showering) rather than from direct consumption. Of the approximately 5,000 to 20,000 lung cancer fatalities estimated to occur annually in the United States because of radon in indoor air, about 1 to 7 percent are attributed to radon gas released from water.

Natural surface water supplies generally carry little threat of human radiation contamination because radon volatilizes into the atmosphere. However, groundwater can have high concentrations of radon because there can be sustained association with naturally occurring radon-emitting rock (uranium and radium), with little chance for removal through volatilization.

Even though relatively little information links adverse health effects to radon in water, limitation of radon has become the focus of major new activities designed to protect drinking water quality.

TABLE 6–1 Public exposure to radiation

Source	Dose Equivalent (mrem/year)
Natural radiation	
Cosmic rays	45
External surroundings	40
Food and drinking water	20
Radon	90
Anthropogenic sources	
Diagnostic X-rays	80
Radiopharmaceuticals	16
Fallout	3
Nuclear power plants	0.1
Color television	1
Mining and milling of uranium and phosphate rock	5
Occupational exposure	0.8
Consumer products	0.3
Approximate total	300

SOURCE: C. R. Cothren, "Estimating the Health Risks of Radon in Drinking Water," *JOURNAL OF AMERICAN WATER WORKS ASSOCIATION* 4(1987):153–58 .

PROTECTING WATER THROUGH GOVERNMENT ACTIONS

A number of federal laws relate to water quality, but two laws (and subsequent amendments) especially focus on this issue. The Federal Water Pollution Control Act and the Safe Drinking Water Act deal primarily with, respectively, ensuring the quality of surface waters and ensuring the quality of domestic supplies. However, for a proper focus on water quality issues, it is important to understand first how rights to use water are obtained in the United States.

Water Rights

Water rights is traditionally a state issue, with only limited involvement on the federal level. Specific policies governing rights to water reflect the tradition brought into the state by its founders and the nature of the state's water resources. Federal activity largely involves situations where water flows or is located between more than one state or country.

Two fundamental doctrines govern the right to use water. In the East and in some of the western states, the right to use water depends on a physical link between the water source and the user. This means that the owner of property on the bank of a stream, river, or lake can make reasonable use of that stream. This is called a riparian right. In many western states, where water is scarce, rights can be claimed for beneficial uses both adjacent to and away from water sources. Rights are prioritized with respect to time; if supply is limited, the first to acquire the right can have all the supply. Only after an earlier right has been exhausted can later rights be met. This is called an appropriated right.

Riparian Rights. Riparian rights are derived from the English tradition, which in turn comes from Roman law. Each owner of riparian land is entitled to receive water undiminished in quality or quantity by upstream users. This entitlement places an obligation on each riparian landowner not to degrade the water source.

Riparian landowners in all states (including those with appropriative water laws) generally have rights to use their adjoining surface waters for such nonconsumptive uses as fishing and recreation. Within states using a riparian system to control consumptive uses, water diversion by a riparian landowner was historically restricted to domestic use. Upstream landowners could not divert water to irrigate fields, to use in mining or industry, or for any other use where the quality or quantity of downstream supply would be reduced.

This limitation to domestic supply prevents water-based development. Thus, to allow growth, this historic restriction has been replaced in most states by restricting diversions to that needed for reasonable use. Under this doctrine a riparian landowner may divert water if the use does not interfere with the legitimate use of the water by other holders of riparian rights. States individually determine reasonable use, based on such factors as the following:[4]

The purpose of the use

The suitability of the use to the watercourse

The economic value of the use

The social value of the use

The harm associated with the use

The practicality of avoiding the harm

The practicality of adjusting the quantity of water use

The protection of existing values of the water and associated land

Equity between the water user and any injured parties

Specific preferred uses depend on state policy, but use has generally been granted for agriculture, mining, and (historically) milling. During times of limited supply, allocation of limited water supplies depends on reasonableness of competing uses.

In states with riparian right systems, eminent domain may be used to acquire water rights by nonriparian water companies or municipalities. These water companies and municipalities can then provide a domestic water supply. Alternatively, if a nonriparian uses a water supply for a sustained and continuous period of time (15 years in many states), a prescriptive right may be established that allows for the continued use of that supply. Furthermore, many states with riparian rights systems also have administrative permit systems for water diversion and allocation. These administrative permits allow for diversion of water for beneficial uses to nonriparians and ensure that riparians' use of water is reasonable.

Riparian rights reflect historic development patterns in wet climates, where water is usually abundant. In areas where water is scarce, riparian rights are not easily adapted to ensure that water is used to maximal benefit. Moreover, riparian rights disadvantage nonriparian land that could productively be developed if a secure water supply were available.

Appropriative Rights. Most of the western United States is much drier than the East, with water supply much more limiting. For development to occur, water must be available and long-term rights secured. The system of appropriative water rights provides a mechanism for obtaining water rights as a function of water use. By making use of water (such as diverting it from a stream for agriculture or industry), a user develops a right to that water supply. Earliest water users have priority to the water supply if the supply is limited; subsequent water users have inferior rights: "First in time is first in right." Rather than sharing burdens during times of limited supply, the right holders who began using water first can satisfy their entire (reasonable) demand before later right holders can take any water.

Water is appropriated, and rights established, through the actual consumptive use of water. Diverting water and returning some portion to the waterway (such as returning power plant cooling water) only establishes a right to the net amount removed. If water is not used where an appropriative right exists, that right can be lost. Appropriative rights are established because of demonstrated needs; without this need, the legal right for future use is superseded by rights of current users.

An appropriative right is not dependent on landownership but on diverting and consumptively using water for a beneficial use. Most states with appropriative rights systems also have statutes that govern how much water can be taken and specify beneficial uses (only Colorado maintains a pure appropriative rights system where rights depend only on using water).[5] Typically, agriculture, industrial, and domestic uses are all accepted uses for which rights may be secured.

Appropriated rights are complicated by the varying availability of water. In a wet year all rights may be satisfied; in a dry year many users may have unmet needs. Further complicating this issue is the need for water to maintain healthy aquatic ecosystems. Is it appropriate for appropriative rights users to take all of a stream's available water for human consumptive use and degrade or destroy the natural ecosystem? In other words, do fish have rights?

A key case demonstrating an interest in protecting quality of waterways by limiting appropriative rights was *National Audubon Society* v. *Superior Court* (Mono Lake), decided by the California Supreme Court in 1983. In 1940, the city of Los Angeles had appropriated for its domestic supply most of the flow of four streams draining into Mono Lake. The Audubon Society filed suit in superior court to stop diversions because of environmental damages resulting from loss of supply to the lake. Mono Lake, the second largest lake in California, is located at the base of the Sierra Nevada mountain range (east of Yosemite National Park) and receives most of its water supply from Sierra snowmelt. Because of the hot arid climate causing rapid evaporation (leaving salts behind to concentrate), the lake is saline. Fish do not live in the lake, but large numbers of waterfowl thrive (most feeding on the abundant population of brine shrimp). By diverting flow away from the lake, the surface elevation has dropped. In addition to reducing the area of the lake, previously submerged bridges have transformed islands into peninsulas. Where island rookeries were once protected, coyotes and other predators now have access to nesting sites and juvenile birds. Continued or increased diversion of feeder streams clearly would cause deterioration of the lake ecosystem, including a large reduction in the waterfowl population.

At issue in the case was whether appropriated rights (even those given some time ago) must consider the public trust doctrine (requiring government protection of important natural resources). The court ruled that the public trust doctrine and appropriated rights are "parts of an integrated system of water law," so both must be considered in determining appropriate use of water. This decision allows legal challenges, based on natural resource values, to state administrative decisions for water appropriation. It forces administrative decisions to include considerations of long-term resource impairment as well as economic development.

A few other states have integrated natural resource values more directly into their systems for appropriating water. For example, Montana has a statutory program that allows water to be appropriated for future uses. These future uses can include maintaining minimum flows needed to protect in-stream water quality. State agencies can establish an appropriated right for water that never is "used" in the traditional sense in being removed from the stream channel.

Protecting Waters of the Nation

Protecting water quality was not a major concern of the federal government until relatively recently. Historically, federal involvement was largely defined by three acts: The Rivers and Harbors Act of 1899 protected navigable water through restrictions on discharge; the Public Health Service Act of 1912 provided for federal investigation of water pollution affecting public health; and the Oil Pollution Act of 1924 prohibited discharge of oil into coastal waters. These acts were not broadly interpreted or widely enforced and so had relatively little impact on water quality.

With a growing population leading to increased rate of waterborne disease, the need for a more active federal role began to be evident. During the 1930s and 1940s, federal money was used to help states and cities construct wastewater treatment plants. In 1948, the Federal Water Pollution Control Act was passed, formalizing government obligations for water pollution control. State governments maintained primary responsibility, with the federal role focusing on providing financial assistance and research support through the U.S. Public Health Service. The federal government took direct action only in response to polluters when the pollution crossed state borders.

The 1956 and 1965 amendments to this act strengthened the role of the federal government but left primary responsibility with the states. Quite important was the increasing funding granted by the federal government for construction of local wastewater treatment plants. The 1965 amendments (also known as the Water Quality Act) moved federal responsibility from the Public Health Service to the newly created Federal Water Pollution Control Administration. (This agency moved, in 1966, from the Department of Health, Education, and Welfare to the Department of Interior to facilitate activities other than those limited to a human health orientation.) The 1965 amendments represented a compromise in the face of clearly deteriorating water quality throughout the United States. Industry opposed federal standard setting as an obstacle to business, and states opposed an increased federal presence in an area of traditional states' rights. Yet something had to be done. These amendments permitted the federal government to establish water quality standards, if states refused to establish their own. However, an effective and enforced set of standards was not developed, and water quality continued to diminish.

During the late 1960s, a series of events directed public attention to the deteriorating environment and a demand for action. Two of the most dramatic incidents occurred on opposite sides of the continent, in Ohio and in California.

In June 1969, the Cuyahoga River, near Cleveland, caught fire! Clearly, this river was little more than an industrial sewer, with oily waste concentrating sufficiently to turn a major waterway into a fire hazard. Soon thereafter, more than 250 million gallons of crude oil leaked from an oil drilling operation offshore of Santa Barbara, California. The media gave substantial coverage to both events, and pictures of dead oil-coated waterfowl, sea otters, and other wildlife crowded the front pages of newspapers. The public was ready to support major changes.

In response, Congress passed the Federal Water Pollution Control Act (FWPCA) of 1972 (over the veto of President Nixon). It mandated major changes in the way water quality would be controlled in the United States and provided the basis for water quality programs today. Three subsequent acts made substantial amendments to the FWPCA: the Clean Water Act of 1977 (CWA), the Water Quality Act of 1987 (WQA), and the Oil Pollution Act of 1990. These amendments followed the basic principles established in the 1972 act and have resulted in a complex, comprehensive system of water pollution control.

A strong federal role is now integral to our system of water quality protection. Ambitious water quality objectives are clearly established for the nation: "The objective of this Act is to restore and maintain the chemical, physical and biological integrity of the Nation's waters." It is important to note that water quality goals include more than maintaining a safe drinking water supply, the primary focus of water quality when the federal role was under the jurisdiction of the Public Health Service. Specific reference is made to providing for "the protection and propagation of fish, shellfish and wildlife, and…recreation in and on the water." Thus, *all* waters of the nation are required to be fishable and swimmable. This goal is very different from that commonly found in other parts of the world, where much of the value of surface waters is the ability to move waste away from production sources.

To protect water quality, either restrictions can be set on pollutant dischargers (assuming that if sufficient restrictions are applied, the water body will be protected) or ambient quality standards can be established (with restrictions imposed to control pollutant sources or other conditions if these standards are not met). This act uses both approaches. All discrete point sources of discharge into surface water, such as factories, pulp and paper mills, food processing plants, and wastewater treatment plants, are required to obtain a discharge permit. These permits are administered through the National Pollution Discharge Elimination System (NPDES), so dischargers must follow specifications of their NPDES permits. Effluent limitations are dependent on the type of pollutant and type of discharger. In setting these limitations, three broad categories of pollutants are identified: conventional pollutants, nonconventional pollutants, and toxic pollutants. The level of required discharge control depends on the category of pollutant. Requirements also vary, depending on whether the discharge is a new or existing source. Furthermore, municipal wastewater treatment plants have somewhat different controls from those of other dischargers.

The least stringent level of control is imposed on existing dischargers of conventional pollutants, requiring only that best conventional pollutant control technology (BCT) standards are met. Only five conventional pollutants are specified: biochemical oxygen demand, suspended solids, pH, and fecal coliform were established in the 1977 amendments, and the EPA subsequently added oil and grease.

In setting BCT standards, the EPA is required to consider the relationship between the costs of pollution control and the derived benefits. Furthermore, these costs have to be compared to the cost of compliance at wastewater treatment plants. Additionally, the EPA is required to consider "the age of equipment and facilities involved, the process employed, the engineering aspects of the application of various types of control techniques, process changes, non-water quality environmental impact (including energy requirements), and such other factors as the Administrator [of the EPA] deems appropriate."[6] Toxic and nonconventional pollutants must be controlled using best available technology (BAT), economically achievable, a more rigorous standard than BCT. A list of toxic chemicals, known as priority pollutants, has been developed by the EPA. The current list, shown in Table 6–2, can be modified by the EPA. Nonconven-

---

TABLE 6–2 Water quality priority pollutants

Acenaphthene
Acrolein
Acrylonitrile
Aldrin/dieldrin
Antimony and compounds
Arsenic and compounds
Asbestos
Benzene
Benzidine
Beryllium and compounds
Cadmium and compounds
Carbon tetrachloride
Chlordane (technical mixture and
   metabolites)
Chlorinated benzenes (other than
   dichlorobenzenes)
Chlorinated ethanes (including 1,2-
   dichloroethane, 1,1,1-trichloroethane,
   and hexachloroethane)
Chloroalkyl ethers (chloroethyl and
   mixed ethers)
Chlorinated napthalene
Chlorinated phenols (other than those
   listed elsewhere; includes
   trichlorophenols and chlorinated
   cresols)
Chloroform
2-Chlorophenol
Chromium and compounds
Copper and compounds
Cyanides
DDT and metabolites
Dichlorobenzenes (1,2-, 1,3-, and 1,4-
   dichlorobenzenes)
Dichlorobenzidine
Dichloroethylenes (1,1- and 1,2-
   dichloroethylene)
2,4-Dichlorophenol
Dichloropropane and dichloropropene
2,4-Dimethylphenol
Dinitrotoluene
Diphenylhydrazine
Endosulfan and metabolites
Endrin and metabolites
Ethylbenzene

Flouranthene
Haloethers (other than those listed
   elsewhere; includes
   chlorophenylphenyl ethers,
   bromophenylphenyl ether, bis-
   (dichloroisopropyl) ether, bis-
   (chloroethoxy) methane, and
   polychlorinated diphenyl ethers)
Halomethanes (other than those listed
   elsewhere; includes methylene
   chloride, methylchloride,
   methylbromide, bromoform,
   dichlorobromomethane)
Heptachlor and metabolites
Hexachlororbutadiene
Hexachlorocyclohexane
Hexachlorocyclopentadiene
Isophorone
Lead and compounds
Mercury and compounds
Napthalene
Nickel and compounds
Nitrophenols (including 2,4-
   dinitrophenol, dinitrocresol)
Nitrosamines
Pentachlorophenol
Phenol
Phthalate esters
Polychlorinated biphenyls (PCBs)
Polynuclear aromatic hydrocarbons
   (including benzanthracenes,
   benzopyrenes, benzofluoranthene,
   chrysenes, dibenzanthracenes, and
   indenopyrenes)
Selenium and compounds
Silver and compounds
2,3,7,8-Tetrachlorodibenzo-p-dioxin
   (TCDD)
Tetrachloroethylene
Thallium and compounds
Toluene
Toxaphene
Trichloroethylene
Vinyl chloride
Zinc and compounds

tional pollutants are anything not included in these other two categories that still may pose a threat (such as thermal pollution).

Whereas BCT standards "shall include consideration of the reasonableness of the relationship between the costs of attaining a reduction in effluents and the effluent reduction benefits derived," BAT standards require only that standard determination "shall take into account...the cost of achieving such effluent reduction." This reduced requirement for cost assessment has resulted in the EPA's establishing BAT standards primarily on health-based criteria. The 1977 amendments to the act specify that effluent standards for toxic pollutants consider "the toxicity of the pollutant, its persistence, degradability, the usual or potential presence of the affected organisms in any waters, the importance of the affected organisms and the nature and extent of the effect of the toxic pollutant on such organisms, and the extent to which effective control is being or may be achieved under other regulatory authority."[7]

The FWPCA and its subsequent amendments do not specifically identify a system for setting standards. The EPA established standards for existing industry based on industrial classifications, assuming that plants performing similar functions should have similar effluent limitations. However, this approach was challenged. E. I. du Pont de Nemours & Co. claimed that the EPA was required to establish uniquely effluent standards on each plant, responsive to the plant's specific conditions. The U.S. Supreme Court decided that it would be impractical to do so (estimating more than 42,000 dischargers), and that the legislative intent of the act would best be upheld by allowing for control based on industry class. However, the establishment of standards must be sufficiently flexible to allow some variation for individual plants.[8]

New sources are subject to more rigorous effluent limits than existing sources, based on the belief that it is cheaper to minimize effluent pollutants if environmental controls are considered during plant design than it is to retrofit existing facilities. New sources include major modifications to existing facilities, as well as new construction. Effluent limits for new sources are based on consideration of an entire process rather than the BAT and BCT approach requiring pollution controls to be imposed following waste generation (commonly known as end-of-pipe treatment). As specified in the FWPCA, standards must consider "control of the discharge of pollutants which reflects the greatest degree of effluent reduction which the Administrator determines to be achievable through application of the best available demonstrated control technology, *processes, operating methods, or other alternative* [emphasis added] including, where practicable, a standard permitting no discharge of pollutants." Congress listed 27 pollution sources in the FWPCA for which the EPA was required to develop performance stands. The EPA was also given the authority to add to this list; the resultant sources for which standards have been promulgated are shown in Table 6–3. The EPA is required periodically to review new source requirements and make amendments reflecting changes in technology and economic conditions.

The system for controlling effluents from public wastewater treatment plants (called publicly owned treatment works, or POTWs) differs slightly from that for other dischargers. POTWs must meet effluent standards characterized by waste receiving "secondary treatment." EPA initially defined secondary treatment so as

---

TABLE 6–3 Industrial categories subject to performance standards

Adhesives and sealants	Aluminum forming
Asbestos manufacturing	Auto and other laundries
Battery manufacturing	Coal mining
Coil coating	Copper forming
Electric and electronic components	Electroplating
Explosives manufacturing	Ferroalloys
Foundries	Gum and wood chemicals
Inorganic chemicals manufacturing	Iron and steel manufacturing
Leather tanning and finishing	Mechanical products manufacturing
Nonferrous metals manufacturing	Ore mining
Organic chemicals manufacturing	Pesticides
Petroleum refining	Pharmaceutical preparations
Photographic equipment and supplies	Plastic and synthetic materials manufacturing
Plastic processing	Porcelain enameling
Printing and publishing	Pulp and paperboard mills
Soap and detergent manufacturing	Steam electric power plants
Textile mills	Timber products processing

---

to effectively limit compliance to those communities using activated sludge technology meeting rigorous performance standards. This requirement was subsequently viewed as excessive in many situations, particularly where small POTWs discharged into waters capable of rapidly assimilating the waste water. Moreover, it was viewed as economically impractical as well as ecologically unnecessary for many small communities. Thus, these requirements were modified.

Communities now attaining secondary treatment by the use of activated sludge must meet standards of 30 milligrams per liter of both suspended solids and BOD as a 30-day average, or 45 milligrams per liter as a 7-day average. Additionally, there must be an overall reduction of at least 85 percent of these pollutants. However, communities can be permitted to use alternative technologies (such as trickling filters and waste stabilization ponds) that remove less contamination. For these alternative technologies, only 65 percent total removal is required, with suspended solid and BOD level standards of 45 milligrams per liter and 65 milligrams per liter as 30-day and 7-day averages, respectively.

Also, a system is in place to control discharges of pollutants into municipal sewage. The EPA's guidance is rather broad, but prohibits discharges that

Create a fire or explosion hazard in the sewers or treatment works

Are corrosive (with a pH lower than 5.0)

Obstruct flow because of solids or viscous materials

Upset the treatment processes

Increase the temperature of wastewater entering the treatment plant to above 104°F (40°C).

Recently, changes were made in these regulations to ensure that the hazardous waste management system could not be circumvented through the use of municipal sewers.[9]

Categorical standards have been promulgated for 25 industry types (see Table 6–4). For each, standards have been adopted specifying limits on pollutants characteristic of that industry. Industries not identified in a category must meet general requirements intended to prevent the discharge of any pollutant detrimental to the treatment system.

Most of the regulatory burden for the pretreatment program is on local POTWs. Each POTW is required to identify all industrial sources, as well as the volume and characteristics of industrial discharge in its wasteshed. Using this information, limits on problem dischargers are imposed that protect the POTW. This program requires the POTWs to expend considerable resources (in industrialized communities) to ensure that pretreatment requirements are met.

In contrast to the pretreatment program, other aspects of the water quality regulatory system are largely controlled at the state and federal levels. The NPDES system is administered through the EPA. However, similar to many environmental statues, most states have assumed active management responsibilities, with the EPA maintaining only an oversight role.

TABLE 6–4   Industrial categories subject to national categorical pretreatment standards

Aluminum forming	Asbestos manufacturing
Battery manufacturing	Builders' paper
Carbon black	Cement manufacturing
Coil coating	Copper forming
Dairy products processing	Electrical and electronic components
Electroplating	Feedlots
Ferroalloy manufacturing	Fertilizer manufacturing
Fruits and vegetables processing	Glass manufacturing
Ink formulating	Grain mills manufacturing
Iron and steel manufacturing	Inorganic chemicals
Meat processing	Leather tanning and finishing
Metal molding and casting	Metal finishing
Nonferrous metals manufacturing	Nonferrous metals forming
Pesticides	Paint formulating
Pharmaceuticals	Paving and roofing
Porcelain enameling	Petroleum refining
Rubber processing	Phosphate manufacturing
Soaps and detergents	Pulp and paper
Sugar processing	Seafood processing
Plastics molding and forming	Steam electric manufacturing
Textile mills manufacturing	Timber products

Another regulatory strategy is based on ambient water quality. Subject to federal review, states are required to establish water quality standards for intrastate waters. If discharge standards are not sufficient to meet these ambient standards, additional discharge standards must be imposed. For example, in a heavily industrialized community, a large number of dischargers all meeting BCT and BAT standards might still result in the receiving water being unfit for swimming or fishing. In such a case, the state would be required to increase discharge restrictions to improve water quality.

This system has resulted in substantial improvements in water quality. "Point sources" of pollution, such as industrial effluents and municipal wastewater treatment plants, have been controlled to such an extent that much of the remaining pollution comes from "nonpoint sources." Nonpoint pollution originates from a variety of small sources that in combination may result in significant pollution. Good examples are agricultural storm water runoff carrying fertilizers and pesticides and oil dripping from cars and trucks. Recent EPA estimates indicate that between 50 and 70 percent of impaired or threatened surface waters are affected by nonpoint source runoff from agriculture, with urban runoff responsible for another 5 to 15 percent.

Nonpoint source pollution from urban areas has partly been addressed by new regulations governing municipal and industrial storm water discharges. Following requirements of the FWPCA, many large industries obtained NPDES permits governing discharge of storm water at discrete point sources—the discharge point of the storm water collection system. The WQA expands the number of industries that have this discharge regulated. Furthermore, the WQA requires municipalities serving populations of at least 100,000 to obtain NPDES permits. Each EPA office has considerable latitude regarding appropriate permit requirements for individual municipalities.

Civil and administrative penalties may be assessed against violators of the FWPCA (and subsequent amendments) regulations, and they may be severe: "Knowing endangerment," whereby someone places another person in imminent danger, carries a maximum penalty of 15 years imprisonment and a $250,000 fine ($1 million for an organization). "Negligent violations" carry a maximum penalty of $25,000 a day, so continued operation of a process not meeting standards can quickly become quite expensive! The EPA may also seek civil penalties, including injunctive relief and fines. The EPA may issue administrative orders directly, and impose fines if these orders are not followed. Citizens' suits are authorized that provide individuals the ability to seek civil remedies against dischargers, or to force the EPA to proceed against dischargers or otherwise to meet its legal responsibilities for protecting water quality. Remedies can include fines and adoption of compliance schedules. To some extent, citizens' suits are encouraged by the ability of the courts to assign the plaintiff's attorney's fees to the violator, thus enabling an individual or interest group with limited financial resources to proceed against large companies.

Protecting Drinking Water

Traditionally, protection of drinking water was the responsibility of individual states, not the federal government. Drinking water quality was governed by local and state boards of health or was not governed at all. The role of the federal government was limited largely to providing research grants, loans for development of treatment works, technical assistance, and involvement in interstate and international quality issues. For example, Public Health Service standards governed the quality of water used in interstate rail travel and served as the basis for many subsequent national water quality standards.

In 1974, the Safe Drinking Water Act (SDWA) was passed in response to growing concern over contamination of domestic supplies with synthetic organic chemicals and other pollutants. The statute forced development of national domestic water quality standards. It also provided for protection of groundwater supplies, the source of domestic water for about 50 percent of the U.S. population.

This act is intended to protect public water supply systems and ensure that the public water systems supply potable water free from biological, chemical, or physical contamination. Public water systems are defined as systems that have at least 15 service connections or serve 25 or more people for at least 60 days annually. Consequently, homes and businesses served by individual wells (common in rural areas) are not regulated. Public water supply systems are further separated into community and noncommunity systems, serving resident and nonresident populations, respectively. Specific standards or compliance schedules are often based on the size of the community system.

The EPA was charged in the SDWA with developing National Interim Primary Drinking Water Regulations to protect human health and "secondary standards" to protect the aesthetic quality of drinking water. Interim standards were required to be proposed by March 1975, with final standards adopted by September 1977. The EPA could not meet this ambitious schedule, and by 1986 had adopted interim standards on only 23 contaminants.

Amendments to the SDWA made in 1986 provided a new timetable for establishing water quality standards and increased the number of contaminants to be considered. For contaminants that may have an adverse effect on human health, the EPA is responsible for developing (concurrently) maximum contaminant level goals (MCLGs) and maximum contaminant levels (MCLs). MCLGs are nonenforceable health goals. They are established at levels for which no adverse health effect should occur. MCLs are enforceable standards set as close to MCLGs as possible but take into account the feasibility of achieving standards based on available technology and the costs of treatment. Congress required that the 83 contaminants listed in the Advanced Notice for Proposed Rule Makings of March 4, 1982 and October 5, 1983 have MCLGs and MCLs established. Seven substitutes are allowed to this list, and the EPA has exchanged

seven of the original chemicals for seven organic contaminants suspected as carcinogens.

In addition to the contaminants specified in the SDWA amendments, the
EPA was required to develop a list of contaminants that need regulation to protect drinking water quality. This "drinking water priority list" (DWPL) contains
an additional 77 substances or groups of substances for which MCLs and
MCLGs need to be developed. Included on the DWPL are trihalomethanes,
which were not part of the original list even though standards had been established (and standards enforced) on the interim list.

From this deluge of statutory requirements and rule making has emerged a
large number of chemicals in drinking water that have been identified as needing regulation, a complex process for establishing specific standards, and strict
deadlines for implementation (most of which have already passed). Not all the
chemicals initially controlled through interim regulations have had final MCLs
established, and so the interim regulations continue to be in force. Yet, final
standards have been promulgated for other chemicals in drinking water more
recently identified as potentially hazardous. To stay current on the status of particular chemical standards, consult the *Federal Register* and *Code of Federal Regulations* or the EPA's Office of Ground Water and Drinking Water.

National primary drinking water standards currently in effect are shown in
Appendix A. In some cases, rather than meeting specific water quality standards
determined by monitoring, an assumption is made that specific standards will
be met if the appropriate treatment technology is used. For example, the protozoan *Giardia lamblia* is difficult to detect in water, yet can be a major threat to
public health. Technology is not available to reliably and cost-effectively monitor for this contaminant. However, appropriate filtering of drinking supplies
will prevent it from entering (finished) drinking water. Thus, public water systems using surface water or groundwater under the direct influence of surface
water must (subject to some exceptions) use filtration as part of their treatment
process and are not required to routinely monitor for these pathogens.

As for most federal environmental programs, compliance and enforcement
responsibility is intended to be done at the state level. State programs must be at
least as stringent as the federal specifications. Monitoring of community systems
is done by the water utilities, following a plan approved by the state (or the federal EPA if the state does not have primacy). Monthly routine monitoring
requirements are based on the system size, with larger systems taking more samples. Noncommunity systems can be monitored quarterly, although local conditions may necessitate the need for additional sampling.

The rapidly expanding requirements for drinking water control are imposing
an enormous burden on water purveyors. In addition to the expense of monitoring, water systems may have to be modified to meet new requirements.
The EPA is authorized by the SDWA to enforce regulations by administrative
orders and to collect administrative penalties for noncompliance. However, this

authorization does not deal with the fundamental question of identifying financial resources needed to meet these new requirements. Additionally, many states are struggling with the increasing administrative burden of enforcing the new requirements. Actively being discussed in several states is discontinuation of state primacy over their drinking water program, reverting direct enforcement authority back to the EPA. Obviously, the EPA does not have the resources to assume this role, for it is the intent of the SDWA to have primacy at the state level.

Individuals may sue public water systems in federal court for failure to meet required standards. Individuals will learn of failures because of a requirement for water systems to notify their service communities of MCL violations. Following the traditional requirements for citizens' suits, individuals must first give 60 days' notice to the EPA, state, and alleged violators before pursuing court remedies. Notification must come after the event has occurred, so this requirement is not directly useful as a preventive tool. However, repeated notification should effectively demonstrate a pattern of failure. Individuals can then respond by pursuing legal remedies, working through the political system to upgrade services, or personally seeking alternative supplies.

CONCLUDING REMARKS

The systems governing the use and quality of water are more mature than in most other areas of environmental law and regulation. Water is one of the basic needs of life, so we have a history of concern coincident with the development of population centers and large pollution sources.

We experienced a period during which many important water systems were substantially degraded. Now we can have confidence almost anywhere in the United States that tap water from a public system is safe to drink and that gross contamination of surface water has been, or is being, eliminated. However, we are just beginning to respond to difficult questions regarding how to manage nonpoint sources of pollution and toxic materials that are difficult to detect. We are also facing the situation where water is becoming an increasingly expensive commodity, because of costs involved in treatment and because of increased demand. We are consuming groundwater at a faster rate than it is being replenished, resulting in a diminishing supply, increased costs of use, and water quality problems. While perhaps not having the notoriety of such environmental issues as hazardous waste management (see Chapter 8), water law and regulation remains an active and vital issue.

QUESTIONS FOR REVIEW AND DISCUSSION

1. Why is cultural eutrophication a problem?
2. Describe the difference between conventional and toxic organics. How do the relative concentrations allowed of each compare?

3. What is the difference between riparian and appropriated water rights? Under what conditions is each more suited?
4. Is the federal water quality control program designed to focus on protection of public health or environmental quality?
5. How does the regulatory burden differ for a discharger into a sanitary sewer from that for a discharger into a natural water body?
6. What is the primary source of contamination to surface water in the United States? What regulatory program has been implemented in response to this problem?
7. What are drinking water secondary standards?
8. Why are technology-based standards sometimes used instead of specific (concentration) standards?

FOR FURTHER READING

Baker, Brian. *Groundwater Protection from Pesticides.* New York: Garland Press, 1990.

Concern, Inc. *Drinking Water: A Guide to Citizen Action.* Washington, D.C.: Citizen Action, Inc., 1984.

Gilbert, Charles E., and Edward J. Calabrese, eds. *Regulating Drinking Water Quality.* Boca Raton, Fla.: Lewis, 1992.

King, Jonathan. *The Poisoning of America's Drinking Water.* Emmaus, Pa.: Rodale Press, 1985.

Pye, Veronica, et al. *Groundwater Contamination in the United States.* Philadelphia: University of Pennsylvania Press, 1983.

Resiner, Marc. *Cadillac Desert: The American West and Its Disappearing Water.* New York: Viking Press, 1986.

NOTES

1. American Public Health Association, *The Nation's Health* (March 1979).
2. Walter J. Coesor, ed., *The Global Ecology Handbook* (Boston: The Beacon Press, 1990).
3. U.S. Department of Health and Human Services, *Healthy People 2000: National Health Promotion and Disease Prevention Objectives,* DHHS Publication. (PHS) 91-50212 (September 1990).
4. David H. Getches, *Water Law in a Nutshell,* (St. Paul, Minn.:West 1984), p. 58.
5. L. Rice and M. D. White, *Engineering Aspects of Water Law* (New York: Wiley, 1987), pp. 25–26.
6. FWPCA, Sec. 304 (b)(4)(B).
7. FWPCA, Sec. 307 (a)(3)(2).
8. *E. I. du Pont Nemours & Co.* v. *Train,* 430 U.S. 112 (1977).
9. 40 CFR 403.

7

Controlling Toxic Substances

In 1948, Swiss chemist Paul Muller received the Nobel Prize in medicine for discovering the insecticidal properties of DDT. Through its use to control mosquito populations, DDT saved untold lives from malaria. But within 10 years, this insecticide had produced so many adverse effects that it had been banned or its use severely restricted in several parts of the world.[1]

The experience with DDT is just one example of the potential risks and benefits of the chemical age in which we live. It also points up the primary problem the U.S. legal system faces in trying to regulate such substances. Many substances that are developed end up having extremely harmful effects; natural chemicals, of course, may also be equally or more toxic than many artificial ones. The legal system's main problem, therefore, is trying to find a way to encourage the development and use of helpful chemicals while preventing inadvertent, widespread use of chemicals with toxic effects. This chapter and Chapter 8 explore the regulatory schemes that have been developed to help identify toxic substances and manage their use and disposal.

This chapter begins with a discussion of toxicity. Then federal regulation of toxic substances under the Toxic Substances Control Act, the Federal Insecticide, Fungicide, and Rodenticide Act, and the Federal Food, Drug, and Cosmetics Act is explained. The last section discusses the use of tort law to control toxic substances, or at least provide compensation for harms resulting from exposure to them.

IDENTIFICATION OF POTENTIALLY TOXIC SUBSTANCES

Toxic substances are regulated by a wide variety of environmental laws, as Table 7–1 illustrates. In Chapters 5 and 6, on air pollution and water pollution, you were introduced to some of these regulations. This chapter

TABLE 7–1   Environmental laws regulating toxic substances

Statute	Regulated Substances
Asbestos Hazard Emergency Response Act	Asbestos
Clean Air Act	Hazardous air pollutants
Clean Water Act	Hazardous water pollutants
Comprehensive Environmental Response, Compensation and Liability Act	Hazardous waste
Federal Food, Drug, and Cosmetics Act	Pesticide residues
Federal Insecticide, Fungicide, and Rodenticide Act	Pesticides
Marine Protection Research and Sanctuaries Act	Toxic waste
Occupational Safety and Health Act	Toxic substances in the workplace
Resource Conservation and Recovery Act	Hazardous waste
Safe Drinking Water Act	Pesticides and other hazardous substances
Toxic Substances Control Act	Toxic substances used in commerce

focuses on the two main laws that regulate potentially toxic substances used in commerce. Before we examine these specific laws, however, we need to ask what is meant by the term *toxic substance*. Generally, toxic refers to something that is directly poisonous to humans. However, nowhere in the Toxic Substances Control Act does Congress specifically define the term; in fact, in none of the acts that regulate potentially toxic substances is the term defined. Instead, some acts, like the FWPCA, list certain substances that must be regulated as toxins; and other statutes focus on the risk of harm imposed by certain substances that makes them subject to regulation as toxins.

Many substances regulated as toxins have certain characteristics that make their regulation especially urgent. For example, extremely low doses of a potentially toxic substance can produce adverse effects in humans, animals, or plants. A conventional pollutant may be harmful in parts per million, whereas a toxic pollutant may be harmful in parts per trillion. Also, the harmful effects of a toxic substance may not show up for decades after the exposure. Further, potentially toxic substances may bioaccumulate. If, for example, the toxin is in the water, that substance may accumulate in the bodies of fish so that it would be much more heavily concentrated in the fish than it would be in the surrounding water. Another, and closely related, characteristic is that toxic substances often persist, that is, they fail to break down biologically for a long time. Or when they do break down, their degradation produces toxic by-products.

Scientific Uncertainty

One of the biggest problems with environmental regulation, and especially the regulation of toxic substances, is that of scientific uncertainty. We can see the smog hanging over the skyline and feel it burning our eyes, but we can neither see nor taste the DDT bioaccumulating in the fish we just ate. And while there are ways to determine when a chemical in a set dosage is harmful, there is no test that can prove beyond a doubt that a chemical will not cause any harm to human health or the environment. There is always the potential for harm in a little higher concentration or in a slightly more prolonged exposure.

So how is a regulatory agency to determine whether a chemical is "safe"? Although they regularly struggle with this issue, the courts have not come to a definitive conclusion. They have not specified precisely what degree of evidence of harm is necessary for a substance to be banned or regulated, but they have said that assessing risk and determining how to regulate involve not only factual evidence but also policy considerations. In *Ethyl Corp.* v. *EPA*,[2] a case involving regulation of a conventional pollutant under the Clean Air Act, the court said:

> Undoubtably certainty is a scientific ideal—to the extent that even science can be certain of its truth. But certainty in the complexities of environmental medicine may be achievable only after the fact, when scientists have the opportunity for leisurely and isolated scrutiny of an entire mechanism. Awaiting certainty will often allow for only reactive, not preventative regulation. Petitioners suggest that anything less than certainty, that any speculation, is irresponsible. But when statutes seek to avoid environmental catastrophe, can preventative, albeit uncertain decisions legitimately be so labeled?

Thus, the courts have tended not to hold the EPA to a rigorous standard of proof when determining when a substance can be regulated.

The District of Columbia Circuit Court, in *Lead Industries Association, Inc.* v. *EPA*,[3] even went so far as to say that "feasibility and cost" were irrelevant when the EPA was determining a reasonable margin of safety to protect the public health. However, in *NRDC* v. *United States EPA*,[4] the same court, in considering the regulation of a hazardous air pollutant, stated that an "ample margin of safety to protect human health" does not have to mean "risk free"; there can be an "acceptable" risk to health.

Still, despite the courts' lack of assistance, agencies such as the EPA and OSHA must determine acceptable risk. They generally do so by using the processes of risk assessment and risk management.

Risk Assessment

Risk assessment is generally defined as the process of characterizing the potentially adverse consequences of human exposure to an environmental hazard. Risk assessment is a necessary preliminary state before risk management, the process by which policy choices are made once the risks have been determined. To understand the process that agencies go through to make these assessments, we can examine the scientific basis for risk assessment.

As noted earlier, one of the risks a potentially toxic substance may pose is that of carcinogenicity. In deciding whether to regulate a chemical in a manner that would sustain judicial scrutiny, an agency may undertake risk assessment. The four-step process detailed in the following sections would be typical of such an assessment. This process was first described and recommended in 1983 by a committee of the National Research Council.[5]

Hazard Identification. Four types of information are generally used at the hazard identification stage of risk assessment: comparisons of molecular structures (there is almost unanimous acceptance of this approach within the scientific community), short-term studies, animal bioassay data, and epidemiological studies.

An initial step that may lead to further identification of a potential carcinogen is the comparison of a substance's physical and chemical properties with those of a known carcinogen. These comparisons are primarily useful in setting priorities concerning which substances most urgently need further investigation. Short-term studies of the effects of the substance on single-cell animals may be the next step. If exposure causes mutation, this result is generally an indicator that a substance is likely to be carcinogenic, and thus further studies are warranted. Because these short-term studies are quick and relatively inexpensive, they provide a good screening device.

The most commonly used data to support regulation of a substance as a carcinogen are obtained from animal bioassays. To support a finding of carcinogenicity, scientists usually look for consistently positive results in both sexes and in several strains and species. Higher incidences at higher doses are also considered important. Although animal bioassays are important, they are viewed cautiously. There are several fundamental biological similarities among all mammals, and so we can expect similarities in response to chemical toxicity. Usually, in cases where human and animal responses can be compared, these similarities are borne out. Thus far, all human carcinogens (except possibly arsenic) have also been shown capable of causing cancer in some (but not all) animal species. Usually, but not always, the same sites of the bodies of both humans and animals are most vulnerable to the carcinogen. Benzidine, for example, is most strongly linked to bladder cancer in dogs and humans, but to liver cancer in rats. So we rely on animals tests, but cautiously.

Another question with respect to animal bioassays is whether it is ethical to use animals to test for carcinogenicity. Increasingly, people are organizing to protest the use of animals in research.

Epidemiological data that show a positive association between exposure to an agent and disease is considered the most convincing evidence about human risk. This evidence, however, is generally very difficult to obtain because the number of people exposed to any particular hazard may be low, exposures may be confound by exposures to other substances, and the latency period may be uncertain. Even if these problems did not exist, we still would not want to risk waiting to regulate until people had been exposed to the potentially hazardous substance.

Dose-Response Assessment. Once the hazardous substance has been identified, the next step is to determine the response of humans to various levels of exposure. In a very limited number of cases, sufficient epidemiological data are available to allow extrapolations from the exposures observed in the studies. A problem with such extrapolations, however, is that the general population may contain some people, such as children and the elderly, who are more sensitive than the people in the studies.

Because epidemiological data are not generally available for most substances that are being assessed, dose-response assessment usually requires assessments of animal studies. One problem with these studies is that the amount to which the animals are exposed in the tests for hazard identification is much higher than the doses to which humans would generally be exposed. Scientists have developed a number of mathematical models that they use to predict risks to humans exposed to lower doses. Adjustments must also be made to account for differences in size and metabolic rates.

Exposure Assessment. The third step in the process is to determine which populations would be exposed to the chemical and the dosages to which they would be exposed. Although in rare cases, especially more structured sites such as workplaces, exposures may be directly measured, more typically, exposure data must be estimated.

When a community's exposure is being assessed, the ambient concentrations of chemicals to which people are exposed are calculated on the basis of emission rates, assuming that transport and conversion processes are known. For some chemicals no data are available, and estimates of exposures must be made. When chemicals are present in food or absorbed when a consumer product is used, the exposure assessment is even more complicated because of people's different dietary and personal habits. Part of the exposure assessment process also involves ascertaining which groups would be exposed to the substances. Some groups, such as children or pregnant women might be especially susceptible. Exposure of a group to a mixture of potential carcinogens is also a factor requiring consideration, although such calculations are nearly impossible to make.

Risk Characterization. The final step, the estimate of the magnitude of the public health problem, requires no further scientific knowledge or concepts. At this stage, the value judgments of the assessors are most likely to come into play. Because of the general deference the courts give agency decision making, following such a procedure as the one just described would give the agency's rule a strong chance of being upheld. Remember, the courts tend to look most carefully at the procedures that agency decision makers follow.

FEDERAL REGULATION OF TOXIC SUBSTANCES

Since the 1950s, global economic activity has quadrupled,[6] and manufacture of synthetic organic chemicals has grown dramatically from a tiny, specialty enterprise to a huge, powerful industry. Organic compounds or chemicals, by definition, are those containing carbon, which bonds easily with itself and other elements. Scientists have learned to take advantage of carbon's unique properties to create hundreds of thousands of new chemical compounds and thus new consumer goods. Between 1945 and 1985, there was a 15-fold increase in the production of synthetic organic chemicals, from 6.7 million to 102 million tons per year.[7] Worldwide, more than 70,000 chemicals are in everyday use,[8] and between 500 and 1000 new ones are added every year.[9] And there is no reason to believe this growth will cease, because people are always searching for something better, and chemicals provide much of the hope for that improvement.

Creation of this plethora of synthetic organic substances is, unfortunately, not without risk. As we know all too well, the toxic effects of a chemical may not become known until several years after people are exposed to the substance. This long latency period, during which time hundreds of thousands of people may be exposed, is one of the main problems of some toxic substances. Other problems were mentioned previously, such as their tendency to bioaccumulate and the fact that sometimes very small amounts may cause tremendous harm. The main problem the legal system faces is trying to find a way to encourage the development and use of helpful chemicals while preventing inadvertent, widespread use of chemicals with toxic effects.

Pesticides, substances designed to eradicate pests such as rodents, insects, fungi, and weeds, are a special category of toxic substances. Undoubtedly, their use has increased crop yields worldwide. However, there are also a number of problems associated with these substances. First of all, because they are toxic, they have the capacity to harm not only targeted pests but also humans and wildlife. In the United States alone, there are approximately 45,000 accidental pesticide poisonings each year, with roughly 3,000 resulting in hospitalization and 50 in death. Further, the National Academy of Sciences estimates that pesticides may cause 20,000 cases of cancer each year. A related problem is that only a small percentage of the pesticide actually reaches the target pests; the rest may contaminate the soil and drinking water.

Another problem associated with pesticide use is that a given pesticide does not retain its effectiveness for a long time. Although a pesticide may be highly effective at first, some of the targeted pests, the strongest ones, will survive and breed. Through natural selection, a newer, stronger strain of the pest that is resistant to the pesticide will evolve, resulting in lower crop yields again until some new, stronger pesticide is developed, one that is potentially more dangerous not only to the pests but to the environment in general.

The remaining sections of this chapter discuss how some of the problems created by potentially toxic substances are addressed, through federal regulation and state common law.

Toxic Substances Control Act

The primary federal law designed to regulate toxic substances is the Toxic Substances Control Act (TSCA). Three significant policies are set forth at the beginning of this act:

1. Data on environmental effects of chemicals must be developed by industry.
2. Government must have adequate authority to prevent unreasonable risk of injury to health or the environment, particularly imminent hazards.
3. Government authority must be exercised so as to not "impede unduly or create unnecessary barriers to technology while fulfilling the primary purpose of the Act."

The policy statement may sound attractive; in fact, it contains language that both environmentalists and laissez-faire businesspersons may embrace. Unfortunately, it is a policy statement full of ambiguity, promoting the often conflicting goals of ensuring environmental safety and encouraging technological development. Many people, however, believe this conflict will always exist because we do want a safe environment, yet we also want the benefits new chemicals may bring, and the act does the best possible job of balancing these conflicting objectives. As you read the following sections on how the act regulates both new and existing chemicals, ask yourself whether the law does indeed perform a good balancing act.

Treatment of Old Chemicals. When we examine the structure of the act, we see that TSCA can be divided into two parts: treatment of old chemicals and treatment of new chemicals. By 1979, the EPA had compiled an inventory of all chemicals commercially used or produced in the United States between January 1975 and July 1979, as required by TSCA. This inventory contained information on more than 62,000 chemicals.

Once the inventory was completed, the Interagency Testing Committee had to categorize all chemicals as high priority or not. Information used to determine whether a chemical is high priority comes from manufacturers and importers and is updated every four years. Putting a chemical on the high priority list means that the chemical is subject to further investigation and testing. The criteria for priority ranking include

1. Quantities in which the chemical or mixture is to be manufactured and amount that will enter environment
2. The number of humans exposed in their workplace, as well as the duration and extent of exposure
3. The extent to which the chemical relates to chemical(s) known to pose an unreasonable risk to human health or the environment
4. The extent to which testing would result in the development of data from which the chemical's effects on health could be predicted or determined
5. The reasonably foreseeable availability of testing facilities and personnel

High priority goes to those chemicals suspected of causing cancer, mutation, or birth defects.

Under TSCA, no more than 50 chemicals can be listed as high priority within a 12-month period. Every six months the list is revised. Once the EPA has placed a chemical on the list, the agency has 12 months to assess the risk of the chemical or issue testing rules if it has insufficient data to assess risk. Using a hybrid form of rule making, the EPA must publish these testing rules within reasonable time limits. The publication must include the purpose of the tests and the methodologies to be used. Test results must be published in the *Federal Register*.

Unfortunately, according to the U.S. National Research Council, the EPA currently has more than 48,000 chemicals on its inventory of toxic substances and has no information on the toxic effects of 79 percent of them. Fewer than one-fifth have been tested for acute effects, and fewer than one-tenth for chronic (e.g., carcinogenic), reproductive, or mutagenic effects.

Many environmentalists object that not all existing chemicals are subject to careful review, with only those on the priority list being reviewed. Of the first 33 chemicals on this list, the EPA decided not to test about half. For those tested, no actual testing rules were adopted; instead, the EPA entered into testing agreements with manufacturers.

Treatment of New Chemicals. The centerpiece of the EPA's regulation of new chemicals is the *premanufacturing notice (PMN)*, sometimes referred to as a "section 5 notice." The PMN must be submitted 90 days in advance of the manufacture or import of any new chemical for sale or use in commerce. This notice must contain a significant amount of information about the chemical, including its chemical name; chemical identity; molecular structure; trade names or synonyms; by-products resulting from its manufacture, processing, use or disposal; intended categories of use by function and application; and the estimated maximum quantity to be manufactured or imported during the first year of production and for any 12-month period during the first three years. Details about the manufacture of the product that must be contained in the notice include the site where the chemical will be manufactured, processed, or used by the manufacturer, as well as information with respect to worker exposure and releases to the environment. Perhaps the most important information in the notice, however, are the test data. The notice must contain all available test data related to the impact of the new chemical on human health and the environment, including effects resulting not only from use of the substance but also from its manufacture, processing, distribution, and disposal. If some of the data was obtained from scientific journals, citations to the journal articles must be included. Any new data gathered or generated subsequent to submission of the PMN must be given to the EPA.

Within five days of receipt of the PMN, the EPA must publish a notice in the *Federal Register* containing the name of the new chemical, its intended use, and the test data submitted by the manufacturer to demonstrate that the chemical does not present an unreasonable risk of harm to health or the human environment. Within 45 days, the EPA must act to limit the amount to be produced, sold, or processed; prohibit the sale or manufacture of the chemical; or require further testing and temporarily enjoin the manufacture or sale until the data are provided. In taking action, the EPA must select the "least burdensome control." If no action is taken, the manufacturer is free to use the new chemical after the 90-day period has transpired.

Environmentalists are highly displeased with the PMN program, for several reasons. First, by 1983, stop or limit orders had been issued for only 13 of 2,300 chemicals. It is highly unlikely that only 13 chemicals had insufficient testing done to ensure their safety. Of course, those who quote that statistic often ignore the fact that several hundred chemicals were actually withdrawn by the manufacturer rather than risk EPA disapproval. Second, the statute is considered weak because it requires only *known* data to be reported; there is no requirement for testing. Some argue that this requirement discourages thorough testing. If a firm is fearful of a certain side effect, it may simply not test for it. Of course, firms reject this criticism, arguing that fear of civil liability to persons harmed from a toxic substance provides them with the incentive to perform the necessary tests.

A 1983 Office of Technology Assessment study of 740 PMNs showed that 47 percent had no toxicity data; the other 53 percent had only limited data. Where were the EPA temporary injunctions for insufficient testing? Further, only 17 percent had any test data about carcinogenic effects, birth defects, or mutations.

But it is not just environmentalists who criticize the PMN process. Chemical firms are also critical. They say the procedure is expensive, requiring unnecessary red tape. After all, the firms argue, they would not produce unsafe chemicals, because if they did, they would be liable in tort for negligence. These situations are not like water or air pollution, they claim, where causation is difficult to prove. There will not be the potential anonymity created by 50 dumpers; only *one* manufacturer made the product that caused the injury. And because chemicals affect so many people, the liability would be enormous.

Federal Insecticide, Fungicide, and Rodenticide Act

Not all potentially toxic chemicals are regulated primarily under TSCA. The first toxic substances to arouse public concern (herbicides, insecticides, fungicides, and rodenticides) are all commonly referred to as pesticides and are regulated primarily under the Federal Insecticide, Fungicide, and Rodenticide Act (FIFRA). Because of the sheer volume of pesticides used in this country, the United States, more than 350 billion tons annually since 1978,[10] their regulation is extremely important.

Registration Under FIFRA. For purposes of FIFRA, an item's being labeled an "economic poison" means that it must be registered and properly labeled before it can be distributed in the United States. As of March 1990, approximately 24,000 such products had been registered by the EPA.[11]

When a pesticide is to be registered, data showing its impact are submitted to the EPA. The EPA will register the pesticide when four factors exist:

1. The pesticide's composition is such as to warrant the proposed claims for it;
2. its labeling complies with the act;
3. the pesticide will perform its intended function without unreasonable risks to people and the environment, (taking into account economic, social, and environmental costs and benefits of the pesticide); and
4. when used in accordance with commonly used practice, the pesticide will not cause unreasonable risk to the environment.

The obvious question that arises with respect to these factors is: What is *unreasonable risk?* Originally, risk referred primarily to carcinogenicity. Today, however, the EPA also examines reproductive, immunological, and neurological effects of the pesticide, as well as its impact on groundwater and on the growth and reproduction of wildlife and fish. The EPA, when determining unreasonable risk, engages in a weighing of the economic, social, and environmental costs and benefits of the pesticide. In other words, if there are few or no substitutes available to do the same job, a greater risk to human health might be considered more reasonable than if there were numerous alternatives available. Some people criticize this standard as being insufficiently protective of health and the environment, noting that most other risk-based environmental standards are lessened only because of a lack of technology.

A second question arises with respect to what constitutes a proper label. This requirement dates back to the original Federal Environmental Pesticide Control Act of 1947, which was simply a labeling act. Today, a proper label is one that contains the warnings necessary to prevent injuries to persons and the environment.

A pesticide can be registered for general or restricted use. General use is by far the most desired form of registration. In essence, a general-use pesticide meets the standards set by the EPA and can be sold to anyone in any quantity. Restricted-use pesticides have the potential to have unreasonable impact. However, these unreasonable effects can be mitigated or prevented if the use and/or sale of the pesticide is restricted in some manner—hence the term restricted use.

The most common restriction is to limit use to certified applicators who take a test. "Use" is defined by the statute as application of the pesticide *by* or *under supervision of* a certified applicator. This definition leaves a lot of room for abuse. Another problem with this restriction is that it contains a private applicator exception: If the pesticide is used only on one's own land, a private applicator has to take the courses only and not the test. This exception assumes that those private applicators will be very knowledgeable and careful. Other possible restrictions include a limit to the frequency of use of the pesticide or to locations in which the substance can be sold or applied. The pests that may be targeted and the amount used per application can also be limited.

Under the 1988 amendments to FIFRA, the EPA is required to expedite its review of applications for pesticides that meet one of two criteria. The first standard is when the pesticide is identical or substantially similar in composition and labeling to a currently registered pesticide (often referred to as a "me-too" application). Alternatively, the pesticide may be one that differs in composition and labeling from a currently registered pesticide only in ways that would not significantly increase the risk of adverse environmental effects.

Registration lasts five years. If the EPA receives no request for renewal within 30 days prior to the end of registration, notice of impending cancellation is published in the *Federal Register*. The manufacturer has 30 days within which to protest the cancellation, or the registration terminates.

The EPA does not always grant registration for five years. Sometimes it grants only *conditional* registration. Conditional registration is given when certain required data are not submitted and two conditions exist:

1. The pesticide and proposed use are substantially similar to a currently used pesticide (i.e., they have similar active ingredients) or differ in ways that would not substantially harm the environment.
2. No significant harm or risk of unreasonable adverse effects would result from the pesticide's use.

If the active ingredient of the pesticide is not currently being used, conditional registration can be granted for the time needed to generate and submit the required data, not to exceed one year. Again, there must be no unreasonable risk (considering costs and benefits), and the granting of the conditional registration must be in the public interest.

If registration is denied, the EPA notifies the applicant of the reasons for denial. The applicant has 30 days to correct the condition (e.g., improper label) that led to the denial. If no correction is made, the notice of denial will be published in the *Federal Register*, along with the reasons for denial. Within 30 days, the applicant may seek an EPA hearing and administrative review of the denial.

Cancellation of Registration. As noted, if a pesticide manufacturer does not request renewal of the registration prior to the end of the five-year period, the process for termination of registration automatically begins. Sometimes, however, the EPA may move to cancel a registration earlier. This action for cancellation will occur whenever the EPA obtains information that an existing pesticide may present an unreasonable risk. The EPA will then undertake an intensive review of the pesticide. If it believes the risk is unreasonable, the agency will issue a notice of intent to cancel registration. Table 7–2 identifies some pesticides that have been removed from the market through this process.

Interested parties, generally users and manufacturers, then have 30 days to contest the cancellation by requesting a hearing. If no such request is made, can-

TABLE 7–2 Some pesticides taken off the market

Pesticides	Use	Concerns
Aldrin	Insecticide	Oncogenicity
Chlordane (agricultural uses; termiticide uses suspended or cancelled)	Insecticide/termites, ants	Oncogenicity; reductions in nontarget and endangered species
Compound 1080 (livestock collar retained; rodenticide use under review)	Coyote control, rodenticide	Reductions in nontarget and endangered species; no known antidote
Dibromochloropropane (DBCP)	Soil fumigant, fruits and vegetables	Oncogenicity; mutagenicity, reproductive effects
DDT and related compounds	Insecticide	Ecological (eggshell thinning); carcinogenicity
Dieldrin	Insecticide	Oncogenicity
Dinoseb (in hearings)	Herbicide/crop dessicant	Fetotoxicity; reproductive effects; acute toxicity
Endrin (avicide use retained)	Insecticide/avicide	Oncogenicity, teratogenicity; reductions in nontarget and endangered species
Ethylene dibromide (EDB) (very minor uses and use on citrus for export retained)	Insecticide/fumigant	Oncogenicity, mutagenicity, reproductive effects
Heptachlor (agricultural uses; termiticide uses suspended or cancelled)	Insecticide	Oncogenicity, reductions in nontarget and endangered species
Kepone	Insecticide	Oncogenicity
Lindane (indoor smoke bomb cancelled; some uses restricted)	Insecticide/vaporizer	Oncogenicity, teratogenicity, reproductive effects, acute toxicity; other chronic effects
Mercury	Microbial uses	Cumulative toxicant causing brain damage
Mirex	Insecticide/fire ant control	Nontarget species; potential oncogenicity
Silvex	Herbicide/forestry, rights-of-way, weed control	Oncogenicity, teratogenicity; fetotoxicity
Strychnine (rodenticide use and livestock colar retained)	Mammalian predator control, rodenticide	Reductions in nontarget and endangered species
2,4,5,-T	Herbicide/forestry, rights-of-way, weed control	Oncogenicity; teratogenicity; fetotoxicity
Toxaphene (livestock dip retained)	Insecticide, cotton	Oncogenicity; reductions in nontarget species; acute toxicity to aquatic organisms; chronic effects on wildlife

Oncogenicity , causes tumors; mutagenicity, causes mutation; carcinogenicity, causes cancer; teratogenicity, causes major birth defects; fetotoxicity, causes toxicity to the unborn fetus.

SOURCE: EPA, *Environmental Progress And Challenges: EPA's Update* (1988).

cellation is effective. If the cancellation is challenged, there must be a hearing to determine whether the registration should be cancelled.

There have been a whole series of opinions resulting from litigation between the EPA and the Environmental Defense Fund concerning the issue of who should have the burden of proof in cancellation hearings. The resultant case law has established that once the EPA issues a notice of cancellation, a presumption arises in favor of cancellation. Issuance of the notice is presumed to mean that a substantial question of safety exists that requires suspension in the absence of proof by the manufacturer that the risk is minimal or that the countervailing benefits outweigh the risks. Once the EPA has obtained evidence that one mode of exposure is hazardous, the presumption also arises that all modes of exposure are hazardous.

If a manufacturer contests a cancellation, the hearing process can be extremely time consuming, often taking up to two years. During this time, the pesticide will continue to be sold. Many believe that in light of the presumption in favor of cancellation, it seems irrational to allow the continued production and sale of the pesticide until the final outcome of the cancellation proceedings has been determined.

There is an important exception to this time-consuming process. Suspension can be immediate if the continued use of the pesticide presents an imminent hazard. When evidence of an imminent hazard comes to light, the administrator of the EPA can issue a notice to the manufacturer of the pesticide that use of the pesticide is being suspended. Findings as to the imminent hazard must be included with the notice. The manufacturer then has five days within which to request an expedited hearing prior to the suspension. If no hearing is requested, the suspension will take place upon termination of the five-day period.

One even stronger action the EPA administrator can take is an *emergency suspension*. If the administrator determines that an emergency exists, he or she may order an immediate suspension of all use, sales, and distribution of the pesticide. The manufacturer, however, is entitled to an expedited hearing to determine whether the suspension was appropriate. As you might guess, emergency suspension has been exercised only a few times.

An interesting issue that arises with respect to cancellation is about what should be done with pesticides that have had their registrations cancelled. The EPA has the authority to allow the sale and use of existing stocks "under such conditions and for such uses as will not unreasonably adversely affect the environment." In many cases, as long as they can use their stock, manufacturers do not protest cancellation. This ability to get an easy cancellation makes it tempting for the EPA to go along with such an arrangement.

Another problem that arises with the cancellation of a registration for a pesticide that has been in use for a long time is that the manufacturer, retailers, and end users may have large supplies of the pesticide on hand. Under the original act, the EPA indemnified or reimbursed the holders (manufactures and users) of the pesticide for the costs of the cancelled/suspended products, plus disposal of the pesticide if requested, and established standards for its disposal. This provision of the act proved costly. In 1986, for example, the EPA spent $1.5 million on a yet untested chemical method to neutralize the pesticide EDB. Unfortunately, this process released toxic vapors into the air, requiring the EPA to find another way to dispose of it. The 1988 amendments to FIFRA modified this indemnification provision. Consequently, only farmers and other end users are now entitled to indemnification. Under certain extraordinary circumstances, Congress may make a specific line-item appropriation to reimburse a manufacturer or retailer. Otherwise, the retailer or other non-end user may seek reimbursement from the seller/manufacturer. The seller/manufacturer may avoid this liability only by notifying the buyer in writing at the time of the sale that there will be no reimbursement.

Once a pesticide is suspended, the EPA must notify foreign governments through the State Department, providing them with reasons for cancellation and alternatives to the cancelled pesticide. However, the pesticide can still be sold to foreigners, leading to one of the criticisms of FIFRA. There seems to be something problematic about saying that a pesticide is too harmful to be sold at home, yet it can be sold abroad. And even if there were no concern about exposure to others, many foreign growers are using those pesticides on crops that will eventually be exported to the United States. This so-called circle of poison is a major issue in environmental ethics today.

Change of Use Registration. If the EPA decides to change use registration, it must publish its intent to do so 45 days in advance in the *Federal Register*. The registrant may request a hearing. If a pesticide is classified for restricted use, the registrant may petition the EPA for a change any time. Before any pesticide to be used on a food or feed crop is registered, the EPA must follow one more step. The agency must establish a "tolerance" to pesticide residue. Both locally grown and imported crops are randomly tested to ensure that these tolerances are not exceeded.

Enforcement. The EPA requires manufacturer to keep records showing the quantity sold, date of delivery, and recipient for all pesticides sold. Upon presentation of credentials and a written reason for inspection, including whether a violation is suspected, the manufacturer or retailer of pesticides must allow an inspection of its facility. Samples may also be taken following the same procedures. The inspection must be prompt, with a receipt given for samples taken.

If there is a violation of FIFRA, the EPA or state agriculture department must notify the defendant of the civil or criminal proceedings in writing, thereby giving that party an opportunity to be heard orally or in writing prior to the agency's filing charges.

For minor violations, when it is in the public interest, the EPA may simply give a written warning to the violator. A warning is likely to be used if the violation occurred despite due care and did not cause significant harm to the environment. A stop sale, use, or removal order may also be issued. Or a seizure order may be obtained in federal court. Civil penalties under FIFRA are up to $5,000 per violation by a registrant, wholesaler, distributor, or retailer and up to $1,000 per violation by private user/applicator. Factors the EPA uses to determine the penalty include a comparison of the size of the fine to the size of the business, the effect a fine would have on the violator's ability to stay in business, and the gravity of violation. A private user may use a guarantee from the seller that the pesticide is lawfully registered as a defense.

Criminal penalties may be imposed when there are knowing violations of the act. These fines are up to $25,000 for a firm and $1,000 for a user or applicator. Officials of the firm may also receive up to a one-year jail sentence, and private users may be required to serve up to 30 days in jail. In 1987, states conducted more than 55,000 inspections and initiated 10,000 enforcement actions.

Federal Food, Drug, and Cosmetics Act

The Federal Food, Drug, and Cosmetics Act aids in the regulation of pesticide use by requiring the administrator of the EPA to establish tolerance levels for concentrations of pesticide residues on commodities consumed in the United States. In establishing these limits, the administrator is to consider "the necessity for the production of an adequate, wholesome, and economic food supply." Theoretically, violations will be caught by the EPA through inspections and by the Food and Drug Administration (FDA) in its routine sampling program. A problem with relying on the FDA, however, is that fewer than 1 percent of fruits and vegetables are inspected. In addition, not all pesticides are tested for. Tests take an average of 28 days; by then, the food is often sold. The shipment from which a sample has been taken is supposed to be held; unfortunately, it rarely is.

Progress Under the Acts

The EPA believes that progress has been considerable. Since the enactment of FIFRA, registrations of 34 potentially hazardous pesticides have been cancelled, and 60 toxic inert ingredients have been eliminated from use. As Figure 7–1 shows, levels of persistent pesticides in humans have significantly declined. A National Pesticide Telecommunications Network has been established. By calling the network's toll-free number—800-858-PEST—one can obtain general information about the use and disposal of pesticides and how to recognize and manage pesticide poisoning.

Not everyone is convinced that pesticide regulation is as effective as it could be, however. Increasingly, FIFRA is coming under fire for one of the protections it offers pesticide manufacturers. Under FIFRA, manufacturers do not have to list on their labels the specific inert ingredients, those ingredients that function only to preserve the active, pest-killing ingredients or make them easier to apply. All they have to cite is the broad term "inert ingredients" and the percentage of

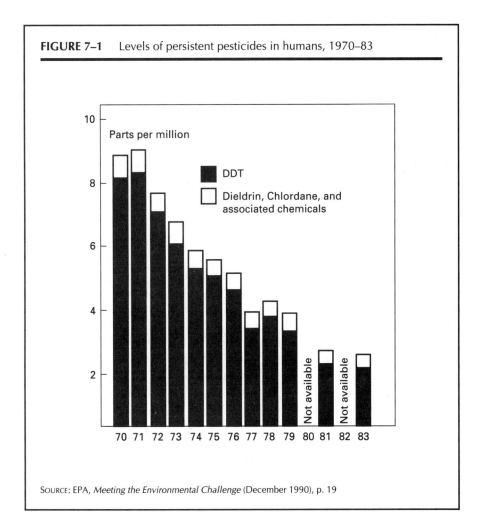

FIGURE 7–1   Levels of persistent pesticides in humans, 1970–83

SOURCE: EPA, *Meeting the Environmental Challenge* (December 1990), p. 19

the total ingredients of all the inert ingredients. This incomplete labeling provides confidentiality for manufacturers to make it more difficult for competitors to discover their formulas.

The problem with confidentiality protection is that many of the inert ingredients are among the most toxic substances, including phenol, toluene, and chlorobenzene, and all have been linked to birth defects, liver and kidney damage, or nervous system disorders. Others are suspected carcinogens. The consumer who buys these pesticides for home and garden use has no way to find out what these inert ingredients are because the EPA is required to keep them confidential. This confidentiality requirement is particularly troublesome because in many instances the inert ingredients constitute 80 to 90 percent of the total ingredients.

TOXIC TORTS

Increasingly, common law tort cases are being used to seek compensation for persons injured or killed as a result of exposure to toxic substances. A wide variety of theories are used to seek recovery in such cases. The most common are negligence and strict product liability. Often these cases are referred to as *toxic torts*, regardless of which theory of liability is being used. In most cases a plaintiff will bring an action attempting to prove both of these theories of liability. This approach is reasonable because this area of the law is very unclear, and it is often difficult to know which theory one will be able to prove.

Theories of Recovery

Negligence. To prove a cause of action based on *negligence*, the plaintiff must prove the following: that the defendant owed a duty of care to the plaintiff; that the defendant failed to meet this duty of care; that this failure to meet the duty of care caused the injury to the plaintiff; and that the plaintiff did indeed incur a compensable injury. The duty of care that a manufacturer generally has is a duty not to expose others to an unreasonable risk of harm. This duty may entail such specific actions as properly testing chemical substances for their potentially harmful effects. In many toxic tort cases the duty that the defendant is alleged to have failed to live up to is a duty to warn the plaintiff of known or knowable dangers resulting from specific uses of the product.

A typical explanation of what a plaintiff needs to demonstrate in a toxic tort case can be seen in a Maryland judge's statement of what the plaintiffs had to prove in the 1984 case of *Chevron Chemical Company* v. *Ferebee.*[12] Ferebee had been exposed on numerous occasions over a three-year period to the pesticide Paraquat, manufactured by the Chevron Corporation. Ten months after his last exposure he developed severe lung fibrosis. During the course of the trial, he died, leaving his family to carry on the lawsuit.

In explaining why he found in the plaintiff's favor, the judge said that the plaintiff had the burden of proving, by a preponderance of the evidence, the following elements:

1. That Paraquat proximately caused Ferebee's illness and death;
2. that Paraquat is inherently dangerous;
3. that Chevron knew, or should have known, at the time it sold Paraquat, used by Ferebee, that the chemical was inherently dangerous;
4. that the resulting duty to provide an adequate warning of the danger was not met; and
5. that the inadequacy of the warning proximately caused Ferebee's illness and death.

Strict Product Liability. A special form of strict liability, *strict product liability,* is most often applicable in cases involving consumers injured by products containing toxic substances. Strict liability, as a general theory of tort liability, requires the plaintiff to demonstrate that the defendant was engaged in an abnormally dangerous activity that caused the plaintiff's harm. The *Restatement (Second) of Torts*, Section 402A, sets out the theory of strict product liability as follows:

1. One who sells any product in a defective condition, unreasonably dangerous, to the user or consumer or to his property, is subject to liability for the physical harm thereby caused to the ultimate user or consumer or to his property, if
   a. the seller is engaged in the business of selling such a product, and
   b. it is expected to reach the consumer without substantial change in the condition in which it is sold.
2. The rule stated in Subsection (1) applies although
   a. the seller has exercised all possible care in the preparation and sale of his product and
   b. the user or consumer has not bought the product from or entered into any contractual relation with the seller.

When looking at the definition of strict product liability, one might naturally ask, When does a defective condition become "unreasonably dangerous"? Because tort law is state law, the precise definition varies from state to state, but most courts rely on one of two tests. The first is the "consumer expectations" test. If a product is more dangerous than the reasonable consumer would expect it to be, then it is unreasonably dangerous. The second test is the feasible alternative test. The court asks whether there was some other, less dangerous, reasonably feasible alternative available but the manufacturer chose not to use it. When applying this test, the manufacturer looks at such factors as the utility of the product, the availability of substitutes, the obviousness of the danger, the role a warning label could have played, the avoidability of danger with careful use, and the viability of eliminating the danger without impairing the usefulness of the product. For example, a knife is dangerous, but it would not be considered unreasonably dangerous to the consumer who got cut using it because the danger is obvious, and the utility would be lost by eliminating the danger.

Problems in Establishing Causation

Regardless of the theory of liability used, the plaintiff must establish that the defendant's conduct caused the plaintiff harm. And proof of causation in toxic tort cases is extremely difficult, for a number of reasons. First, it may be difficult to prove that the chemical in question does cause the harm that has resulted, usually cancer, leukemia, or birth defects. For many of these diseases medical science cannot fully explain their causes. Many times there are multiple causative factors. Animal studies are often used, but these often involve higher doses than the plaintiff received. And then the issue may also be raised of whether one can extrapolate between species. Epidemiological studies may be used, but these are often unavailable or considered inconclusive.

A few courts have even allowed causation to be proven without statistical evidence. In *Chevron Chemical Co. v. Ferebee*, the appellate judges upheld a jury verdict for which the evidence for causation came solely from the testimony of two expert medical witnesses who based their conclusions about causation on their examination of the victim. The court stated that "as long as the basic methodology employed to reach a conclusion is sound, such as the use of tissue samples, standard tests, and patient examination, product liability law does not preclude recovery until a 'statistically significant' number of people have been injured or until science has had the time and resources to complete sophisticated laboratory studies of the chemical." Not all courts, however, have been equally liberal.

Even if the plaintiff establishes a link between the chemical and the harm, it may still be difficult to demonstrate that the particular exposure to the defendant's chemical caused the plaintiff's specific injury, especially when there are a number of factors that could have caused the plaintiff's harm. For example, asbestos may cause lung disease, but what if the victim is also a chain smoker?

The problems associated with establishing causation in toxic tort cases are discussed in great detail in a district court opinion in the case of *Allen v. U. S.*,[13] a case that arose from the federal government's bomb testing at a Nevada test site between 1951 and 1953. Plaintiffs, all of whom had resided in southern Utah, northern Arizona, and southeast Nevada, claimed to have suffered leukemia or cancer as a result of exposure to radioactive fallout from the bomb tests. Plaintiffs alleged that the government was negligent in conducting the open-air testing, failing to monitor the results, failing to warn people who were in danger of the hazards, and failing to inform such persons of what they could do to minimize their risk from the testing.

In addressing the difficulty of proving that the defendant's action definitely caused the harm, the court stated that if the plaintiff could not establish a cause-in-fact connection, the plaintiff should attempt to establish the most exclusive factual connection between the injury and the defendant. If the defendant's conduct can be found to be a "substantial factor," it may then be judged to be a legal cause. With respect to the particular facts of the case before it, the judge wrote:

> Where a defendant who negligently creates a radiological hazard which puts an identifiable population group at increased risk, and a member of that group at risk develops a biological condition which is consistent with having been caused by the hazard to which he has been negligently subjected, such consistency having been demonstrated by substantial, appropriate, persuasive, and connecting factors, a fact finder may reasonably conclude that the hazard caused the condition absent persuasive proof to the contrary offered by the defendant.

The judge went on to quote from the *Restatement (Second) of Torts*, §433, as to what factors would be relevant:

The following considerations are in themselves or in combination with one another important in determining whether the actor's conduct is a substantial factor in bringing about harm to another: a) the number of other factors which contribute in producing the harm and the extent of the effect which they have in producing it; b) whether the actor's conduct has created a force or series of forces which are in continuous and active operation up to the time of the harm, or has created a situation harmless unless acted upon by other forces for which the actor is not responsible, and c) lapse of time.

The court then went on to discuss the problems related to the use of statistics to demonstrate a causal link, saying that in a case where a plaintiff tries to establish a factual connection between a particular "cause" and a delayed, nonspecific effect, such as cancer or leukemia, the strongest evidence of the relationship is likely to be statistical in form. "Where the injuries are causally indistinguishable, and where experts cannot determine whether an individual injury results from culpable human cause or nonculpable natural causes, evidence that there is an increased incidence of injury in a population following exposure to a defendant's risk-creating conduct may justify an inference of causal linkage between the defendant's conduct and the plaintiff's injuries . . . whenever there is an increase of observed cases of a particular cancer or leukemia over the number statistically expected to normally appear, the question arises whether it may be rationally inferred that the increase is causally connected to the specific human activity."

The court then went on to describe the scientists' use of the concept of statistical significance, by which they generally mean that the odds of the event occurring as a result of random chance are or less than 1 in 20; some researchers use an even more stringent standard of 1 in 100 or less. The court was highly critical of the statisticians' requirement of 95 percent probability, and added that the problems of this stringent requirement are exacerbated when the exposed population is fairly small, as is the case with most toxic exposures. The court said that statistical evidence, when combined with other evidence could "supply a useful link in the process of proof." In discussing the evidence, "the value of the available statistical data concerning radiation and cancer in offsite communities is not confined by arbitrary tests of 'statistical significance.'" The court said that whether causal inferences should be drawn that will carry the case to the additional issues of risk, scope of duty, and culpable breach of duty, for example, negligence, is a question of judgment resting in part on policy. The court must determine those risks for which the defendant should be held responsible. Thus, the courts are not going to define causation as rigorously as the scientist might, but they cannot clearly articulate the lesser standard of proof they will require.

Enterprise Liability

An additional problem that sometimes arises in toxic tort cases occurs when the exposure was several years prior to the injury and the toxin was produced by multiple manufacturers. Because of the time lapse, the plaintiff is unable to identify exactly which manufacturer produced the substance to which he or she was exposed. Because of the requirement of establishing the link between the defendant's action and the plaintiff's injury, this lack of knowledge might at first appear to be an insurmountable obstacle. However, some courts felt that to leave a plaintiff in a situation like this would be unfair. So, in the case of *Sindell* v. *Abbott Laboratories*,[14] the court fashioned the concept of enterprise, or market share, liability, whereby a manufacturer that produced a defective product that was sold interchangeably with other brands of the same product could be held responsible for that percentage of the plaintiff's injuries proportionate to the market share the defendant had at the time of the plaintiff's exposure to the product.

In the *Sindell* case, the plaintiffs' mothers had taken DES during pregnancies that had occurred before the drug was banned. The drug caused cancer and other side effects in the plaintiffs. The 11 defendants had collaborated in testing, promoting, and marketing the drug, and none of the plaintiffs could identify the specific manufacturer of the drugs their mothers had taken, to a large extent because doctors prescribed the drugs generically and pharmacists filled prescriptions with whichever brands they had on hand.

The court said, in setting out the novel market share theory:

> In our contemporary complex industrialized society, advances in science and technology create fungible goods which may harm consumers and which cannot be traced to any specific producer. The response of the courts can be either to adhere rigidly to prior doctrine, denying recovery to those injured by such products, or to fashion remedies to meet these changing needs.
>
> The most persuasive reason for finding that plaintiff states a cause of action is . . . as between an innocent plaintiff and negligent defendants, the latter should bear the cost of the injury. . . .
>
> From a broader policy standpoint, defendants are better able to bear the cost of injury resulting from the manufacture of a defective product.

Thus the courts removed a potential hurdle that could arise in many toxic tort cases because of the latency of many effects.

Punitive Damages

In most toxic tort cases, regardless of the theory of liability on which the action is based, the primary goal of the plaintiff is to recover compensatory damages, damages designed to place the plaintiff in the position he or she would have been in if the tort never occurred. Such damages include payment for doctor bills, lost wages, property damages, and pain and suffering. In addition, plaintiffs may also seek *punitive damages* when the defendant's conduct may be described as "willful and wanton" or "extremely egregious." Punitive damages are designed, as their name implies, to punish the defendant for his or her wrongful conduct and to provide a strong deterrent to others who might consider engaging in similar activities. In the toxic tort area, punitive damages may also serve to provide an incentive to encourage private citizens to sue to ensure compliance with environmental regulations.

To meet the goals of deterrence and punishment, the amount of punitive damages awarded in tort cases is based primarily on the wrongfulness of the defendant's act and the resources of the defendant. The more egregious the act, the more substantial is the award. The more resources the defendant has, the more substantial the award must be in order for it to have any punitive effect.

In recent toxic tort cases defendants have tried to argue that punitive damages should not be awarded in cases where a substantial number of potential plaintiffs have been harmed or when the tort occurred in the distant past. Probably the most well publicized of the cases is *Fischer* v. *Johns-Manville Corporation*.[15] The trial court awarded Fischer punitive damages based on an exposure to asbestos that had occurred 40 years prior to the lawsuit. The defendant, on appeal, raised several arguments as to why punitive damages were inappropriate. First, the defendant argued that the remoteness of the claim made the award unfair because at the time the conduct occurred, different social values at that time might have made the conduct less egregious than the same conduct would appear today. The court dismissed that argument, finding that Johns-Manville's conduct, "knowingly and deliberately" subjecting the plaintiff and other asbestos workers to serious health hazards with utter disregard for their safety and well-being, would have been regarded as equally egregious back then.

The defendant then argued that different officers and managers committed the tort, so punishing the corporation today was unfair. The court likewise did not buy this argument, pointing out that while the officers and managers may have changed, Johns-Manville was the same corporate entity. Officers and managers are merely agents of the corporation. Besides, a goal of punitive damages is general deterrence, which will still be accomplished regardless of who is in command.

The court also did not accept the argument that punitive damages were unfair to innocent shareholders. After all, the shareholders benefited from the misconduct in the past, so it was only fair that they now share in the associated losses. Finally, the argument that mass punitive damages could lead to a corporation's inability to pay later claimants because the firm would have lost all its assets caused slightly more concern on the part of the court. However, the court did not believe this potential problem was insurmountable. First, a defendant could introduce evidence at trial of having paid large punitive damage awards in previous cases so that the jury could take those payments into account when deciding whether to assess punitive damages. Second, if any punitive damage award were so high as to make financial disaster imminent, the defendant could file a motion for *remittitur*, which is a request for damages to be reduced.

Thus, it appears that if a plaintiff can overcome the tremendous burden of proving causation, recovery of punitive damages in toxic tort cases is possible. And this threat of potentially unlimited punitive damages awards may provide some incentive for makers of potentially toxic chemicals to test their products more carefully.

CONCLUDING REMARKS

The federal regulatory scheme has been designed both to remove existing toxins from the market and to prevent the introduction of new toxins into commerce. Private law also plays a part in regulating toxins. If one has been harmed by a toxic chemical, he or she can file a toxic tort case, based on either negligence or strict liability. Recovery through such an action will be difficult, although not impossible.

This chapter has focused on toxic chemicals in commerce. We now turn to an examination of toxins in another form—waste—in Chapter 8.

QUESTIONS FOR REVIEW AND DISCUSSION

1. Explain the process of risk assessment.
2. Explain the statutory scheme for the regulation of existing toxic chemicals.
3. Evaluate the criticisms that might be made of TOSCA's regulation of new chemicals.
4. List the criteria for registration of a pesticide under FIFRA.
5. Explain why general-use registration is superior to restricted-use registration.
6. Explain how and when a pesticide's registration may be cancelled.
7. Explain two theories of liability on which a plaintiff exposed to a toxic substance might base a lawsuit.
8. What is the rationale for allowing a private party to recover punitive damages in a toxic tort case?

FOR FURTHER READING

Block, Alan, and Frank Scarpitti. *Poisoning for Profit.* New York: Morrow, 1985.

Brennan, Troyen A. "Causal Chains and Statistical Links: The Role of Scientific Uncertainty in Ultrahazardous Substance Litigation." *Cornell Law Review* 73 (1988):469.

Brodeur, Paul. *Outrageous Misconduct: The Asbestos Industry on Trial.* New York: Pantheon Books, 1985.

Brown Michael. *The Toxic Cloud.* New York: Harper & Row, 1987.

Farber, Daniel A. "Toxic Causation." *Minnesota Law Review* 71 (1987): 1219.

[Note]. "Toxic Tort Litigation and the Causation Element: Is There Any Hope of Reconciliation?" *Southwestern Law Journal* 40 (1986): 909.

Rosenberg, David. "The Causal Connection In Mass Exposure Cases: A 'Public Law' Vision Of The Tort System." *Harvard Law Journal* 97 (1984):851.

Tribe, Lawrence. "Trial by Mathematics: Precision and Ritual in the Legal Process," *Harvard Law Review* 84 (1971):1329.

NOTES

1. Sandra Postel, "Diffusing the Toxics Threat: Controlling Pesticides and Industrial Waste," *Worldwatch Paper* 79 (Worldwatch Institute, 1987), p. 5.

2. 541 F2d 1 (D.C. Cir. 1976) (en banc).

3. 647 F2d 1130 (D.C. Cir. 1980).

4. 824 F2d 1146 (D.C. Cir. 1987).

5. Joseph V. Rodricks, *Calculated Risks: Understanding the Toxicity and Human Health Risks of Chemicals in Our Environment* (Cambridge: Cambridge University Press, 1992).

6. Postel, note 1, p. 7.

7. Ibid.

8. Ibid, p. 8.

9. Ibid.

10. Walter Corson, *The Global Ecology Handbook* (Boston: Beacon Press, 1990), p. 80.

11. Ibid.

12. *Toxic Program Commentary: Ohio (1990)* (Rockville, Md.: Specialty Technical Publishers, 1990).

13. 736 F.2d 1529 (D.C. Cir. Ct. of Appeals 1984).

14. 588 F. Supp. 247 (D. Ct. Utah 1984).

15. 103 N.J. 643, 518 A2d 466 (1986).

8

Waste Management and Hazardous Releases

Waste management is an integral part of pollution control. Improperly handled waste results in contamination of water, air, and land. Moreover, waste generation often means resource mismanagement. Minimization of waste implies maximization of resource value. Recognizing these concepts, Congress adopted the Resource Conservation and Recovery Act (RCRA) in 1976. For the first time, the federal government actively took responsibility for promoting the proper disposal of hazardous and nonhazardous waste and the recovery and reuse of waste. However, as with other environmental management strategies, progress has been slow. Today there are still unsolved questions of how to implement reasonable waste management (not just disposal) strategies that are economically and technologically practicable yet fully protect human health and the environment.

And despite an elaborate system designed to control hazardous materials and wastes, unplanned releases still occur. All too frequently we hear about a tanker truck overturning and dumping its load into a river, about toxic waste discovered at a remote site, about an abandoned field with leaking chemical drums, or about an explosion resulting in a toxic gas cloud. Though we have programs for proper management of hazardous materials and environmental pollutants, these programs are far from being completely effective. Thus, programs have been developed to plan for and respond to things that go wrong, and to remedy things that went wrong before we had adequate regulatory protection.

WASTE CONTROL TECHNIQUES

When you throw something away, where is "away"? In the United States, "away" usually means putting it in the ground (in a landfill) where it is stored indefinitely. However, use of landfills as the primary waste management tool has many disadvantages. Waste entering a landfill may be, or may become, hazardous, and migrate from the site to the groundwater, surface water, or air. Material that is landfilled as waste has lost its potential use as a resource. Furthermore, people do not want landfills in their neighborhoods, as landfills often decrease property values and are perceived as a threat to health. As the amount of waste increases and the available space decreases, it becomes more difficult to find sites for landfill development that are acceptable to local communities.

Rather than throwing waste in the ground, it is better to prevent it from being generated. Reducing waste generation at its source, or source reduction, is the highest priority in the EPA's waste management strategy. Whereas many source reduction techniques may be complex, often they are as simple as using reusable canvas bags rather than disposal plastic bags at the grocery store.

Recycling also can be an effective management tool, although less preferable than source reduction. Recycling typically is a reprocessing of a waste product to recover its inherent resource value. For example, recycling of aluminum cans entails recovering the aluminum to manufacture new cans. Not only does this recovery keep aluminum cans out of landfills, but it also reduces the need to mine for new aluminum.

Resource recovery can also take the form of incineration, whereby some of the potential energy of a waste can be captured as heat or transformed into electricity. For example, waste oil can be used as heating oil. However, in the incineration process, the oil is destroyed. Thus, this form of resource recovery has less potential to maximize fully the resource value inherent in the oil than a reprocessing (recycling) process. Additionally, many times the goal of incineration is limited to waste destruction (particularly when destroying hazardous waste), and no attempt is made to harness the waste's potential energy. Substantial concern exists about the by-products of incineration, which may include toxic chemicals such as dioxins in the exhaust gases. Ashes resulting from incineration may also cause disposal problems, particularly when the waste material contains substantial quantities of heavy metals.

A variety of methods are available to change waste into less hazardous forms, reduce it in quantity, or otherwise cause desirable transformations. For example, organic waste may be degraded biologically. This can take the form of composting yard debris, with resulting compost reapplied to the land. It can also take the form of breeding "superbugs," bacteria that can convert toxic organic waste into less dangerous forms as the bacteria use the waste for energy or as a source of critical growth materials.

Chemical and physical treatment methods are important tools for managing hazardous wastes. Destroying or reducing hazardous characteristics may make the waste easier to place in a landfill or make it practical to reuse. Still, the majority of municipal waste, as well as significant quantities of hazardous waste, are landfilled. Although the quantity of hazardous waste being landfilled is diminishing, municipal waste continues to be deposited in landfills in ever increasing amounts.

THE PROBLEM WITH WASTE

Traditionally waste management has been a local issue. When consumer goods were scarce and people did not live in large communities, the relatively small quantities of waste produced presented little threat. However, the industrial revolution led to growing urban centers and increased amounts of waste material. Individuals could no longer easily dispose of their waste without threatening the health of the community. Beginning in the late 1800s, cities began to assume some responsibility for waste collection and disposal to counter this threat to public health. By 1880, 43 percent of U.S. cities provided some form of garbage collection.[1]

Waste was generally disposed of in open dumps. Dumps provided an excellent habitat for a variety of vermin; furthermore, they were unsightly, stank, and they degraded groundwater and occasionally surface water quality. Hazardous materials could be disposed of with nonhazardous materials, with few concerns regarding the threat to human health and the environment. Beginning in the 1930s, "sanitary landfills" began to replace open dumps. In these early sanitary landfills waste was covered daily with soil, resulting in significant reduction in odor, pests, and loose material blowing from the site. However, this technique did not protect waste material from leaching into groundwater and contaminating important water supplies. Only beginning in the 1980s was serious attention devoted to taking special precautions for hazardous waste.

Incineration of municipal waste was also a popular waste disposal practice by the beginning of the twentieth century. However, many problems emerged as the United States attempted to import European incineration technology. In fact, many early attempts at incineration were abandoned, with only 78 of the 180 incinerators built in the United States between 1885 and 1908 being operational in 1909. However, with improved technology, incineration became more prominent. By the 1930s, more than 600 cities relied on municipal waste incinerators.[2] Since this peak period, the number of incinerators has declined, and communities have become increasingly dependent on sanitary landfills.

During the Great Depression and World War II, both social mores and the economy forced people to extract maximum value out of available resources, wasting as little as possible. After the war, the United States entered a period of consumerism—and of greatly increased per capita generation of waste. As the economy grew, people were encouraged to consume at much greater levels. In addition to the push to buy more products, manufacturers planned many items to fail or become obsolete within a few years. Furthermore, products began to be packaged much more extensively, taking advantage of the rapidly growing plastics technology. The EPA reported in 1986 that one-third of the municipal waste stream resulted from consumer packaging.[3]

Until recently, we had been moving away from recycling and reuse of consumer goods and industrial materials. For example, throughout the 1930s, almost all glass beverage containers were recycled. The practice of selling beverages in refillable containers gradually was replaced by plastic and glass nonrefillable bottles and metal cans. While there has been a market for recycled aluminum cans for some time, markets for recycling plastics are just emerging. Currently, refillable glass bottles are only a tiny fraction of total container use and production.

Data are not available to comprehensively characterize the magnitude of the municipal solid waste stream. Similarly, we do not know the extent of contamination due to municipal solid waste disposal practices, or the resources lost in the "production" of waste. However, enough estimates have been made to show clearly that the municipal solid waste stream represents a major environmental, health, and economic problem. See Table 8–1 for one estimate showing the growing waste stream and the trend toward material recovery.

Estimates made for the Subcommittee on Transportation and Commerce of the House of Representatives, in developing RCRA, indicated that about 135 million tons of municipal solid waste was produced annually in the United States of a total waste stream of about 3 billion to 4 billion tons.[4] Four to six billion dollars was being used annually to dispose of this waste, and 48 major cities were projected to have insufficient landfill capacity by the year 1982. In a later EPA study, the annual municipal waste stream was estimated at about 180 mil-

---

TABLE 8–1   Municipal solid waste, 1960–88

	Gross Discards			Materials Recovery			Net Discards	
Year	Total Million Tons	Per Capita Pounds/Day	Total Million Tons	Per Capita Pounds/Day	Recovery %	Total Million Tons	Per Capita Pounds/Day
1960	87.8	2.66	5.9	0.18	6.7	81.9	2.48
1965	103.4	2.92	6.8	0.19	6.6	96.6	2.73
1970	121.9	3.27	8.6	0.23	7.1	113.3	3.04
1975	128.1	3.26	9.9	0.25	7.7	118.2	3.01
1980	149.6	3.61	14.5	0.35	9.7	135.1	3.26
1985	161.6	3.70	16.4	0.38	10.1	145.2	3.32
1988	179.6	4.00	23.5	0.52	13.1	156.0	3.48

SOURCE: EPA, Office of Solid Waste and Emergency Response, *Characterization of Municipal Solid Waste in the United States, 1990 Update*, (Washington, D.C., 1991).

lion tons, and projected to grow to 216 million tons by the year 2000.[5] Furthermore, another EPA study indicated that 45 percent of operating landfills would reach capacity by 1991.[6] Estimates vary, but it is apparent that increasing quantities of waste are being produced.

In 1989, the EPA published a national strategy for municipal solid waste management. Three goals were identified: (1) increase source reduction and recycling; (2) increase disposal capacity and improve secondary material markets; and (3) improve the safety of solid waste management facilities. The first two goals deal with issues pertaining to waste quantities: how to reduce generation and how to provide enough capacity to manage waste properly. The third goal recognizes that municipal solid waste properly managed from a regulated perspective may still retain substantial environmental and health risks. The EPA strategy clearly states that the current municipal waste management system is inadequate, and that major changes are needed.

Ensuring proper management of hazardous waste, a particular kind (or subset) of solid waste, also presents major challenges to the legal and regulatory system. Prior to 1975, government paid little attention to hazardous waste, with only 25 states even having hazardous waste programs. Within those programs there were only about 50 employees, with one-third working for the state of California.[7] There was no consistency among states regarding these limited programs, so companies faced different requirements depending on where they were doing business.

The significance of the problem of hazardous waste production has never been clear. There have been a variety of "official" estimates of the volume of hazardous waste production in the United States, but these estimates have varied widely. More importantly perhaps, estimates of quantity do little to quantify resultant risk. However, quantifying risk from hazardous waste may be unnecessary; simply knowing that the risk is substantial was sufficient for Congress to demand (through RCRA and its amendments) a national hazardous waste management program. During the 1970s, we began to understand that our industrialized society was producing large amounts of hazardous waste and that much of it was being managed improperly. Locations where improper disposal of hazardous waste had caused, or had the potential to cause, severe health problems became widely known. The Love Canal section of Niagara Falls, New York, Times Beach, Missouri, the "Valley of the Drums" in Kentucky, and the Stringfellow Acid Pits in Riverside, California, among many others, became household words as we learned that mismanaged hazardous wastes presented severe threats.

Such disasters shifted regulatory attention from municipal solid waste to industrial hazardous waste. Whereas initial stages of RCRA development focused on municipal solid waste, hazardous waste became the dominant regulatory (and societal) concern following its passage in 1976. Only recently has the federal government again looked to municipal solid waste with the intent of ensuring that a nationwide program is in place for proper management.

REQUIREMENTS FOR MANAGING WASTE

Municipal Solid Waste

RCRA established the framework for a national system of solid waste control. Subtitle D of the act is dedicated to nonhazardous solid waste requirements, and Subtitle C focuses on hazardous solid waste. It is important to remember that solid waste includes solids, liquids, and gases or, as defined in RCRA:

> any garbage, refuse, sludge from a waste treatment plant, water supply treatment plant, or air pollution control facility and other discarded material, including solid, liquid, semi-solid, or contained gaseous material resulting from industrial, commercial, mining and agricultural operations, and from community activities.

Note that it must be "discarded material" to be considered waste. Thus, if cost considerations warrant the purification of an industrial by-product for reintroduction into a process, then that material may not be a waste. The same by-product will be a waste if the recycling economics are less favorable. Some material is specifically excluded from being classified as solid waste, such as domestic sewage sludge, industrial discharges that are point source discharges regulated under the Clean Water Act, and irrigation return flows.

RCRA directs most of the responsibility for active municipal solid waste management to the states and local governments. The federal role is to set nationwide standards and to provide technical and financial assistance. Resource conservation is specified as an important goal of the act, although most attention has focused on waste disposal.

A key condition is that "no reasonable probability of adverse effects on health or the environment" result from solid waste disposal practices. A facility meeting this requirement is called a sanitary landfill, whereas a facility failing to provide this protection is classified as an open dump. In 1984, Congress, through RCRA amendments, required the EPA to revise disposal criteria for sanitary landfills. Existing regulations were found to be inadequate, in part, because hazardous wastes from very small quantity generators and households can be disposed of (legally) as part of the municipal waste stream. Rather than trying to limit further the types of wastes introduced into sanitary landfills, the EPA elected to require additional landfill controls inhibiting off-site migration of waste.

On October 9, 1991, the EPA promulgated its final rule on municipal solid waste landfills (MSWLFs). These regulations increased requirements on landfill construction, operations, monitoring, and closure. However, these restrictions did not duplicate requirements for hazardous waste landfills (specified in Subtitle C of the act), contrary to the expectations of a number of commentators to the proposed rule. Interest in having MSWLFs meet the same criteria as hazardous waste landfills is based on concern that the two types of disposal facilities share a common potential for damage to human health and the environment. For example, a study by the EPA found that leachates from hazardous waste landfills, older landfills constructed prior to current restrictions, and modern landfills did not vary significantly from one another.[8] Accounting for these similarities may be the ability of hazardous waste to enter the municipal waste stream. For example, very small quantity generators and household hazardous waste can legally be sent to modern MSWLFs. Prior to 1980 (the year the EPA's hazardous waste regulations under RCRA became effective), substantial amounts of industrial hazardous wastes were deposited in municipal landfills.

In establishing the new rules, EPA required MSWLFs to meet more stringent requirements than those previously in place but less stringent than those required for hazardous waste landfills. This distinction was based on the EPA's determination that MSWLFs intrinsically represent a lesser threat than hazardous waste landfills and because the language of the statute and congressional record allowed such a distinction. The EPA argued that the congressional intent of distinguishing between levels of protection at hazardous waste landfills and MSWLFs is evident in RCRA language. For hazardous waste landfills, standards shall be those "necessary for protection of human health and the environment." However, for a facility to be classified as a sanitary landfill, it only must show "no reasonable probability of adverse effects on health or the environment." "Reasonable probability" is interpreted as allowing a less severe standard (that may include economic considerations) than is allowed for hazardous waste landfills.

Hazardous and Solid Waste Amendments of 1984 Requirements

Solid waste management continues to be focused on state and local control. States are encouraged to seek primacy over their solid waste programs, with the federal role being largely one of guidance, financial assistance, oversight, and enforcement. The EPA maintains an active management role for those states unwilling or unable to assume responsibility for their own program.

Each state (with an approved program) is required to prepare a solid waste management plan, which must include methods for encouraging resource conservation or recovery. Each state must also implement a permit program for its solid waste management facilities that receive hazardous waste. Thus, sanitary landfills, which accept such waste as household hazardous waste, must have a permit and meet federal design and operational standards. Substantial flexibility is allowed in the federal standards, however, to allow states to develop specific criteria best suited to the local situation.

The philosophy behind landfill design is that the landfills must prevent movement of any of the waste constituents away from the site. Landfills must be lined with plastic or clay (usually both) as a barrier to waste migration. Liquids must be minimized, because if liquids build up inside a facility, they result in a

force (hydraulic head) that pushes dissolved waste products through the barriers. To keep out water from rain and runoff, closed facilities must have surface liners of the same type as used on the bottom and sides. In the resultant oxygen-deficient, dry environment, little degradation of waste occurs. Thus, modern landfill design effectively preserves the waste. Closure plans must ensure that landfills will not fail (allow leakage from the site) for an extended time period. Although a 30-year postclosure care period is specified in the federal rule, either a reduction or an extension is allowed depending on local conditions.

Four tools are available to ensure that the state plan complies with federal guidelines. The simplest is the denial of federal funding or technical assistance to those states that are not in compliance. This power should force the state and federal governments to negotiate in good faith, because it is advantageous to the state to receive assistance, and it is advantageous to the federal government to have the state maintain its own program. The EPA may seek injunctive relief when solid waste disposal presents an imminent threat to health or the environment, although this authority is somewhat limited because Congress wanted municipal solid waste programs to be solved through local efforts.[9] However, the EPA's power to intervene directly is enhanced by its ability to use hazardous waste enforcement authority in states that do not provide a permit program for MSWLFs receiving household hazardous waste or hazardous waste from small quantity generators.[10]

The fourth enforcement tool is the citizens' suit. Any citizen may bring suit against any government agency or individual alleged to be violating any requirements of the law or the state plan. Suits can be brought against the EPA for failure to perform required duties, as well as for violations of specific facility requirements.[11]

Hazardous Waste

Identification. For material to be regulated as a hazardous waste, it must be found to be a solid waste or a combination of solid wastes. RCRA then specifies that solid waste meeting the following criteria will be considered hazardous waste:

(a) causes, or significantly contributes to an increase in mortality or an increase in serious irreversible, or incapacitating reversible illness; or

(b) poses a substantial present or potential hazard to human health or the environment when improperly treated, stored, transported, or disposed of, or otherwise managed.

The definitions of hazardous waste and solid waste clearly reflect the intent of Congress but are too nonspecific to incorporate directly into a regulatory program. The EPA has developed language to provide specific direction in considering when materials need to be regulated as solid and hazardous wastes.

The EPA originally defined solid waste in 1980 as "any garbage, refuse, sludge or any other waste material," except for material qualifying under this definition but specifically excluded from consideration. Difficulty with this definition arose because other waste material was interpreted to mean material that sometimes is discarded, by anyone in a similar industry, after serving its original purpose. This interpretation led to confusion regarding the status of intermediate products that were used for later processes and to difficulty in comparing processes to determine when similar materials were sometimes discarded. The EPA expanded and simplified its solid waste definition in 1985 to include any discarded material not exempted from such classification. Discarded material consists of material disposed of in landfills, injection wells, or other facilities where the waste is placed in land or in water such that there is potential for migration away from the site. It also includes material that is burned or incinerated, as well as many materials that are recycled.

Hazardous wastes are determined in two ways. Solid waste having characteristics of ignitability, corrosivity, reactivity, or toxicity is considered hazardous. (Notice that toxicity is only one of the characteristics for hazardous waste; many people incorrectly use toxic waste synonymously with hazardous waste.) Alternatively, the EPA has listed certain solid wastes as hazardous, so specific characteristics do not have to be measured.

Solid waste must be evaluated for ignitability and corrosivity following specific EPA-designated test procedures. Ignitability is the characteristic of catching fire.[12] The threat from wastes that can easily catch or cause fires is obvious. An example of an ignitable hazardous waste is a solvent degreaser. Corrosivity is the characteristic of corroding metals and other materials.[13] Corrosive wastes can damage waste containers and cause spills. They can also directly damage people; corrosive materials such as waste acids and bases can cause severe tissue burns. Reactive wastes are those that are unstable under normal conditions and can form toxic fumes or explode.[14] It is difficult to describe a specific procedure that adequately tests reactivity. Therefore, the EPA has promulgated a narrative description of reactivity characteristics to assess waste rather than specify testing criteria.

Toxicity is the most difficult characteristic to assess. Almost everything is toxic in great enough concentrations, so the regulatory definition cannot include all potentially toxic wastes. Although we know that in a great enough dose most things are toxic, we usually do not know what the toxic dose is. Therefore, the EPA had to develop a definition useful as an indicator of potential toxicity rather than one that directly relates to all plausible toxic agents.

Waste is evaluated for toxicity by conducting a testing procedure that somewhat simulates conditions found in a landfill.[15] Liquids in a landfill usually are acidic, a condition favorable to the leaching of many heavy metals and other materials from solids. Because liquids are more mobile than solids, the risk of migration of toxics away from landfills is greatly enhanced when the toxics are solubilized. The required test procedure, called the Toxicity Characteristic Leaching Procedure, or TCLP, puts the solid waste in a liquid acidic solution under rigidly defined operating conditions. At the end of the test period, the acid is tested for 32 organic and 8 inorganic chemicals. If concentrations of any of these chemicals exceed specified levels, the waste is considered toxic.

The EPA has three lists of hazardous wastes. The source specific list identifies wastes from specific industrial processes (such as petroleum refining) where operation is known to produce wastes with known hazards. The nonsource specific list contains hazardous wastes commonly found in a variety of sources, such as degreasing solvents. Discarded commercial chemical products are identified in the third list. Certain solid wastes are exempt from being considered hazardous. These exemptions include household waste; agricultural wastes returned to the ground as fertilizer; mining overburden returned to the mine site and other wastes resulting from the extraction and processing of ores and minerals; utility wastes from coal combustion; oil and natural gas exploration drilling waste; cement kiln dust wastes; and arsenic-treated wood wastes generated by end uses.[16]

Cradle to Grave. Passage of RCRA meant that hazardous waste now needed to be tracked and managed from the point of generation (cradle) to its ultimate fate in the environment (grave). The generator is responsible for identifying whether a material is waste and whether the waste is hazardous. The generator must then ensure that the waste is handled appropriately, even after it leaves the generating facility.

Each generator must obtain an identification number from the state agency responsible for the hazardous waste program (or the EPA, if the state does not have primacy for the program). Waste being sent offsite must be listed by the generator on a waste manifest (see Appendix B). The waste is characterized by a numerical coding system developed by the EPA. The manifest also contains information about the waste quantity, and identifies the generator, transporter, and receiving facility. The generator also must certify that efforts have been taken to minimize the waste quantity and associated hazard. On the manifest, the generator must certify by signature the following statement, indicating that efforts have been taken to minimize the waste quantity and associated hazard:

> I have a program in place to reduce the volume and toxicity of waste generated to the degree I have determined to be economically practicable and I have selected the method of treatment, storage or disposal currently available to me which minimizes the present and future threat to human health and the environment.

The hazardous waste transporter carries this manifest with the load and gives it to the waste recipient. The recipient checks the manifest to ensure that the waste can be properly handled at that facility, and frequently physically checks the waste to make sure it is the same as designated on the manifest. A copy of the manifest is returned to the generator, who is supposed to check to make sure it has not been altered. Thus, the generator should know that the waste has arrived in an unaltered state at the intended designation, with any problems reported to the appropriate agency in an "exception report." The generator is required to retain a copy of the manifest for at least three years, although most generators will retain manifests indefinitely.

It is important to remember that while hazardous waste generators have substantial obligations under RCRA, if they do not treat, store, or dispose of waste, they do not have to obtain a permit. Because permit requirements can be severe (see the next section), many facilities eliminate or avoid practices that would turn them into TSDFs. For example, if waste is stored by a generator for more than 90 days, the generator qualifies as a storage facility. Thus, it is to the generator's advantage to make sure that waste is promptly removed from the facility (and to society's advantage to see that hazardous waste does not stockpile at unregulated facilities).

Facilities generating less than 100 kilograms per month are exempted from almost all RCRA requirements. This means that hazardous waste from these sources may legally be deposited in municipal landfills (although municipal landfills are under no obligation to accept such waste). Before 1984, small quantity generators producing less than 1,000 kilograms per month of hazardous waste were also exempt. However, the Hazardous and Solid Waste Amendments of 1984 (HSWA) modified this situation, so that now these generators must meet almost all the same requirements required for larger facilities.

Permits. Hazardous waste treatment, storage, and disposal facilities are required to obtain a permit. Congress recognized a problem when implementing a permit requirement: If all TSDFs submitted their applications at the onset of the program, the EPA would not have the resources to provide timely permit review. Therefore, a system was specified such that TSDFs could operate under an interim permit, as well as a final permit.

All TSDFs in existence on November 19, 1980, that had submitted a Part A application were given an interim permit. The Part A application contains only basic information, including the facility location, estimates of waste quantities, and waste management practices. This information has been unreliable and of limited value. To obtain a final permit, a Part B permit application needs to be approved by the EPA. Part B permit applications require substantially more operational and organizational detail than Part A permits and may run several volumes in length for major facilities. Initially, Part Bs were submitted only after the EPA requested them for individual facilities. This policy was established to maintain submission of permit applications at a rate coincident with the EPA's ability to provide permit review. However, Congress did not agree with this approach, as few final permits were being issued. After the program's 1980 inception, only 24 facilities (of about 8,000) had been issued final permits by July 31, 1983.[17] Twenty of these permits had been issued to storage facilities. From the more significant waste management units, only one landfill and three incinerators had been given permits.

Congress replaced the EPA's program of calling up final permit applications at the EPA's convenience by setting a schedule for permit issuance. Land disposal facilities were required to submit by November 8, 1988, incinerators by November 8, 1989, and other facilities by November 1992.

Facility Standards. Treatment, storage, and disposal facilities are all governed by minimum standards established by the EPA, which may be further refined (but not weakened) by individual states. Specific design, construction, and operating standards have been established for hazardous waste facilities with containers, tanks, surface impoundments, waste piles, land treatment units, landfills, incinerators, thermal treatment units, chemical, physical, and biological treatment units, underground injection wells, and miscellaneous units.[18] These standards are technically complex, so a more complete discussion is inappropriate in this text. It is vital to recognize, however, that if responsible for a TSDF, these standards must be followed precisely.

It is instructive to look at a few of the facility standards as representative of the kinds of restrictions placed on the management of hazardous waste. The landfill standards have had a major effect on management practices; thus, they provide a good place to start.

Before RCRA, the federal system had little impact on disposal practices. Consequently, much hazardous waste was disposed of in landfills that were not designed for long-term containment of the hazardous constituents. Now landfills must be highly engineered units providing redundant barriers to migration of waste. Furthermore, a comprehensive monitoring program is required to ensure that these barriers are effective.

It is important to recognize that hazardous waste "disposed of" through landfilling often does little to reduce the intrinsic hazard associated with the material. Landfilling keeps people and wildlife away from the waste, and keeps the waste from spreading to uncontrolled parts of the environment. Therefore, the landfill itself must be designed as a facility that retains its hazardous characteristics in perpetuity.

Because landfilling is not destroying waste, landfilling can be viewed as the alternative of choice (along with other land disposal techniques) only after determining that opportunities for reuse, recycling, and treatment are not available or practical. In fact, HSWA banned land disposal of hazardous waste for which alternatives are available. The EPA was directed to determine for all hazardous wastes whether land disposal should be prohibited when pretreatment was not used in accord with the best available demonstrated technology. An aggressive timetable was established by which the EPA would promulgate decisions concerning waste suitability and requirements for land disposal. Failure of the EPA to meet this timetable would have resulted in automatic banning of hazardous waste from land disposal. This gave the EPA the necessary incentive to complete this work by the required May 1990 deadline.

Particularly important to note is the ban on liquids in landfills. Liquids have the capability to leach hazardous waste materials from solids, travel through the landfill, and, under pressure if liquids accumulate, migrate through landfill barriers. Thus, even when a particular liquid is not intrinsically hazardous (such as rainwater), its presence in a landfill may greatly increase the chance of hazardous materials' migrating offsite.

As already described, hazardous waste landfill design is more restrictive than solid waste landfill design. However, the basic principles are identical: Make sure that anything put into the landfill does not migrate out of the landfill. Every new hazardous waste landfill (or expansion of an existing landfill) must have a double liner along the sides and bottom. Above and between the liners a leachate collection system is required—a system for collecting all the liquid that seeps down the landfill until it reaches the impermeable liner barrier. Typically, a landfill will in effect have three liners: a thick clay liner underlying the entire site in addition to two plastic membrane liners. A comprehensive groundwater monitoring program also must be maintained, so that if a leak occurs it would be discovered before large scale movement of waste.

An elaborate procedure must be followed to close a hazardous waste landfill or a section of a landfill. A written closure plan is part of the facility application, although it may be modified during the active life of the landfill. Technical requirements include capping the top with another liner to ensure that water does not infiltrate the site. Groundwater monitoring must continue, and the site must remain secure from people or animals inadvertently coming into contact with the waste or damaging the facility. However, perhaps the most important part of the entire closure process is that someone must remain identifiable as being responsible for the facility, with financial resources available to remedy any problems.

The owner or operator of the facility must provide an appropriate instrument guaranteeing long-term financial ability to manage the site, even after it has been closed. This instrument may be a trust fund, surety bond, letter of credit, insurance policy, or financial worth test. This financial guarantee became necessary because a past practice of some unethical operators was to charge for waste disposal services, but then dump waste illegally and inexpensively. The company would go bankrupt before the practice was discovered, so it could not be forced to pay to clean up the mess. In the meantime, the operators had taken the money for waste disposal and cut their ties with the company.

Enforcement of RCRA

HSWA greatly expanded the scope of criminal liability for RCRA violations. The key to criminal liability is that the violator must have committed the act "knowingly"; no such requirement is necessary for civil action. Violators may be charged penalties of up to $50,000, receive up to two years' imprisonment, or both. Furthermore, anyone who knowingly commits an act that "places another person in imminent danger" may be fined up to $250,000 and face up to 15 years' imprisonment.

The EPA may take a variety of civil actions to obtain compliance with RCRA. Civil penalties for Subtitle C violations can be up to $25,000 for each day of violation. The EPA may also seek injunctive relief in court or issue compliance orders directly. Failure to comply with administrative orders may result in a company's losing its hazardous waste permit.

States (or the EPA in states without primacy over the hazardous waste program) are required to inspect all privately operated TSDFs at least once every two years. This requirement was made part of HSWA because of the lack of an effective existing monitoring program; companies could take the gamble to stay out of compliance because there was a good chance that it would not be discovered. With an increased enforcement presence, plus the threat of criminal penalties being assessed to responsible individuals, Congress has made it much less attractive to choose to violate hazardous waste laws and regulations.

RCRA also established a right for individuals to bring a citizens' suit against alleged violators or against the EPA for alleged failure to meet its responsibility. However, citizens' suits are prohibited when dealing with siting and permitting of a TSDF, where the EPA is prosecuting an action, when the EPA or the responsible state is conducting a remedial action, or when the responsible party is conducting the approved remedial action.

Before leaving this discussion on enforcement, consider why an elaborate program for controlling the fate of hazardous waste is needed. Before RCRA, companies frequently disposed of waste using extremely inexpensive techniques (including just throwing it out the back or putting it into dumpsters going to the local landfills). Complying with hazardous waste regulations imposes a substantial financial burden, which may result in a company's product or service becoming economically noncompetitive (or substantially reduce the profit margin). One response to these new burdens is to ignore them. Firms may gamble that illegal practices will not be detected, or, if they are, that the penalties will be less onerous than the compliance costs.

Much of the rationale for imposing criminal sanctions and having a strong enforcement program is to make illegal practices more expensive than compliance. Criminal penalties may be particularly effective, because the expense of a possible jail term might deter a plant manager or owner much more than the threat of a fine. As compliance costs continue to grow, the expense of noncompliance must keep pace in order to keep waste management programs effective. Ultimately, we will measure success by the magnitude of future problems resulting from today's hazardous waste management practices. As we discuss in the next section, remediation once damage is done is frequently quite expensive, with the most practical solution being prevention.

CERCLA: AN OVERVIEW

The key law that brought active federal government involvement to emergency response, site remediation, and spill prevention is the Comprehensive Environmental Response, Compensation and Liability Act of 1980 (CERCLA). (This act is also commonly referred to as Superfund, for reasons discussed later.) It is informative to closely examine the name of this act. Congress intended CERCLA to be comprehensive in its coverage, encompassing both prevention of and response to uncontrolled hazardous substance releases. The act deals with environmental response, providing mechanisms for reacting to emergency situations and to chronic hazardous material releases. In addition to establishing procedures to prevent and remedy problems, it establishes a system for compensating appropriate individuals and assigning appropriate liability.

EMERGENCY RESPONSE PLANS
AND RIGHT TO KNOW

A good place to start discussing hazardous material releases is to examine the requirement to plan for emergencies, including consideration of prevention. The federal program requiring comprehensive community planning was established in the Emergency Planning and Community Right-to-Know Act of 1986 (EPCRA), which was passed as part of the Superfund Amendments and Reauthorization Act of 1986 (SARA). Further complicating the jargon surrounding the program names is the usual reference to EPCRA as SARA Title III, because it is the third part of SARA. Other aspects of SARA are discussed later.

Strangely, the seminal event that started serious thinking about emergency planning did not occur in the United States, but in India. The release of methyl isocynate gas at Bhopal in December 1984 was a tremendous demonstration of the destructive power of chemicals. While we will never be sure of the magnitude of the disaster, the Bhopal directorate of claims reports 3,828 deaths, 18,922 permanent injuries, and 173,382 temporary injuries.[19] Following the event, substantial efforts were made to guard against such a catastrophe happening here. SARA Title III was the federal response.

SARA Title III is organized into three subtitles. Subtitle A covers emergency planning, Subtitle B specifies hazardous chemical reporting requirements, and Subtitle C describes how the public will have access to facility information.

State and local governments are required to develop emergency response and preparedness plans. Every state must have an emergency response commission, and each commission must appoint local emergency response planning committees and designate emergency planning districts. Each committee must include, at minimum, representatives from "elected State and local officials; law enforcement, civil defense, firefighting, first aid, health, local environmental, hospital, and transportation personnel; broadcast and print media; community groups; and owners and operators of facilities subject to the requirements of this subtitle."[20] This requirement makes the local committees fairly large and cumbersome, but it also ensures that affected parties will have representation.

Each local planning committee was required to have prepared by October 17, 1988 its comprehensive emergency response plan. These plans are required to include the following:[21]

1. Identification of facilities that have any substance designated as an extremely hazardous substance in a quantity above the threshold level, as determined and listed by the EPA. Routes used for transporting these substances and sensitive facilities that may be at particular risk from these substances (such as hospitals or natural gas facilities) must also be identified.
2. Plans followed by facility owners and operators, and local emergency response personnel (including medical teams) in response to any hazardous substance release.
3. Identification of a community emergency coordinator, and emergency coordinators for each regulated facility.
4. Procedures for notifying personnel involved in emergency response, and the public, following a release.
5. Methods for determining when a release occurs and the affected area and population.
6. An identification of the emergency equipment, and people responsible for the equipment, available in the community.
7. Evacuation plans.
8. Training programs from local emergency responses and medical personnel.
9. Methods and schedules for testing the plan.

Emergency plans are not limited to these nine items, and a community may choose to include more activities. At minimum, however, these plans are designed to determine what extremely hazardous substances are located in or go through a community, who is responsible for them, what resources are available to deal with spills, how spill information will be communicated so that the correct response is taken, and how the entire system has been integrated so that it will work. Ideally, much of this planning will be preventive in nature. It will be better to have fewer spills occur rather than just being better prepared for those that happen.

Substantial burden is placed on facilities using extremely hazardous substances. The EPA has published a list of extremely hazardous substances with associated threshold planning quantities. Any facility having an amount of any of these substances above the designated quantity must notify the state planning commission and the local planning committee that it is subject to provisions of this law. Note that there is a duplicative effort required of the facility, because there is not (by law or regulation) a uniform reporting system to ensure that a single report will be transmitted to all involved agencies.

Facilities also are required to report to the local committee, the state commission, and the local fire department if they have any chemicals regulated under OSHA's hazard communication standard in quantities of 10,000 pounds or greater. (Note, again, the redundant reporting requirement.) For each reportable chemical, the facility must submit either a material safety data sheet (MSDS) or a list of the reportable chemicals providing the following information:[22]

1. The chemical or common name of each chemical.
2. A list of the hazardous chemicals grouped by hazard category; whether the chemical can be considered an "immediate health hazard," chronic health hazard (including carcinogens), fire hazard, hazard from sudden pressure release (such as explosives and compressed gases), or chemical reactives.
3. Identification of "any hazardous component of each" chemical as identified on the material safety data sheet.

Ordinarily, the chemical list and associated information will be more useful than receiving MSDS for all chemicals. These lists are intended to identify critical information in an organized fashion. MSDS typically provide such an overwhelming amount of detail as to make them extremely difficult to interpret for pertinent emergency planning and response information.

In addition to this initial reporting requirement, facilities must report annually on the quantities and locations of their hazardous chemicals.[23] To meet "Tier I" requirements this information must include:

1. An estimate of the maximum amount of hazardous chemicals in each category (as described above) at any time during the year. These estimates do not have to be made on a chemical-by-chemical basis; amounts must be estimated only by category.
2. An estimate of the average daily amount of chemicals in each category present at the facility during the year.
3. The general location of chemicals in each category.

Local committees, state commissions, or local fire departments can also request Tier II information. Whereas the Tier I data reporting requirements are to identify categories of chemicals and their general locations, Tier II requirements are to identify individual chemicals by names and to report their specific locations and storage conditions. Companies may elect to protect trade secrets by withholding specific names and locations of chemicals from public reporting. Instead, generic descriptors, such as strong inorganic base or acid, may be used. However, community planning agencies must have access to specific names and locations if they request it. (Tier I and Tier II federal reporting forms are shown in Appendix C.)

Another list of chemicals is used as the basis for reporting on the presence of toxic materials. Facilities with chemicals above threshold quantities on the Toxic Chemicals Subject to Section 313 of the Emergency Planning and Community Right-to-Know Act of 1986 list must report to the EPA annually. In addition to information identifying the facility and on chemical use at that facility, the report must document the "annual quantity of the toxic chemical entering each environmental medium." The EPA must collect this information and maintain a national toxic chemical inventory available to the public. This information has sparked interest in many communities about the activities of local industry. As these data are released by the EPA and reported by local media, many companies have been faced with a local population outraged by the vast quantities of toxic chemicals being discharged regularly as part of their normal operating practices.

The public is given access to data collected under these requirements, which typically is done through requests to the local planning committee or the state planning commission. However, the quantity of information may be overwhelming, and there are no requirements regarding providing data in any organized way or in a form immediately compatible with computerization. Thus, the utility of these data to the public is still somewhat problematic.

In reviewing these requirements for submitting information, be sure to reflect on how obtaining data is different from using data. As an analogy, consider the value of a telephone directory as an aid in finding a number if the names were entered randomly. Then consider the value of volumes of unsorted chemical information sitting in boxes if you were a fire fighter responding to an explosion at an industrial plant. Unfortunately, making the link to useful data from collected data remains a difficult problem in many communities.

Consider, also, the difference between requiring effective prevention programs and implementing them. A dramatic example of this distinction is the 1989 Exxon Valdez disaster in Prince William Sound, Alaska. While it is easy to attribute blame of the release of almost 11 million gallons of crude oil solely to a failure to comply with rules governing the operation of a supertanker, the response plan must also be held culpable. A comprehensive plan had been developed and nominally was in operation to minimize the damage from this type of spill. However, neither the response personnel nor the response equipment was ready for a spill of this magnitude, and the oil was able to spread with little hindrance. It is hoped that good emergency prevention planning in communities will prevent most response plans from being tested, but we must remain aware that requiring response capabilities is different from having these capabilities.

FEDERAL RESPONSE TO CONTAMINATED SITES

Before CERCLA, the federal government had little ability to take an active role in responding to a hazardous spill or to a site contaminated with hazardous material. For example, when hazardous material was found at Love Canal, one of the big obstacles to response was the lack of any federal mechanism to intervene. CERCLA provided both the necessary authority and a funding mechanism to respond to this type of situation.

Two types of responses are identified in CERCLA, removal actions and remedial actions. Removal actions are intended to stabilize or clean up a hazardous site that poses an immediate threat to human health or the environment. Remedial actions are intended to provide permanent remedies. Removal actions may not eliminate the need for remedial actions, because chronic problems may be ignored while providing immediate protection.

The universe of chemicals regulated by CERCLA is much broader than that regulated under RCRA. CERCLA includes not only RCRA hazardous wastes but also hazardous substances designated under the Clean Air Act, Clean Water Act, and Toxic Substances Control Act. CERCLA also requires the EPA to maintain an additional list of substances not included in these other acts that present a potential threat to human health and the environment.

The mechanism for the federal government to finance its emergency response and remedial response activities and to recover costs is the Hazardous Substances Response Trust Fund, or Superfund, established in the 1980 legislation. This was a fund of $1.6 billion, of which 87.5 percent was obtained from the petroleum and chemical industries, with the remaining 12.5 percent coming from general federal revenues. The EPA could use these funds to cover its own costs, or the costs involved with work it ordered, in responding to an immediate threat. However, this fund was intended primarily as a rotating fund, with costs incurred in cleanup recovered from potentially responsible parties (PRPs).

Congress increased the Superfund to $8.5 billion as part of the Superfund Amendments and Reauthorization Act of 1986 (SARA). While the petroleum and chemical industries continued to finance the bulk of this fund, $2.75 billion and $1.4 billion, respectively, corporate income taxes also provided $2.5 billion. The remainder of the fund came from general federal revenues ($1.25 billion), interest ($0.3 billion), and recovery of cleanup costs ($0.3 billion). As the fund runs out, if recoveries from PRPs are insufficient, additional funding will have to be authorized. For example, in 1992 the Superfund received an additional 1.75 billion federal dollars.

CERCLA response requirements put an enormous burden on the EPA to develop a structure to deal with many cumbersome problems. Unfortunately, the EPA got off to a slow start, due in large part to questionable or even illegal conduct from its top officials. The contamination and remediation of Times Beach, Missouri, serves as a good example of the problems that plagued the agency. The town had been sprayed with waste oil to suppress dust, but the oil was later found to contain extremely toxic chemicals, PCBs (polychlorinated biphenyls). The EPA took charge of the cleanup, including a $36.7 million buyout of the entire community! Subsequently, the EPA signed a $7.7 million cleanup contract with Chemical Waste Management, even though Chem Waste had been charged the previous month for pollution violations. Further, the company was represented by an attorney who was a former consultant to Anne Burford, the EPA administrator.

These types of scandals led to the firings of several top officials and the resignation of Anne Burford in March 1983. Though Burford was not indicted, the head of the EPA's hazardous waste cleanup program, Rita Lavelle, was indicted on five felony counts. Four of these counts resulted from congressional testimony concerning her obstruction of an EPA investigation of her former employer, Aerojet General Corporation.[24]

Removal Action

If a material is spilled, the EPA can implement a "removal action." These actions are limited to situations where there is an immediate threat to human health or the environment. Each action is limited to 12 months and $2 million (prior to the passage of SARA, limits were 6 months and $1 million), although extensions can be granted. An example of a removal action is collecting leaking drums of explosive material. If the threat is imminent, the EPA can arrange for immediate removal or containment. If the danger is not immediate, actions must be done under authority given for remedial response.

Removal actions are not meant necessarily to provide permanent solutions. This means that the EPA may take actions that provide immediate protection and then leave with substantial hazard remaining. For example, the immediate hazard at a site where carcinogenic hazardous substances were left leaking from drums might be mitigated by fencing the site. Obviously, the local populace wants the site fully remediated. However, once immediate contact is prevented, the threat becomes chronic rather than acute. Because there are so many sites that present chronic risks, the EPA must follow an elaborate procedure to determine which ones to focus on first. This can leave members of the community believing that the government really does not care about their long-term problems. The EPA reported in 1991 that more than 2,300 cleanups have been started and 1,900 cleanups completed since 1980.[25] More than 70 percent of these responses have taken place at sites not currently eligible for remedial actions.

Whereas the EPA manages most of this work, the U.S. Coast Guard has authority for discharges in coastal waters and inland waterways. Hazardous substance spills must be reported to the National Response Center, operated by the Coast Guard, if they exceed "reportable quantities." Reportable quantities are listed by the EPA for many hazardous substances. Unlisted hazardous substances generally have reportable quantities of 100 pounds, except chemicals that meet EPA criteria for toxicity may have a lower limit.[26] Department of Transportation (DOT) regulations call for transporters to report spills if the spill results in hospitalization or death, if damage exceeds $50,000, if pathogens or radioactive materials are involved, if the area is evacuated for more than an hour, or if the operational flight pattern of an aircraft is altered.[27] Following a spill, the EPA and DOT may reduce regulatory obligations on responders. Transporters without an EPA identification number may be allowed to remove hazardous waste and not prepare a waste manifest. Responders may also be exempted from permit requirements for treatment or containment. These allowances are made to allow for the timely control of the released hazardous material.

It is important to recognize that the Emergency Planning and Community Right-to-Know Act of 1986 should significantly reduce the need for direct federal involvement in spill cleanup and hazardous substance removals. Communities should be prepared for spills and able to mobilize quickly appropriate resources. Local involvement should prevent critical situations from emerging. However, it is too early to assess adequately the effectiveness of EPCRA and learn if it will reduce the need for Superfund removal activities. In evaluating the effectiveness of these programs, you may want to consider the incentives that a spiller might have in *not* reporting an incident.

Remedial Response

Before CERCLA, only common law remedies applied to most sites where hazardous substances had been released and presented a threat to human health and the environment. At many sites there were a host of uncertainties regarding the nature of the threat and the potentially responsible parties. No one seemed to be accountable for determining what kinds of materials were present, how effectively materials were contained, the effects of human exposure to the leaking chemicals, or the long-term effects on the environment. A large variety of different kinds of chemicals have been found, and it is quite difficult to evaluate their risk.

CERCLA required the EPA to develop criteria for prioritizing among sites potentially needing remediation. The EPA developed (through the Mitre Corporation) a hazard ranking system by which sites were evaluated on the basis of relative risk to human health and the environment (notice that there was no attempt to quantify the actual risk). This is necessarily a complex task because of the many routes by which harm may occur. See Figure 8–1 for various kinds of harm that may occur. Those sites scoring high enough on this ranking system, now about 1,200, are included on the National Priorities List (NPL). The number could easily rise, because as of 1985 more than 30,000 potentially contaminated sites had been identified by the EPA, and the states have recognized others that have not been reported to the EPA.[28] Only NPL sites are eligible for EPA remedial action. However, the EPA is not obligated to pursue sites on the NPL in any particular order. Thus, EPA site selection can be a very political process as well as a technically demanding one. For example, would it be better to pursue remediation of a site scoring very high on the list for which remediation is quite expensive, or should the EPA expend the same amount of money to clean three sites with somewhat lower scores?

Once a site on the NPL has been selected for remediation, a formal process must be followed to determine and implement appropriate actions. A Remedial Investigation/Feasibility Study (RI/FS) is done first. The conditions at the site must be determined, including the extent of contamination, migration offsite,

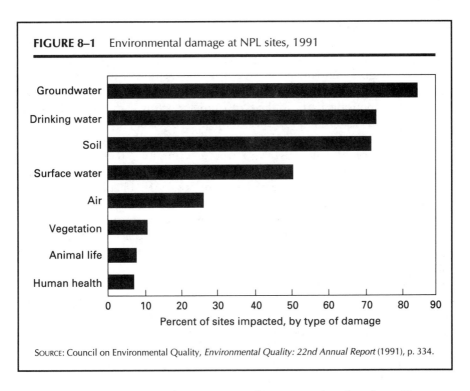

FIGURE 8–1   Environmental damage at NPL sites, 1991

Percent of sites impacted, by type of damage

SOURCE: Council on Environmental Quality, *Environmental Quality: 22nd Annual Report* (1991), p. 334.

and potential for human and environmental exposure. A series of specific remediation alternatives must be developed, including specification of costs, technical feasibility, and environmental impacts. Based on the RI/FS, a Record of
Decision (ROD) is written in which the EPA documents and justifies the selection of a particular cleanup option. This process must include substantial public and state participation. Following the ROD, the detailed engineering plans
are prepared (the Remedial Design), and implementation (Remedial Action)
can begin.

The Superfund can be used to finance remedial response. The intended use of
the fund is to allow activity to begin before potentially responsible parties are
identified. Additionally, if no (financially solvent) potentially responsible party
can be identified, work may be completely financed from the fund. Ultimately,
potentially responsible parties should replenish most of the fund. Between 1980
and 1989, potentially responsible parties agreed to contribute more than $642
million toward cleanups at 441 sites. In 1990, the EPA obtained more than $1
billion in private party contributions to clean up Superfund sites.[29]

Potentially responsible parties may be legally identified as responsible for
waste cleanup even if they had relatively little involvement with the site difficulties. Potentially responsible parties can include present and past owners and

operators of the site, transporters of the substances to the site, and generators who produced the substances. Joint and several liability is assigned, meaning that a responsible party may be assigned all, or any part, of the liability.

Thus, though a company provided only a tiny fraction of the hazardous substances to an NPL site (but perhaps was the most financially solvent of the potentially responsible parties), the EPA would be acting within its authority to assign the total cleanup costs to that company. Of course, that company could then pursue through the courts cost recovery from the other sources of the hazardous substances. Liability is also retroactive, meaning that companies are responsible for their hazardous substances regardless of when they were disposed of (or if they were in compliance with existing laws). Strict liability also applies, meaning that even if a company met all requirements existing at the time of disposal, problems occurring today still put them under the purview of CERCLA.

The definition of potentially responsible party has been very broadly interpreted by the courts to expand the net of those who could be held liable. For example, in *United States* v. *Carolawn Chemical Company*,[30] the district court ruled that a chemical company that had held title to a hazardous waste disposal site for only *one hour* could be held liable as an owner and operator under the act. The court in that case rejected the chemical company's claim that it had not really been an owner but merely a "conduit" in the transfer of title to the site. Other unlikely candidates have also been held responsible as owners. In *United States* v. *Burns*,[31] a district court in New Hampshire found the trustee of a realty trust liable as an owner. And in a widely discussed case, *United States* v. *Fleet Factors Corporation*,[32] the court held that a lender that holds a security interest in a corporation that owns a contaminated site may be liable if that lender is able to "affect hazardous waste disposal decisions" at the site.[33]

Recently, the EPA has provided a mechanism for eliminating liability for owners whose interest in a facility is only financial and does not involve site management.[34] This protection to lending institutions largely applies to "involuntary" acquisitions of property rather than active participation in decisions involving the facility or hazardous material. Thus, a lending institution having no interest in a facility other than holding a mortgage would not be held liable for cleanup.

The EPA can also limit future liability concerns by granting a "covenant not to sue" or by agreeing to a *de minimis* settlement. A potentially responsible party that contributed relatively little of the material causing the hazardous condition of a site may enter into an agreement where it makes a relatively small settlement. As part of this *de minimis* settlement, the EPA may agree that this party will not be responsible for future liability for activities needed beyond those already specified in the ROD. Because the potentially responsible party will not be responsible for future activities, the EPA will agree not to sue the party in the future for cost recovery. These arrangements are intended to allow relatively

quick and complete settlement for companies that had little to do with a site and allow concentration of effort on those parties responsible for the majority of the problem.

Another issue of liability arising under the act is whether an officer of a corporation responsible for dumping waste at a site may be held personally liable. In the 1985 case of *United States* v. *Mottolo*[35] the court held the president of a chemical company personally liable, stating that those persons who actually arranged for or disposed of a hazardous waste under the act did not need to be owners in order to be held responsible. Thus, we can see that the court is attempting to extend liability broadly to ensure that the Superfund will be at least partially replenished.

This assignment of liability may seem totally inequitable at first, because companies with very little involvement in a problem may face substantial financial obligations. However, keep in mind that if a responsible party cannot be found, then the burden falls back on the taxpayer. Probably more important is that these liability burdens provide substantial incentive to the generating facilities to ensure that hazardous substances are properly disposed of. Thus, in addition to regulators' (which are frequently badly understaffed) checking on the performance of treatment, storage, and disposal facilities (TSDFs), companies sending their wastes to these sites have substantial incentive also to make sure that they are properly operating. This brings industry expertise to the task of TSDF inspections.

Earlier discovery of old hazardous waste sites may also result from potential purchasers of property being much more careful to ascertain whether the land they are considering purchasing has been contaminated. Individuals involved with the transfer of waste and even the purchase of property should be much more cautious in their transactions. Additionally, this liability provides industry incentive to minimize waste needing disposal. When a company includes in its economic analysis the potential costs involved in cleaning up someone else's hazardous waste site, that company may look for an alternative to land disposal. If that alternative is waste minimization, recycling, or treatment, the long-term societal risk may be significantly reduced.

Because of the risk of liability, industry has become somewhat hesitant to move to old industrial sites. This hesitancy often conflicts with local and state land use policies, which promote retention of an active industrial zone to prevent economic stagnation or depression. Furthermore, industry locating in traditionally nonindustrial areas often presents other problems, including the elimination of farmland, destruction of wilderness, or conflict with residential land uses. In response, some states are attempting to entice industrial development by reducing liability associated with site redevelopment. For example, in Indiana, legislation recently passed allows the state to enter into agreements with developers that, after appropriate site investigation and remediation, removes the new developer from liabilities for problems subsequently discovered from past site practices. Interestingly, this may be reverting the liability burden back to the taxpayer, in direct opposition to the rationale behind the federal assignment of responsibility.

Furthermore, a recent decision by the third circuit court, *U.S.* v. *Alcan Aluminum Corp.,*[36] may result in an additional mechanism for industry to remove liability from involvement in a hazardous waste site. In this case, the court ruled that Alcan Aluminum must be given an opportunity to demonstrate the portion of harm that it was responsible for rather than having the court indiscriminately impose joint and several liability. If this case serves as a precedent, companies may become less concerned about the status of the disposal sites accepting their wastes, as long as the ultimate fate and impact of their wastes can be clearly identified.

Following passage of CERCLA in 1980, EPA action on remedial cleanup was quite slow. By 1986, only eight sites had been remediated, and the entire Superfund had been spent.[37] This obviously was not the intent of Congress, so it included in SARA a schedule for work to begin at NPL sites. By January 1, 1989, site inspections were required to be completed at all facilities listed on the Comprehensive Environmental Response, Compensation and Liability Information System (a federal system for managing sites identified for possible consideration for hazard ranking, frequently referred to as CERCLIS). By October 17, 1989, at least 275 facilities on the NPL were required to have implemented remedial investigations and feasibility studies. Also by this date, remedial action was required to have begun on 175 NPL facilities, with an additional 200 facilities having remedial action start during the following two years.

CERCLA provided little guidance on how the EPA should determine the level of removal during a site cleanup. This issue of "how clean is clean," was modified in SARA to provide the agency with more direction in determining suitable removal levels during a remedial response. Cleanups must be protective of human health and the environment, be cost-effective, and use permanent solutions, including treatment and resource recovery, as much as practicable. Land disposal is discouraged.

Even within the framework established by SARA, it is difficult to determine appropriate cleanup levels for specific sites. Removal of all of a contaminant is virtually impossible, exceedingly expensive to attempt, and calls for analytical procedures beyond current technical abilities. However, cleaning up to any other level raises issues of dose response; the state of the art linking an amount of a contaminant and the resultant effect is still rather primitive. How much of an effect should be acceptable (a one in a million chance of causing cancer, one in a billion?), and at what cost (how much is a life worth?). EPA's regulations promulgated in 1990 provide detailed guidelines on how to provide more direct guidance, but they may also have resulted in a loss of useful site-specific flexibility.

The EPA may use the Superfund to engage in a cleanup while it is negotiating with potentially responsible parties, and later recover its costs. Alternatively, the EPA may issue an administrative order or go through the courts to force potentially responsible parties to pay directly for site cleanup. Typically, cleanup settlements reflect months or years of negotiations between the EPA and potentially responsible parties to determine appropriate solutions and division of financial responsibility. The EPA encourages potentially responsible parties to decide on their own proper allocation of responsibilities, as long as their settlement covers all costs. Obviously, this is often difficult and the agency must become involved. One big problem in negotiating is that there is great uncertainty about responsibility (what percentage of the problem is due to your company's waste?). Another important complication is that frequently companies that are now insolvent may have contributed significantly. The EPA may use Superfund dollars to cover their portion of the cleanup, although it is not required (or even encouraged) to do so. Obviously, the Superfund will go farther if cleanups can be financed completely from those potentially responsible parties that remain solvent, so the EPA has shown great reluctance to accept a settlement for less than 100 percent of the total cleanup costs.

Citizens' suits permit individuals to sue the government, any company, or individual for alleged violations of SARA.[38] Cases will be heard in the district court in the area where the alleged violation occurred or in the district court for the District of Columbia if the case is against the government. However, to allow time for compliance, no action may begin until at least 60 days after the plaintiff has notified the federal and state governments and the alleged violator of the intent to prosecute. Of great utility to individuals wishing to pursue citizens' suits is that the information gathered about a site becomes part of the public record. As action begins at each NPL site, the remedial investigation/feasibility study and record of decision are published by the EPA. Substantial opportunity and requirement for public involvement is built into this process; the EPA can give grants for up to $50,000 to public groups to hire appropriate people to help them understand the key issues. Obviously, this also makes data available to anyone wishing to pursue litigation.

CERCLA does not remove the owner of contaminated property's common law liability for personal injury or death under applicable principles of toxic tort laws (see Chapter 7). The *Restatement (Second) of Torts* provides the generally accepted standard of liability for hazardous waste releases. The defendant is liable, despite the exercise of due care, if the activity was "abnormally dangerous." The determination of whether an activity is abnormally dangerous is said to require consideration of a number of factors, including the probability and foreseeability of severe harm, whether the activity is unusual, and whether it is inappropriate for the area where it is carried out. Some courts, however, simply say that whenever toxic substances escape from a landowner's property, the landowner will be strictly liable.

In addition to relying on a theory of strict liability, the defendant in a toxic tort case may also use other theories, such as negligence or nuisance. For example, in *Ayers* v. *Township of Jackson*,[39] a judgment of $15,854,392.78 was awarded to 150 plaintiffs who established that the township of Jackson had created a nuisance by operating a landfill in a "palpably unreasonable" manner that allowed varying concentrations of hazardous chemicals, including acetone and benzene, to escape from the landfill and infiltrate plaintiffs' drinking water. This case was particularly interesting because the plaintiffs' damages were not for diseases they had already incurred; rather, their recoveries were for enhanced risk of disease related to toxic exposure and the consequent cost of annual medical surveillance they would now need to detect symptoms of disease at the earliest possible time.

As in the toxic tort cases described in Chapter 7, the plaintiffs injured by releases of toxic substances still face the difficult problem of proving that their harm, especially if it is a disease such as leukemia or cancer, was actually caused by the exposure to the toxic substance. Another problem for plaintiffs in these cases is that their actions may be barred by a statute of limitations. Statutes of limitations are laws that restrict the time frame during which a cause of action can be brought. Time limits vary by type of case. In most states these statutes require that a tort action be filed within two or three years of the time the cause of action arose. The problem in toxic tort cases is determining when the cause of action arises. In New York State, a trial court judge in 1983 dismissed the personal injury cases of 54 out of 91 residents of Love Canal. He ruled that their actions were barred by the statute of limitations because more than three years had passed since their exposure to the toxic chemicals. Judges in most states have made the statute of limitations less of a problem, however, by holding that the cause of action does not arise until all of the necessary elements to prove a cause of action are in existence; obviously the necessary action would include the development of the injury to the plaintiff.

UNDERGROUND STORAGE TANK PROGRAM

A program related to emergency planning, although of different regulatory origin, is the underground storage tank (UST) program. The Hazard and Solid Waste Amendments of 1984 (HSWA) provided the framework for a regulatory program designed to help prevent releases from tanks. It is interesting to note that while this program is within the hazardous waste regulatory statute, it deals with "regulated substances." These substances are those defined in CERCLA, petroleum products (including crude oil), and exempt hazardous wastes (which must be stored following RCRA standards). Thus, the UST program has a similar philosophy to the SARA Title III philosophy of spill *prevention* rather than the RCRA philosophy of hazardous waste *management*.

Most of the underground tanks in the United States store gasoline. However, other flammable industrial chemicals (such as degreasing solvents) are also stored underground, to minimize fire hazards. Various estimates put the number of regulated tanks at 1.5 to 2 million, with between 10 and 30 percent of them leaking. Materials leaking from tanks generally will migrate down to groundwater and can cause significant contamination. Such leaks are not obvious because the tanks are not visible and because contamination effects may not become apparent for many years.

Underground storage tank leaks can contaminate important groundwater supplies and cost millions of dollars to remediate (even partially). One area that has experienced major problems is Silicon Valley in Santa Clara County, California, a hub of the semiconductor industry. In the 18-month period beginning in April 1980, IBM, Hewlett Packard, Intel, Advanced Micro Devices, and Fairchild all reported tanks leaking organic solvents. These solvents moved to drinking-water wells; one well near Fairchild had one organic solvent, 1-1-1-trichloroethane (TCA), at concentrations 29 times the state action level.[40] Cleanup of the groundwater in Silicon Valley will cost millions of dollars, and may never be successfully completed (or accomplished to everyone's satisfaction). Obviously, the best remedy to this problem would have been prevention.

The federal regulatory program works by establishing tank and leak detection standards. New tanks must have spill and overflow protection devices. The tanks must meet performance standards designed to ensure that the stored material will not corrode the tanks. Because responsibility for these programs is being taken over by the states, actual requirements may be more stringent than these federal minimums. Existing tanks have until December 1998 to meet the new tank standards. This can be accomplished by installing a liner or cathodic protection against corrosion. Spill and overflow protection and a leak detection system must be installed. Specific technical guidance regarding acceptable methods to provide this protection have been developed by the EPA. Tanks that store hazardous substances (rather than petroleum products) must have extra protection against hazardous substance release. This may be accomplished through a secondary containment system, a double-walled tank, or an external liner.[41] These devices are intended to keep any release of the inner tank contained as the leak detection system signals that the inner tank has lost its integrity.

A significant burden is placed on the owner/operator of a tank to ensure that adequate financial resources are available to respond to a leak. Financial responsibility can be demonstrated through insurance, a letter of credit, a trust fund, a surety bond, or a state-managed financial assurance device in a state with an approved program. Large facilities, handling more than 10,000 gallons of petroleum per month, must have at least $1 million of coverage per occurrence. All other facilities must have $500,000 coverage per occurrence.

The UST program is still in its infancy. As you drive around your community and see gasoline stations pulling their tanks, realize that this is being done all over the country in response to this law. Companies are struggling to comply, because of the expense and disruption to operations. Tank removal may cost more than $10,000, and complete replacement should cost at least $30,000. Yet, while these costs are high, the costs of remediation following a tank leak may be orders of magnitude higher. Thus, there has been relatively little discussion of the reasonableness of having a UST program, although substantial discussion has focused on specific program provisions and approaches.

CONCLUDING REMARKS

Waste management practices in the United States have changed remarkably over the last two decades. A complex, comprehensive system now governs the fate of waste, with incentives to reduce generation and recycle rather than "dispose" through permanent storage on land or in water. Nevertheless, much of the waste stream continues to be landfilled. Though modern landfills should be effective in containing wastes, even several layers of plastic and clay liners will not last forever. Thus, modern technology may be only deferring liability problems into the future. Clearly, waste management has changed from a minor concern to a major societal issue.

Although progress has been made in providing protection from releases of hazardous materials, it is also easy to open almost any newspaper and read an account of a failure. In addition to the CERCLA and UST provisions, efforts to reduce hazardous waste generation and properly manage waste following RCRA provisions are also important in minimizing risk from hazardous materials. CERCLA followed RCRA because initial concerns focused more on hazardous waste than hazardous materials, perhaps due to a misconception that wastes intrinsically presented more of a hazard than materials. Even after the incident at Bhopal and numerous spills, much of the public probably still views hazardous waste as presenting the larger threat. The regulatory community, however, now clearly recognizes the need to protect the public and the environment from all agents that have a substantial potential to cause harm.

QUESTIONS FOR REVIEW AND DISCUSSION

1. What is the best solution to the growing problem of waste production?
2. Why should we worry about insufficient landfill capacity? Will market forces drive the completion of new landfills?
3. Why would laws exclude hazardous wastes from households and small quantity generators from regulation?
4. Why would a state want to have primacy over its hazardous waste program?
5. Why is CERCLA commonly referred to as Superfund? Is this appropriate?
6. What groups must be represented in emergency planning? Are there other groups that should be represented?
7. What is the difference between a removal action and a remedial action?
8. Does CERCLA protect owners of contaminated property from prosecution under tort law?

FOR FURTHER READING

Arbuckle, J. G., et al. *Environmental Law Handbook,* 11th ed. Rockville, Md.: Government Institutes, 1991.

Cohen, Mark A. "Environmental Crime and Punishment: Legal/Economic Theory and Empirical Evidence on Enforcement of Federal Environmental Statutes." *Journal of Criminal Law and Criminology* 82 (1992): 1054–108.

Hall, Ridgway M., Jr., T. Watson, J. J. Davidson, D. R. Case, and N. S. Bryson. *RCRA Hazardous Wastes Handbook,* 7th ed. Rockville, Md.: Government Institutes, 1987.

Harris, Christopher, William L. Want, and Morris A. Ward. *Hazardous Waste—Confronting the Challenge.* New York: Environmental Law Institute/Quorom Books, 1987.

EPA Office of Solid Waste and Energy Response. *The Solid Waste Dilemma: An Agenda for Action.* EPA/530-SW-89-072. 1989.

Peck, L. "Protection Mechanisms for Lenders Against Hazardous Waste Liability." *Hofstra Law Review* 18 (1989): 89.

Rebovich, Donald L. *Dangerous Ground: The World of Hazardous Waste Crime.* New Brunswick, N.J.: Transaction Books, 1992.

Robinson, W. D., ed. *The Solid Waste Handbook: A Practical Guide.* New York: Wiley, 1986.

Rodgers, W. A. "A Superfund Trivia Test: A Comment on the Complexity of the Environmental Laws." *Environmental Law Journal* 22 (1992): 417.

NOTES

1. Louis Blumberg and Robert Gottlieb, *War On Waste: Can America Win Its Battle with Garbage?* (Washington, D.C.: Island Press, 1989).
2. Ibid.
3. EPA, *Characterization of Municipal Solid Waste in the United States: 1960–2000.* EPA PB 87-178323 (1986).
4. Subcommittee on Transportation and Commerce, Committee on Interstate and Foreign Commerce, U.S. House of Representatives. Materials relating to the Resource Conservation and Recovery Act of 1976, 94th Congress, second session (Comm. Print 20); Waste Control Act of 1975; Hearings on H.R. 5487 and H.R. 406, before Subcommittee on Transportation and Commerce, 94th Congress, first session, 1975.
5. EPA, Office of Solid Waste, Reports to Congress, *Solid Waste Disposal in the United States.* EPA/530-SW-88-011B (1988).
6. EPA, Office of Solid Waste, *Survey of Solid Waste (Municipal) Landfill Facilities* (August 1986).
7. William D. Robinson, ed., *The Solid Waste Handbook: A Practical Guide* (New York: Wiley, 1986).
8. EPA, Office of Solid Waste, *Summary of Data on Municipal Solid Waste Landfill Leachate Characteristics—Criteria for Municipal Solid Waste Landfills* (40 CFR part 258), Subtitle D of the Resource Conservation and Recovery Act (RCRA). EPA/530-SW-88-038, PB88-242-441 (1988).
9. 42 U.S.C. 6073.
10. Pub. L. 898-616, Sec. 302.

11. 42 U.S.C. Sec. 6972.
12. 40 CFR 261.22.
13. 40 CFR 261.22.
14. 40 CFR 261.23.
15. 40 CFR 261.24.
16. 40 CFR 261.4(b).
17. Government Accounting Office, *Interim Report On Inspection, Enforcement, And Permitting Activities At Hazardous Waste Facilities* (September 1983).
18. 40 CFR 264, Subparts J–X, 265, Subparts J–R.
19. W. Lepkowski, "Union Carbide—Bhopal Saga Continues as Criminal Proceedings Begin in India," *Chemical and Engineering News* 70 (1992): 7–14.
20. EPCRA, Sec. 301.
21. EPCRA, Sec. 303.
22. EPCRA, Sec. 311.
23. EPCRA, Sec. 312.
24. Donald Rebovich, *Dangerous Ground: The World of Hazardous Waste Crime* (New Brunswick, N.J.: Transaction Books, 1992), pp. 1–9.
25. EPA, *The Superfund Program: Ten Years of Progress,* EPA/540/8-9/003 (1991).
26. 40 CFR 302.4.
27. 40 CFR 171.5.
28. EPA, *Environmental Progress and Challenge: EPA Update* (1989).
29. EPA, *Environmental Stewardship: EPA's First Two Years in the Bush Administration* (Washington, D.C.: EPA Office of Communications and Public Affairs, 1991).
30. 21 Env't. Rep. Cases 2124 (D.S.C. 1984).
31. No. C-88-94-L (D.N.H. 1988).
32. 901 F2a 155 (11th Cir. 1990), *cert. denied,* 111 S.C5.752 (1991).
33. Ibid., 1557.
34. 40 CFR Part 300.
35. 605 F. Supp. 898 (D.N.H. 1985).
36. 964 F2d 252.
37. Sidney M. Wolf, *Pollution Law Handbook—A Guide to Federal Environmental Laws* (New York: Quorum Books, 1988).
38. SARA, Sec. 310.
39. 106 NJ. 557, 525 A2d 287 (1987).
40. J. M. Logsdon, "Collaboration to Regulate L.U.S.T.: Leaking Underground Storage Tanks in Silicon Valley," *Journal of Business Research* 23 (1991): 99–111.
41. 40 CFR Sec. 280.42 9(a).

9

Energy and Natural Resources

No nation seems more endowed with natural resources than the United States—abundant water, fertile soil, a benign climate, an incredible variety of plant and animal species, and stores of energy resources, including natural gas, coal, oil, and uranium. Yet these resources are not unlimited. Without careful management, many will become depleted or destroyed. This chapter focuses on how we protect these important natural resources, with special emphasis on energy.

We begin by examining energy law and policy, the area of law attempting to manage energy needs. This area is very complex because we must consider not only issues of resource depletion, but also the effects of alternative forms of energy on the environment. Next we examine U.S. policies with respect to preservation of land, protection of coastal areas and wetlands, and the protection of plant and animal species.

ENERGY POLICY: A HISTORICAL OVERVIEW

The U.S. energy policy has been anything but consistent. We seem to bounce back and forth from complacency to crisis to complacency, at least with respect to aspects of energy policy designed to ensure that the nation's demand for energy can be met. Many fear that this cycle may be continuing and we are heading for the next energy crisis.

As you examine energy policy, you should be aware of the major conflict in philosophies that underlies our shifting policies. On the one hand, the belief in unlimited resources or unlimited technological developments tends to encourage the full development of energy resources. On the other hand, the view that energy is a limited resource favors policies that encourage conservation and demand reduction.

Prior to the 1970s, energy policy received little consideration. Although the possibilities of nuclear energy had begun to be explored, we were still complacently relying on what seemed to be an unlimited access to worldwide stores of fossil fuels: coal, petroleum, and natural gas. In fact, in 1900, coal provided 90 percent of the energy in the United States. By 1970, petroleum and natural gas each provided about 35 percent. Coal still remained a significant source, however, providing about 23 percent of our energy.

The Crisis Begins

Not until 1973 did the phrase *energy crisis* enter the American vocabulary. The "crisis," which would last until 1978, began in October 1973, when the United States was importing 38.8 percent of its daily petroleum consumption. The Organization of Petroleum Exporting Countries (OPEC) voted to cut its oil production by 5 percent monthly until Israel made fundamental changes in its Arab policies. The day after that vote, Saudi Arabia, OPEC's major producer, cut its oil exports by 10 percent and ended all petroleum shipments to the United States until the Nixon administration altered its pro-Israel policies. The loss of 2 million barrels of oil a day shocked Americans into suddenly recognizing how dependent they had become on foreign oil and also what political, economic, and military risks this dependence entailed. From an environmental standpoint, the situation was a crisis because if the oil shortage continued for long, the United States might be compelled to increase greatly its mining of coal, with potentially disastrous ecological consequences.[1]

In response to the OPEC oil embargo, Nixon took the first steps in U.S. history toward comprehensive national energy planning. He established the Federal Energy Office (FEA) within the White House staff in late 1973. The next year he established the Federal Energy Administration, which was given authority to initiate federal policy and take whatever steps the White House deemed necessary for national energy needs. Congress, likewise, contributed to a developing national energy policy by creating the Energy Research and Development Administration (ERDA) to consolidate all federal energy research in a single agency.

Until his forced resignation in 1974, Nixon continued to urge legislation designed to increase the federal role in energy management. He proposed laws restricting public and private energy consumption, providing unemployment insurance for those who lost jobs due to the energy crisis, temporarily relaxing air pollution standards for automobile emissions and power plants, and imposing a windfall profits tax to keep companies from making excess profits by rapidly increasing energy prices. He used powers granted to him by Congress to impose mandatory allocations of selected fossil fuels, as well as to set up an allocation program and price guidelines for crude oil and petroleum.

By the end of Nixon's term, he and Congress had also required national day-light savings time and the 55-mile-per-hour speed limit as conservation efforts. They had funded new federal programs for research into solar energy and had encouraged private development of nuclear energy. Nixon had also invented Project Independence, a hastily crafted program designed to ensure that by the end of the decade the United States would be able to meet all of its own energy needs. Many of the proposals were technologically infeasible, and some were contradictory.

The energy crisis continued through the Ford administration, with Ford submitting a package of measures in his 1975 Energy Policy and Conservation Act, focusing on programs designed to give flexibility to the administration in handling energy problems. Carter came into office making energy policy his number one priority. A month after taking office, he set forth his National Energy Plan (NEP), organized around four broad objectives: (1) to centralize federal energy planning through institutional reform; (2) to achieve greater energy efficiency through selective use of market forces and a major expansion of federal regulatory policy; (3) to increase rapidly federal spending on research and development of new technology for energy conservation and productivity; and (4) to ensure that environmental protection and social equity would be important in these new programs.[2] More than 200 separate proposals were considered by Congress in relation to NEP. Many were defeated, and the program was perceived by many as hastily constructed and too complex. But by the end of his term, Carter had made some significant changes in federal energy policy: The Department of Energy (DOE) had been created; domestic gas and petroleum prices had been decontrolled; increased government funding had been provided for federal research and development for new energy technologies; and more environmental safeguards on energy use had been established.

A Return to Complacency

Reagan's victory signaled the end of the energy crisis, at least as perceived by the executive and the general public. In his first National Energy Plan, Reagan informed the public that the forecast for energy supplies was not as bad as some had thought; there were going to be no more "wars on energy." And Reagan's program of regulatory relief was going to be applied to energy policies as well as to other regulatory actions. Within a few years, energy policy had been dramatically altered. There was a return to the pre-embargo days of abundant energy. This new philosophy continued through the Bush administration.

Reagan tried to abolish the DOE, but Congress would not go along and he had to be content with reducing the agency's authority. He slashed the budget of the Office of Strip Mining, weakening its ability to enforce regulations. His secretary of state attempted to lease more public land on the outer continental shelf and in federal wildlands for energy exploration than had been leased in the entire period prior to Nixon's election. Funding for energy conservation programs and research for renewable sources of energy like solar and wind power was slashed.

By mid-1985, energy no longer appeared in public opinion polls as a major concern. Conservation of energy was no longer a concern by the late 1980s; in 1989, Ford Motor Company brought back the V-8 engine in its Mustang, an act representative of the return of the gas-guzzling "muscle cars." By 1990, Americans were no longer interested in energy-efficient houses; many developers had quit building them because of lack of demand. In 1986, residential energy demand had exceeded industrial demand for the first time ever. By the end of Reagan's term, funding for research and development of renewable energy sources had fallen to 18 percent of 1980 levels, and federal tax credits for the use of these alternative energy sources had expired.

What Now?

Today, the energy situation in the United States is similar in many ways to what it was at the time of the 1973 embargo. We seem to have not learned anything about the need for a coherent energy policy. Currently the United States is importing 46 percent of its daily petroleum consumption, an increase over the 38.8 percent that was imported in 1973. Domestic oil production is decreasing; in 1989, U.S. production was at its lowest level since 1963 and was not expected to increase significantly, if at all. Only about 1 percent of U.S. electrical power comes from renewable sources. Many states have increased the 55-mile-per-hour speed limit, and our per capita energy consumption continues to increase.

There were some indications that the 1990s might see a renewed interest in a national energy policy. The 1990 invasion of Kuwait, which made Americans again aware of the danger of dependence on foreign oil, may have served as a partial stimulus. Nonetheless, in February 1991 Bush introduced his National Energy Strategy (NES), an attempt to achieve roughly equal measures of new energy production and conservation. Summaries of the various initiatives under the NES are given in Table 9–1.

In April 1991, Bush issued an Executive Order on Federal Energy Management.[3] If fully implemented, the order is projected to save taxpayers up to $8 million in annual energy costs and cut federal energy consumption by the equivalent of up to 100,000 barrels of oil per day.[4] The three primary elements of the order are the following:

1. Energy use in federal building must be reduced to 25 percent below 1985 levels by 1995.
2. Gasoline and diesel use in government fleets of 300 or more must be reduced to 10 percent below 1991 levels by 1995.

TABLE 9-1   National energy strategy

In February 1991, President George Bush issued a National Energy Strategy (NES) to lay the foundation for a more efficient, less vulnerable, and environmentally sustainable energy future. In barrel-of-oil equivalents, NES initiatives will provide roughly equal measures of new energy supplies and increased conservation. With maximum reliance on markets as a keystone of the strategy, NES initiatives address five interlocking areas:

- *Energy security.* When fully implemented, NES will make the nation less prone to economic damage from sharp fluctuations in either the supply or the price of petroleum.
- *Energy and economic efficiency.* NES initiatives aim to lower energy costs to consumers, reduce energy-related emissions, maintain or enhance standards of living, and promote a strong economy.
- *Energy supplies.* To secure future energy supplies, NES will develop and use renewable energy sources; increase reliance on low-emission energy sources such as natural gas; develop a new generation of safer nuclear technology; and continue development of domestic coal and oil supplies in an environmentally responsible manner.
- *Environmental quality.* Initiatives will increase the efficiency of energy-producing and consuming technologies, reduce solid and hazardous wastes, and improve energy-related practices.
- *Technology and competitiveness.* NES initiatives fortify the nation's foundations in science and engineering research, technology development, and education; establish federal research and development priorities; strengthen research in universities, industries, and international collaboratives; accelerate technology transfer from federal laboratories to private industry; and enhance U.S. mathematics, science technology, and engineering education.

The strategy complements such developments as the 1990 Clean Air Act amendments, natural gas price decontrol in 1989, incentives provided to domestic energy producers in the fiscal 1991 budget agreement, international cooperation forged during the recent Persian Gulf crisis, and the secretary of energy's science and mathematics education initiatives.

SOURCE: Council on Environmental Quality, *Twenty-second Annual Report* (1992), p. 75.

3. All federal agencies must secure the largest practicable number of alternative-fuel vehicles by the end of 1995.[5]

With a new administration in 1993 and a growing awareness of some of the problems associated with fossil fuels, it is possible that the United States may attempt to develop a comprehensive energy plan that incorporates the often conflicting objectives of providing sufficient inexpensive energy to satisfy demands, lessening energy dependency on foreign nations, and not causing further environmental degradation.

In the next sections, we look at where this energy goes. Then we examine the types of energy we have to choose from, along with the problems of each and the temporary solutions arrived at. Though it may seem strange to examine each type of energy independently when we need a strategy combining all of them, you will see that as a nation we have indeed chosen to treat each independently—and perhaps that is part of our inability to establish a coherent energy policy.

ENERGY CONSUMPTION

One of the reasons that lack of a coherent, long-term energy policy is problematic is that as a nation, we have extremely high energy demands,
consuming about one-fourth of the world's energy production. Consumption of
energy is consistent with our high standard of living, large land mass, low population density, and historically abundant low energy, relatively inexpensive
energy resources. The great demand for energy can be understood a little better
if we examine the four economic activities that place the greatest demands on
our energy resources: residential, commercial, industrial, and transportation.

Because of the large number of single-family dwellings, the relative spacious-
ness of these dwellings, relatively small average family size, a desire for heating
and cooling systems to maintain uniform indoor temperatures year-round, and
a wide range of labor saving devices, U.S. energy use per dwelling is among the
highest in the world. More than half of that use is for heat and hot water;
approximately 20 percent is used to run major appliances.

Commercial energy use is primarily for heating and cooling commercial buildings. More than one-third of the nation's energy demands comes from industry.
Seventy percent of that demand can be traced to the nine most energy-intensive
industries, including steel, paper, and chemicals. Finally, transportation of goods
and people accounts for more than one-fourth of energy consumption. Most of
this energy comes from the petroleum used to power automobiles, planes, trains,
ships, and trucks.

From 1949 to 1973, demand for energy in the United States more than dou-
bled. However, from 1973 to 1991, consumption increased by only 10 percent.
Still, in 1991, the DOE projected that by the year 2010 the United States will
need a significantly greater electrical power generating capacity, perhaps requiring 175 to 325 new medium-sized power plants.

In the following sections, we look at the alternative ways to satisfy our vora-
cious demand for energy.

COAL: THE OLDEST ENERGY SOURCE

Coal is this nation's most plentiful fossil fuel, constituting approximately 90 percent of U.S. hydrocarbon reserves. At one time providing more
than 80 percent of our energy needs, today coal supplies about 25 percent. At
present rates of consumption, we have sufficient reserves to last approximately
250 years. Coal is extremely important because it is used to generate more than
half the nation's electrical power, and the percentage of electricity generated by
coal seems to be increasing. Most of the coal reserves are located in three regions
of the country: the seven-state Appalachian region, the midwestern plains, and
the western plains and grasslands. Roughly half the coal reserves are in the west,

and approximately 60 percent of those are on public lands. Most of the coal on these western reserves is low in sulfur content; most of the coal in the eastern reserves is privately owned and has a high sulfur content.

Because coal is so plentiful and its use would therefore reduce U.S. dependence on foreign oil, and because an increase in coal production could increase employment, every president since Nixon has, in some way, sought to increase our reliance on coal. Congress has also jumped on the bandwagon for greater use of coal.

Under the 1978 National Energy Act, five statutes were passed by Congress that were designed to increase dependence on coal. The most significant of these was the Powerplant and Industrial Fuel Use Act (PIFUA).[6] This act required certain electrical power generating plants and major fuel-burning installations to switch from oil or gas to coal. The DOE was authorized to require facilities, both individually and by category, to convert to coal or other alternative fuels when two conditions were met: (1) the conversion was financially feasible and (2) the facilities had the technical capability to be converted without substantial physical modifications or reductions in capacity. Individual plants in categories subject to conversion were to be granted permanent exemptions if the plant would have difficulty, due to its location, in getting access to alternate fuels. Also, conversion would not be required if it would cause a violation of any state or federal environmental regulations. The EPA was charged with making sure that no proposed conversions would result in NAAQS violations.

Problems with Coal

Given the plentiful nature of coal and its positive impact on employment, one may wonder why the United States does not more wholeheartedly endorse a policy that emphasizes the use of coal. The reason is that a number of environmental problems are associated with the use of coal, especially the high-sulfur coal of the eastern reserves. Recall the discussion of acid rain in Chapter 6, and that one of the major factors in acid rain is sulfur dioxide emissions. Increased use of coal, especially high-sulfur coal may increase acid deposition.

One of the biggest problems associated with the use of coal is that coal mining can have disastrous environmental effects, especially strip or surface mining. Roughly 44 percent of the western coal and 18 percent of the eastern coal reserves are accessible by strip mining. There are three basic types of surface mining: contour mining, area mining, and open pit mining.

Contour mining is the main type of mining used in Appalachia. The miner excavates a portion of the hillside where the coal seam intersects the surface. Then the soil that covers the seam is stripped off, following the seam along the contour as far into the mountain as possible. The excess dirt unearthed to reveal the coal is thrown downhill from where the coal is removed. In flat or rolling terrain, area mining is used. The earth is stripped off the coal and piled up to one side in a ridge along the area from which the coal has been removed. Open pit mining is similar to area mining except that the area from which the coal has been stripped is much deeper than the thickness of the land that was stripped off, so the stripped-off land, called the overburden, is not thick enough to replace the coal that was removed; consequently, a deep depression is left.

If unregulated, the results of strip mining are acres of barren, sterile land. Unregulated strip mining may cause soil erosion, pollution of streams from mining runoff, destruction of the land for agricultural purposes, destruction of ecosystems, and loss of habitat for numerous species. By some estimates, more than 1.5 million acres in more than 30 states have been disturbed by strip mining, and more than a million of these acres remain abandoned wasteland, no longer claimed by those who took the coal and no longer productive.[7] More than 1,000 more acres are being ravaged each week by further mining.

Given these disastrous environmental consequences, why has strip mining remained such a viable activity? The answer lies to a large extent in the fact that surface mining is much cheaper, less labor intensive, more efficient, more profitable, and safer than underground mining.

Regulation of the Mining Industry

In an attempt to contain some of the disastrous consequences of strip mining, Congress passed the Surface Mining Control and Reclamation Act of 1977 (SMCRA). Vetoed twice by President Ford and strongly opposed by the mining industry, the act was finally signed into law by President Carter. The primary objective of the act, as indicated by its name, was to force the mining industry to return the land from which it stripped the coal to a level of productivity equal or superior to its condition prior to mining.

The act contains very strong provisions that were extremely pleasing to environmentalists; but the implementation of the act, from an environmentalist perspective, has been a disaster. Under the act, a number of environmental protection performance standards were established, regulating a broad range of activities including the removal, storage, and redistribution of topsoil; citing and erosion control; and drainage and protection of water. These standards were to be implemented in two stages: an interim and a permanent phase.

The interim standards were published in 1977 and require mine operators to meet standards that include restoring the land to its prior or a superior condition, returning the land to its original contour, segregating and preserving topsoil, minimizing disturbance of the hydrologic balance in the mined area, and revegetation. Permanent regulations for all performance standards were published in 1979. These have not yet been adopted by all states because of a provision providing that the final regulations will be enforceable when the state adopts a permanent program. This program may contain equal or more stringent provisions than the federal regulations provide. Special, more stringent performance and reclamation standards were to be established under the act for mining on alluvial valley floors in arid and semiarid regions, on prime farmland, and on steep slopes. Mining was to be prohibited on land deemed unsuitable for mining.

A new executive agency, the Office of Surface Mining Reclamation and Enforcement (OSM), was created within the Department of the Interior to enforce the act. To ensure that this agency was not captured by the mining industry, the OSM could, by statute, employ only individuals from other agencies who had no association with any authority, program, or function intended to promote the use or development of coal. The primary means of enforcing the SMCRA is through a permit system that can be administered by the states if they adopt programs for enforcing the act that are at least as stringent as the federal program. By the mid-1980s, 25 of the 27 states with regulated mining under the act had adopted their own programs.

As noted, despite the fact that the SMCRA reads like a strong piece of environmental regulation, its effectiveness is highly questionable. The act has been fraught with problems from the beginning. Under the Carter administration, many strong regulations were drafted, a number of which were strongly opposed by the mining industry. One of the industry's most common arguments was that the OSM exceeded its authority to establish performance standards for mine sites when it set standards for both the types of controls to be used and the standard of performance to be met. It also argued that standards were too rigid and did not allow for enough local flexibility.

Industry's complaints were heeded shortly after the Reagan administration came to power. Under the auspices of Interior Department Secretary James Watt, approximately 90 percent of the regulations promulgated under the Carter administration were rewritten. The OSM also underwent massive downsizing, making serious enforcement of the law almost impossible. Seventeen of the 37 field offices were closed. The five regional offices that had received much criticism for their "tough" enforcement from coal companies were replaced by two technical service centers. The agency's penalty assessment office was eliminated, as were several hundred regional and field staff positions. The number of full-time federal mine inspectors was cut in half.[8] The OSM also suffered from instability at the top; in its first eight years it had six acting directors.

The OSM's record of enforcement, especially under the Reagan administration, has been abysmal and has subjected the agency to congressional investigations and litigation by environmental groups. In 1983 and 1984, congressional hearings revealed that state enforcement was inadequate in several states in light of evidence that mining activities were causing severe environmental deterioration. There was, obviously, a strong incentive for states *not* to strictly enforce the regulations. Compliance was costly, so mining companies in those states with loose enforcement would be at a competitive advantage.

In 1984, in response to a lawsuit brought by a number of environmental groups, the Department of the Interior agreed to establish a computerized system to monitor mine operators that violated the act and prevent them from obtaining permits in the future. The settlement also allowed plaintiffs to monitor the Interior Department's enforcement actions. This settlement took place at a time when there were about 1,700 cease and desist orders against violators that had never been enforced.[9] In 1985, a House Government Operations subcommittee cited the OSM for failing to collect more than $150 million in fines for violation of the SMCRA.[10] What is incredible about the OSM's inaction is that approximately $72 million of the fines were fully processed, undisputed, and unappealable.[11] In 1986, the Government Accounting Office (GAO) reported that its study of program enforcement in four states demonstrated that enforcement was weak. State officials did not even accept evidence of violations observed by federal inspectors during oversight inspections, when this evidence could have been used to cite mine operators that were violating the act.[12] A GAO study of three additional states one year later was equally critical. One state collected fines on only one-tenth of the violations it discovered and another on less than one-third.

Clearly, the SMCRA is not the success for which its advocates had hoped. There is some evidence that the act has helped maintain environmentally safe conditions in some states, such as Montana, Pennsylvania, and Wyoming,[13] but in states like West Virginia and Kentucky minimal enforcement means minimal impact.[14] Some people, however, question whether the act's overall objective can actually be accomplished, even with the most vigorous enforcement program. Some scientists believe that the disruption of subsurface hydrology and the drainage of acids and salts that occurs during mining may cause irreparable damages.[15]

In light of all the controversy over the potential environmental destruction resulting from strip mining, it is no wonder that another problem with the use of coal is over the extent to which the federal government should lease exploration and mining rights to coal companies. Remember that over half the coal reserves in the western states are on public lands.

Under the Mineral Leasing Act of 1920, the secretary of the Interior may lease federal lands to private companies for oil, gas, and mineral exploration and production. Until the 1960s, very few leases were sought for energy production. There was a slight increase in interest in leases for coal production during the 1970s. During the Reagan administration's tenure, however, Secretary of the Interior James Watt announced his intention to increase lease sales from the Carter administration's 771 million tons of new coal to 2.2 billion tons. In 1982, Interior received almost $55 million in bids on almost 1.6 million acres of reserves, the largest coal lease sale in U.S. history. Congressional Democrats fiercely opposed the leases, as did the governors of many western coal states.

Some congressional staff reports alleged that the leases were being offered for far less than fair market value.

Because of the controversy, Watt appointed a special panel to study federal coal leasing policies. The panel, called the Linowes Commission, after its chairman, concluded that the government had offered too many leases, many at less than fair market value. The commission recommended that Interior revise its schedule of leases to respond better to changes in the coal market. Shortly before the commission issued its report, Watt resigned. Since his resignation, other Interior secretaries have been less eager to lease federal coal reserves. Thus, for now, at least, leasing federal lands is not a major concern. An increase in demand for coal, however, could reignite the controversy.

PETROLEUM AND NATURAL GAS

Since 1955, petroleum and natural gas have been the primary sources of energy for the United States, supplying more than two-thirds of our energy needs. Petroleum has been a chief energy source primarily because of its low cost. Natural gas is a fossil fuel that, like petroleum, burns cleanly and efficiently, producing few pollutants. It constitutes about 30 percent of domestic energy production. Approximately one-fourth of this domestic production satisfies about 40 percent of residential energy needs. Reserves of natural gas in the United States, however, are not extensive. In the mid-1980s, known reserves of natural gas were sufficient to last for 20 to 40 years at then current rates of consumption.

Petroleum and natural gas share common problems, primarily related to production and transportation.

Onshore Development Problems

Production and transportation of petroleum and natural gas necessitate large refineries and terminals, as well as miles of pipelines. Construction of these facilities often causes conflicts over land use. Many times the terminals and refineries are near coastal areas, which many people believe should be preserved as natural areas or used only for recreation. The environmental balance in these areas is delicate, and many fear disruption of this balance from the construction.

There are those who are fearful of spills at these facilities. Even though such spills are not common, their environmental consequences can be devastating. For example, in 1988, a storage tank in Pennsylvania collapsed, spilling more than a million gallons of diesel fuel into the Monogahela River and causing an oil slick that eventually spread into the Ohio River and caused the disruption of numerous communities' drinking water systems. Large numbers of birds and other wildlife were also killed by the spill.

Fears of pipeline ruptures causing similar ecological disasters have made it difficult for firms to obtain permission to construct pipelines to transport oil across land. The Alaskan Pipeline was constructed only after great controversy. Additional segments of that pipeline, from Port Angeles, Washington, to Clearbrook, Minnesota, generated so much dispute that ultimately the project was cancelled.

Offshore Development Problems

Even more controversies have been generated over offshore development, primarily in conjunction with the federal leasing of land in the outer continental shelf (OCS) for energy exploration. The federal government, primarily through the Department of the Interior, exercises authority over the approximately 1.1 billion acres of the continental shelf beginning three miles from the coastline and extending ten to twelve miles farther offshore. As custodian of this public land, the government leases some of it to private firms for exploration and production of oil. To ensure that states have some say in the development of submerged land off their shores, and to help ensure that multiple interests are taken into account when leasing decisions were made, Congress passed the Outer Continental Shelf Leasing Act (OCSLA).

As amended in 1978, OCSLA requires the secretary of the Interior to establish a five-year leasing program that includes as many details as possible about plans for leases during that time period. Details include the time, location, and sizes of leases that the secretary believes are necessary to meet the nation's energy needs. In developing the leasing plan, the secretary is to take into account four basic principles. First, the OCS must be managed in a manner that reflects a balancing of economic, social, and environmental values. The impact of exploration on the marine, coastal, and human environment must be taken into account. Second, choice of locations for development must be based on an equitable sharing of developmental benefits and environmental risks among the various regions, with special attention given to the laws, goals, and policies of the affected states as communicated by their governors to the secretary. In selecting timing and location of leases, the secretary must balance the potential for environmental damage, the potential for the discovery of oil and gas, and the potential for adverse impact on the coastal zone. Finally, the federal government must receive fair market value for the land.

The steps for developing the leasing program are laid out by the act. When initially drafting the program, the secretary of the Interior must "invite and consider suggestions" from governors of any states that might be affected by the leasing program. The proposed program finally drafted must then be submitted to the governors of the affected states for their comments. If any governor makes any suggestions that the secretary denies, the reasons for the denial must be provided, in writing, to the governor.

The next step is publication of the proposed program in the *Federal Register.* Any interested parties, including representatives of the affected states, have 90 days to submit written comments to the secretary. The secretary will then forward the proposed program, along with the comments, to Congress and the president. If any suggestions from a state were not incorporated, the secretary must include an explanation for rejecting the state's advice.

Sixty days after submitting the proposed program to the president and Congress, the secretary may finally approve the program. Anyone who participated in the administrative process that led to the adoption of the leasing program and who will be adversely affected by it then has 60 days to challenge the program in the Circuit Court of Appeals for the District of Columbia. When reviewing the actions of the secretary, the court must take the secretary's findings as conclusive if supported by substantial evidence on the record. After the process of judicial review has been completed, the secretary of the Interior will then propose and conduct competitive bidding lease sales. Once land has been leased, leasees submit to the secretary their exploration plans, followed by development and production plans. Throughout these stages, the secretary must still operate in accordance with the four principles described previously.

President Reagan's Interior Secretary James Watt caused a great deal of controversy by suggesting that all OCS lands might be open for leasing. The actual program he proposed was not so dramatic, but still it offered almost 1 billion acres of OCS land for oil and gas leasing during 1982–87. His program was challenged in a combined action brought by eight environmental groups and several state and local governments. Their primary claim was a lack of balance among the competing factors of potential for environmental damage, hydrocarbon discovery, and adverse coastal effects. The legality of Watt's plan was upheld, but the next secretary of the Interior, William Clark, feeling pressure from Congress, removed some areas from the program and cancelled some leases. Congress helped prevent some leasing along the coasts by denying appropriations for the administration of the program. The 1987–92 plan, finally approved in 1985 by Secretary of the Interior Donald Hodel, removed from planned leasing 650 millon of the 1.4 billion acres Watt had proposed. However, other new areas that had previously been protected were proposed under Hodel's plan. Some of these controversial areas include the fishing area of Georges Bank off the New England coast and other sensitive areas off the Pacific and Atlantic coasts.

OCSLA is not the only law designed to ensure a balanced development of coastal and subcoastal lands. The Coastal Zone Management Act (CZMA) aids in this process by providing financial assistance for states that develop and administer management programs that achieve a balance between energy development and environmental and coastal zone factors. NEPA also comes into play, because leasing is a major federal activity. Therefore, the secretary of the

Interior generally will have to prepare an EIS when proposing a lease sale. Many times, in fact, environmental groups will challenge an EIS as a way to at least delay proposed lease sales.

Oil Spills

One of the worst problems associated with oil and petroleum, or at least one that captures the public's attention, is oil spills. In March 1989, the Exxon Valdez dumped 11 million gallons of oil into Alaska's Prince William Sound, when it ran aground. Since that gigantic spill, there have been other spills that were even worse. In Scotland's Shetland Islands, for example, in 1992, the oil tanker Braer ran aground in hurricane force winds while carrying 25 million gallons of light crude oil.

To try and reduce the harm from oil spills when tankers run aground, break up in heavy weather, or collide with other vessels, President Carter issued an executive order in 1976 requiring all tankers over 20,000 tons that sailed in American waters to be fitted with double hulls and bottoms by 1982. As of 1992, the order has not been fully implemented. Congress has been considering legislation to effectuate the same goal by 2005. Shipowners argue that the expense is too great considering the low likelihood of a wreck; and these costs, they add, would have to be passed on to the consumers.

Oil spills in conjunction with production of oil on the OCS are also a concern. The 1978 amendments to OCSLA impose strict liability for cleanup costs and damages resulting from OCS activities on owners and operators of offshore facilities and vessels carrying oil from such facilities. Liability is limited to $250,000 for a vessel and $35 million plus government removal costs for a facility. The act also created the Offshore Oil Spill Pollution Protection Fund, which pays for all losses that cannot be covered by the responsible parties. The fund receives its income from per barrel tax imposed on purchasers of OCS oil.

Additional liability was also imposed by the Clean Water Act. Section 311 held vessel operators strictly liable for cleanup costs incurred by the government unless the operator can prove that the cause of the spill was an act of God, act of war, act or omission of a third party, or negligence of the federal government. Government removal costs under this act include restoration or replacement of natural resources damaged or destroyed by the spill. Damages were limited, however, to $125,000 for inland barges, $250,000 for other vessels, and $50 million for onshore and offshore facilities. The limits would not apply if the accident were caused by "willful negligence or willful misconduct within the privity and knowledge of the owner."

Liability of responsible parties was broadened by the Oil Pollution Control Act of 1990, which replaces the foregoing liability provisions. Under this new law, each responsible party, defined as owners and operators of vessels, onshore facilities, or pipelines, is liable for removal costs, damage to natural resources, damages for injury to or economic losses from destruction of real or personal property, and lost profits due to the injury or destruction of any real property, personal property, or natural resources. The measure of damages to natural resources was clearly spelled out under the act. It includes the cost of restoring, rehabilitating, rejecting, or acquiring the equivalent of the damaged resources; the diminution of value of those resources pending restoration; and the reasonable cost of assessing those damages.

Liability limits under the Oil Pollution Control Act were increased to $10 millon for ships weighing more than 3,000 gross tons and $75 million for owners of offshore facilities. Limits are inapplicable if the spill is caused by gross negligence, willful misconduct, or a safety violation. A one-billion-dollar oil spill trust fund is also established under the act.

NUCLEAR ENERGY

Nuclear energy once offered a dream of cheap, unlimited electrical power. In many people's opinion that dream has now been dimmed as numerous problems have developed during the almost 40 years of attempts to harness nuclear power to satisfy energy needs. As originally conceived, uranium ore would be mined, processed, used in nuclear reactors, reprocessed, and used again in nuclear reactors—all in a continuous, closed cycle. The cycle did not work that way, however, leading to perhaps the most serious problem of nuclear energy: nuclear waste.

History of Nuclear Energy Development

Development of nuclear energy as a fuel really began in the mid-1950s. The federal government invested a great deal of money to subsidize early research and development. To encourage industry further in developing nuclear power, Congress even passed the Price-Anderson Act in 1957 to limit liability for any nuclear reactor accident. By 1975, the high point of nuclear energy, 56 commercial reactors had been built, 69 were under construction, and there were plans for 111 more. By 1986, 95 nuclear reactors were licensed and operating. Then came the near-catastrophe of Three Mile Island, which alerted the public to the potential risks of nuclear accidents and also called attention to a lot of other problems in the nuclear industry. The core meltdown at Chernobyl, in the Soviet Union, further turned public opinion away from nuclear energy.

By 1990, 112 commercial reactors were generating electricity in the United States, providing about 20 percent of the energy for peak summer consumption. Half these generators are scheduled to be closed down between 2005 and 2015; the remainder will be shut down by 2075. No new reactors have been ordered since 1979, so it is conceivable that nuclear energy will be only a memory by the year 2075. Still, another oil crisis might spur the development of this industry once again.

Problems with Nuclear Energy

A major problem with the nuclear industry is safety. Many of the materials and designs currently in use in reactors have failed safety tests; and many reactor parts have aged faster than projected. A 1988 survey by the GAO revealed that one-third of the plants it inspected had prematurely deteriorating pipes; the GAO consequently recommended inspection of pipes at all facilities. Horror stories about mismanagement and incompetence of managers and technicians in the industry abound. Those within the industry, however, point out that, in terms of accidents, the nuclear industry has a good safety record.

While not environmentally related, per se, the nuclear industry has been beset with economic problems. Costs were underestimated, and many of the facilities completed during the 1980s and early 1990s were 500 to 1,000 percent over budget. The licensing procedures caused costly delays in start-ups, with many plants taking four to eight years to obtain all the necessary permits.

The most troublesome problem with nuclear energy, perhaps, is nuclear waste. Four types of wastes are created, all of which present problems. First are the high-level radioactive liquids created during the reprocessing of reactor fuels. More than 100 million gallons of these highly dangerous wastes currently are being stored in temporary containment facilities in New York, North Carolina, Idaho, and Washington. Stored along with the high-level wastes are transuranic wastes. These are by-products of reactor fuel and military waste processing. Some have a half-life of more than 200,000 years. The most well known of these dangerous by-products is probably plutonium-239, with a half-life of 24,000 years. A third category is spent nuclear fuel, which is currently being stored in cooling ponds at reactor sites. Many of these ponds are nearly full. This category of waste was never expected to be so large, as this spent fuel was supposed to have been recyclable. Unfortunately, the necessary technology for recycling did not develop. More than 63,000 metric tons of this waste is expected to exist by 1995. Finally, there are low-level radioactive wastes. This category includes such items as clothing, tools, and equipment that have become radioactive through exposure at reactors. These wastes are currently being stored at repositories in Nevada, New York, and South Carolina.

As the nuclear industry was developing, those in the industry assumed they would discover the technology to reprocess and then safely contain the waste. When the technology did not develop, the industry was, and still is, unprepared to handle all the hazardous wastes. A major problem is finding permanent sites to dispose of the waste.

Not only is waste disposal a problem, but the cost of decommissioning these plants now appears to be much higher than anticipated. The first nuclear plant to be taken apart began being decommissioned in 1993. That relatively small plant, located at Fort St. Vrain, in Colorado, cost $224 million to build in the 1970s; it is now being taken apart at a cost of $333 millon. The Nuclear Regulatory Commission (NRC) requires utilities to put aside up to $130 million for each of their nuclear plants to cover the costs of dismantling them. Not only is this amount apparently going to be far less than needed, the NRC estimates that the total amount that utilities have set aside falls far short of even this inadequate sum. To make matters still worse, many plants are wearing out far earlier than their projected 40-year life span, after having never consistently produced the low-cost energy they were designed to produce. Closed plants now operate an average of 12.7 years.

Currently, at least 14 nuclear plants have closed and are being mothballed until a lower cost method of dismantling them can be developed. The NRC will allow plants to sit idle for up to 60 years before the owners must dismantle them. However, maintaining, inspecting, and securing a closed nuclear facility can cost up to $15 million a year.

Regulation of the Nuclear Industry

The Atomic Energy Act of 1954 is the primary legislation that gives the federal government the authority to protect human health and the environment from excessive exposure to radiation. The agency responsible for regulating the nuclear industry is the Nuclear Regulatory Commission. Created in 1978 to replace the old Atomic Energy Commission, the NRC issues licenses for the construction and operation of nuclear facilities, as well as for the possession, use, handling, and disposal of nuclear wastes. The NRC has generally been staffed by people who believe in nuclear energy, and is cited by some as an example of a captured agency.

In 1979, after the accident at Three Mile Island, the Kemeny Commission, was established to investigate the accident. Chief among the commission's findings was that to prevent similar accidents in the future, changes would be necessary in the organization, procedures, practices, and attitudes of the NRC. The commission felt that the NRC had grown too firmly convinced that nuclear plants were sufficiently safe. The NRC was too preoccupied with regulations and equipment, and was not paying enough attention to human factors. Workers were not being well trained to respond to equipment malfunctions, especially severe or multiple malfunctions. The commission said that the NRC was not paying enough attention to the ongoing process of ensuring nuclear safety.

In 1980, in partial response to the accident at Three Mile Island and the Kemeny Commission's report, Congress passed Public Law 96-295. The law provided funding to train additional federal inspectors who would be stationed at nuclear power plants. The law also required the agency to draw up a plan for agency responses to nuclear accidents, as well as to issue new regulations to improve safety at reactors.

The Nuclear Waste Policy Act of 1982 was passed to resolve the problem of siting and developing permanent repositories for high-level nuclear waste. By 1985, the DOE was to nominate five sites. After extensive public hearings, the president was to make a recommendation to Congress. If the site were approved by the selected state or Congress, the DOE was to apply to the NRC for a repository license. Until the permanent facility was established, an interim storage program was to be maintained.

Nomination of three sites, in volcanic rock in Nye County Nevada, salt beds in Deaf Smith County, Texas, and basalt deposits at Hanaford Reservation in Washington, led to an uproar among local citizens. Congress, in 1987, perhaps in frustration over the political opposition created by the site selection process, passed legislation directing the DOE to examine a site in Yucca Mountain, Nevada. The department was to also look for a site for an intermediate storage facility, if it believed one was necessary. After spending two years and $500 million on preliminary work, the DOE announced that it was abandoning its initial repository plan. The DOE projected it would be at least the year 2010 before it would have a repository ready to accept high-level waste.

RENEWABLE FUELS

Because the so-called traditional fuels present a number of environmental problems—and they are bound to be depleted someday—many argue that the government needs to encourage more research into renewable fuels, sources of energy that are continuously renewed. Those renewables most heavily used today include hydropower, solar power, wind, and the burning of waste for steam. Briefly, these sources offer the benefits of generally being less polluting and being available domestically, so they reduce dependence on foreign oil. Different sources estimate that considering all of the various types of renewable energy together, they constitute about 8 to 10 percent of U.S. energy needs.[16] Some predict that this figure could rise to 15 percent by 2030,[17] assuming no further federal support. The same sources project that with federal research and development and demonstration funding, a possible increase to 28 percent within that time frame is not unrealistic.[18]

Hydropower

The most popular is hydropower, that is, the power to generate electricity from running water. In 1990, hydropower from dams generated about 10 percent of the electricity used in the United States. Increasingly, however, environmental groups have been raising concerns about the environmental effects of dams.

Dams are licensed by the Federal Energy Regulatory Commission (FERC). The 1986 Electric Consumers Act requires the FERC to give environmental and recreational factors equal weight with power generation when granting and reviewing licenses. Federal licenses for 16 percent of the dams overseen by FERC

(157 hydroelectric projects) were up for renewal in 1993, and many people are watching FERC to see how it will interpret the law. Some environmental groups have even argued that dam relicensing is going to be the hottest environmental issue. They want FERC to require dam operators to engage in environmentally conscious actions, such as adding more fish ladders around dams, protecting areas around the dams from development, and engaging in other conservation activities such as updating equipment at the dam if it is old and less energy efficient than currently available technology permits. Dam owners, as one might expect, oppose such requirements, maintaining that such measures are too costly.

Solar Energy

The sun can provide energy in different ways. Solar energy can be used at one centralized location to create electricity, or it can be used in individual residences or commercial buildings to directly satisfy energy needs.

Because solar energy requires sunshine, it is obviously not a source that could satisfy anyone's energy needs completely. And places where there is sufficient sunlight year-round to justify construction of a solar energy plant are extremely limited. Currently, California is the only state that has solar thermal power plants. These plants use trough collectors to focus sunlight onto pipes that carry a synthetic oil-based heat transfer fluid. When heated, this oil creates the steam that drives a turbine to generate electricity. In southern California, in 1990, these solar thermal plants generated enough electricity to satisfy the energy needs of more than 500,000 people.

Solar energy systems used at individual sites are generally referred to as passive or active. Passive solar energy is really a matter of designing a structure so that it will become a solar collector. For example, you would have big south-facing energy-efficient windows that would capture the heat of the sunlight. Active systems are ones that use moving parts to generate energy for heating, producing hot water and sometimes even powering air conditioning. Active systems generally use some sort of collector to absorb the sunlight and transfer its heat to some other medium for distribution or storage.

The legal system can encourage or discourage the use of solar energy, primarily through the funding of research into solar energy and through the tax system—directly by providing tax breaks for installing solar technologies or indirectly by increasing taxes on the use of fossil fuels. For example, in 1977, Congress provided a tax break for homeowners who installed solar technology, which was ended in 1984. During that time, about 924,000 claimed the tax break. When Carter was president, he saw great merit in solar technology research and funded it accordingly. When Reagan came into office, he saw no need for government support of an energy technology that did not appear to offer much of a private sector profit opportunity and drastically reduced funding.

Wind Energy

Another form of renewable energy, which, again, can be used in only appropriate climates, is energy from the wind. By 1989, California was using wind to create approximately 1 percent of its electricity. California has five windparks, or windfarms, where wind turbines generate electricity. Hawaii has one. Again, because federal support for this nontraditional technology is not strong, its development is unlikely.

Biomass Energy

Biomass conversion simply means burning organic matter to generate energy: agricultural waste, municipal garbage, grains, animal manure, and wood. Burning of wood creates pollution problems, but other biofuels are much cleaner than fossil fuels. As air pollution standards become more stringent, use of these alternative fuels becomes more desirable.

Geothermal Energy

Geothermal energy refers to the use of heat that is trapped within the earth. Technically, it is not a renewable fuel, but is often thought of as one because it is such a vast source. The most common form of geothermal energy is hydrothermal energy. Naturally occurring hot water reservoirs are tapped for their energy. This type of energy supplies 7 percent of California's energy.

PROTECTING PUBLIC LANDS

As the preceding sections have revealed, use of one of our major energy resources—fossil fuels—often comes into conflict with alternative uses of one of our most important natural resources, the land. This section focuses on a particular segment of land resources—public lands. When examining the laws developed to regulate our public lands, it is important to remember that, historically, the purpose of these laws was to preserve the land for sustained exploitation.

More than a half billion acres of public lands are managed by federal agencies. Many conflicts arise over the appropriate use of these lands. Some argue that we should take a purely economic view of the use of public lands. If the Sierra Club is willing to pay more for Yellowstone National Park, then it should have it to preserve for nature lovers' enjoyment. But if the strip mining companies will pay more, then perhaps the best disposition of the land is to sell it to the strip mining companies.

Of course, many people will say that we cannot take a purely economic viewpoint with respect to use of public lands. Those who advocate consideration of other values tend to fall into two categories—conservationists and preservationists. Conservationists tend to focus on conserving resources, using them in a sustainable way, so that they will be available for future generations. Plant and animal species should not be reduced to the extent that they can no longer serve human needs. Conservationists have an instrumental view of nature; its purpose is to serve humans. Preservationists, on the other hand, want to preserve wilderness areas just as they are for their inherent value. They see nature as having value beyond its usefulness to humans. Both preservationists and conservationists tend to be especially concerned about protecting certain types of land, namely, forests and wilderness.

Forests

Forests are complex ecosystems, made up of interdependent communities of plants, animals, and microbes. They are vital because they provide recreational opportunities, watersheds, wildlife habitats, wilderness, timber, and minerals. Forests also provide food and raw materials for pharmaceuticals.

There are numerous types of forest, from the scrub forests of the arid interior West to the lush forests on the coasts. A major concern today is the declining amount of forests in the United States. Obviously, when the nation was young, forests were cleared with abandon. But even during the 1970s and 1980s many acres of forestland were lost. Many were cleared for agricultural use as a result of a rapid growth of agricultural exports during that time period. Despite consequent recognition of the need to protect these areas, their acreage loss has been slowed, but not halted. The EPA in 1990 estimated a further decline of 4 percent by 2040. This figure represents an annual decline of half a million acres per year, an improvement over the decline of 1.5 million acres per year from 1970 through 1987.

Of particular concern is the loss of a special type of forest, old-growth forests. Old-growth forests contain trees that are hundreds, and even thousands, of years old—great stands of Douglas firs and giant sequoias and redwoods. Some of the firs are up to 300 feet tall. These old-growth forests are considered valuable by conservationists because they contain a much greater diversity of plant and animal species than do younger, so-called secondary forests. In 1990, only about 15 percent of the old-growth forests that once covered the United States remained, and some conservation groups fear that at current rates of cutting, most of the old-growth forests of the United States will be gone within 15 to 20 years.

One of the causes of the rapid depletion of forestland is a process known as clear-cutting. Clear-cutting occurs when a logging firm moves into a 25- to 50-acre area and cuts down every tree in that area. Clear-cutting is favored by the timber industry over the alternative, selective cutting of individual trees in a forest, for several reasons. With selective cutting, the company must search through the forest to identify small groups of single intermediate or mature trees to be cut. This method, which preserves a "whole" forest with multiple-aged trees, is extremely expensive and time-consuming. Clear-cutting is cheaper and requires less skill. Fewer roads must be built into the area, and replanting is relatively easy. Also, the company knows that in a given number of years it can come back and reharvest a huge acreage of relatively similar size trees. Clear-cutting does not require a great amount of planning.

When clear-cutting was initially proposed, some thought that it would be ecologically superior. After all, it left some areas of forest completely undisturbed. Soon, however, problems began to materialize. First, removal of big swatches of trees affects the ecological balance in the adjacent areas. If the clearing is done on sloped land, there can be extreme erosion problems: flooding from melting snow and heavy rains, and landslides. From an aesthetic viewpoint, it is ugly. Today, an estimated two-thirds of the annual timber harvest is done by clear-cutting. At present, there are no viable measures available to limit this ecologically devastating process.

Rangelands

Much of public land is rangeland. The Bureau of Land Management oversees more than 170 million acres of range. The Forest Service also manages 104 million acres, about half of which is timbered. The primary issue with respect to rangeland is the extent to which such land should be leased to farmers for grazing. While the government takes in a substantial amount of revenue from grazing fees, more than $18 million in 1991, there is a question over the extent to which grazing should be viewed as the dominant use of these lands, especially when the land is to be managed under a multiple-use concept (described in the next section).

Regulation of Public Lands

No comprehensive statutory scheme for regulation of public lands exists, and management of these lands is fragmented among a number of agencies housed under different departments. The primary agencies responsible for land management are the Bureau of Land Management, Forest Service, Fish and Wildlife Service, and National Park Services. Also, the Department of Defense is responsible for managing 6 million acres of forestland.

The Bureau of Land Management, within the Department of the Interior, is responsible for managing approximately 270 million acres of public lands, of which 48 million are forestlands. Another Interior Department agency, the Fish and Wildlife Service, manages approximately 92 million acres, 16 million of which are national forestlands. The National Forest Service, of the Agriculture Department, manages 191 million acres of forestland, and the National Park Service manages 80 million acres.

The management activities of these agencies are directed by diverse statutes. To discuss all of them would take an entire book, so our discussion will be limited to the most influential laws affecting the management of public lands, starting with the earliest laws, so that you can follow the historical development of public lands policies.

Initially, the attitude of the federal government toward public lands was "sell and develop." Early homestead acts conveyed large tracts of public lands to farmers and ranchers who were willing to develop those lands. The Mining Law of 1872 provided that anyone who discovered a valuable mineral deposit (excluding oil, gas, coal, and oil shale) on public land could obtain a mining claim on that land; further provisions of the act allowed the miner also to obtain title to the land on which the claim was located, hence encouraging mining of formerly public lands.

In 1891, the president was first authorized to set aside land for national forests.[19] An 1897 statute declared the purposes for establishing such forests were to be water control and "a continuous supply of timber."[20] In 1920, the exploitation of land for the extraction of oil and gas was encouraged by the Mineral Leasing Act of 1920, described earlier in this chapter.

In more recent years, land use regulation took on a less singularly developmental tone. In 1960, Congress passed the Multiple-Use Sustained Yield Act. This act provides that national forests should be managed to fulfill a multiplicity of purposes: outdoor recreation, timber, and provision of wildlife habitats. No particular weight is given to any of these uses by the act.

In 1964, Congress passed what many preservationists consider one of the most significant pieces of legislation for the protection of land—the Wilderness Act, the law that created the National Wilderness Preservation System. The act defines a wilderness as having four characteristics. First, there has been no noticeable human impact on the land. Second, the area offers opportunities for solitude or primitive recreation. Third, the area consists of at least 5,000 acres or a sufficient size to make preservation possible. Finally, although this characteristic is not mandatory, the area has ecological, geological, or other value. The act itself specifies certain areas to be designated wilderness and other forests to be reviewed for consideration as wilderness in the future. Under this law, once land is designated wilderness, its use is sharply restricted. The agency administering the land must preserve the "wilderness character" of the area and make sure that the area is devoted to "the public purposes of recreational, scenic, scientific, education, conservation, and historical use." Unless specifically provided for by statute, no commercial enterprises or permanent roads may be constructed in any wilderness area. An exception in the act, however, provided for the continuation of mining in wilderness areas until 1983. By 1990, 94 million acres had been designated wilderness under the National Wilderness Preservation System.

In 1976, greater protection for public lands was encouraged by the Federal Land Policy and Management Act. This act requires the secretary of the Interior, when managing the public lands, to take any action necessary to "prevent unnecessary or undue degradation of the lands."[21] This act also requires the Bureau of Land Management to prepare land management plans for the 450 million acres of land it administers.[22] Similar management plans for national forests were required of the secretary of Agriculture in legislation passed by Congress in 1974 and 1978.[23]

WETLANDS, ESTUARIES, AND COASTAL AREAS

Although the need to regulate public lands has been recognized, to some extent, since the late 1800s, preservation of wetlands, estuaries, and coastal areas is of more recent vintage. A wetlands is an area of land covered with water all or part of the year. When covered with saltwater, these areas are known as coastal wetlands; when covered with fresh water, they are inland wetlands. The wet tundra that covers 58 percent of Alaska is also a wetlands. Figure 9–1 depicts the typical features of a wetlands.

An estuary is a coastal area where the fresh water of rivers and streams mixes with seawater.

Coastal wetlands make up about 30 percent of the wetlands and 16 percent of the coastline. Figure 9–2 shows the types of coastal wetlands, the regions where they are located, and the states with the greatest coastal wetlands acreage. Despite the fact that they are viewed by many as useless homes for mosquitoes, coastal wetlands are highly productive ecosystems. They provide a habitat for numerous plant and animal species, including a number of endangered species.

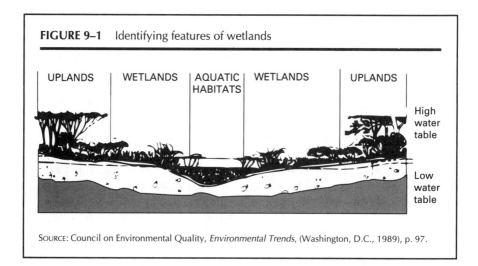

FIGURE 9–1   Identifying features of wetlands

UPLANDS   WETLANDS   AQUATIC HABITATS   WETLANDS   UPLANDS

High water table

Low water table

SOURCE: Council on Environmental Quality, *Environmental Trends*, (Washington, D.C., 1989), p. 97.

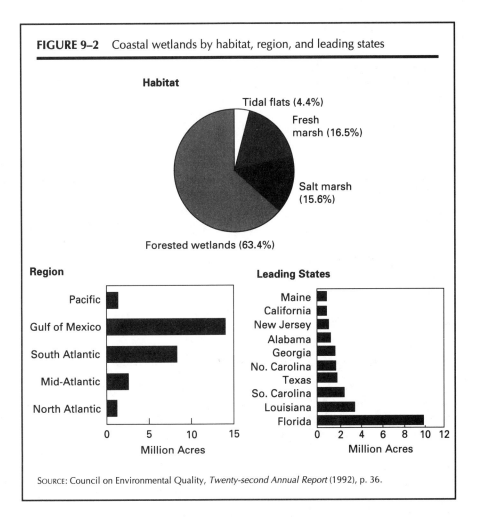

FIGURE 9–2   Coastal wetlands by habitat, region, and leading states

Source: Council on Environmental Quality, *Twenty-second Annual Report* (1992), p. 36.

Roughly 70 percent of the nation's commercial seafood is spawned in coastal wetlands. Coastal wetlands also dilute water pollutants, thereby helping to improve the quality of the adjacent water.

Both coastal wetlands and estuaries help prevent erosion of coastlines. When hurricanes and tropical storms hit coastlines, estuaries and wetlands help to absorb the impact of the waves. Inland wetlands, commonly referred to as bogs and marshes, are important as habitats for a number of fish (most inland sport fish spawn in inland wetlands), waterfowl, and wildlife. Inland wetlands also help to prevent riverbank erosion and flooding.

Destruction of Wetlands

Wetlands were once plentiful in the United States, but since the eighteenth century, over half of them have been lost, with some states losing up to 80 percent of their wetlands. From the mid-1950s to the mid-1970s, wetlands in the lower 48 states were lost at a rate of approximately 458,000 acres per year. During the next decade, this loss fell to approximately 290,000 acres per year.[24] Alaska's wetlands losses have not been as severe, with only about 1 percent being lost. However, in coastal areas around major cities, losses have been about 50 percent.[25]

Coastal wetlands and estuaries are being lost in part because of development exacerbated by increasing coastal populations. Almost half the country's population in 1990 lived in coastal counties, which make up only 11 percent of the nation's total land. By the year 2010, this coastal population of 110 million is projected to grow to 127 million. Not only are wetlands being filled on for development, but runoff, including sewer overflows, are polluting these fragile areas. The heavier the population, the more severe the pollution problem becomes.

Loss of inland wetlands can be primarily attributable to filling in the wetlands for agricultural use. Additional losses are due to a desire to develop wetlands for industrial or residential use.

Regulations to Preserve Coastal Areas and Wetlands

A number of regulations and federal programs have been implemented to preserve wetlands and coastal areas. Preservation of wetlands is in some ways more difficult than protecting wilderness and forest areas because many of the wetlands are on private property. The main regulatory tool for preserving wetlands is Section 404 of the Clean Water Act. This provision requires that any landowner seeking to add dredged or filled material to a wetland must receive a permit from the Army Corps of Engineers or risk being subject to both civil and criminal penalties. To obtain such a permit, the landowner must demonstrate that the activity satisfies the environmental criteria established by the EPA and that the activity is in the public interest. In many states the landowner must also comply with state regulations governing wetlands.

Marine Protection, Research, and Sanctuaries Act. The 1972 Marine Protection, Research, and Sanctuaries Act allows the National Oceanic and Atmospheric Administration to designate specific areas as marine sanctuaries. Such sanctuaries are the marine equivalent to national parks, and they are to have protective management of their recreational, ecological, historical, education, and aesthetic values. Figure 9–3 shows where existing and proposed marine sanctuaries were located as of 1991 and provides a description of some of them.

Coastal Zone Management Act (CZMA). In 1972, to encourage the prudent management and conservation of the coastal zone, defined as state land near the shorelines of the coastal states and the coastal waters, extending to the outer lim-

FIGURE 9–3   National marine sanctuaries system

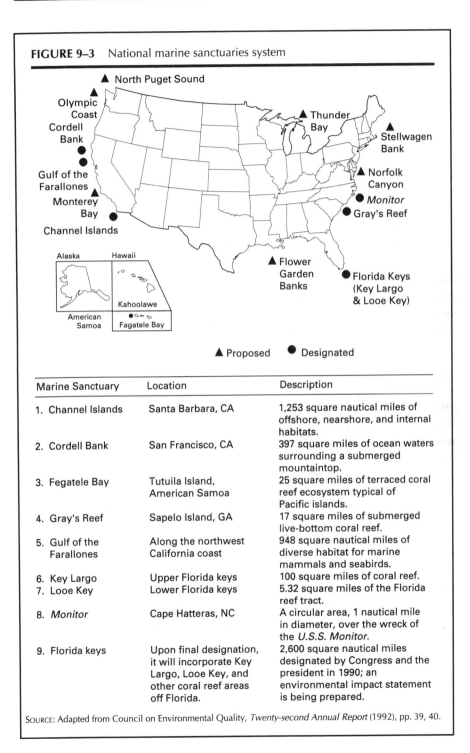

Marine Sanctuary	Location	Description
1. Channel Islands	Santa Barbara, CA	1,253 square nautical miles of offshore, nearshore, and internal habitats.
2. Cordell Bank	San Francisco, CA	397 square miles of ocean waters surrounding a submerged mountaintop.
3. Fegatele Bay	Tutuila Island, American Samoa	25 square miles of terraced coral reef ecosystem typical of Pacific islands.
4. Gray's Reef	Sapelo Island, GA	17 square miles of submerged live-bottom coral reef.
5. Gulf of the Farallones	Along the northwest California coast	948 square nautical miles of diverse habitat for marine mammals and seabirds.
6. Key Largo	Upper Florida keys	100 square miles of coral reef.
7. Looe Key	Lower Florida keys	5.32 square miles of the Florida reef tract.
8. *Monitor*	Cape Hatteras, NC	A circular area, 1 nautical mile in diameter, over the wreck of the *U.S.S. Monitor*.
9. Florida keys	Upon final designation, it will incorporate Key Largo, Looe Key, and other coral reef areas off Florida.	2,600 square nautical miles designated by Congress and the president in 1990; an environmental impact statement is being prepared.

SOURCE: Adapted from Council on Environmental Quality, *Twenty-second Annual Report* (1992), pp. 39, 40.

its of the U.S. territorial sea, Congress passed the Coastal Zone Management Act. The act, like NEPA, is a planning statute. Under CZMA, the federal government will provide matching funds to a coastal state, including Great Lakes states, to assist the state in developing a management plant for its coastal lands and waters. CZMA specifies nine elements that must be included in the plan. Some of the more substantive elements include:

- A definition of what will constitute permissible land uses within the coastal zone that will have direct and significant impact on coastal waters
- Broad guidelines on the priorities of uses in particular areas
- A description of the organizational structure to implement the proposed management plan
- A definition of "beach" and a planning process for protection of and access to public beaches and other public coastal areas of environmental, recreational, historical, aesthetic, ecological, or cultural value
- A planning process for studying and controlling erosion.

The plan must give full consideration to ecological, cultural, historical, and aesthetic values, as well as to needs for economic development. The National Oceanographic and Atmospheric Administration reviews the plans submitted by the states. If the plan is approved, the state will receive additional funds to administer the plan. Approval of a state plan also means that any federal activity within the state's coastal zone must be consistent with that state's management plan, "to the maximum extent possible." As an incentive to the state to adhere to its plan, funding can be withdrawn if the state fails to do so.

In 1990, CZMA was amended to require each state to develop a nonpoint source pollution-control program. Recall that one of the major problems along the coasts is nonpoint source pollution.

"Swampbuster" Provisions of the 1985 Food Security Act. Many people argue that one of the most effective measures for protecting wetlands, particularly inland wetlands, has been what is commonly referred to as the "Swampbuster bill." This provision was an attempt by Congress to slow the conversion of wetlands to agricultural land. It provides that any persons who produce crops on wetlands that were converted after December 23, 1985 will be ineligible for most federal farm benefits.

"No-net-loss" Policy. In August 1989, President Bush announced a no-net-loss of wetlands policy. The policy, however, has been criticized by many as sounding better than it actually is. Much of the policy involved improving funding with respect to existing nonregulatory wetlands programs, such as the North American Waterfowl Management Plan, which was designed to help restore declining waterfowl population by the acquisition and restoration of wetlands that provided breeding grounds and resting areas for these waterfowl.

Bush's policy of no-net-loss of wetlands was mitigated by fact that no-net-loss really meant except when the loss was "unavoidable." If the loss were unavoidable, the developer had the option of creating roughly the same amount of wetlands elsewhere. This option completely overlooks the significance of a loss in a particular area. Also, if the loss were "insignificant," a clearly vague term, then no replacement was necessary. Finally, in a move many believed was clearly directed toward Alaska, replacement was unnecessary if it would be impracticable to create more.

ENDANGERED SPECIES

In 1973, Congress recognized that the wide variety of plants and animals do indeed constitute an important natural resource. In setting forth its findings to justify the Endangered Species Act (ESA), Congress declared that

(1) various species of fish, wildlife, and plants in the United States have been rendered extinct as a consequence of economic growth and development untempered by adequate concern and conservation;

(2) other species of fish, wildlife, and plants have become so depleted in numbers that they are in danger of or threatened with extinction;

(3) these species of fish, wildlife, and plants are of aesthetic, ecological, educational, historical, recreational, and scientific value to the Nation and its people[26]

Congress went on to state that the purpose of the ESA was to provide a means to preserve the ecosystems in which endangered species survive, to provide a program to conserve such species, and to enter into appropriate treaties for species protection on an international level.

The ESA has both a national focus and an international one. This chapter discusses the national aspect; Chapter 10 addresses the international aspect.

Under this act, the secretary of the Interior is required to list species of animals and plants that are both threatened and endangered. A species can become threatened or endangered because of a number of factors: "present or threatened destruction, modification, or curtailment of its habitat or range; overutilization for commercial recreation, scientific, or educational purposes; disease or predation, the inadequacy of existing statutory mechanisms; or other natural or manmade factors affecting its continued existence."[27] Once a species is listed as endangered, it cannot be "taken," that is, it cannot be harassed, harmed, pursued, hunted, shot, wounded, killed, trapped, captured, or collected. Nor can anyone attempt to engage in any of those activities with respect to an endangered species. Violation of the prohibition against "taking" can result in criminal sanctions.

Perhaps more important, Section 7 of the ESA requires all federal agencies to take actions necessary to ensure that activities authorized, funded, or carried out by them do not jeopardize the continued existence of endangered or threatened species. This section of the act has ended up being a powerful tool to protect the habitat of endangered species, which many environmentalists believe is the key to protecting the species. So powerful is this section that many accuse environmentalists of using, or abusing, it to prohibit developments they primarily oppose for other environmental reasons.

There is no doubt but that because many habitats are on public lands, this law also helps regulate the use of public lands and protect old-growth forests and wilderness areas. Most Americans probably became aware of the controversy over protection of old-growth forests as well as endangered species as a result of the application of the ESA in a highly publicized case involving the northern spotted owl.

The controversy began during the late 1980s, when the Forest Service, charged with perpetuating vertebrae species native to the national forests, discovered through its research that the population of the northern spotted owl was shrinking because of the destruction of its forest habitat by logging. The Forest Service recognized that if the spotted owl were placed on the endangered species list, a virtual cessation of logging in the Northwest could be mandated. So the agency proposed setting aside 550 spotted owl habitats in Oregon and Washington, along with 200 areas in northwestern California. Each habitat area consisted of approximately 2,200 acres of old-growth forest. The plan was criticized immediately by environmentalists, who claimed that this was insufficient habitat area.

After discussing in its findings of fact the importance of logging, and the record of violations by the Fish and Wildlife Service, the court acknowledged the likelihood of irreparable harm from continued logging: the extinction of a species. The court then discussed the balancing of equities necessary in an environmental case, and issued an injunction ordering the Forest Service to come up with a plan to preserve the species by March 5, 1992, and to prohibit the selling of further logging rights in spotted owl habitats until they were in compliance with the law.

That same year, the issue became more than "owls v. jobs." Environmental groups sought to have the Pacific Yew, the bark of which provides an extract that can be used in a potent drug to fight cancer, listed as an endangered species. The tree, one of the slowest-growing species in the world, is found exclusively in old-growth forests. In February 1991, an interagency team of federal, state, and university representatives met to develop a plan for the recovery of the species. In January 1992, the Fish and Wildlife Service adopted regulations designating 6.9 million acres in Oregon, Washington, and California critical habitat for the owls.

Thus, a tentative resolution was reached. Loggers were allowed to exercise the logging rights they had previously obtained, but future logging right sales, at least in a limited area, were temporarily halted.

The controversy will never really end, however, because the timber industry may always return to argue that logging in this or that area will not adversely affect the owl's habitat.

In June 1990, after considerable controversy, and under court order, the Fish and Wildlife Service listed the northern spotted owl as a threatened species under the Endangered Species Act. This precipitated a massive publicity campaign by the timber industry, forecasting the loss of thousands of jobs. On February 26, 1991, the federal district court once again ruled that the FWS had violated the law. This time, it had violated the ESA by failing to designate critical habitat with the listing of the spotted owl, and it had failed to comply with the deadline of September 30, 1990, for adopting a plan for ensuring the owl's survival.

The Audobon Society then filed an action seeking a permanent injunction against any further sales of logging rights in northern spotted owl habitat until the Forest Service adopted guidelines and regulations to ensure that a viable population of the species is maintained in the forest.

The controversy continued into 1993, when President Clinton called a special summit for affected interests to try to discuss the ongoing controversy. Whether any real changes will result from this attempt to get the parties talking to one another remains to be seen.

CONCLUDING REMARKS

Energy policy and resource protection, while often not thought of as part of traditional environmental law, are important to environmental conditions. We need energy, and though some say that the United States uses more than its share, our consumptive behaviors are not likely to change soon. Therefore, the best the law can do is to try to regulate use of energy in ways that allow us to extend the life of current resources and not create environmental damage through the extraction and use of those resources.

Other natural resources besides energy also need protection. Therefore legislation attempts to protect the forests, ranges, wetlands, and estuaries. We have even come to recognize species of plants and animals as natural resources, and are according them protection under the Endangered Species Act. When we think about issues of resource protection, however, it really makes no sense to think in terms of national resources alone. Resource protection is really a global issue, as you will realize when reading Chapter 10.

QUESTIONS FOR REVIEW AND DISCUSSION

1. Explain why we have come to rely so heavily on coal as an energy source at so many times in our history.

2. Explain the main problems associated with coal as a fuel and how we try to solve those problems.
3. Explain the primary problems associated with petroleum as a fuel and how we try to solve those problems.
4. Explain the primary problems associated with nuclear energy as a fuel and how we try to solve those problems.
5. What is an old-growth forest, and why are such forests important?
6. What are wetlands, and why are they important?
7. Explain the purpose of the Coastal Zone Management Act.
8. Explain the similarities and differences between Section 7 of the ESA and the EIS requirement of NEPA.

FOR FURTHER READING

Burchell, Robert, and David Listokin. *Energy and Land Use.* New York: Transaction Publishers, 1981.

Byrne, John, and Daniel Rich, eds. *Energy and Global Environmental Change.* New York: Transaction Publishers, 1992.

Clarke, Lee. *Acceptable Risk: Making Decisions in a Toxic Environment.* Berkeley: University of California Press, 1989.

Hall, Charles, et al. *Energy and Resource Quality: The Ecology of the Economic Process.* Boulder: University of Colorado Press, 1992.

Keeler, Barbara. *Energy Alternatives.* San Diego: Lucent Books, 1990.

Mane, Christopher. *Green Rage.* Boston: Little Browne & Co., 1991.

Munasingne, Mohan. *Energy Analysis and Policy.* Stoneham, Mass.: Butterworth-Heinemann, 1990.

Nash, Roderick. *Wilderness and the American Mind.* New Haven: Yale University Press, 1967.

NOTES

1. U.S. Department of Commerce, Bureau of the Census, *Statistical Abstract of the United States* (1989), p. 563.
2. Walter A. Rosenbaum, *Energy, Politics, and Public Policy* (Washington, D.C.: Congressional Quarterly, 1987), p. 6.
3. Council on Environmental Quality, *Environmental Quality: the Twenty-second Annual Report* (1991), p. 80.
4. Ibid.
5. Ibid.
6. 42 USCA §§ 8301–8433 (1978).
7. Walter A. Rosenbaum, *Environmental Politics and Policy,* 2d ed. (Washington, D.C.: Congressional Quarterly, 1991).
8. *New York Times,* November 5, 1983.

9. Rosenbaum, *Energy, Politics, and Policy.*

10. Ibid.

11. Ibid.

12. Ibid.

13. Rosenbaum, *Environmental Politics and Policy,* p. 264.

14. Ibid.

15. Ibid., p. 265.

16. See Council on Environmental Quality, p. 23; see alsoWorld Resources Institute, *The 1992 Information Please Environmental Almanac* (1992), p. 83.

17. World Resources Institute.

18. Ibid.

19. 16 USCA §471.

20. 16 USCA §475.

21. 43 USCA §1732(b).

22. 43 USCA §1701–1784.

23. 16 USCA §1601 et seq.

24. Council on Environmental Quality, pp. 193–94.

25. Ibid., p. 194.

26. 16 USCA §1531.

27. 16 USCA §1533.

10

International
Environmental
Law

Thus far, we have been examining the environmental law of the United States. Environmental protection, however, if it is to be truly effective, must have an international dimension.

THE NEED FOR INTERNATIONAL ENVIRONMENTAL LAW

Over the past two decades there has been growing recognition of the need for international environmental law, primarily because of an increasing awareness of the severity of certain worldwide environmental problems. These problems are discussed first. The next section explains the unique nature of international law, followed by descriptions of the sources of environmental law and the primary institutions that carry out those laws. The final sections address how international environmental law is attempting to remedy some specific environmental problems and speculate about the future of international environmental law.

Overpopulation

One of the most severe problems in the world today is overpopulation. This problem necessitates an international solution because without a worldwide solution, extremely adverse consequences will result. The threat of overpopulation was set forth originally in the now famous book of Thomas Robert Malthus, *On the Principle of Population*. Published in 1798, Malthus's work argued that population, which grows geometrically, will eventually outstrip food production, which grows arithmetically, resulting in mass starvation.

Though Malthus's timetable for disaster may have been disrupted by unanticipated agricultural developments, many believe that the ultimate impact of those developments is simply to delay the point at which our inability to provide sufficient foodstuffs will occur.

Added to this original concern, and more important to stimulating the development of international environmental law, is the effect that a larger population has on the overall ability of the planet to sustain life: More people use more energy, more land, and more water. This greater use of resources may lead to their depletion. A huge influx in population also creates more pollution. Burning wood and low-sulfur coal contributes to the buildup of carbon monoxide. Rapid urbanization, occurring in most Third World nations today, leads to massive traffic jams, overcrowded slums, and clogged waste disposal systems, all of which degrade the environment.

Some social scientists, most notably Julian Simon, believe that population growth is good for humanity, primarily because human intellect is our most valuable resource: The more people, the greater the intellect pool from which society can draw. Those who do not believe there is a population problem point out that whenever apparently fixed resources become scarce, we seem to figure out a way to replace them. For example, when horse-powered transportation became a problem, we developed the railroad and the motor car. When trees became scarce in the sixteenth century, we learned to burn coal. Hence, it could be argued from history that every apparent shortage is just a stimulus for the development of new resources, new resources that in the long run may be cheaper than the old ones.[1]

Whether we agree with those who see increased population as a blessing or a curse, we can all agree that the population of the planet is increasing at an unprecedented pace. Every year the population is more than the previous year. Today's population of 5.3 billion is expected to reach 6 billion by the middle of this decade and then *double* in 40 years. The population in 1930 was 2 billion, 3 billion by 1960, 4 billion by 1975, and just over 5 billion by 1987. In 1989, the world population grew by 92 million—the largest annual increase ever recorded.[2]

Perhaps as a society we have always been able to handle increases in population and increasing demands on resources, but it is only logical that at some level a breaking point must be reached. For years the air managed to cleanse itself, but then its self-cleansing properties were overcome by excess pollutants. The same phenomenon occurs with bodies of water. And many fear that despite our successes in the past, we are nearing the carrying capacity for Earth.

If indeed overpopulation is as great a problem as many, such as Paul Ehlich, author of *The Population Bomb*, believe, then perhaps the most important international environmental issue may be one we do not often think of as an environmental issue: population control.

Regardless of whether we perceive population increases as nearing crisis levels, certainly the fact that an increasing number of people are using common resources means that we are more likely to interfere with one another's use of these resources. Hence there is a need for an international body of law to respond to questions regarding use and abuse of the global environment.

Loss of Biological Diversity

Whereas some see overpopulation as the preeminent global problem today, others consider loss of biological diversity an even greater problem. Scientists have classified approximately 1.4 million living species, of which roughly 750,000 are insects, 41,000 are vertebrates, 265,000 are plants, and the rest are invertebrates.[3] No one knows how many millions more exist that have not been classified. The more we learn about these diverse species, the more we discover ways that they can improve and maintain our lives. Some plants and animals provide food, medicine, and industrial raw materials. For example, more than 40 percent of prescription drugs contain chemicals originally derived from wild species. Other species provide flood control, pest control, and natural recycling of waste. Ninety percent of agricultural crops are pollinated exclusively by insects.

Yet, just as we are starting to learn about many of these species and how they can benefit the planet, we are destroying them. At least two-thirds of all land-dwelling species inhabit the tropical rain forests that are being rapidly destroyed. As the rain forests are being destroyed, so are the species that inhabit these areas. Estimates of species loss vary, and it would be impossible to know the precise figure, but they range from 400[4] to 17,500[5] species per year. Some researchers project that by the year 2000, we may lose more than 1 million species.[6] In Germany, the Netherlands, Denmark, and Spain, more than 20 percent of the bird species[7] and 40 percent of the mammalian species are classified as threatened.[8]

As noted, however, the greatest losses are occurring in tropical forests, where most of the various species reside. These losses are occurring because increases in population, endemic poverty, the need for fuel wood, and the failure to use sustainable agriculture methods have led to massive clearing of these forests. Essentially, it is human activity that destroys habitats and leads to the loss of species.

The Global Commons

The term *biosphere* refers to the thin shell where the atmosphere, hydrosphere, and lithosphere connect; in this context life and its products exist. The biosphere constitutes a symbol of the unity and interrelationships of living things and their physical setting. The biosphere calls to mind a complementary relationship between humans and the physical environment. That environment is not viewed primarily as a set of independent, strictly bounded territories but, rather, as one related unit, divided if at all, into natural components—air, water, and land—each having interactive relationships with one another and with humans. Space travel permitted the first real view of Earth as a biosphere. From outer space we could see Earth as a single, unitary whole, set against the blackness of the universe. When we view Earth as a biosphere, we can see that the land, air, and water are interconnected and, in fact, represent a sort of global commons.

Obviously, the oceans and seas constitute a major part of the global commons. Problems associated with the destruction of these shared resources are potentially numerous: Human health may be placed directly at risk by contamination of seafood; reproductive cycles of species of animal life may be disrupted; human health may also be adversely affected as a result of direct contact with polluted water; aesthetic qualities of coastal environments may be destroyed.

Potential destruction of the ocean environment comes primarily from three basic sources: ocean shipping, land-based pollution, and the dumping of wastes in the oceans. The primary problem caused by marine shipping is pollution created by marine oil. Ninety percent of this oil is from standard ship operations, deballasting and tank washings. Only about 10 percent results from tanker accidents, although it is these accidents that tend to generate the greatest publicity. Recall from Chapter 6 that water pollution from land-based activities can be point or nonpoint source. The same two categories apply to pollution of oceans. Point source discharges occur when manufacturers along a coast discharge insufficiently treated or untreated water directly into the ocean. Nonpoint source pollution comes primarily from runoff from cropland, urban areas, and construction and mining sites. Wastes being dumped at sea include sewage sludge, industrial waste, and dredge spoils. These wastes may contain a plethora of heavy metals, synthetic chemicals, and other toxic materials. Ocean dumping of low-level radioactive waste was a problem at one time, but no longer is.

Air is another important part of the global commons. Because of air currents, substances one country emits into the atmosphere are likely to travel to other countries. The three primary global problems associated with air (described in Chapter 5) are acid deposition, depletion of the ozone layer, and the greenhouse effect.

Environmental Disasters and Transboundary Pollution

During the past 20 years, a number of dramatic environmental disasters have made people recognize the potential that our advanced levels of technology have for allowing one nation to wreak havoc on the environment worldwide. These catastrophes make it very clear that no nation, regardless of the precautions it takes, can protect its environment by itself. Some of these disastrous incidents include nuclear accidents such as the Chernobyl incident in the Soviet Union and the nearly catastrophic Three Mile Island accident in the

United States. Others are the industrial accident in Sevesko, Italy, and the Exxon Valdez oil spill in Alaska. The combined effect of these incidents has been to make people question whether there should be some international agreement on how to respond to such disasters when they arise and, even more importantly, how to prevent their occurrence.

Transboundary pollution, on the other hand, has been around for years. Transboundary pollution generally arises in two ways. First, pollution is generated in one area and transported a great distance before falling to earth in another nation. A typical example would be where a U.S. firm uses tall stacks to disperse air pollutants, which causes the air pollutants to settle in Canada. The second type of transboundary pollution occurs when two or more nations border on a common resource and one nation pollutes the common resource to the detriment of the other. An example would be Mexico's dumping sewage into the Tiajuana River, resulting in damage to wells and crops in California.

Solutions to these wide-ranging problems are being sought through international environmental law. Before we examine international environmental law, per se, however, we need to understand how international law in general compares to domestic law.

THE NATURE OF INTERNATIONAL LAW

International law is unlike any other area of law in that there is disagreement over whether indeed there can even *be* a body of law known as international law, and if there is, what those laws are. There is no international superlegislature to establish these laws and no effective international mechanism with enforcement authority.

International law is generally viewed as being derived from two sources: treaties and other agreements freely entered into by nation states and principles derived from long-standing practices. Laws from treaties are referred to as conventional laws; those from long-standing practice are called customary laws. The primary actors in the international law system are the nation-states, as represented by their governments. Intergovernmental agencies also play an important role in the international law system, as do nongovernmental organizations (NGOs). Also, individuals and corporations are sometimes participants.

Enforcement is where international law presents the greatest difficulty. The Security Council of the United Nations is most often viewed as the primary source of enforcement of international law. The council has limited executive authority to enforce the provisions of its charter and to maintain peace and security. However, it does not have any enforcement authority over international law in general. It is also limited because it requires unanimity of all of its members before acting.

The United Nations has established an International Court of Justice. However, the impact of this court has been limited by the fact that it decides only cases submitted by parties who agree to be there. The parties between whom there is the greatest disagreement are therefore unlikely to be before the court because they will not agree to submit their dispute. Thus the parties who need the court the most arguably will be the least likely to use it. In some cases the court has the authority to issue advisory opinions only, which may be, and frequently are, freely ignored.

Given the ineffectiveness of these sources of enforcement, parties have sometimes turned to the courts of the nation-states to seek enforcement of international law. As long as the court will assume jurisdiction, this approach may be the most effective. (This approach is discussed in somewhat greater detail later on.)

SOURCES OF INTERNATIONAL ENVIRONMENTAL LAW

As noted in the preceding section, international law comes from both treaties and practices. International environmental law likewise draws from these two sources. Its conventional law comprises some 20 multilateral treaties governing environmental issues and more than 275 bilateral agreements that contain references to environmental issues.

Conventional Law

Conventional international environmental law can trace its roots back to the UN Conference on the Human Environment in Stockholm in 1972. This two-week meeting produced the Stockholm Declaration of the conference, which was subsequently adopted by the twenty-seventh session of the UN General Assembly by a vote of 114 to 0, with 10 abstentions. This document contained 26 principles, an action plan consisting of 109 recommendations, and a resolution on institutional and financial arrangements. The topics covered by the principles included fundamental human rights (Principle 1), management of human resources (Principles 2–7), the relationship between development and the environment (Principles 8–12), planning and demographic policy (Principles 13–17), science and technology (Principles 18–20), state responsibility (Principles 21–22), respect for national environmental standards along with the need for state cooperation (Principles 23–25), and the threat of nuclear weapons to the environment.[9]

The principles are important because they consolidated the existing rules of international environmental law while also providing guidance for the future of this body of law. Principle 22 is a good example of the tone of these principles and also reflects a recognition by the drafters of the existence of a body of international environmental law. Principle 21 reads as follows:

> States shall cooperate to develop further the international law regarding liability and compensation for the victims of pollution and other environmental damage caused by activities within the jurisdiction or control of such states to areas beyond their jurisdiction.

A second important agreement, the World Charter for Nature,[10] was adopted by the UN General Assembly in 1982, by a vote of 111 to 1, with the United States casting the only dissenting vote. The charter contains a preamble and 25 principles. The first five are general principles. Principles 6 through 13 provide detailed rules for planning and management of the natural environment. Finally, Principles 14 through 24 contain implementation rules that specify obligations for members of the international community.

Customary Law

Customary law is defined by the statute of the International Court of Justice, Article 38,[11] as having its source in state practice, in the "general principles of law that are recognized by civilized nations, and in the judicial decisions and teachings of respected jurists." Think of customary law as analogous to common law in the U.S. legal system.

Four basic principles seem to have evolved as customary international environmental laws. These customary laws are reinforced by treaty provisions. Attempts to codify these customary rules have been undertaken by two private organizations: the International Law Association and the International Law Commission.

A first principle is that of *good neighborliness*—the rule that no state is entitled to use its land in a way that would infringe on the rights of others. This principle, often cited in its Latin form, *sic uter tuo alienum non laedas*, can be viewed as an international application of the U.S. common law of nuisance, discussed in Chapter 4. The doctrine of good neighborliness seems to have been initially granted its status as a customary law in the *Trail Smelter* arbitration.[12] *Trail Smelter* arose from a situation wherein sulfur dioxide fumes from a smelter in Trail, British Columbia, were damaging farmland and crops in the state of Washington. The United States complained to Canada in 1927. After years of negotiations, Canada accepted liability and agreed to arbitrate the issue of damages. In 1941, the decision was handed down that contains the often quoted principle of good neighborliness as applied to transboundary pollution: "Under principles of international law, as well as the law of the United States, no state has the right to permit the use of its territory in such a manner as to cause injury by fumes to another country or to the properties or persons therein where the case is of serious consequence and the injury is established by clear and convincing evidence." This decision is sometimes criticized because of two requirements that limit the rule's application: the description of the consequences as serious and the standard of clear and convincing evidence.

Further support for this customary law can be found in several treaties that incorporate the principle of good neighborliness. For example, the preamble to the Charter of the United Nations states the desire of member states to "live together in peace with one another as good neighbors." Article 74 of the same document encourages member states to conduct their social, economic, and commercial policies in accordance with "general principles of good neighborliness."

A second principle is the *duty of due diligence*—the obligation to protect the rights of other states. In the environmental area, this duty has been extended to mean a duty to use due diligence to prevent and abate pollution. This principle has not been interpreted as an absolute prohibition on pollution but, rather, a mandate that the state take the measures expected under "good government" to prevent pollution. Numerous cases exemplify this principle. For example, France was going to build an ammonia plant that would have generated odorous emissions that could have created a nuisance for several health spas in southern Germany. A French-German commission negotiated an agreement that resulted in France's installing technology that would prevent the creation of a transboundary nuisance.[13]

Another important principle is that of the *equitable utilization of shared resources*—the requirement of the reasonable use of shared resources. The obvious question that arises with respect to this principle is how one decides whether a use is reasonable. In fact, if one decides that reasonable may be derived from past practice, one may in fact be sanctioning the very activities that gave rise to the environmental problems in the first place.

This customary law of equitable utilization was first set out in the *River Oder* case.[14] In that case the Permanent Court of International Justice laid down the rule by stating that "this community of interest (of riparian states) in a navigable river becomes the basis of a common legal right, the essential features of which are the perfect equality of all riparian states in the use of the whole course of the river."

This principle was reinforced by its inclusion in the Helsinki Rules.[15] Article IV states: "Each basin state is entitled, within its territory, to a reasonable and equitable share in the beneficial uses of the waters of an international drainage basin." The Helsinki Rules attempt to provide some guidance as to what is considered reasonable use by listing some factors that should be taken into account—for instance, geographic and climatic conditions, social and economic needs of the neighboring states, comparative costs of alternative ways to satisfy those needs, availability of the technological means to reduce the impact on the environment, and the practicality of compensation as a means of adjusting the burden. The rules do not suggest any order of importance for these factors, indicating that their relevance depends on the individual circumstances of each case.[16]

A final principle is the *duty to inform and cooperate*. The duty to give prior notice is recognized in such often cited cases as the *Corfu Channel* case.[17] This case arose when two British warships traveling through the Corfu Channel, part of Albania's water, were damaged by mines that had been placed there by the Germans. Albania was believed to have, at minimum, knowledge of the mining. The International Court of Justice, in ruling that Albania had to compensate the British for the damage to property and life, stated that "the obligations incumbent upon the Albanian authorities consisted in notifying . . . the existence of a minefield in Albanian territorial waters and in warning the approaching British warships of the immediate danger to which the minefield exposed them."

Adoption of the duty to inform is evidenced by this principle's inclusion in many treaties. For example, Article XXX of the Helsinki Rules recommends that states "furnish any other basin state the interests of which may be substantially affected, notice of a proposed construction or installation which would alter the regime of the basin."[18]

INSTITUTIONS THAT EFFECTUATE AND INFLUENCE INTERNATIONAL ENVIRONMENTAL LAW

United Nations

The most influential intergovernmental organization in the development of international environmental law is the United Nations, an organization established in 1945. Its primary bodies include the General Assembly, the Security Council, and the Economic and Social Council. Technically, all the United Nations can do is make recommendations; the individual members must adopt their own policies. However, the articulation of treaties and policies by the United Nations is a powerful first step toward the worldwide adoption of environmental policies. The United Nations also sponsors several programs that have a significant impact on international environmental law.

United Nations Environmental Program. The United Nations Environmental Program (UNEP) is a special body created by the UN General Assembly that has done much to effectuate worldwide environmental policies. Created at the same time was the Environmental Fund. Both UNEP and the Environmental Fund were mandated by Resolution 2997 (XXVII) in 1972 to effectuate the action plan set forth in the Stockholm Declaration.

UNEP's structure has three distinct entities: the Governing Council, the Environment Secretariat, and the Environment Fund. The Governing Council comprises delegates from the 58 member states that are elected on a rotating basis by the General Assembly. The main responsibilities of the Governing Council are to promote international cooperation in environmental matters and provide general policy guidance for the direction and coordination of environmental programs within the UN system. The council also annually reviews and approves the allocation of money from the Environment Fund. Every year the council receives from the executive director, the state of the environment report, which it uses to identify environmental issues and to decide on future initiatives. The Governing Council reviews the impact of environmental policies on developing countries, as well as promotes contributions from the scientific and other communities to program formulation and development. The council reports

UNEP's activities to the General Assembly through the Economic and Social Council, with special attention being paid to questions of coordination and to the relationship of environmental policies and programs within the UN system to overall economic and social policies and priorities.

The Environment Secretariat is composed of approximately 200 people and is headed by UNEP's executive director, who is elected by the General Assembly. The tasks of the secretariat include coordinating environment programs in the UN system and reviewing and evaluating their effectiveness, providing advisory services for promotion of international cooperation, advising intergovernmental bodies of the UN system on environmental programs, and administering the Environment Fund.

The Environment Fund receives about $5 million in funds annually from the United Nations to cover operating expenses, but relies on voluntary contributions from governments to build up funds to be used for financing initiatives taken within the United Nations and to sponsor many of their programs of general interest that are described in the following paragraphs.

UNEP's mandate is to assess, monitor, and protect the human environment by seeking solutions to pollution and man-made contamination, promoting environmentally sound economic and social developments in urban and rural areas. UNEP is primarily a catalyst and coordinating agency. As such, it collaborates with other environmental agencies, as well as runs some of its own programs.

The Global Environmental Monitoring System (GEMS) is one of the most important UNEP programs. GEMS is responsible for the collection, storage, retrieval, analysis, and dissemination of environmental data related to a wide range of potential pollutants. It functions through a network of national monitoring stations, each of which is coordinated by an appropriate UN specialized agency; for example, climate-related monitoring is done by the World Meteorological Society. A component of GEMS is the Global Resource Information Project (GRID). This project began in 1985 to assimilate and reference data geographically from a wide variety of sources, including satellite observations.

The Regional Seas and Oceans Program (renamed Oceans and Coastal Areas Program) is one of UNEP's most successful. This program involves more than 120 countries through 11 regional sea treaty agreements. The objectives of the program are to foster communications among nations sharing coastal and marine problems, to provide training in oil spill management and emergency response, and to develop marine science centers. The program is also attempting to create common calibrations for monitoring coastal water pollution.

UNEP also engages in a wide range of cooperative ventures with other organizations such as the International Council of Scientific Unions. For example, UNEP publishes the *International Register of Potentially Toxic Chemicals*, which provides detailed information and policy proposals for more than 80,000 chemicals.

World Commission on Economic Development. The World Commission on Economic Development (WCED, sometimes referred to as the Brundtland Commission) was created by the General Assembly of the United Nations in fall 1983 to formulate long-term strategies to attain sustainable development by the year 2000 and beyond. The prime minister of Norway was named chair; the prime minister of the Sudan was named vice chair. These two appointed the remaining 21 members, with more than half being from developing nations.

On October 1–3, 1984, the newly organized WCED met and adopted a mandate to "re-examine critical issues of environment and development and formulate innovative, concrete, and realistic action proposals to address them, strengthen international cooperation on environment and development and assess and propose new forms of cooperation that can reshape existing economic patterns and influence policies and events in the direction of needed change; and raise the level of understanding and commitment to action on the part of individuals, voluntary associations, businesses, institutions, and governments."[19]

The major accomplishment of WCED, thus far, has been the publication of *Our Common Future.* The report was based on data gathered from public hearings in a dozen cities around the world and information from several advisory panels. The report concluded that "humanity has the ability to make development sustainable—to ensure that it meets the needs of the present without compromising the ability of future generations to meet their own needs."

World Bank

The World Bank is one of the primary sources of funding for projects in developing countries. As such, it has the potential to play an extremely influential role in environmental policies worldwide.

Prior to the mid-1980s, environmental factors were not a consideration in the World Bank's lending decisions. And, in fact, many have criticized the bank for lending money without considering the social impacts of the projects, for example, lending money for projects that led to deforestation and to governments that do not care about indigenous tribal minorities. In 1987, however, the bank was reorganized and an environmental department was established. As a result, potential borrowers were asked to prepare an environmental issues paper for each loan they wished to obtain. The contents of these papers were to be considered when loans were being made.

In 1979, the impact of potential environmental effects was given even more prominence by an operational directive on environmental assessments of proposed projects. Now, when a project is being considered, a preliminary screening is done by the environmental department of the World Bank. The project is rated according to its potential impact on the environment. Category A has the greatest potential, so it would require that a full environmental assessment be done by the potential borrower. Category B would require only limited assessment of specific impacts. Category C would not necessitate any assessment because it is unlikely to have environmental impacts. Category D does not require any assessment because the environment is the focus of the project. Not only are these assessments taken into account when the bank is considering action on loan requests, but a summary of the project's environmental impact is included in a supplement to the bank's monthly operational summary, the main document the bank uses to convey its future plans to interested parties.

In 1991, the World Bank's commitment to environmentally sound lending practices was strengthened by its adoption of a new policy on tropical rain forests. No further bank funding is to be made available for commercial logging in the remaining tropical forests. The World Bank, while not a party to making law, still has a tremendous influence on international environmental policy. A law prohibiting logging in tropical rain forests may be evaded, but if the funding for such projects is not readily available, evasion will be much more difficult.

European Community

The European Community (EC) is a "community" originally established by six European nations and now embraces 12. The EC has been given the authority, by its member states, to negotiate treaties that directly bind the members without further ratification by members' separate legislatures. The EC consists of a council, whose members are ministers from the member nations, a commission, and a parliament, which is made up of representatives directly elected by member states. The commission proposes legislation, and the council adopts it after receiving input from the parliament. The legislation passed by the EC is in two forms—regulations and directives. Regulations have the force of a national law and are directly enforceable in each nation's court. Directives are broader and bind nations to ends that are to be achieved.

The EC first began to address environmental policy explicitly in 1972, influenced to a great extent by the Stockholm Conference. Legislation is adopted in accordance with the EC's environmental action program. The program, which has been redefined four times since its inception, establishes principles in accordance with which environmental legislation is to be adopted. Eleven principles have been established; the following are typical examples of those principles: Activities in one nation should not cause a deterioration of the environment of another, and the effects of environmental policies in member states should take into account the interests of developing nations. By 1992, the EC had adopted more than 280 pieces of environmental legislation. These regulations cover a broad range of environmental issues, from drinking water standards to limits on sulfur dioxide emissions for controlling acid rain.

The EC also acts as negotiator for its member states in negotiations for treaties (often referred to as conventions) with nonmember nations. As a representative of many nations, the EC has greater clout than any single nation would have. Although the EC is an active and influential participant in these treaty negotiations, the EC does not actually bind member states to most conventions; member states independently determine whether they will become signatories to such agreements. In some cases, however, member states do give the EC the authority to bind them to a proposed treaty. When given such authority, the EC has even greater power at the negotiating table. The Montreal Protocol, the treaty to reduce chlorofluorocarbons, is one example of a treaty to which the EC was a signatory, binding all member states.

ADDRESSING SPECIFIC INTERNATIONAL ENVIRONMENTAL PROBLEMS

In this section we examine how international environmental law attempts to solve some specific problems. Treatment of these problem areas relies on both customary and conventional law, neither of which is very satisfactory. The customary law is plagued by the uncertainty of its principles. Treaties, because they require agreement of parties with conflicting interests, are often very weak, imposing few absolute rights or obligations. Both types of law are victims of the overall problem of weak enforceability.

Transboundary Pollution

Transboundary pollution occurs when pollution generated in one nation is transported to another nation, or when two countries share a common resource and one contaminates that resource to the detriment of the other. Establishing an international law for transboundary pollution is difficult because of two conflicting perspectives on state sovereignty. One is a concept of absolute sovereignty, under which a nation is free to do whatever it wishes with resources within its boundaries. Most nations denounce this absolutist position, but, still, in practice, it describes many nations' behavior. The opposing view is that of absolute territorial integrity. This view holds that no state may engage in activities that would in any way damage the territory of another nation.

The development of international environmental law regarding transboundary pollution can be seen as an attempt to find a way to recognize these two competing notions of territoriality. The current tentative resolution of this conflict seems to be that the rights emanating from territorial sovereignty imply a reciprocal duty to take into account the impact of one nation's behavior on other nations. Recognition of the need to incorporate both concepts of territoriality is perhaps best exemplified by Principle 21 of the Stockholm Declaration. The principle reads as follows: "States have, in accordance with the Charter of the United Nations and the principles of international law, the *sovereign right to exploit their own resources pursuant to their environmental principles, and the responsibility to ensure that activities within their jurisdiction or control do not cause damage to the environment of other states* [emphasis added] or areas beyond the limits of national jurisdiction."

Finding a definitive statement of the law of transboundary pollution is not easy. However, we can look to a couple of sources: *Legal Principles and Recommendations Adopted by the Experts Group on Environmental Law of the World Commission on Environment and Development (Legal Principles)* and *Restatement (Third) of the Foreign Relations of the United States.*

Article 10 of *Legal Principles*, Prevention and Abatement of a Transboundary Environmental Interference, provides as follows: "States shall prevent or abate any transboundary environmental interference or a significant risk thereof which causes substantial harm—i.e., harm which is not minor or insignificant." In the comments to this section the drafters explained that this duty did not impose on countries an absolute duty to prevent every possible harm, nor was the duty to undertake heroic measures. Rather, states were to take "to the fullest extent practical" measures that would prevent such "excessive pollution" as would "substantially impair" customary use of a shared resource.

Article 11, Liability for Transboundary Interferences Resulting from Lawful Activities, provides that:

1. If one or more activities create a significant risk of substantial harm as a result of a transboundary environmental interference, and if the overall technical and socio-economic cost or loss of benefits involved in preventing or reducing such risk far exceeds in the long run the advantage which such prevention or reduction would entail, the State which carried out or permitted the activities shall ensure that compensation is provided should substantial harm occur in an area under national jurisdiction of another State or in an area beyond the limits of national jurisdiction.

2. A state shall ensure that compensation is provided for substantial harm caused by transboundary environmental interferences resulting from activities carried out or permitted by that state notwithstanding that the activities were not initially known to cause such interferences.

The comments to this section point out that liability for transboundary pollution is under the doctrine of strict liability. In other words, even if the polluting state is not violating any law in terms of the activity in which it is engaged, it may still be liable if those activities result in harm that outweighs the benefits.

In *Restatement (Third) of the Foreign Relations of the United States*, we find the following statement of liability for transboundary pollution:

§902 Interstate Claims and Remedies

(1) A state may bring a claim against another state for violation of an international obligation owed to the claimant state or to states generally, either through diplomatic channels, or through any procedure to which the two states have agreed.

(2) Under Subsection (1), a state may bring claims, *inter alia* for violations of international obligations resulting in injury to its nationals or to other persons on whose behalf it is entitled to make a claim under international law.

Because of the confusion surrounding the issue of liability of nations for transboundary pollution, the UN General Assembly requested that the International Law Commission (ILC) report on liability for transboundary pollution when the acts giving rise to the injury were not illegal, per se. (The ILC is a body of the United Nations composed of 35 representatives that are elected by the General Assembly by geographic location.) The conclusions reached by the ILC seem to be reflective of what we have seen as the principles of customary international environmental law.

Four duties appear to be imposed on nations: to prevent transboundary harm, to inform other nations of accidents that might cause transboundary harm, to enter into negotiations to attempt to develop a convention to determine how the situation should be handled, and, if no convention can be adopted, to negotiate in good faith with respect to the rights and obligations of the parties. When harm has resulted, liability should be determined by considering a number of factors, including the amount of damage, the degree of control exercised by the responsible state, the reasonableness of the parties' conduct, and the relative costs of preventing the injury.

Choice of Forums

A question may arise when one reads that statement of law in the preceding paragraph: Where should such a case be brought? Earlier we made reference to the fact that one of the problems of international law is its lack of an effective forum for both dispute resolution and the subsequent enforcement of any judgment that may be obtained. That problem is reaffirmed in our examination of the alternative forums in which transboundary pollution disputes may be brought.

Whenever one thinks of resolving a transboundary pollution dispute, the first forum that comes to mind is the International Court of Justice. The International Court of Justice has the jurisdiction to decide cases that are submitted to it. Also, the court may render advisory opinions at the request of the General Assembly or any other competent body of the United Nations. One major obvious problem is that when one party is the transgressor, that party is obviously going to be reluctant to submit the dispute to the court. And if the court is asked to render a nonbinding advisory opinion, the effect of that advice is likely to be nil, especially if the opinion suggests the payment of reparations. The rarity of disputes coming before this forum is reflected by the low number of opinions rendered by this court. From 1945 to 1986, only 72 cases were submitted, with 45 judgments and 17 advisory opinions issued.[20]

Even if a judgment is rendered, enforcement is difficult. The UN Security Council can, "if it deems necessary, make recommendations or decide upon measures to be taken to give effect to the judgment."[21] However, because of the uncertainty of this clause, the Security Council has been reluctant to take action under it. Therefore, states have felt fairly free simply to ignore the judgments of the International Court of Justice.

Perhaps the most effective forum for resolution of these disputes is the court of the nation in which the harmful conduct took place. The major problem addressed by this approach is that there exists an effective means of enforcement. The power of the state lies behind the judgment. This approach, however, is most likely to be effective when the victim state is suing a private party residing in the offending state rather than actually suing the state itself.

The UNEP Draft Principles of Conduct express a preference for the use of national courts for the resolution of transboundary pollution problems. Principle 14 provides as follows:

> States should endeavor, in accordance with their legal systems and where appropriate, on a basis agreed by them, to provide persons in other states who have been or may be adversely affected by environmental damage resulting from the utilizations of shared resources with equivalent access and treatment in the same judicial and administrative proceedings and make available to them the same remedies as are available to persons within their own jurisdiction who may have been or may be similarly situated.

The UN Organization for Economic Cooperation and Development (OECD), in its 1977 Recommendation for Implementation of a Regime of Equal Right of Access and Non-Discrimination in Relation to Transfrontier Pollution, reflects a similar view. The OECD recommends that equal access to information be given to foreign nations, as well as equal access to all public authorities, courts, and administrative agencies. In private treaties, some nations are adopting this equal access approach with respect to transboundary pollution. One example of such a treaty is the Convention on Protection of the Environment, the so-called Nordic Convention, entered into by Sweden, Denmark, Finland, and Norway. Article 3 of the convention provides that any person who is

> affected or may be affected by a nuisance caused by environmentally harmful activities in another contracting state shall have the right to bring before the appropriate court or administrative authority of that state the question of the permissibility of measures to prevent damage, and to appeal against the decision of the court or administrative agency to the same extent and on the same terms as a legal entity of the state in which the activities are being carried out.
>
> (2) The provisions of the first paragraph . . . are equally applicable in the case of proceedings concerning compensation for damage caused by environmentally harmful activities. The question of compensation shall not be judged by rules that are less favorable to the injured party than are the rules of compensation of the state in which the activities are being carried out.

An alternative forum to the courts themselves is the use of international arbitration. To make the decision binding, disputants enter into a compromise or agreement that sets forth the subject matter of the dispute, the method for selecting the arbitration panel, and the procedures to be followed during the arbitration. Again, however, because of the need for an agreement to arbitrate, the most hotly contested cases may not come before the arbitrator. Also, once the award is made, if one of the parties disagrees with the award and refuses to comply, there's no available mechanism for enforcement.

A final, and perhaps most common way of resolving conflicts arising out of transboundary pollution is diplomacy. Diplomatic solutions are generally compromises brought about through negotiations between the countries in conflict. Frequently they are aided by representatives from an international or regional organization, so that the procedure for resolution in fact becomes a form of mediation.

The Global Commons

Recall that the global commons refers to those areas of Earth that cannot easily be partitioned, those resources that belong to no one but preserve and maintain the lives of us all. If we all simply use the commons without taking care to preserve it, the global commons will be destroyed. The primary problems associated with the global commons have been discussed earlier in this chapter. Here we will consider attempts to solve some of these problems. As you will see, the primary approach has been through multilateral treaties.

Destruction of the Ozone Layer. Although this problem has been considered a national problem, it is, in fact, global in nature. The United States could totally ban the use of ozone-destroying CFCs, but if other nations did not follow suit, the ozone layer would still be destroyed. We cannot separate "our" portion of the ozone layer.

The worldwide response to ozone depletion has been remarkably swift. On September 16, 1987, 24 nations and the EC signed the Montreal Protocol on Substances That Deplete the Ozone Layer. The primary objectives of the treaty were as follows:

1. In 1987, to hold increases of ozone depleting chlorofluorocarbons and halons to 10 percent of 1986 levels.
2. Within four more years, to reduce the production of CFCs and halons to 80 percent of 1986 levels.
3. By July 1, 1999, to reduce CFC and halon production to 50 percent of 1986 levels.

The protocol provided an exception for developing countries. The treaty also provided that there would be no trade in controlled substances with any nation not a party to the treaty. A Montreal Protocol Multilateral Fund was also set up in conjunction with the treaty. This fund provides aid to assist developing nations in the transition from ozone-depleting chemicals. At a June 1990 meeting in London, the parties to the protocol agreed to phase out CFCs, carbon tetrachloride, and nonessential uses of halons by the year 2000 and the use of methyl chloroform by 2005.

Global Warming. Figure 10–1 depicts the global warming or greenhouse effect. As you can see from the figure, carbon dioxide is the primary contributor to global warming, and the United States is a primary source. In May 1992, the problem of greenhouse gas emissions was temporarily resolved by the signing of a treaty by representatives of 142 nations to attempt to reduce the level of emissions of greenhouse gases (carbon dioxide, methane, nitrous oxide) by developed nations back to 1990 levels by the year 2000. The treaty will set up a procedure for monitoring scientific advances so that modifications can be undertaken if necessary. Developing nations will adopt policies that will limit the increase in their emissions, although these emissions will still increase substantially, and developed nations will provide financial and technical aid to developing countries.

This treaty was actually much less stringent than originally proposed; many environmentalists argued that the treaty had been gutted by the United States. President Bush had used this treaty for leverage to bargain with other nations at the Earth Summit. Bush agreed to attend this major international conference on the environment only if stipulations in the original treaty that absolute curbs on carbon dioxide levels would be enforced were removed.

Marine Pollution. As with most global commons problems, the primary approach to protecting the oceans and seas has been through the use of treaties, with one of the more important treaties being the 1982 Convention on the Law of the Sea. *Restatement (Third) of Foreign Relations Law of the United States, Part VI, the Law of the Environment* (1988) reiterates some of the important aspects of this convention.

Section 603, State Responsibility for Marine Pollution, obligates a state to "adopt laws and regulations to prevent, reduce and control any significant pollution of the marine environment that are no less effective than generally accepted international rules and standards," and to "ensure compliance with the foregoing by ships flying its flag, imposing adequate penalties on the captain or owner of the ship that violates such rules." Part (2) of Section 603 provides that "a state is obligated to take, individually and jointly with other states, such measures as may be necessary, to the extent practicable under the circumstances, to prevent, reduce, and control pollution causing or threatening to cause significant injury to the marine environment."

Remedies for marine pollution caused by violating Section 603 are given in Section 604, which provides that any state responsible to another state for violating Section 603 is subject to general interstate remedies "to prevent, reduce, or terminate the activity threatening or causing pollution and to pay reparation for

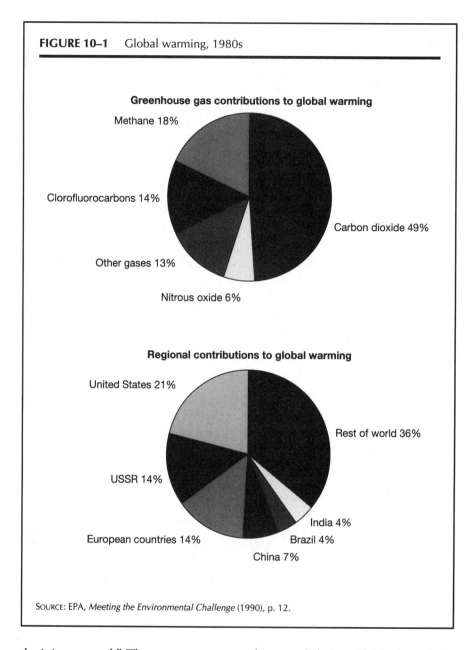

FIGURE 10–1   Global warming, 1980s

Greenhouse gas contributions to global warming

Methane 18%

Clorofluorocarbons 14%

Carbon dioxide 49%

Other gases 13%

Nitrous oxide 6%

Regional contributions to global warming

United States 21%

Rest of world 36%

USSR 14%

India 4%

European countries 14%   Brazil 4%

China 7%

SOURCE: EPA, *Meeting the Environmental Challenge* (1990), p. 12.

the injury caused." The state must ensure that a remedy is available through its legal system "to provide prompt and adequate compensation or other relief for an injury to private interests caused by pollution of the marine environment."

This section gives coastal states the additional authority to detain and institute proceedings against foreign states navigating its territorial seas and violating one of the state's antipollution laws or violating international antipollution laws that resulted in a discharge that caused or threatened a major injury to the state. A port state may institute proceedings against a foreign ship that voluntarily entered its port for "a violation of that states anti-pollution laws . . . if the violation occurred in the port state's territorial sea or exclusive economic zone"; or for "a discharge in violation of applicable international anti-pollution rules and standards that occurred beyond the limits of national jurisdiction of any state." A port state also has the obligation, as far as practicable, under Section 604(c), to investigate whether a ship that voluntarily entered into its port was responsible for a discharge in violation of applicable antipollution rules and standards, when asked to do so by either the states in whose waters the discharge allegedly occurred or by the flag state.

Another important international treaty dealing with marine pollution is the International Convention for the Prevention of Pollution from Ships of 1973, as modified by its protocol of 1978, and generally referred to as the MARPOL Convention. The MARPOL Convention has been ratified by more than 40 countries and thereby regulates more than 80 percent of the world's merchant fleet. The convention is divided into five sections, called annexes, with each attempting to regulate a different potential problem: pollution by oil; noxious liquid substances carried in bulk; harmful substances carried in packages; ship sewage; and ship garbage. Many of the treaty's directives involve standards for design and equipment. For example, Annex I requires ballast tanks of all oil-carrying vessels to be strategically located around the outer periphery of the hull of the vessel.

Discharges are also regulated under the MARPOL Convention. For example, oil tankers may discharge no more than 60 liters of oil per mile, and discharges must take place at least 50 miles from land. Under the convention the disposal of plastics at sea is completely prohibited. The disposal of other types of garbage is restricted to certain distances from land. Domestic garbage cannot be dumped within 3 miles of land, and if it is to be dumped within 12 miles, it must first be sent through a grinder.

Ocean dumping is regulated by the London Convention on the Prevention of Marine Pollution by Dumping of Wastes and Other Matter, effective since December 29, 1972. This treaty prohibits the deliberate dumping of high-level radioactive waste at sea. Other compounds that parties may wish to dump are divided into annexes and regulated accordingly: Matter from Annex I cannot be dumped. Matter listed in Annex II can be dumped only with a "special permit," the criteria for which are specified in Annex III. All matter not mentioned in Annex I or II may be dumped with a prior general permit.

Land-based pollution, in general, is simply regulated by the state of origin. Article 207 of the UN Law of the Sea Convention, however, does oblige parties to adopt necessary laws to prevent and control land-based sources of marine pollution.

By 1991, the United States had ratified three additional treaties that are important for protecting the marine environment. The first was the International Convention on Oil Pollution Preparedness, Response, and Cooperation; this treaty establishes a worldwide network of expertise and resources to prevent and respond to oil spills. The second treaty, the 1989 Salvage Convention, provides compensation for persons who take steps to preserve the environment while salvaging a ship or cargo at sea. The third treaty was the International Convention on Standards of Training, Certification, and Watchkeeping for Seafarers, which sets standards for ship officers and crew so that accidents will be less likely to occur.

Preservation of Biological Diversity

The primary way that we are attempting to preserve biological diversity is through treaties. See Table 10–1 for a listing of some of these treaties.

Convention on International Trade in Endangered Fauna and Flora (CITES). The Convention on International Trade in Endangered Species of Wild Fauna and Flora has been characterized by some as "perhaps the most successful of all international treaties concerned with the conservation of wildlife."[22] Ratified by 96 nations as of 1987, the treaty is designed to prohibit the international trafficking in wildlife species and products that are endangered. Under the CITES,

TABLE 10–1   Treaties that help preserve the global commons and biological diversity

Treaty	Purpose
Convention on Regulation of Antarctic Mineral Resource Activity	Regulate exploitation of mineral resources in Antarctica
Declaration on Arctic Environmental Protection	Encourage cooperation in areas of pollution, marine environmental protection, emergency response, conservation of flora and fauna, and research and monitoring in the Arctic
Convention for the Protection of the Environment in the South Pacific	Encourage cooperation in addressing water treatment programs, management of coastal zones and wastes, lagoon and coral reef restoration, and climate change issue
International Whaling Convention	Phase out commercial whaling by 1986, except when meat and products are used for local consumption by aborigines
Treaty for Amazonian Cooperation	Obtain agreement among eight countries with territories in Amazon to balance economic growth and environment protection
Convention in International Trade in Endangered Species	Prohibits international trade of endangered plants and animals

species are listed under Appendices I, II, and III. Appendix I species are endangered, and trade in these species will be authorized under only the most extraordinary circumstances. Appendix II contains those species that are not now threatened with extinction but may become so if traded. Appendix III consists of species that a nation protects within its jurisdiction and is seeking the cooperation of other nations to protect that species from exploitation. Only under extremely strict conditions specified in CITES can a listed species be traded. Enforcement is left to the signatory parties.

Although the CITES looks good, the problem with it lies in its enforcement, which is almost nil. Studies of enforcement of the treaty have found that most inspectors in signatory nations are not trained well enough to be able to enforce the treaty.

In the United States, CITES is implemented through the Endangered Species Act, which many call the most stringent environmental statute in the world. As explained in Chapter 9, it prohibits the import, export, sale, or shipment of any endangered or threatened species in the course of a commercial activity, as well as the possession of any species taken in violation of the act. Only with a special permit can one cause any harm to an endangered species or its habitat. The act is enforced by the U.S. Fish and Wildlife Service with respect to animals and by the Animal and Plant Health Inspection Service with respect to plants.

Today, 681 domestic species are listed in the act as threatened or endangered. Another 3,800 are candidates for listing, but the Fish and Wildlife Service has not yet had time to study them or add them to the list. Since the law's passage, only one species—the American alligator—has recovered as a result of being protected. Seven listed species have become extinct, 10 percent are recovering, and 37 percent are declining.

The act is up for reauthorization and is generating considerable debate. Some argue that there is not enough money to save all species, as the act tries to do, and that under the new law certain species should be targeted so that the money can be used more efficiently to save the targeted species. Many argue that the way the decision as to what biological species or subspecies are to be preserved must be revised. Currently subspecies and even distinct populations of subspecies may be listed. This issue was raised when the preservation of one of 25 subspecies of the red squirrel halted the construction of an observatory. Some people are even arguing that the species-by-species approach is wrong; instead, focus should be on creating and preserving habitats. Given all these conflicting views, it should be an interesting reauthorization process.

Man and the Biosphere Program. The United Nations Educational, Scientific and Cultural Organization (UNESCO) has tried another approach to preserving our biological diversity. In 1976, UNESCO's Man and the Biosphere (MAB) program became operational. Participating countries create and protect biosphere reserves—protected areas designed to combine conservation and sustainable use. In the center of a reserve is a core area where there is minimal disturbance of an ecosystem characteristic of a major type of natural environment. This core is surrounded by a buffer zone wherein activities are managed in ways that will help protect the core. Outside the buffer zone is the transition area, which combines conservation and sustainable activities like forestry and recreation. As of early 1987, more than 110 countries were participating in the MAB program, and 260 biospheres reserves had been created. The United States established its first reserve in 1974 and now has 44.

Debt for Nature Swaps. One new way to try to protect diversity is an innovative contractual arrangement called debt for nature swaps. In simplest terms, a debt for nature swap occurs when conservation parks or sustainable use areas are set aside and legally protected by a foreign government in exchange for which a portion of that country's foreign debt is cancelled. An intermediary group, generally a conservation organization facilitates the swap by paying off the debt at a deeply discounted rate.

The first such debt for nature swap occurred in Bolivia. Conservation International (CI), a nonprofit organization, obtained a $100,000 grant from the Frank Weeden Foundation, a charitable organization in California that donates money exclusively to environmental causes. CI used this grant to purchase $650,000 of discounted Bolivian debt from a Swiss bank. In exchange for the $650,000 face value debt from CI, the Bolivian government agreed to establish three conservation and sustainable use areas consisting of 3.7 million acres, adjacent to an existing biosphere reserve.

By November 1991, 21 debt for nature swaps had been completed in 11 countries, and several other swaps were being negotiated. The three conservation organizations most frequently involved in swaps, Conservation International, the Nature Conservatory, and the World Wildlife Foundation, were responsible for 19 of the 22 swaps. With $17 million of privately raised funds, they retired $99 million worth of debt through these swaps.

The typical debt for nature contract attempts to achieve its environmental goals by specifying the environmental activities that are to be undertaken by the host government. Many include provisions allowing the conservation organization to undertake specific activities on the newly protected area. The debtor nation is usually required to set aside a specific fund of money to be used in managing the protected area.

These projects seem to have potential, but, again, the major problem is their enforceability. The developing country may mismanage the funds set aside for protecting the area; the host country may simply be incompetent and not manage the area appropriately. Or, in some less stable nations, the government that agreed to the swap may be overthrown and the new government unwilling to carry out the contract.

If the host country breaches the agreement, the organization that retired the debt may always sue for breach of contract in the host country. That country's willingness to rule against its own government is somewhat unlikely, however. Alternatively, the conservation group may hold out the threat of refusing to carry out any further swaps with the nation in question if compliance is not attained. Another possibility is to include in the contract a provision that if compliance by the host country is lacking, that country becomes liable to the conservation organization for the amount of debt retired by the organization.

Another problem with the debt for nature swaps is that their use on a large scale may be impossible. Part of the reason why these swaps can be done is the willingness of banks to discount debt. Banks may do so when they feel they will never get full payment anyway. But their willingness to discount loans is not unlimited.

In spite of these potential problems, many believe debt for nature swaps are an important tool for retaining biodiversity. First, when successful, land is set aside that otherwise might have been developed. Second, deforestation in areas other than the swapped region may be prevented because one of the reasons for deforestation is that developing countries are often forced to exploit their natural resources to service their debt. Without the massive debt, much exploitation may be unnecessary. Because swaps are new, it is too early to speculate as to their effectiveness. For now, we can only wait and see.

THE FUTURE OF INTERNATIONAL ENVIRONMENTAL LAW

The Rio Summit

From June 1 through June 12, 1992, delegates from more than 120 nations met in Rio de Janeiro for the United Nations Conference on Environment and Development (UNCED), commonly referred to as the Rio Summit. With two years of negotiations leading up to the summit, the participants in the meeting had established a lofty goal for themselves: to agree on a set of principles and conventions to set the world on a new environmental course, and perhaps some day eradicate the pollution that is threatening our planet.

It is too early to know what real impact, if any, the summit will have on worldwide environmental policies. Some participants are claiming that it has already been a success because, if nothing else, the two years of preparation brought the idea of sustainable development—progress without destruction of the environment—before hundreds of officials from developing nations. Others applauded the creation of a UN Sustainable Development Commission, modeled on the Human Rights Commission, that will use public criticism and pressure to hold governments accountable for achieving the goals laid out at the summit.

Five documents came out of the summit. Whether the agreements will have any impact on international environmental law depends on the agreements' ratification and enforcement.

Agenda 21. Agenda 21, an 800-page blueprint for environment-friendly development, covers a diverse range of issues, including hazardous waste, human health, ocean pollution, and advancement for women. The heart of this document is a program of aid to Third World nations to help them clean up their pollution and replant their forests, at an estimated cost of $125 billion per year.

Rio Declaration. The Rio Declaration is a six-page statement containing 27 principles that calls for a link between environmental protection and development, spelling out the "rights" of poor nations to develop in responsible ways. This document was designed to encourage new levels of cooperation among states.

Biodiversity. The agreement that aroused the most debate in the United States was the biodiversity agreement. This treaty requires signatory nations to establish policies to slow the loss of plant and animal species. Developed nations with technology will cooperate with nondeveloped nations that have the diverse species of rain forest flora and fauna to develop new pharmaceuticals. President Bush created an uproar among environmentalists by opposing the treaty on the grounds that it would not adequately protect biotechnology and other patents and would excessively regulate the biotechnology industry. He also argued that the treaty was unnecessary because the U.S. Endangered Species Act was already providing much greater protection than would be provided under this treaty. Thirty nations are needed to ratify this treaty.

Climate Change. The industrialized nations, including the United States, agreed to reduce emissions of greenhouse gases to 1990 levels by the year 2000. Developing nations are to develop policies to control their emissions. When 50 nations sign, this treaty becomes effective.

Forest Protection. A statement of principles called for sustainable forest management and asked nations to avoid excessive cutting of trees.

It was clear from the meeting that some changes from all nations are going to be needed if Rio's agreements are to be successfully ratified and implemented. Poor nations tended to place all blame for the world's woes on developed nations and asserted that the polluters should pay developing countries to protect their ecosystems. Clearly, the World Bank, the primary distributor of money to developing nations, will have to do a better job of integrating environment and development in its investments. Only time will tell, however, whether the world will be able to live up to the goals set forth at the Rio Summit.

Environmentalism and Trade

Traditionally, the only treaties environmentalists really worried about were those designed to address specific environmental problems, such as the treaties we have examined in this chapter. Increasingly, however, some environmental groups are beginning to see the value of having input into international trade agreements, although not surprisingly, not all environmental organizations agree about how environmental interests can best be protected through these treaties.

The negotiations of two treaties designed to make trade freer—the 103-nation General Agreement on Tariffs and Trade (GATT) (previously negotiated but now being revised) and the North American Free Trade Agreement (NAFTA)—have caught the interest of environmentalists. One issue that negotiators must resolve is the potential conflict that arises when a nation's "green" laws have an adverse effect on commerce. For example, Germany recently passed a law requiring that all packaging be recyclable. Because other nations do not require recyclable (and, thus, more expensive) packaging, an extra burden is placed on foreign competitors that do not do a significant amount of business in Germany yet would probably, for efficiency, have to change the packaging of their products or leave the market.

The key provision of GATT related to this issue is the statement that nations have the right to enact any environmental, health, and safety laws they choose, as long as the laws are "necessary" and are the "least trade restrictive" way of resolving the problem. NAFTA additionally requires that the laws be based on "scientific principles" and "risk assessment." Because U.S. laws are often based on political compromise as well as science, one can see how some of this nations' laws might not meet these standards.

In fact, the United States has already lost one environmental law battle under GATT. GATT disputes are resolved by a GATT panel of trade judges. In 1991, such a panel ruled that the United States violated GATT by banning the import of tuna caught in the type net that kills dolphins, a ban required by the Marine Mammal Protection Act. Fortunately, the United States and Mexico, the nation challenging the ban, reached a settlement satisfactory to both. But this adverse ruling was sufficient to alarm many environmentalists.

Some people, including Max Baucus, the head of the U.S. Senate's trade subcommittee, argue that for purposes of trade, lax environmental regulation should be seen as a governmental subsidy because it will be cheaper to produce products when a firm does not have to meet stringent environmental standards. Therefore, many argue, nations with strict environmental standards should be able to place a duty on those goods made under relaxed regulations to increase their price to what it would have been without the subsidy. Whether such provisions may be included in future trade agreements is uncertain, but certainly environmental groups are going to pay a lot more attention to trade agreements in the future.

CONCLUDING REMARKS

This chapter clearly demonstrates that many of our major environmental concerns—acid rain, the greenhouse effect, transboundary pollution, and the loss of biodiversity—are really global problems. World population is growing at an unprecedented rate, and this increase in population only exacerbates these problems. International environmental agreements appear to be the best approach to solving these problems. As we see how these treaties work, we may begin to understand the extent to which we may be able, through international cooperation, to solve the most pressing environmental problems. We can also continue to try innovative ideas such as the debt for nature swaps. The United States is a small part of a complex biosphere; thus we must remember that we cannot solve our environmental problems in isolation.

QUESTIONS FOR REVIEW AND DISCUSSION

1. Identify four major problems that international environmental law needs to address.
2. Discuss the two primary sources of international law.
3. Why does international law tend to be ineffective?
4. Explain the four primary principles of customary international environmental law.
5. How does UNEP function?
6. Explain why it has been difficult to establish a satisfactory way to handle transboundary pollution problems.
7. What are the purpose and provisions of the Montreal Protocol?
8. Explain how international law is addressing the problem of pollution of the oceans and seas.

FOR FURTHER READING

Favre, David. "Tension Points Within the Language of the CITES Treaty." *Boston University International Law Journal* 5 (1987):247.

Reilly, William K. "Debt-for-Nature Swaps: The Time Has Come." *Environmental Affairs* 2 (1990):134.

Springer, Allen. *The International Law of Pollution.* Westport, Conn.: Quorom Books, 1983.

Wagner, Rodney. "Doing More with Debt for Nature Swaps." *International Environmental Affairs* 2 (1990):160.

Williams, Brock. "Trade and the Environment." *Foreign Affairs* 62 (1988):1037.

World Commission on Environment and Development. *Our Common Future.* New York: Oxford University Press, 1987.

Zang, Donald. "Frozen in Time: The Antarctic Mineral Resource Convention." *Cornell Law Review* 76 (1991):722.

NOTES

1. Julian Simon, "Population Growth Is Not Bad for Humanity," *Phi Kappa Phi Journal* (Winter 1990):12.
2. Werner Fornos, "Gaining People, Losing Ground," *The Humanist* (May/June 1990).
3. Edward Wilson, "The Current State of Biological Diversity," in *Biodiversity*, ed. Edward O. Wilson. (Washington, D.C.: National Academy Press, 1988).
4. Norman Myers, *An Atlas of Planet Management.* (Garden City, N.Y.: Anchor Press, 1988).
5. Wilson, "Current State of Biological Diversity."
6. Ibid., p. 13.
7. United Nations, Organization for Economic Cooperation and Development, *The State of the Environment* (1985).
8. Ibid.
9. Louis Sohn, "The Stockholm Declaration on the Human Environment," *Harvard Journal of Environmental Law* 14 (1973):423.
10. GA Res. 37/7, 37 UN. GAOR SUPP. (No. 51) at 7, U.N. DOC. A/37/51 (1982).
11. I.J. Acts and Documents 77 (1978).
12. "Trail Smelter Arbitration," *Encyclopedia of Public International Law* Installment 2 (1983), pp. 267–80.
13. International Law Association, "Legal Aspects of the Conservation of the Environment," *Report of the Fifty-eighth Conference* (Manila, 1978), p. 401.
14. P.I.C.J. Ser. A. No. 23 at 27 (1929).
15. Comment to Article IV, Helsinki Rules on the Uses of Waters of International Rivers, ILA, Report of the Fifty-second Conference (Helsinki, 1966), p. 487.
16. Ibid., comment to Article X, p. 497.
17. *I.C.J. Reports* (1949):4.
18. International Law Association, "Legal Aspects of the Conservation of the Environment."
19. Council on Environmental Quality, *Environmental Quality: Twentieth Annual Report* (1990).
20. Richard Levy, "International Law and the Chernobyl Accident, Reflections on an Important but Imperfect System," *Kansas Law Review* 36 (1987):81.
21, Ibid.
22. John Heppes and Eric McFadden, "The Convention on International Trade in Endangered Species of Wild Fauna and Flora: Improving the Prospects for Preserving Our Biological Heritage," *Boston University International Law Journal* 5 (1987):22.

Appendix A   National Primary Drinking Water Standards

ORGANIC CHEMICALS

Contaminants	Health Effects	MCL[1]	Sources
Acrylamide[2]	probable cancer nervous system	TT[3]	flocculents in sewage/wastewater treatment
Alachlor[2]	probable cancer	0.002	herbicide on corn and soybeans; under review for cancellation
Aldicarb[4]	nervous system	0.003	insecticide on cotton, potatoes; restricted in many areas due to groundwater contamination
Aldicarb sulfone[4]	nervous system	0.002	degraded from aldicarb by plants
Aldicarb sulfoxide[4]	nervous system	0.004	degraded from aldicarb by plants
Atrazine[2]	reproductive and cardiac	0.003	widely used herbicide on corn and on noncropland
Benzene	cancer	0.005	fuel (leaking tanks); solvent used in manufacture of industrial chemicals, pharmaceuticals, pesticides, paints, and plastics
Carbofuran[2]	nervous and reproductive systems	0.04	soil fumigant/insecticide on corn/cotton; restricted in some areas
Carbon tetrachloride	possible cancer	0.005	commonly used in cleaning agents, industrial wastes from manufacture of coolants
Chlordane	probable cancer	0.002	soil insecticide for termite control, corn; potatoes; most uses cancelled in 1980
2,4-D[2] (current MCL = 0.1)	liver, kidney, nervous system	0.07	herbicide for wheat, corn, rangelands
Dibromochloropropane (DBCP)[2]	probable cancer	0.0002	soil fumigant on soybeans, cotton; cancelled in 1977
Dichlorobenzene p-[2]	possible cancer	0.075	used in insecticides, mothballs, air deodorizers
Dichlorobenzene o-[2]	nervous system, lung, liver, kidney	0.6	industrial solvent; chemical manufacturing
Dichloroethane (1,2-)	possible cancer	0.005	used in manufacture of insecticides, gasoline
Dichloroethylene (1,1-)[2]	liver/kidney effects	0.007	used in manufacture of plastics, dyes, perfumes, paints, SOCs (synthetic organic chemicals)
Dichloroethylene (cis-1,2-)[2]	nervous system, liver, circulatory	0.07	industrial extraction solvent
Dichloroethylene (trans-1,2-)[2]	nervous system, liver, circulatory	0.1	industrial extraction solvent
Dichloropropane (1,2-)[2]	probable cancer, liver, lungs, kidney	0.005	soil fumigant; industrial solvent
Endrin[5]	nervous system/ kidney effects	0.0002	insecticide used on cotton, small grains, orchards (cancelled)

INORGANIC CHEMICALS

Contaminants	Health Effects	MCL[1]	Sources
Arsenic[6]	dermal and nervous system toxicity effects	0.05	geological, pesticide residues, industrial waste and smelter operations
Asbestos[2]	benign tumors	7 MFL[7]	natural mineral deposits; also in asbestos/cement pipe
Barium[4] (current MCL = 1.0 mg/liter)	circulatory system	2	natural mineral deposits; oil/gas drilling operations; paint and other industrial uses
Cadmium[2]	kidney	0.005	natural mineral deposits; metal finishing; corrosion product plumbing
Chromium[2] (current MCL = 0.05)	liver/kidney, skin and digestive system	0.1	natural mineral deposits; metal finishing, textile, tanning and leather industries
Copper[8]	stomach and intestinal distress; Wilson's disease	TT[3]	corrosion of interior household and building pipes
Fluoride	skeletal damage	4	geological; drinking water; toothpaste; foods processed with fluorinated water
Lead[8] (current MCL = 0.05)	central and peripheral nervous system damage; kidney; highly toxic to infants and pregnant women	TT[3]	corrosion of lead solder and brass faucets and fixtures; corrosion of lead service lines
Mercury	kidney, nervous system	0.002	industrial/chemical manufacturing; fungicide; natural mineral deposits
Nitrate	methemoglobinemia (blue baby syndrome)	10	fertilizers, feedlots, sewage; naturally in soil, mineral deposits
Nitrite[2]	methemoglobinemia (blue baby syndrome)	1	unstable, rapidly converted to nitrate; prohibited in working metal fluids
Total (nitrate nitrite)[2]	not applicable	10	not applicable
Selenium (mining/smelting)	nervous system	0.05	natural mineral deposits; by-product of copper

RADIONUCLIDES

Contaminants	Health Effects	MCL[1]	Sources
Beta particle and activity	cancer	4 mrem/yr[9]	radioactive waste, uranium photon deposits, nuclear facilities

Contaminant	MCL[1]	Health effects	Sources
Epichlorohydrin[2]	TT[3]	probable cancer, liver, kidney, lungs; nervous system	epoxy resins and coatings, flocculents used in treatment
Ethylbenzene[2]	0.7	nervous system	present in gasoline and insecticides; chemical manufacturing
Ethylene dibromide (EDB)[2]	0.00005	probable cancer	gasoline additive; soil fumigant, solvent cancelled in 1984; limited uses continue
Heptachlor[2]	0.0004	probable cancer	insecticide on corn; cancelled in 1983 for all but termite control
Heptachlor epoxide[2]	0.0002	probable cancer	soil and water organisms convert heptachlor to the epoxide
Lindane[2] (current MCL = 0.004)	0.0002	nervous system, liver, kidney	insecticide for seed/lumber/livestock pest control; most uses restricted in 1983
Methoxychlor[2] (current MCL = 0.1)	0.04	nervous system, liver, kidney, nervous system	insecticide on alfalfa, livestock
Monochlorobenzene[2]	0.1		pesticide manufacturing; metal cleaner, industrial solvent
Pentachlorophenol[2]	0.001	probable cancer, liver, kidney	wood preservative and herbicide; nonwood uses banned in 1987
Polychlorinated biphenyls (PCBs)[2]	0.0005	probable cancer	electrical transformers, plasticizers; banned in 1979
Styrene[2]	0.1	liver, nervous system	plastic manufacturing; resins used in water treatment equipment
Tetrachloroethylene[2]	0.005	probable cancer kidney, nervous system, lung	dry cleaning/industrial solvent
Toluene[2]	1		chemical manufacturing; gasoline additive; industrial solvent
Total trihalomethanes (TTHM) (chloroform, bromodichloromethane, bromoform, dibromochloromethane)	0.1	cancer risk	primarily formed when surface water containing organic matter is treated with chlorine
Toxaphene[2] (current MCL = 0.005)	0.003	probable cancer	insecticide/herbicide for cotton, soybeans; cancelled in 1982
2-4-5-TP (Silvex)[2] (current MCL = 0.01)	0.05	nervous system, liver, kidney	herbicide on rangelands, sugarcane, golf courses; cancelled in 1983
Trichloroethane (1,1,1)	0.2	nervous system problems	used in manufacture of food wrappings, synthetic fibers
Trichloroethylene (TCE)	0.005	possible cancer	waste from disposal of dry cleaning materials and manufacturing of pesticides, paints, waxes and varnishes, paint stripper, metal degreaser
Vinyl chloride	0.002	cancer risk	polyvinyl chloride pipes and solvents used to join them; industrial waste from manufacture of plastics and synthetic rubber
Xylenes[2]	10	liver, kidney, nervous system	paint/ink solvent; gasoline refining by-product; component of detergents

Contaminant	MCL[1]	Health effects	Sources
Gross alpha particle	15 pCi/liter[10]	cancer	radioactive waste, uranium deposits, geological/natural
Radium 226/228	5 pCi/liter[10]	bone cancer	radioactive waste, geological/natural

MICROBIOLOGICAL

Contaminant	MCL[1]	Health effects	Sources
Giardia lamblia	TT[3]	stomach cramps, intestinal distress (giardiasis)	human and animal fecal matter
Legionella	TT[3]	Legionnaires' disease, Pontiac fever	water aerosols such as vegetable misters
Total coliforms	see note 11	not necessarily disease-causing themselves, coliforms can be indicators of organisms that can cause gastroenteric infections, dysentery, hepatitis, typhoid fever, cholera, and other. Also, coliforms interfere with disinfection.	human and animal fecal matter
Turbidity	0.5–1.0 NTU (nephelometric turbidity unit)	interferes with disinfection	erosion, runoff, discharges
Viruses	TT[3]	gastroenteritis (intestinal)	human and animal fecal matter

OTHER SUBSTANCES

Contaminant	MCL[1]	Health effects	Sources
Sodium	none (20 mg/liter reporting level)[12]	possible increase in blood pressure in susceptible individuals	geological, road salting

[1] In milligrams per liter, unless otherwise noted.
[2] Effective date July 30, 1992.
[3] TT = treatment technique requirement in effect.
[4] Effective date January 1, 1993.
[5] Phase V proposes changing MCL for endrin to 0.002.
[6] MCL for arsenic currently under review.
[7] Million fibers per liter, with fiber length > 10 microns.
[8] Effective date December 7, 1992.
[9] Rem = unit of dose equivalent from ionizing radiation to the total body of any internal organ or organ system. A millirem=1/1,000 of a rem.
[10] Picocurie (pCi) = quantity of radioactive material producing 2.22 nuclear transformations per minute.
[11] For large systems (40 or more routine samples per month), no more than 5.0 percent of the samples can be positive. For small systems (39 or fewer routine samples per month), no more than one sample can be positive.
[12] Monitoring is required and data are reported to health officials to protect individuals on highly restricted sodium diets.

Appendix B
Uniform Hazardous Waste Manifest

Please print or type. (Form designed for use on elite (12-pitch) typewriter.)

Form Approved. OMB No. 2050-0039. Expires 9-30-91

UNIFORM HAZARDOUS WASTE MANIFEST	1. Generator's US EPA ID No.	Manifest Document No.	Page 1 of	Information in the shaded areas is not required by Federal law.

3. Generator's Name and Mailing Address	A. State Manifest Document Number
	B. State Generator's ID
4. Generator's Phone ( )	
5. Transporter 1 Company Name 6. US EPA ID NUMBER	C. State Transporter's ID
	D. Transporter's Phone
7. Transporter 2 Company Name 8. US EPA ID NUMBER	E. State Transporter's ID
	F. Transporter's Phone
9. Designated Facility Name and Site Address 10. US EPA ID NUMBER	G. State Facility's ID
	H. Facility's Phone

	11. US DOT Description (including Proper Shipping Name, Hazard Class and ID Number)		12. Containers		13. Total Quantity	14. Unit Wt/Vol	I. Waste No.
		HM	No.	Type			
G E N E R A T O R	a.						
	b.						
	c.						
	d.						

J. Additional Descriptions for Materials Listed Above	K. Handling Codes for Wastes Listed Above

15. Special Handling Instructions and Additional Information

16. GENERATOR'S CERTIFICATION: I hereby declare that the contents of this consignment are fully and accurately described above by proper shipping name and are classified, packed, marked, and labeled, and are in all respects in proper condition for transport by highway according to applicable international and national government regulations.

If I am a large quantity generator, I certify that I have a program in place to reudce the volume and toxicity of waste generated to the degree I have determined to be economically practicable and that I have selected the practicable method of treatment, storage, or disposal currently available to me which minimizes the present and future threat to human health and the environment; OR, if I am a small quantity generator, I have made a good faith effort to minimize my waste generation and select the best waste management method that is available to me and that I can afford.

Printed/Typed Name	Signature	Date Month Day Year

T R A N S P O R T E R	17. Transporter 1 Acknowledgement of Receipt of Materials		
	Printed/Typed Name	Signature	Month Day Year
	18. Transporter 2 Acknowledgement of Receipt of Materials		
	Printed/Typed Name	Signature	Month Day Year

F A C I L I T Y	19. Discrepancy Indication Space		
	20. Facility Owner or Operator: Certification of receipt of hazardous materials covered by this manifest except as noted in Item 19.		
	Printed/Typed Name	Signature	Month Day Year

EPA Form 6700-22 (Rev. 9-88) previous editions obsolete

90290

284

Please print or type.
(Form designed for use on elite (12-pitch) typewriter.)

Form Approved. OMB No. 2050-0039. Expires 9-30-91

UNIFORM HAZARDOUS WASTE MANIFEST
(Continuation Sheet)

21. Generator's US EPA ID No. ....

Manifest Document No. ....

Page

Information in the shaded areas is not required by Federal law.

23. Generator's Name

L. State Manifest Document Number

M. State Generator's ID

24. Transporter ______ Company Name

25. US EPA ID NUMBER

N. State Transporter's ID

O. Transporter's Phone

26. Transporter ______ Company Name

27. US EPA ID NUMBER

P. State Transporter's ID

Q. Transporter's Phone

GENERATOR

28. US DOT Description *(including Proper Shipping Name, Hazard Class and ID Number)*	29. Containers No.	Type	30. Total Quantity	10. Unit Wt/Vol	R. Waste No.
a.					
b.					
c.					
d.					
e.					
f.					
g.					
h.					
i.					

S. Additional Descriptions for Materials Listed Above

T. Handling Codes for Wastes Listed Above

32. Special Handling Instructions and Additional Information

TRANSPORTER

17. Transporter 1 Acknowledgement of Receipt of Materials

Printed/Typed Name	Signature	Date: Month Day Year

18. Transporter 2 Acknowledgement of Receipt of Materials

Printed/Typed Name	Signature	Date: Month Day Year

FACILITY

19. Discrepancy Indication Space

EPA Form 6700-22 (Rev. 9-88) previous editions obsolete

20-FS-C6

Appendix C
Emergency and Hazardous Chemical Inventory

Revised June 1990

Form Approved OMB No. 2050-0072

| **Tier One** | EMERGENCY AND HAZARDOUS CHEMICAL INVENTORY | FOR OFFICIAL USE ONLY | ID# |
| | *Aggregate Information by Hazard Type* | | Date Received |

Important: Read instructions before completing form Reporting Period From January 1 to December 31, 19____

Facility Identification

Name _____

Street _____

City _____ County _____ State _____ Zip _____

SIC Code [ ][ ][ ][ ]   Dun & Brad Number [ ][ ]-[ ][ ][ ]-[ ][ ][ ][ ]

Emergency Contacts

Name _____

Mail Address _____

Phone (____)

Emergency Contacts

Name _____

Title _____

Phone (____)

24 Hour Phone (____)

Name _____

Title _____

Phone (____)

24 Hour Phone (____)

[ ] Check if information below is identical to the information submitted last year.

[ ] Check if site plan is attached

Physical Hazards

Hazard Type	Max Amount*	Average Daily Amount*	Number of Days On-Site	General Location
Fire	[ ][ ]	[ ][ ]	[ ][ ][ ]	_____
Sudden Release of Pressure	[ ][ ]	[ ][ ]	[ ][ ][ ]	_____
Reactivity	[ ][ ]	[ ][ ]	[ ][ ][ ]	_____

Health Hazards

Immediate (acute)	[ ][ ]	[ ][ ]	[ ][ ][ ]	_____
Delayed (Chronic)	[ ][ ]	[ ][ ]	[ ][ ][ ]	_____

Certification (Read and sign after completing all sections)

I certify under penalty of law that I have personally examined and am familiar with the information submitted in pages one through _____, and that based on my inquiry of those individuals responsible for obtaining the information, I believe that the submitted information is true, accurate and complete.

_____
Name and official title of owner/operator OR owner operator's authroized representative

_____   _____
Signature   Date signed

* Reporting Ranges

Range Code	Weight Range in Pounds From...	To...
01	0	99
02	100	999
03	1000	9,999
04	10,000	99,999
05	100,000	999,999
06	1,000,000	9,999,999
07	10,000,000	49,999,999
08	50,000,000	99,999,999
09	100,000,000	499,999,999
10	500,000,000	999,999,999
11	1 billion	higher than 1 billion

Page _____ of _____ pages
Form Approved OMB No. 2050-0072

Revised November 1990

Tier Two

EMERGENCY AND HAZARDOUS CHEMICAL INVENTORY

Specific Information by Chemical

Facility Identification

Name _____
Street _____
City _____ County _____ State _____ Zip _____

SIC Code [ ][ ][ ]   Dun & Brad [ ][ ]-[ ][ ][ ]-[ ][ ][ ][ ]
Number

FOR OFFICIAL USE ONLY   ID# _____
Date Received _____

Owner/Operator Name

Name _____ Phone (___)
Mail Address _____

Emergency Contact

Name _____ Title _____
Phone (___) _____ 24 Hr. Phone (___)

Name _____ Title _____
Phone (___) _____ 24 Hr. Phone (___)

Important: Read all instructions before completing form   Reporting Period   From January 1 to December 31, 19 ___

☐ Check if information below is identical to the information submitted last year

Chemical Description	Physical and Health Hazards (check all that apply)	Inventory	Container Type / Pressure / Temperature	Storage Codes and Locations (Non-Confidential) Storage Locations	Optional
CAS [ ][ ][ ][ ][ ][ ][ ] ☐ Trade Secret Chem. Name _____ ☐ ☐ ☐ ☐ ☐ ☐ Pure Mix Solid Liquid Gas EHS EHS. Name _____	☐ Fire ☐ Sudden Release of Pressure ☐ Reactivity ☐ Immediate (acute) ☐ Delayed (chronic)	☐ Max. Daily Amount (code) ☐ Avg. Daily Amount (code) ☐ No. of Days On-site (days)		_____ _____ _____ _____ _____	☐
CAS [ ][ ][ ][ ][ ][ ][ ] ☐ Trade Secret Chem. Name _____ ☐ ☐ ☐ ☐ ☐ ☐ Pure Mix Solid Liquid Gas EHS EHS. Name _____	☐ Fire ☐ Sudden Release of Pressure ☐ Reactivity ☐ Immediate (acute) ☐ Delayed (chronic)	☐ Max. Daily Amount (code) ☐ Avg. Daily Amount (code) ☐ No. of Days On-site (days)		_____ _____ _____ _____ _____	☐
CAS [ ][ ][ ][ ][ ][ ][ ] ☐ Trade Secret Chem. Name _____ ☐ ☐ ☐ ☐ ☐ ☐ Pure Mix Solid Liquid Gas EHS EHS. Name _____	☐ Fire ☐ Sudden Release of Pressure ☐ Reactivity ☐ Immediate (acute) ☐ Delayed (chronic)	☐ Max. Daily Amount (code) ☐ Avg. Daily Amount (code) ☐ No. of Days On-site (days)		_____ _____ _____ _____ _____	☐

Certification (Read and sign after completing all sections)

I certify under penalty of law that I have personally examined and am familiar with the information submitted in pages one through _____, and that based on my inquiry of those individuals responsible for obtaining the information, I believe that the submitted information is true, accurate and complete.

_____   _____   _____
Name and official title of owner/operator OR owner operator's authroized representative   Signature   Date signed

Optional Attachments
☐ I have attached a site plan
☐ I have attached a list of site coordinate abbreviations
☐ I have attached a description of dikes and other safeguard measures

---

Tier Two

EMERGENCY AND HAZARDOUS CHEMICAL INVENTORY

Specific Information by Chemical

Facility Identification

Name _____
Street _____
City _____ County _____ State _____ Zip _____

SIC Code [ ][ ][ ]   Dun & Brad [ ][ ]-[ ][ ][ ]-[ ][ ][ ][ ]
Number

FOR OFFICIAL USE ONLY   ID# _____
Date Received# _____

Owner/Operator Name

Name _____ Phone (___)
Mail Address _____

Emergency Contact

Name _____ Title _____
Phone (___) _____ 24 Hr. Phone (___)

Name _____ Title _____
Phone (___) _____ 24 Hr. Phone (___)

Important: Read all instructions before completing form   Reporting Period   From January 1 to December 31, 19 ___

☐ Check if information below is identical to the information submitted last year

Confidential Location Information Sheet

		Container Type / Pressure / Temperature	Storage Codes and Locations (Non-Confidential) Storage Locations	Optional
CAS [ ][ ][ ][ ][ ][ ][ ] Chem. Name			_____ _____ _____ _____ _____	☐
CAS [ ][ ][ ][ ][ ][ ][ ] Chem. Name			_____ _____ _____ _____ _____	☐
CAS [ ][ ][ ][ ][ ][ ][ ] Chem. Name			_____ _____ _____ _____ _____	☐

Certification (Read and sign after completing all sections)

I certify under penalty of law that I have personally examined and am familiar with the information submitted in pages one through _____, and that based on my inquiry of those individuals responsible for obtaining the information, I believe that the submitted information is true, accurate and complete.

_____   _____   _____
Name and official title of owner/operator OR owner operator's authorized representative   Signature   Date signed

Optional Attachments
☐ I have attached a site plan
☐ I have attached a list of site coordinate abbreviations
☐ I have attached a description of dikes and other safeguard measures

Appendix D
Abbreviations and Acronyms

ACO	Administrative Consent Order
ADR	Alternate Dispute Resolution
AEC	Atomic Energy Commission (now NRC)
APA	Administrative Procedures Act
AQCR	Air Quality Control Regions (CAA)
BAT	Best Available Technology or Best Available Technology Economically Achievable
BCT	Best Conventional Control Technology
BDAT	Best Demonstrated Available Technology
BDT	Best Available Demonstrated Control Technology
BLM	Bureau of Land Management
BMP	Best Management Practices
BNA	Bureau of National Affairs
BPT	Best Practicable Control Technology Currently Available
CAA	Clean Air Act
CEQ	Council on Environmental Quality (executive office of the president)
CERCLA	Comprehensive Environmental Response, Compensation, and Liability Act
CFR	Code of Federal Regulations
CWA	Clean Water Act
DNR	Department of Natural Resources
DOA	U.S. Department of Agriculture
DOI	U.S. Department of Interior
DOJ	U.S. Department of Justice
DOT	U.S. Department of Transportation
EA	Environmental Assessment
EC	European Community
ECRA	Environmental Cleanup Responsibility Act
EDF	Environmental Defense Fund
EIS	Environmental Impact Statement
ELR	Environmental Law Reporter
EO	Executive Order
EPA	U.S. Environmental Protection Agency
EPCRA	Emergency Planning and Community Right to Know Act
EPCRTKA	EPCRA—Emergency Planning and Community Right to Know Act
ERC	BNA Environmental Reporter—Cases
ESA	Endangered Species Act
FDA	U.S. Food and Drug Administration
FEPCA	Federal Environmental Pesticide Control Act
FHWA	Federal Highway Administration
FIFRA	Federal Insecticide, Fungicide, Rodenticide Act
FLPMA	Federal Land Policy and Management Act
FOE	Friends of the Earth
FOIA	Freedom of Information Act
FONSI	Finding of No Significant Impact (NEPA)
FR	Federal Register
FRCP	Federal Rules of Civil
FWPCA	Federal Water Pollution Control Act (CWA)
FWS	Fish and Wildlife Service
GAO	General Accounting Office (congressional)
HRS	Hazard Ranking System (CERCLA)
HSWA	Hazardous and Solid Waste Amendments (of 1984)
ICJ	International Court of Justice (The Hague)
IGO	Intergovernmental Organization
IJC	International Joint Commission (U.S.-Canada)
ILM	International Legal Materials

IPM	Integrated Pest Management
ISC	Interagency Scientific Committee (ESA)
IWC	International Whaling Commission
LAER	Lowest Achievable Emissions Rate
MACT	Maximum Available Control Technology
MCL	Maximum Contaminant Level (CWA)
MCLG	Maximum Contaminant Level Goals
NAAQS	National Ambient Air Quality Standards
NAM	National Association of Manufacturers
NCP	National Contingency Plan (Superfund)
NEPA	National Environmental Policy Act of 1969
NESHAP	National Emissions Standards for Hazardous Air Pollutants
NFMA	National Forest Management Act
NGO	Non-Governmental Organization
NOAA	National Oceanographic and Atmospheric Administration (Department of Commerce)
NPDES	National Pollutant Discharge Elimination System (CWA)
NPL	National Priority List (Superfund)
NPS	National Park Service
NRC	U.S. Nuclear Regulatory Commission or (state) Natural Resources Commission
NRDC	National Resources Defense Council
NSPS	New Source Performance Standards (Air)
NFW	National Wildlife Foundation
NWQS	National Water Quality Standards (CWA)
OCS	Outer Continental Shelf
OMB	Office of Management and Budget (executive offices of the President)
OSHA	Occupational Safety and Health Act, Occupational Safety and Health Administration
OSWER	Office of Solid Waste and Energy Response
OTA	Office of Technology Assessment (congressional)
PMNs	Pre-marketing Notifications
POTW	Publicly Owned Treatment Works (CWA)
PRP	Potentially Responsible Party (Superfund)
PSD	Prevention of Significant Deterioration
RCRA	Resource Conservation and Recovery Act
SARA	Superfund Amendment and Reauthorization Act
SCS	U.S. Soil Conservation Service
SDWA	Safe Drinking Water Act
SIP	State Implementation Plan (CAA)
SMCRA	Surface Mining Control and Reclamation Act
Superfund	CERCLA
SWDA	Solid Waste Disposal Act
ToSCA or TSCA	Toxic Substance Control Act
TRO	Temporary Restraining Order
TSD	Treatment, Storage, and Disposal (CERCLA)
TVA	Tennessee Valley Authority
USDA	U.S. Department of Agriculture
USFS	United States Forest Service
WQS	Water Quality Standards (CWA)

Index